Errata

P. 97, l. 1: ref. should be to Deut. 13:13 not 3

THE
PAULINE ESCHATOLOGY

BY

GEERHARDUS VOS, Ph.D., D.D.

Late Professor of Biblical Theology
in Princeton Theological Seminary

WM. B. EERDMANS PUBLISHING COMPANY

GRAND RAPIDS 1961 MICHIGAN

Second printing, January, 1961

PHOTOLITHOPRINTED BY CUSHING - MALLOY, INC.
ANN ARBOR, MICHIGAN, UNITED STATES OF AMERICA
1961

DEUS CREATOR REDEMPTOR CONSUMMATOR
IN HIS TRIBUS RELIGIO NOSTRA UNIVERSA PENDET

PREFACE

CHRISTIAN faith has at various times put widely varying appraisals on biblical eschatology. The latter was first held in esteem because of the service it was able to render to early apologetics. The two at the outset were practically identical. The vindication of the new-born faith depended on the proof that the Messiah, that great Agent and Consummator of God's world-purpose, had appeared upon the scene. Whosoever believed in this found himself drawn into the center of the eschatological movement, by prophets long foretold. It is true, this apologetic subserviency did not always work in even measure to the advantage of the Scriptural scheme of Eschatology. The Old Testament was the chief armory from which weapons had to be drawn. Even Virgil's Fourth Eclogue could not quite replace this, whatever its ultimate provenience. And as to the Old Testament, who can deny that sometimes minor and isolated correspondences were subjected to a harder strain than they ought to have been asked to bear.

At all times through the life of the Church the eschatological hope remained securely fixed upon her mind. It was an uncontroverted, accepted belief. Perhaps the retention of it may sometimes have been largely of a formal nature. But there is something about these expectations and visions of the last things, that will send them into the light and focus of the consciousness of believers, whenever storms of persecution arise and hard distresses invade. The mediaeval Roman Church seemed so unshakably fixed beyond every chance of transitoriness, and it moreover so clearly typified the true image of the ultimate city of God, that in it, one would suppose, only little soil could have been left for the cultivation of super-terrestrial fields. And yet this appearance was to some extent deceptive. The finest products of the hymnody of that Church, with their unearthly aroma still clinging to them after so many ages, are here to prove how rich a vein of piety ran through the hearts of their authors, derivable from the living waters of Paradise alone. Its hills still stood and the birds were still delighting the saints of God with jubilance from their leafy trees.

In the period of the Reformation the problem of the obtaining of righteousness before God filled hearts and minds. For the time this forced the eschatological hope into the background, although even then it would have been by no means paradoxical to say that the two strands of the justifying faith and the eschatological outlook remained closely intertwined. Paul knew the inevitableness of this and knew it better, perhaps, than the foremost heroes of the Reformation, not even Luther or Calvin excepted. While the Reformers were by no means unacquainted with the melodies of eschatological music, theirs was by preference martial music drawn from the storm and stress of the Psalter. But they received something better from Paul than either prophet or Psalmist had been able to give. Paul had been the first to grasp with his master-mind the single items of eschatological belief scattered through Scripture, and to weave them into a compact, well-rounded system, so coherent, that, speaking after the manner of man, it became next to impossible for any of the precious texture henceforth to be lost. He it was who made the single items of hope find themselves and group themselves into crystal formations with symmetrical shapes. Truly for this, not his smallest gift, he may justly be called the father of Christian eschatology.

With the rise of Rationalism Eschatology was bound to drift into troubled waters. Eschatology is preëminently historical, and Rationalism is from its cradle devoid of historic sense. It despises tradition; the past it ignores and the future it barely tolerates with a supercilious conceit of self. Moreover Rationalism is bent upon and enamored of the inward. To it the essence and value of all religion lie in purely-subjective ethico-religious experiences. Now in the eschatological process from the nature of the case, the forces of propulsion must come from *ab extra*. No nature-force can possibly be conceived as producing them. All that remains of interest for Eschatology in such circles can spring from a "historicizing" curiosity only. Piety it is no longer capable of kindling. And yet, there was and may still further appear to be something good from the Lord in this modernistic setback. Driven by such a storm of denial from the old pastures, not a few of the pious sought refuge out of this chill-grown world into anticipations of the world to come. We cannot help but recoil from much distorted thought and morbid emotion, that makes present-day eschatologizing propaganda unlovable. But let us be sure not to overlook even the smallest grain of golden piety that may linger in it.

And meanwhile let us learn to reconcile ourselves to this outstanding sign of the times: Eschatology has become the large mountain of offense lying across the pathway of modern unbelief. That part of it which we call Messiahship was already a piece broken from that rock in the days of Jesus. The double offense was one at bottom. Neither will be tolerated in modern religious thought. And the results will inevitably be the same. Paul divorced from his Eschatology becomes unfit for his Apostleship; Jesus divested of his Messiahship can no longer serve us as a Saviour. What boots it to strive for minor (although in themselves sufficiently important) things, when we see all these treasures the Church has gloried in and all this nourishment we have lived on, burned up before our eyes in one and the same fire? Here, certainly, is the test-limit of what shall warrant a claim to continuity with historic Christianity and the right to further retention of the name of "Christian."

GEERHARDUS VOS.

Princeton, January 21, 1930.

CHAPTER I

THE STRUCTURE OF THE PAULINE ESCHATOLOGY

Eschatology is "the doctrine of the last things." It deals with the teaching or belief, that the world-movement, religiously considered, tends towards a definite final goal, beyond which a new order of affairs will be established, frequently with the further implication, that this new order of affairs will not be subject to any further change, but will partake of the static character of the eternal. Eschatology is a term of Greek derivation, which leads us to look for its linguistic antecedents first of all to the Greek Old Testament. Here we find the two phrases ἔσχαται ἡμέραι (occurring Gen. xlix. 1; Isa. ii. 2; Jer. xxxvii. 24;[1] Ezek. xxxviii. 16; Hos. iii. 5; Mic. iv. 1; Dan. x. 14) and ἔσχατον τῶν ἡμερῶν (occurring Num. xxiv. 14; Deut. iv. 30; xxxi. 29; Jer. xxiii. 20; xxv. 18).[2]

Back of these Greek phrases lies the Hebrew phrase הימים אחרית.[3] It is important to determine the precise import of the term אחרית, both etymologically and conceptually. "Acherith" is a derivation from "achar" and the latter means "hindmost." "Acherith" is applied to space as well as to time in the sense of "the hindmost part." An example of the application to space is Ps. cxxxix. 9: "the uttermost parts of the sea." Applied to time, as is the case in the phrase under review, it would proximately signify "the farthermost parts of the days." The question arises, however, whether this is a purely chronological designation, or whether there enters

[1] In the arrangement of the Hebrew text this passage occurs xxx. 24.

[2] The last two in the Hebrew text, xlix. 39. Heb. Jer. xlviii. 47 has no corresponding Greek passage in Sept. Chap. xxxi.

[3] Besides *"acherith hajjamim,"* the combinations *"acherith hazza'am"* "of the wrath" and *"acherith hashshanim"* "of the years" are also found, the former in Dan. viii. 19, the latter in Ezek. xxxviii. 8.

into it likewise the idea of "eventuation," "issue of a foregoing process." In ordinary untechnical usage such a sense sometimes does attach to the word: Job viii. 7 draws a contrast between the small beginnings of prosperity and its abundant issue; the former is "reshith," the latter "acherith"; similarly xlii. 12; Prov. v. 4, 11 speak of the bitterness of the end of a man's relation with "the strange woman," implying that this bitter "acherith" is the inevitable outcome of the whole course of conduct involved. In the same way it is said of wine that "it goes down smoothly," but that "at the last ("acherith") it bites like a serpent and stings like an adder," xxiii. 31, 32; the "reward" hoped for is an "acherith," xxiii. 18; xxiv. 14. There can not, therefore, be drawn any objection *a priori* from the common usage of the word to its having carried a similar pregnant sense in technical eschatological language. The sole question is whether the presence of this climacteric element can be pointed out in the eschatological passages. The "Blessing of Jacob," Gen. xlix, contains an approach to this point of view in what it predicts concerning Judah, vs. 10. The "Shiloh," that is "the One to whom Judah's sceptre and ruler's staff belong" appears here as the ultimate embodiment and virtually as the eternalizer of Judah's preëminence among the tribes. In other words the One later called the Messiah is a Consummator in more than a purely chronological sense. This is still clearer if the Ezekielian reference to this prophecy is laid by the side of it, for here a succession of acts of overturning is held in prospect until shall come "He whose right it is," and to whom Jehovah gives the final government, Ezek. xxi. 32;[4] both in Genesis and in the reproduction of the thought by Ezekiel the idea of progression towards a fixed end is marked by the word "until." To be sure the term "acherith" stands in Gen. xlix. 1 at the head of the prophecy with general reference to what is foretold concerning all the tribes, yet it is meant virtually so that in Judah's destiny alone it is realized to the full

[4] Vs. 27 in English text.

extent of its import.[5] The same phenomenon meets us in Nu. xxiv. 14: Balaam says to Balak, "I will advertise thee what this people (Israel) shall do to thy people in the acherith hajjamim." Upon this follows the vision of the star out of Jacob and the sceptre out of Israel, projected into the dim future ("not now" and "not nigh"). The introduction is abrupt; no intervening events nor preparatory stages are mentioned. In the last *mashal,* however, (vss. 20-24), there is a concatenation of successive overthrows befalling successive powers, in regard to which the idea of historico-causal connection suggests itself. The representation of one power overtaking and replacing another reminds strongly of the later prevision of political developments in Daniel, with this difference that Daniel places the kingdom of God at the close of the rise and rule of the profane kingdoms as something in which the entire movement comes to rest, whilst with Balaam, the Messianic culmination stands in the preceding *mashal* by itself, and before the picture of the intervening destinies in vss. 20-24. The occurrence of the simple "acherith" without determination in the first of Balaam's *meshalim,* xxiii. 10, ought not to be overlooked; it is here ostensibly applied to the individual, and used synonymously with "death": "Let me die the death of the righteous, and let my acherith be like his." In Deut. iv. 30 the "acherith hajjamim" denotes the time of the return of Israel to Jehovah after all the calamities described in the foregoing discourse shall have come upon them; among these is the captivity, so that the use is from the O.T. standpoint truly eschatological. In Chap. xxxi. 29, on the other hand, it marks the period of the calamities themselves, and these are placed by Moses at the end of a process of corruption beginning immediately after his death; in this Deuteronomy anticipates some of the prophetic representations. No mention is here made of return, so that only the negative side of the eschatological outcome is touched upon. Isa. ii. 2-4 and Mic. iv. 1-3 are identical prophecies with this difference only that

[5] Gen. xlix. 1, "Gather yourselves together, that I may tell you that which shall befall you in the latter (acherith) days."

the idyllic picture of the new paradise in vs. 4 is added by Micah. In both the reference is to the last issue of things. Isaiah makes no direct connection between the events of the "acherith" and the preceding developments; the prophecy is introduced abruptly. In Micah, however, through the attachment to the exceedingly ominous close of Chap. iii a contrast seems to be suggested between the depth and the height in Israel's future; the translators of the English Bible (A.V., R.V., A.R.V.) express this view of it by giving the conjunction "waw" the sense of "but."[6] Of the Jeremiah-passages two (xxiii. 20; xxxvii. 24, corresponding to Hebrew and English xxx. 24) link with the "acherith" (placed in or after the captivity) a new understanding of the divine judgment come upon the people. The two others (xxv. 18; found in Hebrew and English xlix. 39 and xlviii. 47, lacking in the Greek) speak of the return at the end of Elam and Moab. To these may be added the interesting statement in Hebrew and English xxxi. 17,[7] to the effect that there is "hope" for the people's "acherith," thus associating the latter with a state of favor; this renders it probable that the "new understanding" of the judgment, predicted for the "acherith" in the references given above, is meant to bear the same auspicious meaning. Ezek. xxxviii. 16 represents the last great attack made by Gog upon the people as taking place in the "acherith"; this attack happens when the state of security has already become an established state for Israel (vs. 14).[8] Hos. iii. 5 fixes the "acherith" as the point after the exile, when the children of Israel return and seek Jehovah their God and David their King, and come with fear to Jehovah and to

[6] The *waw* occurs also in Isaiah; to be certain of its force as "but," we should have to know that the prophecy was taken from Micah by Isaiah, or that the connection of contrast found by the English Versions was intended in an assumed third source lying back of both Isaiah and Micah.

[7] In Sep. xxxviii. 16, corresponding to the Hebrew above cited, the text is greatly different and the word "acherith" does not occur.

[8] Cp. Mic. iv. 1, 11, where the attack of the "many nations" is mentioned after the description of the "acherith" as a state of blessedness. But the arrangement need not be strictly chronological; vs. 11 says "and now."

His goodness. Finally, according to Dan. x. 14, the interpreter proceeds to make the prophet understand what shall befall the people in the "latter (post-Persian) days."

The above survey includes all the Greek Old Testament instances of occurrence of the phrase. Certain conclusions can be drawn from it, which here may be briefly set down: *In the first place* the phrase belongs strictly to the field of eschatology. It does not signify some indefinitely subsequent point or period or complication of events. The note of epochal finality is never missing in it. This should, however, not be confounded with the idea of chronological fixity. It is peculiar to the Old Testament that it makes this "acherith" a sort of movable complex, capable of being pushed forward along the line of prophetic vision. Here is not the place to treat of the principle of the philosophy of revelation underlying this phenomenon; it may suffice to point to it as a fact borne out by exegetical induction.[9] *In the second place* the conception relates to the *collective* aspect of eschatology: it deals with the fortunes and destinies of the people, not with the prospect and future of the individual.[10] This, however, does not mean that the Old Testament, as sometimes alleged, is wholly lacking in individual eschatology, it only means that whatever approach to or teaching of such a doctrine there is has not found expression through the "acherith"-concept. *Thirdly* the idea is elastic as to its extent, no less than movable as to its position. It covers, as has been shown, unfavor-

[9] Cp. Delitzsch, *Commentar über die Genesis,*[4] 1872, pp. 498-501.

[10] A possible exception is Num. xxiii. 10; here "the death of the righteous" (parallel to his "acherith") is spoken of as something devoutly to be desired. Can this refer to Israel as the connection would seem to indicate? There is nothing strange in "the righteous" as a name for Israel; "Jeshurun" occurs as a name of the people in Deut. xxxii. 15; xxxiii. 5, 26; Isa. xliv. 2. For the idea of the death of Israel cp. Hos. xiii. 13, but there the representation is ominous. Even when individualistically interpreted, Balaam's words are eschatological; the blessedness is pronounced in view of the future after death (hence "*the righteous*"), not in view of things left behind (children or property). Individually interpreted the passage would yield an early instance of the eschatological conception of the state after death; Gen. v. 24 would furnish the only analogue.

able and favorable happenings occurring in the farthest visible plane to which the prophetic vision extends, and there is no clear marking of the sequence of these in time. This is what might be expected, taking into consideration the whole tenor of Old Testament prophecy with regard to the future. Sometimes *points* are mentioned as falling within the "acherith," sometimes *a condensation of events* occupying apparently a certain stretch of time. The principal question is whether the static outcome, the permanent state of blessedness predicted, is actually included, sometimes at least, in the "acherith." If so, then this would extend the latter indefinitely, in fact render it synonymous with what the New Testament considers the state of eternity, although, of course, the language of time would still be employed to describe it, the latter feature being inherent in the etymology of the phrase itself. Deut. iv. 30 has been quoted as an instance of this (on the usual construction): "When thou art in tribulation and all these things are come upon thee, in the latter days thou shalt return to Jehovah thy God." Thus construe R.V. and A.R.V., but A.V. has: "When all these things are come upon thee (i.e., the calamities spoken of) even in the latter days," etc. This, as an alternative construction, is also offered by R.V. and A.R.V. in the margin. The Greek Text is not clear; it reads: "and all these words (things) shall find thee in the "acherith of the days." The Hebrew represents the "acherith" as the period of adversity. But even if the construction of R.V. and A.R.V. be adopted, the passage still falls short of placing the blessed age in the "acherith"; what it puts there explicitly is only the act of conversion. And no more than this can be said for the passage in Hos. iii. 3: the people's coming unto Jehovah and unto His "goodness" is put in the "acherith." Here, however, it is possible, if "coming to his goodness" be taken in the pregnant sense of enjoying God's favor, to make the "acherith" cover the resulting permanent eschatological state. The only passage which unequivocally puts consummated eschatological things within the "acherith" is the duplicate prophecy, Isa. ii. 2; Mic. iv. 1. Here we read that in the "acherith" the mountain of Jehovah's house shall be established (*"nakhon jihjeh"*) at the head (= on the top) of the mountains; the Niphal Participle must be understood of an enduring condition, and the same is implied in the representation in vss. 3, 4 of Jehovah's teaching function, of his judging between many nations and of the state of peace and security prevailing, every man sitting under his vine and fig-tree, and none to make them afraid (the last in Micah only).[11]

Coming now to the N.T., and first to the extra-Pauline New Testament material, we notice the fact that in the Synoptical Gospels the terminology of *ἔσχατον* does not appear with eschatological reference. In John it occurs; here we meet with *"eschate hemera,"* vi. 39, 40, 44, 54; xi. 24. On account of both the noun and the adjective being in the singular, and through the specific reference to the act of the resurrection, the Old Testament phrase has here become contracted in meaning. Acts has but one instance of the use of the phrase, ii. 17, and this in a quotation by Peter from Joel iii. 1, where the Hebrew does not contain it, but simply says "after that." But this easy substitution proves that the formula was thoroughly familiar in early-Christian circles. Apart from Paul the other N.T. references are Heb. i. 2; Jas. v. 3; 1 Pet. i. 5, 20; 2 Pet. iii. 3; 1 Jno. ii. 18 (bis); Jude 18. In these passages the noun varies between "hemerai" and "kairos,"[12] or "chronos," "chronoi," "time," "times"; 1 Jno. ii. 18 the phrase runs, as in the Gospel, "eschate hora," with this difference only that what figures in the saying of Jesus as a *point* of time (the point of the resurrection) becomes in the Epistle the last *stretch* of time.

The characteristic feature of these New Testament ap-

[11] Cp. Stark, *"Der Gebrauch der Wendung Beacherith Hajjamim im alttestamentlichen Kanon, Z. f. A. W.* 1891, pp. 247; Giesebrecht, *Beiträge zur Jesajakritik, Anhang,* pp. 187-220.

[12] The difference between "eschatai hemerai" and "kairos eschatos" can best be felt through 2 Tim. iii. 1, "in the last days grievous times (kairoi chalepoi) shall come"; the former is purely chronological, the latter carries the note of qualitatively complexioned and specifically appointed seasons. This passage in 2 Tim. is the only case of technical use of "eschatai hemerai" with Paul.

plications of the phrase consists in the idea accompanying them that the writers and readers are conscious of the last days being upon them, or at least close at hand. Indeed, this has to such an extent become inseparable from the phrase, that no longer any particular pains are taken to separate by means of precision of statement present from future or semi-present from present. Herein lies a very marked difference from the Old Testament mode of representation. Sometimes belief in the imminence of final happenings and the pervasive eschatological state of mind engendered by this, seem to lead to scrutiny of the contemporary state of things for possible symptoms of the approach of the end, 2 Tim. iii. 1; 2 Pet. iii. 3; Jud. 18. At other times the observation of the symptoms leads to the conclusion, or at least the strengthening of the conclusion, that the last hour is there, 1 Jno. ii. 18. Again at other times the thought has a thickly ominous coloring, Jas. v. 3. It also may appear in more theoretical form, though even then never wholly detached from the present practical situation, 1 Pet. i. 5, 20. An interesting example of combination of the two motifs appears in Heb. i. 2: "God has spoken in the last days in a Son"; to this, which is so far a merely chronological construction of the history of revelation, the writer then as a sort of afterthought, by means of the pronoun "these" loosely attached at the close, adds the reflection that these days are the present days of himself and his readers; were it not for the subsequent supervention of that thought, the sense would have naturally been expressed by "ep' eschatōn (plural) tōn hemerōn." By all this the phrase which previously hovered in the mist of more or less remote futurity, has obtained a fixed appurtenance to the present and closely impending future. It is due to the correct perception of this that in our English Bible the Old Testament and Septuagint phrases are rendered by "the *latter* days," whereas the New Testament speaking of itself translates the identical phrases by "the *last* days."[13]

[13] In thus rendering from the Old Testament A.V., R.V. and A.R.V. agree with the two exceptions of Gen. xlix. 1 and Isa. ii. 2 (Mic. iv. 1).

A feature which this extra-Pauline New Testament usage and that of the Greek Old Testament have in common is what might be called the "non-comparative" character of both. There is no conscious reflection upon the qualitatively specific complexion of "early" or "earlier" days: the attention is wholly fixed upon the future final segment of time, so as to make the contrast an almost entirely chronological one. In result of this the rendering by "latter days" might easily create a misunderstanding, the comparative degree inviting the idea that two *sorts* of days, the earlier and the latter ones were, at least by implication, set over against each other. But this is not necessarily implied; yet neither is it allowable to draw the conclusion, that the static result of the crisis foreseen will again be made up of "days," although that would suit the Old Testament perspective of a Messianic state in time quite well. The "eternal" as the negation of time is not envisaged here. What is envisaged is a point or stretch lying at the end of history; it forms part of what are called "days"; that thereafter there shall be no more days, but something of a different nature is not implied. The acherith, the eschaton have the stress, not the jamim or the hemerai. The phrase *"last days"* does not as yet carry the implication, that the time-order is soon to be ended to make place for a non-diurnal state of existence.

Now examining Paul with the technical phrases just discussed in mind, it is immediately apparent that his terminology is differently oriented than that attaching itself to the eschaton-idea.[14] To be sure, Paul joins the adjective "eschatos"

In these two passages A.V. has "the last days." So far as Isaiah and Micah are concerned, this anticipation, as it were, of the New Testament usage may be due to the static character of what is located in the "acherith"; cp. above "the mountain of Jehovah's house shall *be* (and *remain*) established"; as a permanent, non-transitory phenomenon this seemed better expressible by "last" than by "latter." Num. xxiii. 10, where all three versions have "last end" is hardly an exception to the rule, for here the translators obviously found the death of the righteous *person* referred to; in xxiv. 14 where the point of view is nationally-collective, all three version have again "latter days."

[14] If anywhere, then the phrase "the last days" might have been ex-

to a number of nouns and that with eschatological connotation. I Cor. iv. 9, the Apostles are represented as set forth *eschatoi* to death, which certainly can not mean that they are the most recent examples of such a destination; it relates to their place in the final tribulation impending. I Cor. xv. 26, "last" (with reference to death) in the order of enemies to be abolished seems to be purely numerical, although, of course, the eschatological association could not be entirely kept out of the word. The latter is distinctly present in "the last trumpet," vs. 52, for this does not refer to all the several trumpets blown in the course of the world's history, but it either means the counterpart to the tremendous trumpet-blast that accompanied the giving of the law, or it is named "last" because of a series of eschatological trumpets immediately preceding it, in which case there is no reflection upon ordinary, so to speak secular, trumpets.[15] Most significant of all, however, is the designation of Christ as "the eschatos Adam," vs. 45, where "last" is entirely steeped in eschatological meaning, for this "last Adam" is the fountain-head of the resurrection, vss. 22, 23, a "quickening Spirit," "of heaven" and "heavenly," vss. 47-49, all this referring to the final celestial state and the conditions pertaining thereto, such as the peculiar kind of (bodily) image to be borne by believers after their resurrection. In how far this use of "eschatos" by Paul has its roots in the ancient idea of "the last days," can not here be determined.

In distinction from the O.T. point of view the structure of Paul's eschatology appears antithetical. It places the end

pected in the "Man-of-Sin" prophecy, 2 Thess. ii; its absence from this piece seems significant. "The day of the Lord" is here the central conception; cp. also "in his own season" vs. 6.

15 How thoroughly "eschatologized" the trumpet is appears from its occurrence without the term "last" I Thess. iv. 16, and the verb I Cor. xv. 52; cp. Matt. xxiv. 31, "a great trumpet"; in Thess. "the trump of God"; in Rev. viii.-xi. 15, the seven trumpets are numerically distinguished, but, collectively speaking, they all belong to "the end." Rev. xv. I and xxi. 9, the attribute eschatai belongs to the seven plagues because "in them is *finished* the wrath of God."

under the control of one principle with the sway of which an opposite principle of equally comprehensive rule and of primordial origin is contrasted, so as to make the two, when taken together, yield a bisection of universal history. By giving the soteric movement this cosmical setting it claims for it the significance of a central world-process, around the core of which all happenings in the course of time group themselves.[16] By this one stroke order is brought into the disconnected multitudinousness of events. The eschatology, without losing touch with history, nevertheless, owing to the large sweep of its historical reach, becomes philosophico-theological. It no longer forms one item in the sum-total of revealed teaching, but draws within its circle as correlated and eschatologically-complexioned parts practically all of the fundamental tenets of Pauline Christianity. Here this can only be briefly premised; it will have to be shown by detailed investigation at subsequent points. It will appear throughout that to unfold the Apostle's eschatology means to set forth his theology as a whole. Through a conceptual retroversion the end will be seen to give birth to the beginning in the emergence of truth. What we are here concerned with more immediately is the specific terminology in which this mode of thought has come to express itself. In I Cor. xv. 45-47, the presence of this antithetical orientation is clearly seen in the correspondence of the two names for Christ, "the eschatos Adam" and "the deuteros Man," the opposite to the former no less than to the latter being "the protos Man." "Eschatos" here bears technical meaning; it designates not so much the Adam that belongs to the order of the "eschata," but pointedly the One who is the last in contrast with one other who is the first; it is antithetical no less than "deuteros." As backward of "the protos" there was no other, so beyond "the eschatos" there can be none further. Typologi-

[16] In the Epistle to the Hebrews there is a similar bisection of history with eschatological issue, but here this pertains to the sphere of redemption; the first age is the Old Diatheke, the second the New Diatheke, cp. ii. 5; (oikoomene melloosa); vi. 5 ("mellon aion") cp. "Hebrews, the Epistle of the Diatheke," P.T.R., 1914, 1915.

cally the same principle finds expression Rom. v. 14: "who is a figure (type) of him that was to come."

More comprehensively the antithetical structure appears in the distinction between the two *ages* or *worlds*. The only passage in Paul where this contrast is explicitly drawn is Eph. i. 21: "far above . . . every name that is named, not only in this world (or age), but also in that which is to come." There are, however, quite a number of other passages where, although only "this age" (ὁ αἰὼν οὗτος) appears the other member of the contrast is nevertheless present by implication. Thus Rom. xii. 2; 1 Cor. i. 20; ii. 6, 8; iii. 18; 2 Cor. iv. 4; Gal. i. 4; Eph. ii. 2; 1 Tim. vi. 17; Tit. ii. 12. In Eph. i. 21 there is a special reason for naming both terms, because the supremacy of the name of Christ above all other names was to be affirmed without restriction either as to time or sphere. The other passages deal with some feature or element within the pre-eschatological period, so that there was no need of naming the opposite. Still, apart from this, Paul might have in certain connections spoken of the "coming aeon" by itself, but the less formal, more expressive phrase "kingdom of God" was naturally preferred in such cases, just as we more easily speak of "heaven" or "eternity" than of "the future age"; cp. 1 Cor. vi. 9, 10; xv. 50; Gal. v. 21; Eph. v. 5; 1 Thess. ii. 12; 2 Thess. i. 5; 2 Tim. iv. 18. The scarcity of explicit reference to "the coming aeon" should not, therefore, be counted an instance against the familiarity of Paul with the correlated contrast nor against the importance of the part played by it in his eschatological scheme. There is no evidence that the term *"aion"* had *per se* an evil flavor, which would have rendered it unfit to the Apostle's mind for association with the perfect future life; Eph. i. 21 proves the contrary. And yet it cannot be denied that as a rule the phrases "this age," "this world" were apt to call up evil associations. Such is plainly the case in 1 Cor. i. 20; ii. 6-8; in both these instances the evil implied or expressed has a peculiar noëtic reference. Satan is in 2 Cor. iv. 4 called outright "the god of this aion." According to Gal. i. 4, Christ gave Himself for our sins that He might rescue us out of this present evil aion. 2 Tim. iv. 10, Demas is said to have forsaken Paul, because he loved this aion. The Apostle warns the readers, Rom. xii. 2, not to assume or bear *"the schema"* of this aion, but to let themselves be transformed in the opposite direction. The degradation of the concept of "aion" in these cases is probably a reflex of the evil meaning of *"kosmos."* Other passages like 1 Tim. vi. 17; Tit. ii. 12 are more neutral from an ethical point of view.[17]

There are two problems connected with this terminology, being to some extent interdependent. The first problem concerns the antiquity and origin of the contrast in general; the second concerns the relation of *"aion"* to *"kosmos."* The Johannine writings do not employ "this aion" or "the coming aion" for the purpose of eschatological contrast. Wherever "aion" occurs in them either in the purely-temporal or in the eternity-sense, the associations are thoroughly favorable; the pronoun "this" is not prefixed to it. The standing phrase is "eis ton aiona," "until eternity." This receives sufficient explanation from the older Scriptural time-use of "'olam" and the plural "'olamim." On the other hand, for the evil member of the antithesis the word "kosmos," "ho kosmos hootos" finds characteristic employment with John.[18] Now this word "kosmos" with Paul also occasionally occurs synonymously with "ho aion hootos." So we find it Rom. iii. 6; 1 Cor. i. 20, 21; ii. 12; iii. 19; xi. 32; 2 Cor. vii. 10; Phil. ii. 15. That the word "kosmos" had evil coloring, when used in ethico-religious connections appears most clearly from the fact of its never being transferred to the state to come; "ho kosmos ekeinos," "that age," is neither Johannine nor Pauline. Jesus in his speech to the Jews shows conscious avoidance of it, Jno. viii. 23: "Ye are of this world; I *am not of this world"* instead of: "I am of that world." This

[17] The wicked nature implied in the contrast to the other aion marks a further point of difference between the Pauline antithesis and that in Hebrews.

[18] Cp. Jno. xii. 31; xiv. 30; xvi. 11, "ho archon too kosmoo tootoo"; cp. with "the god of this aeon," 2 Cor. iv. 4.

does not, of course, prevent either with John or Paul the ethically-neutral use of "world" as a comprehensive quantitative designation of the lower creation. For Paul, cp. Rom. i. 8; v. 12; 1 Cor. iv. 9 (vii. 31); xiv. 10; Eph. i. 4; Col. i. 6; 1 Tim. vi. 7; for John, cp. i. 9, 10; iii. 19; vi. 14; viii. 26; ix. 5; x. 36; xi. 27; xiii. 1; xvi. 21; xvii. 5, 24; xviii. 37; xxi. 25; 1 Jno. ii. 2; iv. 1, 3, 9; 2 Jno. 7.

The usage of both terms in Paul leaves the impression that the antithesis is not of the Apostle's own coining. The evil aspect of "the present age" he may have accentuated more than was done previously, but he certainly did not frame *de novo* either the phrase itself nor its close association with "ho kosmos." In the Jewish writing 4 Ezr., scarcely a generation later than Paul, it is said "that God made two aions," vii. 50; further, the present age and the future age are contrasted in a number of passages. The same appears in the Apocalypse of Baruch (of approximately the same period). Hillel speaks of "the life of the future aion." Jochanan ben Zakkai (about 80 A.D.) states that God revealed to Abraham "this aion" but not "the coming aion." To these may be joined, as a Jewish witness for the way of speaking, Eleazar from Modiim (somewhat later than Jochanan) who enumerates among the six good gifts bestowed upon Israel the coming aion and the new world. These Jewish authorities would certainly not have borrowed a phrase of this kind from Paul nor from the vocabulary of Christian eschatology in general. So that, even if earlier indubitable instances of occurrence could not be quoted, the ones just mentioned will suffice to prove the Pauline usage a derived one. Dalman, who is on the whole disinclined to carry the phrases farther back than is absolutely necessary, here also has critical suspicions, but is compelled to admit: "the existence of the phrases 'this aion,' 'the future aion' is at any rate established for the close of the first post-Christian century."[19]

Ascending backwards from Paul to the speech of Jesus in the Synoptical Gospels, we find the distinction between the two

[19] Cp. Dalman, *Die Worte Jesu,* I, pp. 122, 123.

ages both explicitly drawn and assumed by implication. The explicit contrast occurs Matt. xii. 32; Mk. x. 30; Lk. xx. 34 ff. Semi-explicit is Lk. xvi. 8, where as the contrast to "the children of this age (or world)" appears "the children of light." Impliedly the antithesis seems to be present Matt. xiii. 22 (Mk. iv. 19) "the care (Mk. cares) of the age (or world)" and in Matt. xiii. 39, 40, 49; xxiv. 3; xxviii. 20. "the end συντέλεια of the age (or world).[20] Dalman concludes that from a comparison of these parallels the occurrence of the phrase in the speech of Jesus cannot with any degree of certainty be inferred, and that, moreover, even should Jesus have actually employed it, it must have been for his mode of speaking of no significance. The inference of later intrusion of such a phrase from the mere fact of absence or variation in one or more parallel Gospel-texts seems precarious, because condensation no less than amplification on the writer's part may possibly account for the facts. But, even if one, with Dalman, were to call in doubt the presence of the phrase in the eschatological vocabulary of Jesus, its employment by the Evangelists, or by the antecedent bearers of the Gospel-tradition, would none the less retain considerable significance. For that the Evangelists or the tradition did not all borrow this phraseology from Paul seems certain. At their time of repeating or committing to writing, therefore, the terminology must have lain, so to speak, in the air, and this time was not so very far removed from the time of Paul or even of Jesus. In regard to the coloring of the contrast in the Gospel-passages we note that in certain instances it is chronological; so Matt. xii. 32: "it shall not be forgiven him, neither in this aion, neither in that to come." In Mk. x. 29, 30, "this aion" and "the aion to come" are the two time-instalments for restitution, the latter of which, to be sure, far surpasses the former. But in Lk. xx. 34 ff., it is implied that the children of "this aion" are ethico-religiously inferior, because unworthy to obtain the other aion. From

20 Besides here, the phrase "synteleia too aiōnos" is found in Heb. ix. 26 only.

the point of view of inherent distinctiveness "the children of this aion in their generation" are in Lk. xvi. 8 set over against "the children of the light"; "light" here is certainly not a mere figurative characterization, but points to the element pervasive of the future aion (or world). "The care (cares) of this aion" in Matt. xiii. 22; Mk. iv. 19 seem to reflect an unfavorable estimate of the influence and tendency of the aion (or world) with which some of the hearers of the gospel are preoccupied.[21] On the other hand, the five passages in Matthew containing the phrase "sunteleia too aiōnos" obviously take aion in a strictly chronological sense without admixture of a depreciating judgment.

Can this usage of the contrasting two ages (or worlds) be traced much farther back before the time of Jesus? In Sir. xviii. 10 the translated Syrian text distinguishes between "this aion" and "the aion of the pious," which yields both the formal opposition of the two and the different appraisal of each. But Dalman thinks that "in the day of the aion," corresponding to this in the Greek text, means no more than "in the life-time," and moreover considers the entire verse a later interpolation shedding no light upon the usage in the author's own time (about 175 B.C.). The Apocalypse of Enoch likewise speaks in lxxi. 15 of "the future aion," and in xlviii. 7 of "the aion of unrighteousness," but again these passages are regarded by Dalman subsequent additions to the text. The harvest thus gleaned from the pre-Christian sources is not plentiful; indeed after Dalman's critical sifting it dwindles to practically nothing. We would thus seem to be forced down to the Jewish period about contemporary to Jesus and Paul for reliable attestation of the existence of the terminology, always keeping in mind that it must be somewhat older than this time in view of the easy way in which Paul handles it.

Before tracing the antiquity of "kosmos" as found with Paul, and in the Greek Gospels, partly as a comprehensive

[21] Some textual authorities read "too aionos *tootoo*" in this passage; cp. Dalman, p. 125.

term for all that exists, partly as an evil-complexioned designation of the system opposed to God, and therefore doomed to pass away, i.e., more or less eschatologically colored, we shall have to put to ourselves the question what lies back of it in the Hebrew or the Aramaic vernacular. As is well known these languages originally possessed no word for "world," but helped themselves, where the idea of "the all" was to be expressed by roundabout ways of speaking; e.g., Gen. i. 1 says: "in the beginning God created *the heaven and the earth.*" In later times, through the contact with and influence of other languages and modes of thought, it was found necessary to employ a single word for the concept of "the world." The word that entered into this vacant place of speech was the word Ha-'Olām. But this word was from its very etymology a *time*-designation; in being adopted for "world" it was put to an extraneous new use. And yet the choice of precisely this word for that particular use can not have been purely arbitrary; there must have been some reason in the *time*-meaning that invited the transition to the *world*-meaning. Probably the inducement lay in the consideration that the time-course of things unrolling itself successively up to an expected end could be comprehensively surveyed so as to appear a coherent totality of specific character: the age constituted, as it were, a world when regarded as to its complexion. It will be observed, however, that this could scarcely have happened, had not "the age" appeared as strictly terminating at the farther end. In other words belief in a fixed nature and a temporal duration of the present order of things is inherent in the word "aion," where it inclines to pass over from the time- into the world-category.[22] From that point on an "age" and a "world" had become so closely cognate as to be well-nigh inseparable, both being expressible by the same word. In this chronological semi-qualitative condensation of the entire content of a temporal development from beginning to end seems to lie the seed out

[22] Dalman, *Die Worte Jesu,* p. 134, thinks that no reflection upon the *terminus ad quem* was necessary to account for the new point of view:

of which the full-grown scheme of the two ages and the two worlds grew up.

It is obvious that the twofold meaning of the one word "'olam" thus established was bound to produce a degree of uncertainty in the understanding and rendering of the word in not a few cases. And this uncertainty attached not only to the term in the Hebrew or Aramaic original; it likewise passed over to the Greek employment. The Greek had a separate word for "world," and therefore was quite able to distinguish in each case. But this was not done in all instances. As 'Olam "age" had received 'Olam "world" for its twin-brother, so the Greek term aion for "age" was liable to be pressed into the same double service. Originally a pure time-concept, it now became an all-comprehensive space-concept as well. "Aion" may mean "age" in the New Testament and it may mean "world." In some cases the decision may be difficult, in other cases the sense "world" is from the context unmistakable. Matt. xiii. 22, "care of the aion"; Lk. xvi. 8, "the children of this aion" (as contrasted with "the children of the light") are examples of the former; 2 Tim. iv. 10, "having loved the present aion" and Heb. i. 2 and xi. 3 will illustrate the latter. The two last-named references from Hebrews illustrate the inevitable grammatical incongruousness arising from carrying over "aion" "world" into the Greek. "Aion" in its time-sense stood in the Semitic idiom not seldom in the plural, naturally so, since there were many ages or sections of time, or because the concept was subject to pluralization for the sake of stressing endlessness or majesty. Where with "aion" in the sense of "world" this pluralization was retained, we find the mode of speech that God *made* the *"aionas," "worlds."*

The equivocalness of the word "'Olam," or its Aramaic equivalent, has something to do also with the difficulty of

the *unsurveyableness* of the course of things sufficed to suggest it. He admits, however, that "'Olam" in such a case is distinguished from "world" by its temporal conception only; as to content, the two are equal.

ascertaining how old exactly the world-idea is in the religious sources, where it first with certainty emerges in them. In the Old Testament there is no assured instance; Daniel still says "the whole earth," where to us the whole "world" would have seemed to be in place; obviously the writer did not have the latter at his disposal; cp. ii. 35, 39; iii. 31; iv. 8, 19. Sir. xxxviii. 4 is a doubtful instance; the Greek "ktisma aionos" would naturally suggest "creation of the world," especially in view of the Syriac rendering with "da-ʿalmah" for the second word. Still it is possible to maintain, as Dalman prefers doing, that "aionos" here goes back to the meaning of "eternity" for "ʿOlam" which would yield "the eternal creation," thus eliminating the idea of "world." En. i-xxxvi contains several times the designation of God as "the God of the aion," or "the King of the aiones," "the Ruler of the aion." Here again the first impulse would be to render "King of the world" or "God of the worlds." Dalman, however, objects to this on the ground of the obvious dependence of such phrases on the O.T. "God of the age," "Rock of the ages," "King of the age," "kingdom of all the ages," Gen. xxi, 33; Isa. xxvi. 4, xl. 28; Jer. x. 10; Ps. cxlv. 13, all expressive of the eternity of God. To be sure, in none of these phrases does the article stand before the second word, whilst in the Greek combinations it is found regularly. The force of this, however, is somewhat lessened by the observation, that the article need not have been intended to render "aion" by itself determinate, but only for the determination of the compound name. Or again, the qualification "(ha-)ʿolam" might have meant no more than to describe God as *God forever,* "(ha-)ʿolam" being used adverbially. But, while all this may be possible, it at the utmost allows bare possibility, of not-yet-existence of the world-concept; for disproving its existence it is insufficient, and on the whole unconvincing.[23] In the *Similitudes of Enoch* several times "the creation of the world" occurs; here the idea of creation forbids to think of "age." The passages are xlviii. 6, 7; lxix. 16, 17, 18;

[23] *Die Worte Jesu,* pp. 133-134.

lxxi. 15. Dalman regards them as later additions, without, however, giving his reasons except in the case of the first. Be this as it may, the mere suspicion thrown upon them is bound to render them doubtful witnesses. In the Book of Visions (En. lxxxiii-xc) occurs "God of the entire world," lxxxiv. 2; because it stands in "a very verbose doxology" belonging to the introduction of the Visions, Dalman speaks dubiously about this; he thinks it may be later than the other parts. Besides, of the Visions as a whole he remarks, that their date cannot be determined with certainty. And his conclusion of the whole matter, to our mind somewhat rash, is that the use of the word 'Olam for "world" in the pre-Christian period is subject to strong doubt.[24]

The Synoptical passages containing "world" (kosmos) are the following: Matt. iv. 8; v. 14; xiii. 38; xvi. 26; (Mk. viii. 36; Lk. ix. 25); xviii. 7; xxiv. 21; xxv. 34; (Lk. xi. 50); xxvi. 13; (Mk. xiv. 9); Mk. xvi. 15; Lk. xii. 30. Even these are attacked, so far as an underlying 'Olam for kosmos is concerned. The reasons adduced do not carry weight. That the appropriateness of "kingdoms of the *earth*" in the temptation-narrative is as great as that of "kingdoms of the world" not many exegetes, coming to the phrase without particular linguistic preoccupation would affirm. Was Satan's influence in its wide range, let us say at the time of the writing of this account, not more graphically depicted by "world" than by "aion"? Luke has for "kosmos" "oikoomene," which admits of the same remark. Where Matthew, Mark and Luke agree in rendering their original with "gaining the whole world," Matt. xvi. 26; Mk. viii. 36; Lk. ix. 25 the argument from absence of kosmos in a parallel text is eliminated. Hence Dalman acknowledges that from the saying some plausibility may be obtained for the use of the Aramaic term "world," but he thereupon straightway weakens the grudgingly granted concession by observing at the close "that the possibility exists to remove also this example of the use of ''alam' for 'kosmos' from the speech of Jesus,

[24] *Die Worte Jesu*, p. 135.

by either taking ' ʿalma' in the sense of 'Zeitlichkeit' (time-expanse), or putting back of 'the whole kosmos' 'all the *earth*' (arʿa)." That in the combination "light of the *kosmos*" and "salt of the *earth*," Matt. v. 14, the translator must have found two different words in his original, is self-evident. There is a presumption in favor of light having been associated with "world" and salt with "earth." While as a matter of fact in both figures humanity is meant as that which is to be enlightened and to be salted, yet the diffusion of light as the more volatile element is more naturally joined to the idea of "world" and that of salt as a materially penetrating element joins itself most easily to "earth." The "woe" that is proclaimed upon the kosmos, could not very well, without falling into extremely realistic apocalyptic, have been called down upon the *earth*. The phrases descriptive of the preaching of the gospel to the kosmos, Matt. xiii. 38; xxvi. 13; Mk. xiv. 9; xvi. 15 would allow equally well of the rendering "to the (whole) *earth*," and therefore do not help to a decision. Quite synonymously with these are used "in the whole oikoomene," Matt. xxiv. 14, and "to all the ethne (nations)," Mk. xiii. 10; Matt. xxviii. 19; "to the whole ktisis"[25] Lk. xvi. 15, cp. "ta ethne too kosmoo," Lk. xii. 30; "from the foundation of the kosmos," Matt. xxv. 34; Lk. xi. 50; "from the beginning of the kosmos," Matt. xxiv. 41; "from the beginning of the ktisis," Mk. x. 6; xiii. 19; these are certainly more natural expressions when understood of "the world" than of "the earth"; the quotation in Matt. xiii. 35 from Ps. lxxviii. 2 puts "foundation of the world" for the Sept. "from the beginning" which has no further specification as to the beginning of what is meant. Taking all the evidence together it seems hard to escape the conclusion, that the Aramaic original of the Evangelist was not unfamiliar with "Alma" as "world." It would be highly precarious to assume that in all the instances quoted Jesus employed the word with a time-

[25] It ought to be remembered that "ktisis" can designate "the created *race* of men"; Dalman, *Die Worte Jesu*, p. 144.

meaning only, or did not speak the sayings in their present form at all.[26]

Before dismissing these Synoptical cases the question may be put, whether the *kosmos*-ʿolam, if assumed to be present in them, carries with it any association of evil. Is "the world" in the parlance of Jesus a bad or a neutral name? The kingdoms of the world offered by Satan are undoubtedly conceived as making up an evil world.[27] The kosmos upon which the "woe" is pronounced on account of the offenses bound to come in it, Matt. xviii. 7, is, at least in a potential sense, an object of condemnation, but to what extent this enters into the word "kosmos" itself is harder to determine.[28] the kosmos that needs to derive its light from the disciples is a darkened world in a moral sense. The kosmos comparable to the field into which the seed is sown is likewise a sphere outside the pale of salvation. The nations of the kosmos seek after the things of this life in distinction from the disciples who seek after the kingdom of God, and the character of these nations which are thus described can scarcely avoid impressing itself upon the world they compose. Into the other cases no ethical or religious appraisal need enter.[29]

About to return to Paul we may cast a look around in the earlier or contemporary Jewish (non-canonical) literature.[30]

[26] To think of "ʿOlam," "ʿAlam" as time-concepts exclusively is forbidden by the nature of the reference, e.g., "foundation of the world," where "foundation of the age" yields no sense. The choice lies among three things: "world," "earth," and the critical denial of the expressions to Jesus.

[27] Rev. xi. 15, "The kingdom of the world is become of our Lord and of his Christ," furnishes a parallel, although "kingdom" is here in the singular and might mean "kingship."

[28] The latter half of the verse individualizes the application "woe to that man," showing the evil nature of the object affected.

[29] The above survey shows that the evil connotation of "ho kosmos," so prominent in John, is not entirely absent from the Synoptics. It further indicates that Jesus' use of the concept "world" contains the same elements as that of Paul; although the ethical coloring is neither so emphatic nor so systematic as with the Apostle.

[30] Hellenistic writings like 2 Macc., 4 Macc., Wisdom, need not be considered here; they use "kosmos" freely. What we are endeavoring to trace is the *Semitic* equivalent back of "kosmos."

The section lxxii-lxxxii of the Book of Enoch (about 100 B.C.) refers several times to the created "world," lxxii. 1; lxxv. 3, 8; lxxxi. 1, 5, 7. In another division of the same book, xci-civ (about the same date), "the revelation of the judgment to the whole world" is spoken of, xci. 14; the ideas of totality and of wickedness mingle here. The Assumptio Mosis (preserved in Latin, about A.D. 50-100) speaks of the "orbis terrarum," and also of "saeculum."[31] Both of these rest on the world-sense of the underlying original. The Apocalypse of Baruch (believed to contain sections of varying dates) has even in its older parts, not perhaps so very far removed from Paul, the Syriac term in the sense of "world"; the Greek lying back of the Syriac must have read "kosmos," liv. 1; lvi. 2, 3; lxxiii. 1, 5. The Book of Jubilees (last century before Christ) speaks of the "generations of the saeculum," and God is called "the God of the saeculum," phrases in which the Latin "saeculum" plainly seems intended to render the Greek "kosmos," although the time-conception is not wholly excluded, x. 17; xxv. 23; also the possibility that "earth was meant in the original may have to be reckoned with. Finally, 4 Ezra (Apoc. of Ezra), in the main dating at the latest from the close of the First or the beginning of the Second Century A.D., makes frequent mention of "the created saeculum" (in the Syriac text "ʿalma"), and while in some instances "aion" may be the word presupposed

[31] In Christian Latin the noun "saeculum" signifies both "age" (from sequi "to follow") and "world," the latter with a sub-flavor of inferiority from the other-worldly point of view. Hence "secular," from "saecularis," "pertaining to the world." The saeculum is the transitory in its nature—no less than in its time-aspect. This way of speaking is not indigenously Latin; it seems to have been imported into the language from the Jewish or the Christian vocabulary. The phrase "in saecula saeculorum" of the liturgy means, quite after the Scriptural (both Hebrew and Greek) pattern "unto endless ages." It acquires a strange sound only when for the version into English "world" is used: "*world without end.*" This seems at first to imply a confusion between the two meanings of "saeculum," choosing "world" where "age" was indicated. But we are told by lexicographers, that in old English likewise the word "world" already had a time-meaning. Owing to this, "world without end" may not have sounded so strange to the first users as it does to us now.

in the original Greek, even this would not bar out the sense of "world," as Heb. i. 2; xi. 3 prove. The reason why Dalman thinks that "aion" must have stood everywhere in the Greek is not plain.[32]

The later Jewish literature has no further bearing on the situation in the words of Jesus or the writings of Paul. After having looked around in the environment, nearer or more remote, of our Lord and his Apostle, we now proceed to take up certain points yet undetermined and on which perhaps the enquiry just concluded may cast some light. The question naturally arises, whether, if in the surrounding literature (Jewish or Christian) "aion" was made to render double service for "age" and "world," traces of the latter are discoverable with Paul. For Rom. xii. 2; 1 Cor. ii. 6, 8; iii. 18; 2 Cor. iv. 4; Gal. i. 4; 1 Tim. vi. 17 the possibility of this must be admitted; on the other hand where not "this aion," but the present age ("ho nun aion") appears, the strict time-reference has more plausibility. With "kosmos" this "nun" is not found, whilst "hootos" is, 1 Cor. iii. 19. That Paul, though closely associating "this age" and "this world," yet did not quite promiscuously employ them follows from their joint-occurrence in Eph. ii. 2; "wherein ye once walked according to the aion of this kosmos"; here the supposition is that to the kosmos (conceived as evil) an evil time- or life-complexion belongs, the one affecting the other and being inseparable from the other, but none the less conceptually and linguistically distinguishable the one from the other. On the whole we shall have to say that the world-scheme follows the time-scheme, not the reverse; this is not without theological importance for the interpretation of the Apostle's idea of the kosmos as evil.[33]

[32] *Die Worte Jesu,* p. 140.

[33] It may be of some interest to note the attitude of the Versions of the English Bible towards the more or less equivocal "aion." A.V. has rendered "aion" everywhere by "world," except in Eph. ii. 2, where "aion" and "kosmos" occur together in the phrase "aion too kosmoo," and consequently the former required some other term for which "course" was chosen; this would not badly render "aion" in its temporal sense, but

We have already seen that the distinction between "this age" and "the age to come" lies in the line of successiveness. Where, and as soon as, the one ceases, the other begins, or at least is at the point of beginning. Even pre-millennarians can have no objection to this statement, inasmuch as under their scheme the millennium could in part be identified with the age to come as the beginning thereof. The very name "coming aion" is not merely expressive of futurity, but also carries within itself the element of direct successiveness. Were this otherwise, then the entire closely-knit scheme intended to comprehend all happenings in the universe from beginning to end would fall into pieces, because of the lacking link in the

"course" inevitably awakens the erroneous impression as though "manner of conduct" were intended, which is not quite so large a concept as Paul wished to express. In Matt. xiii. 22 (Mk. iv. 19) "the cares of this world" A.V. has added the pronoun "this" which is not in the original; the adverb "nun" in 1 Tim. vi. 17 and 2 Tim. iv. 10, Tit. ii. 12, has not prevented the rendering "world"; nor has the pointed contrast between "this aion" and "the aion to come," in Matt. xii. 33, induced abandonment of "world"; in "synteleia too aionos," "world" is likewise retained; in Heb. ix. 26, the plural "aiones" did not prevent the rendering "world" (singular), which to be sure was warranted in view of i. 2 and xi. 3, where, however, the plural "worlds" is given; the case of ix. 26 and that of the two other passages is not alike, because in the latter the idea of "*making*" the "aiones" enters, which positively demands "world"; in the other passage (ix. 26) the matter is doubtful; R.V. has "ages" in the second half of the verse; this procedure of A.V. has the merit of uniformity; in some cases it is undoubtedly correct, in others certainly incorrect; the worst is that it covers up a problem to the reader who is unfamiliar with the original. R.V. and A.R.V., so far as the text-reading is concerned, have, in, the main, conformed themselves to A.V., but by the marginal reading "age" in nearly all cases remind of the problem which linguistic investigation in modern times has more clearly brought to light. Still, they might have shown less conservatism in the matter; it would have been perfectly safe to place "age" in the text in more than one instance, where it now must put up with a place in the margin, e.g., Matt. xii. 32; Mk. x. 30; Eph. i. 21; Eph. ii. 2, on the other hand, "course of this age" would be scarcely an improvement on "course of this world"; here the marginal suggestion of "age" would have better been omitted. On the whole the Revisions are better guides, not so much because in their text-rendering they are more correct, but because in their margin they reflect the uncertainty of interpretation, which also may be an interpreter's legitimate function.

middle. To say that a sin will not be forgiven either in this age or in the age to come could never have served as a formula for absolute unforgivableness *ad infinitum,* Matt. xii. 32, if there were conceivable a gap between the two aions. "The rulers of this age" are in process of being brought to nought (present participle), 1 or. ii. 6, which implies that after their conquest the aion in which they have ruled ceases. We should also remember that Paul, no less than our Lord, inherited this distinction from Jewish theology or Apocalyptic, where it undoubtedly had the meaning of successiveness. Even, were one to deny its pre-Pauline currency in Judaism, the successiveness plainly belonging to it soon afterwards would be decisive on this point. The close association between aion and kosmos compels the same conclusion, for of the kosmos it is said, 1 Cor. vii. 31 that its *schema* passes away: it passes away to make room for another *schema.* "The ends of the aions" have come upon believers, 1 Cor. x. 11. As will be afterwards shown the "pleroma too chronoo," "the fulness of time" has nothing to do in the first place with the idea of "ripeness of the times"; it designates the arrival of the present dispensation of time at its predetermined goal of fulfilment through the appearance of the Messiah, Gal. iv. 4; cp. Eph. i. 10. Thus understood it signifies the immediate transition from chronos to something else.

This straight horizontal way of looking at the eschatological progress was not with Paul a purely-formal thing. There belong to it a grandiose sweep and impressive inclusiveness with regard to the whole of history. When filled with the content of the latter it acquires the character of the most intense dramatic realism. It is drama, and, besides that, drama hastening on with accelerated movement to the point of dénouement and consummation. Hence it engages the Apostle's most practical religious interest no less than that it moulds his theoretical view concerning the structure of the Christian faith. Some writers have held, to be sure, that nothing but purely-Jewish, or at best primitive-Christian, eschatology is with slight modifications reproduced in this teaching.[34] Even if this were correct, it would not necessarily prove the otioseness or perfunctoriness of such an inheritance of thought and life. Jewish religion was not entirely barren of genuine enthusiasm. Especially in its Apocalyptic phase it reveals a heartfelt interest in the final issues to come, such as went far beyond pessimistic other-worldliness or morbid curiosity inciting to speculation.[35] And, what is more than this, Paul's relation to these matters could never be as distant and at bottom speculative as was that of Judaism.[36] For to

[34] Cp. Pfleiderer, *Paulinism,* I, 259; Brückner, *Entstehung der Paulinischen Christologie,* pp. 173 ff.; Johannes Hoffmann, *Das Abendmahl im Urchristenthum,* p. 139; Deissmann, *Th.L.Z.,* 1898, Sp. 14.

[35] Baldensperger, *Das Selbstbewusstsein Jesu im Lichte der Messianischen Hoffnungen seiner Zeit,* 3d ed. 1903, credits Apocalyptic with a considerable influence towards that transcendentalizing and spiritualizing of religion which in his opinion found its supreme expression in Christianity.

[36] This may be the proper place to add a few remarks about the relation of the Pauline to the Jewish eschatology. That the formal contrast between the present age and the coming age was derived by Paul (or by Jesus) from that source has already been shown. Nor is this contrast purely formal, for it implies a relative depreciation of the ethico-religious quality of the present age. But there are not a few other points of agreement between the Pauline and the Jewish teaching, although these relate rather to details than to comprehensive issues. We mention the following without laying claim to completeness of statement. The **ἅγιοι,** saints or angels, will accompany the Messiah at his coming, En. i. 9; 4 Ezr. vii. 28; xiii. 52; xiv. 9. There will be the sound of a trumpet to wake the dead, Orac. Sib. iv. 173; 4 Ezr. vi. 23. Both God and the Messiah bring about the resurrection, Apoc. Bar. lxxxv. 15; Psa. Sol. xi. 96. A distinction is drawn between the dead to be raised and the gathering to the Messiah of those found alive at His appearance, Apoc. Bar. xiv. 2; 4 Ezr. vii. 28. A change will take place both in the raised and in the living, En. cviii. 11; 4 Macc. iv. 22, although the exact point in time of the change is not fixed with uniformity (on which cp. later); the impossibility of having part in the future world without such a change is recognized; the conception of being "absent" from the body in death appears, Test. Abr. lxxxiv. 21; xcv. 23; the representations that God will be the Judge, that the Messiah will be, that the saints will judge the world, are found En. c. 4; 4 Ezr. xii. 32; Sap. Sol. iii. 8. Fire is named as the means of testing man's work, Apoc. Bar. xliii. 39. Of course, the Jewish eschatology has its basis in the Old Testament. This, however, can not wholly account for the agreement between it and Paul

Paul the chief actor in this drama *had come* upon the scene; the Messiah had been made present, and could not but be looked upon as henceforth the dominating figure in all further developments. And Christ was to Paul so close, so all-comprehensive and all-pervasive, that nothing could remain peripheral wherein He occupied the central place. We hope presently to show that, as a matter of fact, not only the

as to data going beyond the O.T. There is no escape from the conclusion that a piece of Jewish theology has been here by Revelation incorporated into the Apostle's teaching. Paul had none less than Jesus Himself as a predecessor in this. The main structure of the Jewish Apocalyptic is embodied in our Lord's teaching as well as in Paul's. And further, 1 Thess. iv. 15 shows that in an important point of his eschatological program Paul was directly dependent on a word from the Lord. Cp. also the figure of the Lord's coming as a thief in the night, 1 Thess. v. 2, which seems to have no parallel in Jewish literature, Matt. xxiv. 43. The exhortation to be watchful, 1 Thess. v. 6 ff.; 1 Cor. xvi. 13; Eph. vi. 18, may well be a reminiscence of similar words by Jesus. The term "episynagoge" "our gathering together," 2 Thess. ii. 1 is perhaps reminiscent of Matt. xxiv. 31, ἐπισυνάξουσι "they shall gather together." The prophecy of great sufferings and persecution as preceding the end may have been derived, at least in some of its details from Matt. xxiv. 19 ff., cp. 1 Thess. iii. 4; 1 Cor. vii. 26, 28. The thought that the saints shall judge the world offers a partial analogy to the promise of Jesus about the Apostles' judging the tribes of Israel. The doctrine concerning the change in the body finds a point of contact in our Lord's argument with the Sadducees.

On the whole, however, it should not be overlooked that the Pauline eschatology differs from the Jewish Apocalypses in certain fundamental characteristics. For one thing it is non-political. As will afterwards be shown, there is no place in the Apostle's scheme for an earthly, provisional kingdom of the Messiah. Paul's polemic against heathenism is of a strictly religious nature, Rom. xiii. 1 ff. The great powers to be destroyed are "Sin" and "Death"; the victory to be won over them proceeds from "Grace" and "Life," Rom. v. 17, 21; 1 Cor. iv. 8. The Pauline Eschatology (though by no means preponderatingly so) is yet more individualistic than the Jewish. It is also much more restrained and sober, less luxuriant than the latter in which the over-heated phantasy plays no small part. With Paul the specifically-religious interest rules supreme. In such matters the imagination always tends to multiply and elaborate; the religious interest tends in precisely the opposite direction: it simplifies and concentrates. Hence the phenomenon, that the Jewish eschatology offers a multitude of unharmonized, and even unharmonizable, details, whilst with Paul we find a comparatively simple and consistent scheme; cp. Wernle, *Die Anfänge unserer Religion,* p. 173.

Christology but also the Soteriology of the Apostle's teaching is so closely interwoven with the Eschatology, that, were the question put, which of the strands is more central, which more peripheral, the eschatology would have as good a claim to the central place as the others. In reality, however, there is no alternative here; there is backward and forward movement in the order of thought in both directions.

That the Apostle's religious mentality was of a forward-looking character appears first of all from the rôle played in his Epistles by the conception of "hope." The rôle would undoubtedly have been more prominent still, had it not been for the necessity of stressing the idea of faith on account of its controversial importance. In hope the believer must abound through the Holy Spirit, Rom. xv. 13. Together with faith and love it enters into the triad of abiding things, 1 Cor. xiii. 13.[37] The proximate fruit of the ripening Christian experience consists in such hope as does not put to shame, inasmuch as the foretaste of the life to come is shed abroad in the believer's heart through the preliminary gift of the Holy Spirit, Rom. v. 4. The Christian *is* saved "upon the basis of hope" (ep' elpidi), for hope and the things upon which it terminates constitute the supreme goal of salvation,

[37] That "*now*" in "now abideth" can not be restricted to the temporal state is clear from the contrast between the provisional and temporary charismata and the abiding three graces. That love, the greatest of the three, remains in the final state is easy to understand. With regard to faith the matter is more difficult, because Paul elsewhere (2 Cor. v. 7) puts the present walk in faith (or: through the region of faith) over against the future walk through or in sight (or: through the region of sight); cp. also vs. 12 in the same context. The presupposition might be that, side by side with the promises fulfilled, and as such requiring no further functioning of faith, there will always be elements in the apprehension and possession of God which must remain inaccessible to the creature except through faith. God, as God, by his own Being, under all circumstances, must to a large extent remain apprehensible by faith alone. But it is different with regard to hope. Hope ordinarily has its very terminus and object in the final state as such, and would accordingly with the arrival of the latter seem to supersede itself. Hence the word becomes suggestive of still ulterior vistas of realization within the final state. Nor is it sufficient to say that the abiding, assured *retention* of the attained things appears as an object of ceaseless hoping; this would introduce a

Rom. viii. 24. The pre-Christian pagan state is characterized by the absence of God and of hope, and these two are not meant as two simply-coördinated items of religious destitution; the second arises from the first and the implication is that foremost among the benefits of religion (that is of "having God") is to have hope, Eph. ii. 12; 1 Thess. iv. 13. God is called the God of hope, Rom. xv. 13. Hence the double theme of the Apostle's missionary preaching to the Thessalonians is to turn "unto God from idols, to serve a living and true God, and to wait for his Son from heaven, who delivers from the wrath to come," 1 Thess. i. 9, 10. Hope is one of the great telic categories of the divine vocation, Eph. i. 18; iv. 4. In the Christian armor it constitutes the helmet, as connected with salvation, 1 Thess. v. 8. Still in the Pastoral Epistles it occurs as "the blessed hope and appearing of our great God and Saviour Jesus Christ," Tit. ii. 13, and as "the hope of eternal life," Tit. iii. 7. In Gal. v. 5 Christians "through the Spirit by faith wait for the hope of righteousness" (that is for the realization of the hoped for things pertaining to the state of righteousness conferred in justification).

A mere survey of the above references places in very clear light the vividness and vitality pertaining to hope and the complex of future realities it calls up and keeps present to the Christian mind. So far from resembling a quiescent, non-productive capital, merely carried pro forma on the ledger of consciousness, it contains energy and actual no less than potential force. The etymological coloring of such words as "*apokaradokia*" and "*apekdechesthai*" in itself bears witness to the eager state of mind depicted, Rom. viii. 19, 23, 25; 1 Cor. i. 7; Gal. v. 5; Phil. i. 20; iii. 20; cp. also the duplication by synonymy in Phil. i. 20.[38] The quiet, but none the less

discordant note into the Pauline idea of consummation, and be moreover in direct contradiction to the statement of Rom. viii. 24: "Who hopes for that which he sees?" Cp. Bachmann in Zahn's *Kom. z. N.T.*, Vol. VII, p. 405. The same triad of faith, love and hope occurs also 1 Thess. i. 3, where hope occupies the third place, and 1 Thess. v. 8, with the same sequence.

intense, energy of hoping appears most strikingly in this that it is equal to transforming the natural protest against pain and tribulation into that submission of patience which the word "*hypomone*" expresses.[39] The suffusion of the hoping state of mind with profound feeling and the strong concentration of interest upon it as a life-concern are well illustrated by 1 Cor. xv. 19, a statement which needs some paraphrasing in order to bring out its full force and exact meaning. It might be paraphrased approximately as follows: If we have turned out to be no more than Christ-hopers and staked on that our whole present life, then we are of all men most pitiable. In this one sentence the Apostle has woven two thoughts together at some expense of syntactical perspicuity. The one thought is that hope without corresponding reality, or at least a principle of realization, is the most futile and ill-fated frustration of life-purpose; the other is that when this futile hope so engrosses a man as to monopolize him for an unreal world such a state of mind involves the forfeit of all palpable realities of life, a sacrifice at bottom of all this-worldliness for an other-worldliness that has no substance.[40]

[38] Cp. Hodge, *Comm. on Rom.* p. 423 (ad Rom. viii. 19): *"The earnest expectation,* ἀποκαραδοκία from *καραδοκεῖν, erecto capite prospicere,* to look for with the head erect. The ἀπό is intensive; so that ἀποκαραδοκία is earnest or persistent expectation." The same idea is in the other word, although here the figures of the erect head and the stretching forward are not explicitly present.

[39] *"Hypomone"* literally signifies "staying under" as the opposite of "withdrawing from underneath" some burden or hardship. This metaphorical, and in particular N.T. spiritualized, meaning is not to be confounded with the Stoic "apathy," for the latter is an artificial indifference forced by the will, whilst the Christian patience is an inward submission inspired by other positive gains and satisfactions in view. Hence "hope" and "patience" in the Christian sequence of thought naturally go together. Cp. Rom. v. 3, 4; viii. 25; xv. 4; 1 Thess. i. 3.

[40] The *"monon"* at the end of the hypothetical clause is intended to apply equally much to the words "in this life (*only*)" as to the phrase "having had hope (*only*)." The text which places ἠλπικότες ἐσμὲν after ἐν χριστῷ and directly before μόνον brings this out better than the ordinary sequence: ἠλπικότες ἐν Χριστῷ μόνον. The force of the periphrastic perfect, "have been hopers," will be noted; it describes such as have acquired hope and continued to live on that basis ever since; this looks backward to "in this life"; it suggests the idea of a whole life thrown away on *mere* hope.

The pagan, who lives without God and without hope in the world, has at least the enjoyment of the earthly and transitory; the Christian whose hope puts him to shame has not even this: he has lost what he had and received nothing in return, cp. vs. 32. It is significant also in the present connection that Paul makes hope the source of that peculiar exaltation which he calls "kauchāsthai." If the distinction between the so-called "enthusiastic" and the more stabilized elements in the Christian religiousness must needs be drawn, it will be necessary, on account of this association with kauchāsthai to recognize in the experience of hoping a genuinely enthusiastic element; cp. for this combination Rom. v. 2, 3; 1 Thess. ii. 19.[41] Whatever relative appraisal Paul might put upon the two categories named, the fact stated makes it at any rate certain, if further assurance were required, that the believer's hope is a most potent ferment and stimulant in the religious consciousness of the early Christian, and not the least in the Pauline churches. After all, what is most convincing in this respect is the indubitable expectation of the nearness of the parousia which pervaded the Christian mind, and can, both as an expectation and a wish, be traced in the consciousness of the Apostle himself. It is a pity that through the chronological problem in its bearing upon the infallibleness of the teaching, the far more important aspect of the fact as exponential of Paul's attitude towards the futurity-side of Christianity has been too little considered. A *mere* chronological datum the feature certainly is not. It would not be out of the way to suggest that the chronological element has been just as much affected by the eagerness of

[41] It is true kauchāsthai is not descriptive of Christian states of mind exclusively. Paul reminds the Jew that it is his habit to practise this feeling with reference to God and the law, Rom. ii. 17, 20. With apparent allusion to the former he predicates the act of believers as exercised in God *through Jesus Christ,* Rom. v. 11; Phil. iii. 3. In the majority of cases it is used in a depreciating sense either of Jews or Christians, therefore negatively and often metaphorically; cp. 1 Cor. i. 29, 31; iii. 21; iv. 7; 2 Cor. v. 12; but cp. also 2 Cor. x. 15, 17; xi. 16, and the paradoxical vs. 30; xii. 9.

the intent upon eschatological consummation as the reverse. It is a not uncommon phenomenon till the present day that the acuteness or over-acuteness of the eschatological sensorium, brings with itself an inevitable foreshortening of the vista in time. To look contemptuously at the latter can never serve as an excuse for the practical neglect of the true principle of Christian hope as such.

In still another way the predominance of the eschatological note evinces itself through the disparaging judgment passed upon the present age or world. This is by no means to be interpreted as a reflex effect of the eschatological state of mind, as though preoccupation with the future had produced first indifference to and next dissatisfaction with or condemnation of the existing state of things. The attitude towards the world has its own reason, altogether apart from eschatological interest, although the latter may be nourished by the former. In this point eschatology is not so much the active as the passive factor. Nevertheless the intense revulsion from the world and the age, such as they are, affords convincing proof that without a secure anchorage in the world beyond the spiritual poise which the Apostle everywhere maintains would have been impossible. It has become customary to speak of "pessimism" in this connection. The term is badly chosen, not because it is too strong in degree, but because in philosophical nomenclature it denotes the assumption of an absolute, irremediable, metaphysically grounded despair of things. Such a belief was *a priori* impossible to Paul; in fact it forms a contradiction in terms with the concept of eschatology itself. As to the outcome of the eschatological process nothing but unqualified optimism could have existed in the Apostle's mind, not to speak now of the optimistic, because soteric, implications of the substance of his teaching as a whole. The idea of the creation of the world by God already is incompatible with even that qualified pessimism which is symptomatic of Gnostic speculation. Absolute pessimism would have had to attach itself within the scheme of Paul's thinking to the conception of the σάρξ, and there is no evidence whatever either of the primordial origin of the σάρξ in creation or of its lasting persistence in the end. On the contrary, wherever Paul speaks of the two stages of existence he avoids the mention of the σάρξ.[42] The real source of this so-called pessimism lies in the Apostle's acute and pervasive sense of sin. It is the burdensomeness and depressive power of sin that impels irresistibly towards the thought of hope with regard to the eschatological deliverance.[43] Nor should it

[42] Cp. 1 Cor. xv. 45-49, the one passage in which Paul goes back of the fact of sin to find the determining basis for the relatively inferior state of man, as compared with his eschatological destiny, in the mode of his creation. But the technical term for this is not here "sarkikos," it is "psychikos"; the idea of sin does not enter.

[43] A parallel to this intensification of the eschatological hope through the acute sense of sin and evil is furnished among the Apocalyptic writings by *4 Ezra* and *Apoc. Baruch,* both written not too far apart from the date of Paul. In both there is a depreciating judgment on the present state of the world. True, there appears between these two writings a difference in the severity of judgment expressed. *4 Ezra* is more sweeping in his view than the writer of Baruch. This appears in the explanation of the origin of sin. In the former Apocalypse the nexus between Adam's sin and that of humanity as a whole is much more direct: with Adam was *created* a principle of evil, the so-called *"yezer-ra,"* and it was by yielding to this that the *"cor malignum"* was developed; hence Adam is the cause of spiritual death as well as of physical death in mankind, because all were made to share in this evil propensity. The scheme of justification through the law proved, and could not but prove, a total failure. All this, except the idea of concreated evil propensity, reminds of Paul. As a matter of fact the opinion is held that *4 Ezra* stood under Christian, specifically Pauline, influence. Box (*The Ezra-Apocalypse, Introd.* p. lxxi) reaches this conclusion all the more easily, because he inclines to the opinion that Paul likewise in some way associated the first beginnings of evil with creation, on which more below. On the other hand, Bar. keeps in line with the Jewish-Rabbinical theology; every man is his own Adam; there are at least a few who have kept the law and been justified thereby. But notwithstanding these differences as to the genesis of evil, the fact remains that the outlook upon the present world is a highly unfavorable one, in Bar. no less than in *4 Ezra.* The recognition of physical death alone as inseparable from this world was sufficient to effect this. To the righteous also, according to Bar. xv. 8, "this world is a trouble and a weariness with much labor"; it sounds like an echo of Paul's statement of 1 Cor. xv. 19, when Baruch declares: "For if there were this life only, which here belongs to all men, nothing could be more bitter than it." If this be not pessimism (in the specific sense of the word) it certainly is a most pessimistic kind

be overlooked that the drift towards the future was promoted by what the Apostle, and for that matter the nascent Church as a whole, were given to taste of the hostility of the world in its bitterest form of persecution. Rom. viii. 35-39; 1 Cor. xv. 19-34; 2 Cor. iv. 7-v. 10 clearly illustrate the force of this motive. Such passages are precisely the center of the great contexts in which, taking its departure from the fact of sin,

of optimism, Bar. xxi. 13. It remains true, however, that this sentiment of hopeless involvement in evil is stronger in the other Apocalypse. It is stressed that few are saved, ix. 159; there is none not a sinner, viii. 35; this age is full of sorrow and impotence, iv. 27; the ways of this world have become narrow and sorrowful and painful, vii. 12. Box truly says that the theology of such statements "is essentially other-worldly." The point, however, here most interesting us is the obvious connection between this despairing world-outlook and the liveliness of the eschatological hope, for it is in this respect that the two Apocalypses come nearest to the Pauline representation. We find in them likewise the eschatology *per contrarium,* that of the spring forcibly held down, but on that very account evincing a high degree of resiliency. Where the hope of renovation of the present world is given up, there precisely the gaze is fixed with intensity on the future world: "corruption is passed away, weariness is abolished, infidelity is cut off, while righteousness is grown, and faithfulness is sprung up," *4 Ezra* vii. 114. In the future age (which is already prepared) "the evil root is sealed up from you, infirmity from your path extinguished; and Death is hidden, Hades fled away; corruption become forgotten, sorrow passed away; and in the end the treasures of immortality are made manifest, viii. 53, 54. Even the note of eager hope for imminence of the future in view of the intolerable situation of the present is not wanting: "The underworld and the chambers of souls are like the womb; for just as she who is in travail makes haste to escape the anguish of the travail, even so do these places hasten to deliver what has been entrusted to them from the beginning," iv. 41, 42. And: "If I have found favor in thy sight, and if it be possible, and if I be sufficient, show me this also: whether there be more to come than is past, or whether the more part is already gone by us," vss. 44, 45. Still at this point, speaking even without regard to revelation, the Apocalypses were bound to fall short of Paul and the New Testament in general; to the latter the appearance and eschatologizing of the post-resurrection state of the Messiah changes all this anxious, half-querulous questioning into an enthusiastic hope. Cp. for the Jewish teaching in the documents named: Baldensperger, *Das Selbstewusstsein Jesu im Lichte der Messianischen Hoffnungen seiner Zeit,* 3d ed.; Charles, *The Apocalypse of Baruch,* 1896; Box, *The Ezra-Apocalypse,* 1912; Charles, *A Critical History of the Doctrine of a Future Life,* 2d ed. 1913; Oesterley, *The Books of the Apocrypha,* 1914.

the discourse rises through the consciousness of redemption to the highest summits of eschatological eloquence.

Thus far we have considered the structure of the Apostle's eschatology as built on the plan of consecutiveness. The antithesis is between a world (age) that *is* and a world (age) that *is to come*. The point of view is dramatic, the new being the outcome and termination of the forces of supernatural history propelling towards it in the old. This ancient point of view, while quite in accord with the Old Testament (and the Jewish) perspective to which the arrival of the Messiah still lay in the future, ceased to be in perfect harmony with a state of fact and belief looking back upon the arrival of the Messiah, and which in consequence had to recognize the eschatological process as in principle already begun. That nevertheless the scheme of successiveness was not straightway discarded, nor the full consequences from its abeyance drawn was due to more than one reason. An ancient scheme like this that had become an age-long tradition to the eschatological consciousness is not abruptly changed by the mere turning of a hand; revelation here as elsewhere prefers the mode of gradual transition to that of violent supersedure. Still this does not wholly explain the retention and continuing vitality of a point of view, which might appear to have been in principle overcome through the stupendous event of the Messiah's introduction into the process of history. The real and deeper reason lay doubtless in this that the Messianic appearance again had unfolded itself into two successive epochs, so that, even after the first appearance, and after making full allowance for its stupendous effect, the second epoch had, after the fashion of cell-separation, begun to form a new complex of hope moving forward into the future. In this way it will be seen that the scheme of successiveness had not been entirely abrogated but simply been reäpplied to the latter half of the original scheme: the age to come was perceived to bear in its womb another age to come, so that with reference to the mother and the as yet unborn child, as it were, the category of what is and what is to be not only could, but had to be retained. In accordance with this we find the Apostle speaking of "the age to come," not merely in his earlier Epistles but likewise in the later ones, cp. Eph. i. 21; ii. 2; 1 Tim. vi. 17; 2 Tim. iv. 10; Tit. ii. 12.

Side by side, however, with the continuation of this older scheme the emergence of a new one, involving a coëxistence of the two worlds or states, can be observed. From the nature of the case this principle did not allow of application to the age-concept, for the two sequences of time are mutually exclusive. So long as one age lasts no other can supervene.[44] It is different with regard to worlds or states, for here the existence of one does not exclude the contemporary existence of another, and there is nothing logically impossible either in the believer's belonging to both or at least preëminently to one rather than to the other. And what was logically possible became practically unavoidable through the shifting of the center of gravity from the lower to the higher sphere, as brought about by the removal of the Messiah to the higher world and his abiding there in permanence. The bond between the believer and Christ is so close that, from Paul's point of view, a detachment of the Christian's *interest* not only, but even a severance of his *actual life* from the celestial Christ-centered sphere is unthinkable. The latter consideration counts for more than the mere fact that through the appearance or resurrection of Christ the eschatological process has been set in motion. As soon as the direction of the actual spiritual life-contact becomes involved, the horizontal movement of thought on the time-plane must give way immediately to a vertical projection of the eschatological interest into the supernal region, because there, even more than in the historical development below, the center of all religious values and

[44] This furnishes a certain test for determining whether in certain cases *αἰών* has the age-sense or the world-sense, where otherwise the choice might be dubious. For instance, in Gal. i. 4, the idea of lifting the believer from one age into an other would be hyper-paradoxical, and for that reason "world" is indicated: "Who gave himself . . . that he might deliver us out of this present evil world." To be sure, in the idea of a removal out of the present world enough of the paradox remains.

forces has come to lie. The other, the higher world is in existence there, and there is no escape for the Christian from its supreme dominion over his life. Thus the other world, hitherto future, has become present. Now, if the present world had at the same moment ceased to exist, then the straight line would have been carried through unbrokenly, and for a concurrent unrolling of two lines of existence there would have been no call. As it was, a duplication had to ensue. The two diagrams at the foot of this page will make the principle in question visually plain to the reader.[45]

The point of view thus attained may be described as *semi-eschatological.* It is characteristic of the Epistles of the First Imprisonment, Ephesians, Colossians, Philippians. We can not expect that Paul should have used for it the formula of the Christian's belonging in principle to a higher "kosmos," for the word "kosmos" had through its evil associations become unfit for such usage. It is true "aion" in its world-sense might have served the purpose, and is by implication actually so employed in passages as early as Rom. xii. 2 and Gal. i. 4. But "aion" had to continue in use for the continued older simple distinction between "this age" and "the age to come." Consequently the idea of "heaven" and such metaphorical locally-oriented phrases as "the things above" had to take the place of the older technical terms. "Heaven" offered moreover the advantage of expressing that the provisionally-

45 I. The Original Scheme

This age or world | The age or world to come

II. The Modified Scheme

The world to come, realized in principle

[in Heaven]

Resurrection of Christ

[on earth]

Parousia

Future age and world fully realized in solid existence

This age or world

realized final state lies on a higher plane than the preceding world-development. Thus we find the Apostle declaring that the Christian is blessed in Christ with every spiritual blessing "in the heavenly regions," Eph. i. 3, a way of expression, clearly indicating the Christological basis of the transfer of the believer's domicile and possessions to heaven: it is "in Christ," i.e., because of his being in heaven, that the affirmation can be made, cp. i. 20. Still stronger is the statement of ii. 6 to the effect that the believer is raised up with Christ, and made to sit with Him in the heavenly regions, and here the repetition of the phrase "in Christ Jesus" at the end of the sentence emphasizes with additional stress how the lever of the whole upward movement lies in the removal of Christ to the supernal sphere consequent upon his resurrection. In the Epistle to the Philippians the Christians' "πολιτεία" "commonwealth" or "citizenship" is said to be in heaven for the reason of Christ's being there, which, however, does not alter the other aspect of the believer's attitude described in the words: "from whence also we wait for a Saviour, the Lord Jesus Christ," iii. 20. From the Epistle to the Colossians may be added to this the translation of the readers into the Kingdom of the Son of God's love, because as a rule the phrase "Kingdom of God" bears for Paul eschatological significance, i. 13; 2 Tim. iv. 18; further the stress on the Christian's duty to seek the things above, and that from the motive of Christ's being there, and in consideration of the believers' life being there hid with Christ in God, Col. iii. 1, 2, is to be noted here.

It has sometimes been asserted that this deflection from the straight prospective line of vision to the upward bent towards the heavenly world represents a toning down of the eschatological interest. Nothing could be farther from the truth. In reality this whole representation of the Christian state as centrally and potentially anchored in heaven is not the abrogation, it is the most intense and the most practical assertion of the other-worldly tenor of the believer's life. Precisely because it is to a large degree *incipient* realization, it bears the signature of eschatology written clear on its face. And because there is in it no *going back upon,* but a *reaffirmation of* the absolute ultimate hope, the other, more simple line of projection into the future continues to exist side by side with it in full validity. The idea of the future by no means recedes into the background; the *coming* of Christ is in continuance and without the slightest abatement of interest dwelt upon. The only thing that may be conceded to the view criticized is that the eager forward-stretching movement of the former period, characterized by a certain degree of restlessness, here gives place to a more quiet and serene attitude of contemplation of the other world and its content. But this is not the state of mind of one who has unlearned to hunger because of an often failure of his hope in the beginning of the feast. On the contrary it betokens the passing away of the acute, to some degree painful, sense of hunger as a result of the ample provisional satisfaction obtained. The partial enjoyment has rather whetted the appetite for the true food in its abundance. What gives rise to misunderstanding at this point is the confusion of eschatological two-sidedness with the philosophical bisection of the universe into a higher and lower sphere. While this cosmical distinction is presupposed by the view in question, it is in no wise identical with it. The heaven in which the Christian by anticipation dwells is not the cosmical heaven, it is a thoroughly redemptive heaven, a heaven become what it is through the progressive upbuilding and enrichment pertaining to the age-long work of God in the sphere of redemption. As such it not only in principle beatifies but also still beckons onward the believer to its final consummation. Heaven, so to speak, has received time and history into itself, no less than time has received unchangeableness and eternity into itself. Herein lies the inner significance of the repatriation of Christ into heaven, carrying thither with Himself all the historical time-matured fruit of his earthly stage of work, and now from there guiding with impartial solicitude the two lines of terrestrial and celestial development of his Church. Besides the Christ the Spirit holds the two aspects of the Christian's double life-process together, for the Spirit in all his working and in all his present-state manifestations here is, as we shall afterwards have occasion to show, at bottom naught but the earnest and first-fruits of the adequate final possession of the celestial state. That is his fundamental significance, the focus from which all the Spirit's activities proceed and in which they consequently meet again. Notwithstanding a certain formal resemblance in the two-sidedness of the Christian life, it stands at a far remove from Greek philosophical dualism.[46] Its very genesis forbids identification with this even to the slightest degree. Its mother-soil lies in eschatological revelation, not in metaphysical speculation. For this reason it is important to be able to show that the horizontal historical line of perspective is the older one, out of which only through an eminently-historical event the parallel structure of the two spheres was begotten. The historical was first, then the theological. And because the latter came from the former every possibility of conflict was from the outset excluded, neither of the two could interfere with the other. Nor could the rearrangement of the perspective result in abatement of the eschatological interest, as inherent in the Christian faith. For this to take place would have meant a primal apostasy from the origins of Christianity. What is usually charged against the age of Constantine and the rise of Protestantism would actually have its root in a Pauline Hellenizing speculation, which under the guise of directing to heaven would have in its actual effect meant a worldly recurrence from the future upon the present. There is nothing of this in the Apostle's intent: the Christian has only his members upon earth, which are to be mortified; himself, and as a whole, he belongs to the high mountain-land above, Col. iii. 5.

[46] The same charge of infection with Hellenic (Alexandrian) dualism to the effect of softening down primitive Christian eschatologism has been brought against the Fourth Gospel and the Epistle to the Hebrews. In regard to both the answer to the charge will have to be the same as that given above with regard to Paul. In John, no less than in Hebrews, the chronological perspective is retained without impairment. It is true, however, that the spiritualizing tendency of Hebrews assumes in part the form of correcting a too externalized, and consequently impatient, form of eschatological preoccupation.

CHAPTER II

THE INTERACTION BETWEEN ESCHATOLOGY AND SOTERIOLOGY

In Dogmatics the chapter devoted to Eschatology is ordinarily given the last place. The sequence in the actual process predetermines the scientific arrangement. The developments at the end are naturally viewed in the light of a consummation of the redemptive acts and experiences dealt with in Soteriology. The interest attaching to them, if not wholly, yet most frequently, arises from the desire to see "perfected" what has been begun, a desire fully justified both from a theoretical and a practical point of view. At bottom, of course, the desire springs and gathers momentum from the habitual consciousness of the Christian state as an unfinished state with which the protracted abode of the Church in this world, and our own life under preliminary conditions have familiarized but not satisfied us. This provisional state of affairs has been crystallized in a theological system with its own laws of perspective. We think and theologize out of the present into the future, because our base of existence is in the present. Whether this is as it ought to be need not be here considered; it certainly is a matter-of-fact state of mind. To the early Christians a different orientation had been given, and that not merely as a matter of practical religious outlook, but likewise through the teaching of Revelation. The ultimate things were brought forward in their consciousness, in order that in the light of these they might learn the better to understand the provisional and the preparatory. For the ultimate is in a very important sense the normative, that to which every preceding stage will have to conform itself to prove the genuineness of its Christian character. When we speak of the pervasive influence exerted by the hope of the world to come upon the earliest generation of believers, this ought not to be confined to the stimulating and uplifting effect of the other-worldly atmosphere of those days in general. There was an influence exerted upon the doctrinal understanding of the Christian realities likewise. The light of the world to come cast its clarifying and glorifying radiance backward into the present through the medium of teaching and prophecy concerning the future. The picture drawn of what lay ahead was by no means exclusively produced by a prolongation and enlargement and intensification of the vision already attained; the reverse method also was to no small degree put into practice, that of illumining the imperfect by the colors in which the perfect was steeped to the eye of faith. If the Christian hope had been of an imaginative type, such as is apt to lose itself in concrete details of a future state, the danger of such a contemplation of the present life with the mind upon the transcendental world would have been only too obvious. But the Christian hope bore a different character. It was sufficiently spiritualized to fasten itself upon the inward potencies of what was in the womb of the life to come. This eternal treasure with which the true hope occupied itself was not different from but homogeneous with the treasures that had already been imparted to the present state. What Augustine so strikingly formulated concerning the relation of the two historic economies of the history of redemption: "*Novum Testamentum in Vetere latet, Vetus in Novo patet*" permits of application to the subject in hand. Here also there was a "new" and an "old," but the substance was the same, not different in principle, and thus it came about that the one could be used to interpret the other. Revelation could make use of the preëstablished harmony which it had itself laid at the basis of its scheme.

Living, then, in a world of semi-futurities there is every reason to expect that the thought of the earliest Christians should have moved backwards from the anticipated attainment in its fulness to the present partial experiences and interpreted these in terms of the former. Just as natural as it appears to us to regard eschatology the crown of soteriology, it must have felt to them to scan the endowments and enjoyments already in their possession as veritable precursors of the inheritance outstanding. All the more was this natural, because theirs was a most vivid realization of the comparative importance of the two, such as would inevitably make the future entitled to the prime place in the scale of values.

So far, however, all this, while creating a strong presumption in favor of our thesis, is of an *a priori* nature. It will be necessary to examine somewhat in detail after a comparative fashion the material and the vocabulary of the Apostle's teaching both in the sphere of eschatalogy and in that of soterics. To this we now proceed. Before entering upon it, however, it may not be superfluous to remind ourselves, that what we endeavor to ascertain is not the chronology of the emergence of Pauline ideas. That would be a far easier process than the one we actually have in view. Our task consists of ascertaining the perspective of thought in the revealed Gospel delivered by the Apostle. An eschatological and soteriological verity might have been disclosed to Paul in the same moment of time, and yet their mutual adjustment might have remained for that moment unclarified and unappreciated, being reserved as a subject for further revelation and apprehension. Nevertheless the correlation of things in their logical order could in no case have been indefinitely postponed in a mind like Paul's. It is the subtle weaving of these threads of perspective into the doctrinal fabric of thought as a whole that we must endeavor, so far as possible, to unravel.

There are in the Pauline teaching four important structural lines and in connection with these it will prove easiest and most convincing to test our thesis. These consist of the idea of the resurrection, the thought of salvation, the doctrine of the judgment and justification, the conception of the Spirit. It is natural to put the first of these first, because here the eschatological priority of origin and the actual influence upon the soteric teaching are most palpable. That the resurrection is something specifically eschatological needs no pointing out. Nor is it necessary to show that Paul regards the resurrection of Jesus as the actual beginning of this general epochal event. Christ through his resurrection is the *firstfruits* of them that sleep, 1 Cor. xv. 20. When now we find that the soteric experience, whereby believers are introduced into a new state, is characterized by the Apostle as a "rising with Christ," or "being raised with Christ" and find, moreover, that this is not an occasional, figurative description of the experience, but obviously a piece of fixed doctrinal terminology, then the retroactive formative influence exerted by eschatology upon a central part of the saving process is placed beyond all question. A soteriological terminology of this kind was unknown before in Scripture. Previously to Paul no one could nor would have defined "regeneration" or "conversion" as a species of resurrection. The explanation of this way of speaking from a general metaphorical usage is here excluded. Nothing remains but turning things round and according eschatology the precedence in order. It might be urged that in some instances the affirmative is accompanied by the phrase "with Christ," and that consequently there is a borrowing here from Christology rather than from eschatology, Col. iii. 1. This would, however, be plausible only in case Christ's resurrection appeared invested anywhere with other than eschatological associations. This not being the case, the phrases "to be raised in or with Christ" can bear only the one meaning: to have through a radical change of life one of the two fundamental acts of eschatology applied to one's self. This becomes plainer still by observing that Paul in this way of speaking does not mean to affirm merely a general analogy between the resurrection of Jesus and the religious reconstructive vitalism of the Christian life, but most realistically derives from the risen Christ, that is from the resurrection-force stored up in Him the quickening in question. It is in the most literal sense of the word an anticipative effect produced by the eschatological world upon such who are still abiding in the present world. In other words the shaping of soteriology by eschatology is not so much in the terminology; it proceeds from the actual realities themselves and the language simply is adjusted to that. Much that is customarily ascribed to the influence of the mystical factor in the Apostle's thought or experience is undoubtedly, after a far more simple fashion, derived from this source. Eschatology was pregnant with mysticism, to a larger extent than is commonly appreciated. For, be it observed, the mystical element does not on this explanation disappear: it is only reduced, as to its origin, to the fundamental problem, how there can be from the heavenly, to all intents eschatological, world a projection into and a vital interaction with the life that is still lived in the world below.[1]

We may here attach some other representations containing the same fundamental thought, although not explicitly naming the concept of resurrection. One of these is the idea of the *καινὴ κτίσις*, another the idea of *παλιγγενεσία*. The former is met with in 2 Cor. v, vi and Gal. vi. 15, the latter in Tit. iii. 5. The recognition of the eschatological provenience of the term "new ktisis" has been held back by its assumed individual use in 2 Cor. v. 17: "Wherefore if any man is in Christ, *he is a new creature*," and likewise by the exclusively subjective-soteriological reference the representation seemed to suggest. Both obstacles also make themselves felt in regard Tit. iii. 5. But in regard to neither of the two passages can these objections obscure the quite perceptible eschatology texture. That Paul in Corinthians means something far more specific than the metaphorical statement about some one's having been made "a new man" would ordinarily convey, the context clearly shows. For the one who has undergone this experience of having become "in Christ," not merely individual

[1] Cp. Rom. vi. 6, 11; vii. 4; viii. 10, 11; xiii. 11; 2 Cor. i. 9, 10; iv. 12 (here even of the resurrection-power of Jesus as manifesting itself in the miraculous support of Paul's body in the midst of dangers and exhausting labors); v. 15; Eph. i. 19, 20; v. 14 (here more metaphorically, but even so plainly presupposing the literalistic terminology); Col. ii. 12, 13; passages illustrating the causal influence of Jesus' resurrection upon the future raising of the believer's body are, of course, more numerous.

subjective conditions have been changed, but "the old things are passed away, new things have come into being." There has been created a totally new environment, or, more accurately speaking, a totally new world, in which the person spoken of is an inhabitant and participator. It is not in the first place the interiority of the subject that has undergone the change, although that, of course, is not to be excluded. The whole surrounding world has assumed a new aspect and complexion. That the efficient cause for the thing described lies "in Christ" clearly indicates that such is the fact. Christ nowhere with the Apostle figures merely as a productive center of new individuals: He is everywhere, where the formula in question occurs, the central dominating factor of a new order of affairs, in fact nothing less than the originator and representative of a new world-order. A mere glance at the Pauline (and generally N.T.) usage of "ktisis" will further bear out the comprehensive and objective associations of the word; cp. Rom. viii. 19, 20; Col. i. 15; Heb. ix. 11; Rev. iii. 14. Nor does the context permit any restriction to the renovated inner nature of the Christian subjectively considered. The whole argument of the passage revolves around the substitution of one objective status and environment for another. It belongs to the chapter on "justification" equally much as to that on inward renewal. Vs. 18 speaks of "all things" as "being of God," which again is not naturally understood of the subjective internal condition of the believer alone. Also the term "*καταλλάσσεσθαι*," "to reconcile," points to the objective sphere, and in its Greek import, as distinct from the English-Bible rendering, is quite flexible and broad enough to allow of this widening out of the concept to the idea of a "change" affecting the whole world. In view of all this there is ample reason for favoring the rendering "a new creation," which, when once substituted, directly points to the eschatological antecedents of the idea and opens up the perspective of its other-worldly far-reaching significance. Hence the Apostle speaks in vs. 18 of *all things,* indicating that not a single point but a comprehensive range of renewal stands before his mind. The whole antithesis spoken of is for him determined by the complexion of the Christ who stands in the center of it: to know of, that is to reckon with, a Christ κατὰ σάρκα means one constitution of things, to reckon with a differently complexioned Christ (the Christ κατὰ πνεῦμα is meant, though not explicitly named) means a different, an opposite constitution of things, which in this case can only be the eschatological one. How the reference to justification, lying on the surface of the argument, can fit into this eschatologically-colored interpretation will appear presently.

Not so strongly reminiscent of eschatological origins is the phrase καινὴ κτίσις in the second instance of its occurrence, Gal. vi. 16: "For neither is circumcision anything nor uncircumcision, but a new creation." Still even here the thought of the new final order of affairs with new values of enduring equalizing character is by no means absent. On the negative side it clearly finds expression in the immediately preceding avowal: "Far be it from me to glory, save in the cross of our Lord Jesus Christ, through whom (or which) the world has been crucified unto me and I unto the world." The cross is here represented as effecting an absolute separation between two worlds, so as to have cut loose the Apostle from the world to which he at first belonged, and having transplanted him into another. And this separation was so radical that the two parts between whom it took place were afterwards equally unable to have community of interests one with the other: the world was no less crucified to Paul than Paul was to the world. At first it naturally seems difficult to fit in this conception of the effect of the cross with the usual modes of teaching developed concerning the same in other contexts of the Epistles. The difficulty disappears if we call to mind the Christologico-eschatological background of the statement. It is first of all with reference to Christ and the kosmos that such a sharp divorce has taken place through the cross. The cross, that is to say his death under the peculiar circumstances in which it took place, cut through the bond which for a definite period of time had tied Him to the kosmos; it threw Him out from the world, and He departed from it to enter another world, which was his real home. It needs no pointing out that in Christ's case this exchange of one world for another possessed before aught else eschatological features and proportions. It made Him not so much a "new creature," as the veritable beginner of a "new creation." Now, if in conscious assimilation of his own experience to this train of thought, the Apostle affirms of himself that he is crucified to the world, as the world is to him, and further that henceforth in his new sphere of existence a new creation is the decisive, all-important factor, it will hardly do justice to Paul's intent to confine it to the idea of endowment with a new and higher nature or personality; the conception is too weighty for that; the fundamental underlying idea must be that of an incorporation into a new system of reality, a fact which renders it in principle eschatological. How the Apostle would have expressed himself without conscious side-reference to the objective eschatological situation can be seen from Gal. v. 6: "For in Christ Jesus neither circumcision avails anything nor uncircumcision, but faith working through love." Here, it will be observed, where the thought is subjectively turned, the opposite to circumcision and uncircumcision is not "a new creation," but "faith working through love."

It is not different with the term "palingenesia" occurring in Tit. iii. 5. To be sure, here the indigenous soteriological meaning seems to be so strongly attested through the combination with "loutron," the *washing* of palingenesia and of anakoinosis (which are both) of the Holy Spirit." Baptism to our consciousness certainly is something pertaining to the present Christian state. Nevertheless the very fact of its being joined to palingenesia proves that it must have in its conception a definite bearing on the future life. Within the New Testament this is indicated by 1 Pet. iii. 21, where the world-overwhelming flood appears as its type, has ascribed to it a power saving from the antitypical judgment. In extra-biblical sources already the eschatological meaning appears in evidence, and that not as a derived metaphorical usage; on the contrary, the philosophico-mythological meaning is the prius, and an occasional figurative use is felt as having been derived from that. Of individual eschatology it is used in connection with the Dionysiac myth in referring to which Plutarch speaks of the "*ἀποβιώσεις*" and the "*παλιγγενέσθαι*."[2] In the Pythagorean doctrine of the transmigration of souls the term was used technically as the opposite of the "*πρώτη γένεσις*" or "*νῦν γένεσις*." With Philo it signifies the life after death, individually conceived, but also is applied to the future world collectively. Subsequently, however, the metaphorical meaning developed, even in Philo. Cicero calls his return from banishment his palingenesia.[3] Eschatological likewise is the single occurrence in the Septuagint: Job xiv. 14: "All the days of my warfare would I wait *ἕως πάλιν γένωμαι*. Besides by pagan authorities, the eschatological sense is attested by the saying of our Lord in the New Testament itself, Matt. xix. 28: "Ye who have followed me shall in the regeneration, when the Son-of-Man shall sit on the throne of his glory, also sit upon twelve thrones, judging the twelve tribes of Israel."[4] In this saying the word cannot be restricted to the more or less individualizing application of the resurrection; it covers the resurrection as a whole and even the renewal of the universe as is shown from the parallels in Mark and Luke which have as its equivalent descriptions of the final state, Mk. x. 29, 30; Lk. xxii. 29, 30. Thus also Josephus understands the term, making it interchangeable with apokatastasis.[5] Under these circum-

[2] *De Delph.* 9 (389 A); *De Is. et Os.* 35 (364).

[3] *De Cherub.* (ed Mangey), 159, 45; *Leg. ad Caj.* 593, 32; Cic. *Ad Attic.* 6, 6.

[4] The construction above given is to be preferred to that in A.V. and R.V. "who have followed me in the regeneration." This would refer to the following of Jesus by the disciples during his earthly ministry. Even this, however, would not necessarily take the eschatological reference out of it, inasmuch as Jesus' labors on earth meant a veritable beginning of the eschatological kingdom.

[5] Ant. xi. 3-9.

stances the eschatological reference in connection with baptism in Tit. iii. 5 can create no surprise. It made itself so naturally felt that Origen on Matt. xix. 28 declares baptism to be the prooimion (prelude) to *that* palingenesia (i.e., the great palingenesia of the resurrection). Even Clem. Rom. still says that Noah preached a palingenesia to the kosmos.[6] The familiar soteriological sense appears first with Clem. Alex.

The second idea in the handling of which the close nexus between present and future appears is that of salvation. Owing to the eminently practical concern attaching to this matter, it could hardly be expected otherwise than that here the soteriological present usage should more easily detach itself from the earlier eschatological meaning of the term. In the Pauline teaching, however, this was not accomplished by a clean-cut separation of the present experience from its original setting. What happened was the emergence of an idea in which without clear distinction present enjoyment and joyful anticipation of the final deliverance mingle. The sense of salvation was never entirely deëschatologized. Even the most practical religious consciousness found it impossible to think of the one aspect without more or less clearly remembering the other. The mind of the early Christian reveals a constant oscillation from the one pole to the other. Only the multitudinousness of concerns with the world that is, has somewhat deflected the religious interest from that beyond. The movement of thought and the movement of aspiration have both somewhat changed their original point of departure and their habitual direction. Believers followed the chronological order, which after all appears so largely the normal one to time-circumscribed minds. Paul and his converts by a sort of reversion thought themselves saved as in the future so in the present. Precisely because the two states of consciousness, that of being destined to an impending salvation and that of having the prelibation of the same each day, so naturally coälesced, the necessity for

[6] *Ad Cor.* i. 9.

sharp distinction was less strongly felt. Hence there are a number of passages, which it is easy to construe as referring to the simple sense of possession in the present, whilst in all probability the mixture of feeling just referred to is voiced in them, and in consequence half their shade of significance is obscured through an overlaying with our own color of piety. Fortunately statements are not lacking which embody the pure futuristic manner of conceiving the thing in its original force. According to Rom. v. 9, 10, after and because being justified by Christ's blood, the readers *shall* be saved from the wrath of the judgment through Him, and that particularly through his (resurrection-) life. The Christian is saved "by hope," viii. 24, 25; here the past tense (Aorist) joined to the idea of "hope" strikingly portrays the mixed mental attitude towards the idea of salvation; how strongly present and active the ingredient of hope is may be felt from the appended remark: "hope that is seen is not hope," a remark which might seem to deny, if not explicitly the pre-potency, at least the visual actuality of salvation. The strongest passage is Rom. xiii. 11: "for now is salvation nearer to us than when we first believed." The representation of 1 Cor. iii. 15 places both the destruction of the bad builder's work, and his personal salvation "as through fire" in "the day," i.e., the day of judgment, cp. vs. 13. The much-mooted exhortation, Phil. ii. 12: "Work out your own salvation with fear and trembling" is most easily relieved of its difficulty through allowing "salvation" its future reference. At any rate the verb "work out" does not as a rule bear the sense, so frequently given it in the exposition of this text, of unfolding through strenuous effort the potentialities contained in something, but rather that of achieving, accomplishing a thing: the readers are exhorted to fit themselves through the diligent practice of obedience for and assure themselves of the salvation at the end with its varying degrees of glory; cp. 2 Cor. iv. 17; v. 5; vii. 10, 11. His own salvation Paul makes dependent on his own affliction and that of the readers on theirs, and in so far assigns it to the future, 1 Thess. v. 8, 9; in the believer's armor "the hope of salvation" is figuratively described as the helmet. God has appointed believers unto the obtaining of salvation and that this is said with reference to the end appears from the opposite "not unto wrath," the latter term having eschatological meaning throughout with Paul. The foregoing quotations do not prove, of course, that the obtaining of salvation was placed by Paul entirely in the future. There are not a few instances where the application to the present life lies plainly on the surface. The most unequivocal of these are Eph. ii. 5: "By grace are ye saved ones (Perfect Tense)"; cp. vs. 8: "For by grace are ye saved ones through faith"; Tit. iii. 5: "According to his mercy He saved us (Aorist Tense); 2 Tim. i. 9: "According to the power of Him who saved us" (Aorist Tense). The mere use of Present or Future does not have the same convincing force as that of Perfect, because the Present can be void of chronological significance, expressing only the fact that God performs or will perform the act and the Future can be a Future of logical sequence; consequently in some passages the question cannot be answered with certainty to which of the two rubrics they belong: Rom. x. 9: "If thou shalt confess . . . and shalt believe . . . thou shalt be saved." In 2 Cor. ii. 15 the idea seems to stand midway between the "having been saved," and the "being destined to be saved," for here the Apostle declares: "For we are a sweet savor of Christ unto God in them that are being saved (in process of salvation) and in them that are perishing (in process of being lost); to the one a savor of death unto death; to the other a savor of life unto life."

A survey of the facts registered leaves little doubt but that between the two aspects of the matter, the priority belongs in the Apostle's mind to the eschatological aspect. If the starting-point had lain at the other end, we might surely expect some qualifying phrase to appear in the futurity-passages to intimate that not salvation as such, but only its perfection or consummation was associated with the end; the opposite is the case: salvation at the end is spoken of in an absolute way, as though it were the only conception customary; it is "ἡ σωτηρία." In fact, the phenomenon furnishes a strict analogy to the manner after which in our Lord's teaching such things as "the Kingdom of God" and "the Parousia of the Son-of-Man" are referred to as future things in an absolute way, as though no other Kingdom, no other Parousia were reckoned with. There is a continuity in the writings of the New Testament of this way of speaking: the feeling expressed in the word of our Lord, "the hour comes and is now" reëchoes everywhere. The lower air was so surcharged with the sense of what great things had already come to pass and what greater things were on the wings in the upper air ready to come down, that the precision in speaking of the several parts and phases of the whole was for the moment in abeyance. Keen hope had projected itself into the future, and there the habit of speech about salvation had been to no small extent acquired. Afterwards it required some effort to translate such language back into the more sober dialect of the life of a protracted waiting on earth. How unfortunate that we, after waiting so long, seem to have forgotten the semi-celestial accents of Christianity's childhood!

In the matter of justification it requires closer scrutiny, perhaps, to discover the eschatological origins that have shaped it at the beginning and the interdependence with the outlook into the future life characterizing it in continuance. The controversial history through which the doctrine passed and the anti-Judaistic stamp as a result put upon it tended to make it more than aught else a truth of present generally-religious importance. It became in the Pauline type of teaching the very foundation of all Christian belief and experience. And Protestantism, especially of the Lutheran kind, has certainly not been wrong in making its true interpretation, over against Romanism, the comprehensive basis of Christian truth generically conceived. And yet, with the large place occupied in the early-Christian consciousness by the thought of the life to come, it is easy to see, that two such all-covering planes could not fail to intersect. There exists, however, sufficient evidence for the eschatological stamp borne by the idea of justification even at that controversial stage. It is sometimes alleged that Paul was the first to frame the concept of a comprehensive adjustment of all sins in the accounting of God. In this form the thought is not correct, because Judaism had already worked out the doctrine of a daily balance struck by God taking into account the works performed up to the point of reckoning, both as to merit and demerit, and not omitting to introduce the element of imputed righteousness from the fathers, who had a surplus of merit. Only this formal similarity overlooks the specific difference between the two schemes compared. Under the Judaistic scheme the balance struck is unstable, subject to constant modification, each new moment introducing new items to be reckoned with changing the momentary credit or debit from day to day. For this relativity and uncertainty Paul substituted absoluteness and certainty. And here lies precisely the point where eschatology and justification intersect. By making both the negative element of the forgiveness of sin and the positive element of bestowal of the benefits of salvation unqualified, the Apostle made the act of justification to all intents, so far as the believer is concerned, a last judgment anticipated. If the act dealt with present and past sins only, leaving the future product in uncertainty, it could not be regarded as possessing such absoluteness, and the comparison with the last judgment would break down at the decisive point. This interpretation of the Pauline doctrine as bearing a purely-retrospective significance has been actually advocated of late. It has been contended that in the Apostle's view justification is in the main a missionary doctrine, it enabling the convert to begin with a clean record, but with the clear understanding that the question of salvation in the end shall be by no means prejudiced by it, the final issue no longer made dependent on the forgiving grace of God, but on the holiness of the post-baptismal life. The Christian cannot be saved unless successful in his striving to stand blameless before God in the judgment-day. At bottom Paul's teaching so interpreted would have as much, if not more, in common with the Romanist than with the common Protestant doctrine.[7] The main proof for this is said to lie in the fact that the Apostle nowhere consoles the readers of his Epistles, when fallen into sin, with the free, abundant pardon of justification, but requires instantaneous conversion, and in the opposite case insists upon their excommunication from the fellowship of believers. Both his personal practical experience and his doctrinal conviction were that the Christian can and ought to be sinless. Hence his doctrine of the new creature under the control of the Spirit. There is a grain of truth in this representation, but taken as a whole it bristles with impossibilities. True, the pastoral practice of the Apostle does not seem to make as abundant use of the consolatory aspect of justification for allaying the consciousness of sin as from the Protestant standpoint might have been *a priori* expected. In seeking to explain this, however, it should be remembered that the Pauline converts had been to no small extent in their pre-Christian state gross pagan sinners, with whom special caution had to be exercised, lest the doctrine of free grace should become an occasion for antinomianism. When Paul speaks of sin such as *ipso facto* excludes from tolerance and is inconsistent with the Christian state, consequently falling outside the pale of the church, he has in mind these gross types of sin. A scrutiny of the catalogues of sins in 1 Cor. v. 11; vi. 9, 10; Gal. v. 19-21 immediately reveals the pertinence of this observation. But surely, Paul did not consider anything remaining below these terms of excessive and persistent and Christianity-excluding sins as negligible and exempt from the reach of justification. The Apostle not seldom does speak of the consciousness of justification as needful for those who, within the Christian sphere, are subject to a daily sense of sin. In Rom. v. 2 he affirms that believers through Christ have received and now are in actual possession of (ἐσχήκαμεν) access to the grace

[7] Wernle, *Der Christ und die Sünde bei Paulus,* 1897. Cp. Gottschick, *Paulinismus und die Reformation, Z. f. Th. u. K.,* 1897, pp. 398ff.

wherein they stand, i.e., the grace of peace through justification; cp. also the Present Tense ἔχομεν in Eph. i. 7; Col. i. 14. According to Gal. ii. 20 the life which the Apostle now lives in the flesh he lives through the faith of (in) the Son of God, who loved him and gave Himself for him. In Phil. iii. 7-9 he represents it as his constant striving to be found in Christ, not having a righteousness of his own . . . but that which is through faith in Christ. It is also extremely doubtful whether the forgiveness of trespasses spoken of in Eph. i. 7 and Col. i. 14 refers to sins of the pre-Christian state only. The argument, therefore, derived from scanty recourse to justification in pastoral practice does not prove that Paul excluded sins committed after conversion from the scope of the justifying pronouncement of God. To be sure, were Wernle's view correct and justification purely-retrospective, then the vital nexus between it and the final judgment would be broken. But in favor of the intimate connection between the future and the present, and the backward movement in thought from the former to the latter much more may be said than is directly affected by this controversy. The language of Rom. viii. 33, 34: "Who shall lay anything to the charge of God's elect? It is God that justifies; who is he that condemns" could not be more absolute than the sentence rendered in the last judgment; in fact it is so absolute as to be indifferent to the categories of present, past or future. In this respect the fact of justification is only the reverse side of the facts of prognosis and predestination and it would be out of place in the *catena salutis* of vs. 29, if its scope were less unlimited and unconditional than that of the other conceptions enumerated. Justification is a "δικαίωσις ζωῆς" (justification of life), and the "life" thus declared to be its consequent is the endless life, that of which it is promised that the saints "shall reign" in it, Rom. v. 18-21. In general the certainty of salvation so emphatically affirmed by the Apostle with regard to the Christian as such would not be possible, if the central act of the divine saving procedure bore with regard to the future an aspect of relativity. Instead of being, what it actually is, the backbone of the sureness of the religious consummation, it would become the one weak point exposing all the remainder to uncertainty, and in so far worse than void of value. Ultimately the absoluteness of the divine self-committal inhering in this one act of justifying the sinner is due to the feature of its being a "God-interesting" act in the strongest sense of the word. It is the act in which religion celebrates its triumph, and therefore the act in which the religious and the eschatological are inseparably united. But for this same reason it is in principle incapable of being an eschatological act in the *exclusive* sense of the word, an act incapable of anticipation. An experience which was lacking in the *foretaste* of the ultimate enjoyment of God would be to that extent lacking the innermost core of religion itself.[8]

The fourth line along which an influence of the eschatological teaching upon the Apostle's soteriological doctrine can be observed is that of the significance and function of the Spirit. As this subject will afterwards at various points in our investigation obtrude itself, we here content ourselves with a mere sketch of the argument. As is generally recognized, the specific character of Paul's doctrine of the Spirit lies in the universal and equable distribution of his operation over the entire circle of believers, and within the life of every believer over the entire range, subconscious and conscious, religious and ethical, of this life. In this particular the Pauline pneumatology is clearly marked off from the phases of Revelation preceding it, not only in the Old Testament, but also from earlier New Testament types of teaching, not even the Johannine type of our Lord's teaching excluded, although in the last-mentioned a certain preformation of Paul's doctrine may be found. The problem is how to account for this immense widening out of the subject. It might be answered, and not unjustly, that the extraordinary bestowal of the Spirit at Pentecost, or to use more strictly-

[8] Cp. Titius, *Die neutestamentliche Lehre von der Seligkeit,* Vol. II, *Der Paulinismus unter dem Gesichtspunkt der Seligkeit,* p. 162.

Pauline language, the new phase of the Spirit's influence connected with the resurrection of Christ, are sufficient to account for this, the practical enlargement being merely the inevitable result of the speeding up of the factual progress of events. Still this will not wholly account for the peculiarity in question, for the main peculiarity consists in the enveloping, circumambient, one might almost say atmospheric character of the Spirit's working, a feature first clearly emerging with Paul, and that so strongly as to give at times almost the impression as though the personal character of the Spirit's mode of existence were obscured by it. To recur upon what the Old Testament teaches about the Spirit's universally distributed influence in the sphere of natural life does not help to a solution, because this idea of the quickening power of the Spirit in nature, while nowhere denied in the New Testament, and by no means entirely absent from Paul, has nevertheless to a large extent been eclipsed by the soteric pneumatology. And particularly, so far as Paul himself is concerned, this soteriologizing aspect of the Spirit's working has been carried to a point, where it can scarcely be understood as a simple prolongation of the line of his working in the sphere of nature. The "pneumatic" with Paul is practically equivalent to the "supernatural." It is consequently rather the opposite to than the analogue of the natural, after the manner of the antithesis expressed by Jesus in Jno. iii. 8. A natural solution offers itself by supposing that the "Pneuma" was in the mind of the Apostle before all else the element of the eschatological or the celestial sphere, that which characterizes the mode of existence and life in the world to come and consequently of that anticipated form in which the world to come is even now realized in heaven. As pervading this sphere it would cease to exercise a spasmodic activity to be confined to certain groups of phenomena; its presence and operation would of necessity appear constant and universal within the sphere of redemption. The detailed phenomena pointing to the actual existence of this point of view will be investigated later. If their presence may be taken for granted here, they prove that in a very large aspect, second to none in its importance for the Pauline system of thought, the eschatological appears as predeterminative both the substance and form of the soteriological.[9]

What has been found is important not merely by reason of the light it throws upon the genesis of Paul's teaching on its intellectual side, it likewise helps to answer the charge of the absence of systematic coherence brought particularly against the eschatological teaching. It were far more accurate to say that the eschatological strand is the most systematic in the entire fabric of the Pauline thought-world. For it now appears that the closely interwoven soteric tissue derives its pattern from the eschatological scheme, which bears all the marks of having had precedence in his mind. Among all the other factors usually reckoned with as sources or determinants of the Apostle's theological system, there is none that can lay equal claim to self-evidencing character with this. No doubt Paul's mind had by nature a certain systematic bent, which made him pursue with great resoluteness the consequences of given premises. No doubt also some influence should be attributed to his Jewish scholastic training. As to the latter, however, the influence of the Rabbinical cast of mind has, if we may believe Jewish writers, been greatly overestimated. The Rabbinical teaching was not particularly systematic. Even where it tended towards logical correlation, it contented itself with more or less superficial attempts at harmonizing, and did not feel disturbed even by serious antinomies.[10] It is safe to assume that far more than all this counted the eschatological mould into which the Apostle's thought had been cast from the beginning. What gives dogmatic coloring to his teaching is largely derived from its antithetical structure, as exhibited in the comprehensive antitheses of the First Adam and the Last Adam, sin and righteousness, the flesh and the Spirit,

[9] Cp. the author's article entitled "*The Eschatological Aspect of the Pauline Conception of the Spirit*" in *Princeton Theological Studies,* 1912, pp. 209-259.

[10] Cp. C. G. Montefiore, *Judaism and St Paul,* 1914.

law and faith, and these are precisely the historic reflections of the one great transcendental antithesis between this world and the world-to-come. It is no wonder that such energetic eschatological thinking tended towards consolidation in an orb of compact theological structure. For in it the world-process is viewed as a unit. The end is placed in the light of the beginning, and all intermediate developments are construed with reference to the purpose *a quo* and the terminus *ad quem*. Eschatology, in other words, even that of the most primitive kind, yields *ipso facto* a philosophy of history, be it of the most rudimentary sort. And every philosophy of history bears in itself the seed of a theology. To this must be added that the Pauline outline of history possessed in the Messianic concept a centralizing factor of extraordinary potency, an element whereby the antitheses above named were dissolved into an exceptionally harmonious synthesis. Only one thing more, and that of supreme importance, needs to be remembered: all eschatological interpretation of history, when united to a strong religious mentality cannot but produce the finest practical theological fruitage. To take God as source and end of all that exists and happens, and to hold such a view suffused with the warmth of genuine devotion, stands not only related to theology as the fruit stands to the tree: is is by reason of its essence a veritable theological tree of life.

CHAPTER III

THE RELIGIOUS AND ETHICAL MOTIVATION OF PAUL'S ESCHATOLOGY

The eschatological part of the Pauline teaching has not escaped the general opprobrium cast upon the teaching as a whole, that of being un-modernly theological, and hence partaking of all the blemishes and inadequacies, which the flesh of all theology is heir to. There is a difference, however, between the general dislike attaching to the whole fabric and the special attack made against this one piece in particular. The offensive carried on along the line as a whole is of a more formal, theological nature, and, as a rule, disavows antagonism on principle to the religious spirit pervading the teaching as such, provided only the substance be thoroughly divested of its antiquated form. The polemic against the eschatology is of a different kind. Here a positive ethico-religious blame is believed to attach to the animus and content of the ideas considered in themselves. At the outset, in view of what we have found concerning the close interweaving of eschatology with the entire structure of the soteriology, it would seem preposterous to praise in one and the same breath the evangelically-religious and high-mindedly ethical Paul, and yet to make bitter charges against his doctrine concerning the end of the world. It is *a priori* probable that in the circles where such dualistic appraisal appears, either the general trend of Paulinism has been profoundly misunderstood, or the motivation of the eschatology misapprehended, or both defects are present in equal degree. The charges against the eschatology find various forms of expression. Foremost stands the revulsion from the supernaturalism in the eschatology, for with Paul, as elsewhere in Scripture, eschatology is supernaturalism in the *n*th degree. Most uncompromising, further, is the fault found with the other-worldliness of the Apostle's eschatology. To be sure, this is a fault found not with Paul only, but with every type of New Testament eschatology at any point. Paul may have carried the matter to an extreme, but no one of the other writers of the New Testament, not even the Evangelists or the Jesus speaking through them, is exempt from this criticism. At bottom the disagreement here is not one between two types of religion and theology; it concerns the health of religion over against its decline. It is inherent in religion to seek the highest and closest approach to God; where this has become a matter of indifference, to however small a degree, there the genuineness and vigor of the religious impulse have suffered impairment, and been replaced by interests of a lower nature, religiously considered; the change of outlook is symptomatic of a movement away from God, though this may not be always consciously realized. Where the extreme of the tendency in question has been reached it deserves to be qualified as in principle anti-religious. A so-called Christianity proving cold or hostile towards the interests of the life to come has ceased to be Christianity in the historic sense of the word.

A second factor working for the disparagement of Biblical Eschatology, and of the Pauline type in particular, springs from the modern striving after autonomy in ethics and religion. Here again the element criticized is not confined to Paul but covers the entire range of Biblical religion, and, in common with the tendency just discussed, points to a deep-rooted perverseness in the religious mind. There sometimes enters a "too proud to receive" in the relationship between God and man, after the same manner as it appears in social human intercourse. Only in the latter case the fault is more excusable than in the former, because in religion the giver and the receiver are so inevitably unequal in position, as to lift the whole question of what the proprieties allow and forbid above the sphere of reasonable consideration. In our Lord's teaching the two great principles of the sovereignty of God, and of the fatherhood of God, at one stroke rule out the impious concept of human autonomy in deciding the terms on which man shall deal with God. The one who has given all is still at the close of the process (*sub specie juris divini*) an "unprofitable" (not a "useless") servant, since the master has gotten out of him no more than he was at the outset entitled to or, to speak in terms of the slave-market, than had been paid for him at the beginning. Everyone feels that in a relationship thus construed the problem of what is consistent or non-consistent with the dignity of human nature to offer, or to receive, loses all significance. The same regard for divine sovereignty appears likewise in the insistence upon the principle that God without injustice can give the same remuneration to those who labor less than to those who labor more. At best this could be a question of equity; the idea that "the pride of labor" were justified in denying the *more* to the others, beyond what these have strictly earned, remains entirely out of the question. Apart from the element of the divine sovereignty, however, our Lord appeals likewise to the idea of the divine fatherhood, which as such is incompatible with the enforcement of inherent rights. The child refusing to do for its parents aught else than a spirit of autonomous choice may allow it to, acts from the very opposite of filial piety, which amounts to saying that the action would be irreligious and unethical in principle. In this matter grace intertwines with justice, but the recurrence upon either one to the exclusion of the other implies that the autonomous desire of the creature is made the regnant principle in intercourse with God.

The above said holds true in general. It is, however, in the province of eschatology that the two ideas of autonomy and heteronomy stand out in sharpest contrast. The web of biblical eschatology is shot through with the strand of reward.[1] In the teaching of Jesus, where one might least expect it, it is particularly in evidence, to such an extent indeed,

[1] It ought to be observed that the Gospels not unfrequently introduce the idea of reward in connection with eschatological material: Matt. v. 12; vi. 1, 2; x. 41; Mk. ix. 41; Lk. vi. 35.

that its authenticity has been called in question, on the mere ground of the irreconcilableness of such ideas with the ideal ethics of the Great Teacher of Nazareth. Where the presence and authenticity of the element admit of no denial, the issue is glossed over through declaring all such utterances a lingering remnant of Judaism, which Jesus had not been able to throw off completely. Were the thought confined to isolated contexts, an attempt to this effect might perhaps be made with some approach to plausibleness, but even then the fact would remain that in certain recurrent figures, taken from the sphere of labor in the harvest field or elsewhere, the idea is irremovable. If one so choose, he may consider it tares of teaching, but to weed it out from the grain is impossible. Sometimes it occurs in the most tender religious setting, as where a reward is promised for prayer in secret.[2] Plainly this is not an outworn fringe of Judaism; it belongs to the innermost core of Jesus' religious consciousness.

With Paul particularly Jesus' reward-concept shows striking, mostly eschatological, affinities. If there be any reward at all, then the great epoch of summing up and allotting destinies must be pregnant with it. Nevertheless the idea is by no means confined to eschatology, no more than it is with Jesus. How deep-seated an idea it is appears especially from the circumstance that it has succeeded in maintaining itself upon the background of the Apostle's insistence upon the principle of absolute grace in redemption. In spite of the doctrine of justification through faith alone, the factor of works does not cease to play a rôle in the teaching on the Last Judgment, not even so far as the Christian is concerned. How far these two apparently discordant notes are capable of being reduced to harmony we shall have to consider at a later point. Here we simply note that the conflict most stubbornly obtrudes itself at the high points of Paul's eschatological teaching. That the idea of eschatological reward can be made to render service as a powerful incentive towards religious and, in particular missionary, zeal, the grand climax of the

[2] Matt. vi. 5.

resurrection argument in 1 Cor. xv proves: "Wherefore, my beloved brethren, be ye steadfast, unmovable, always abounding in the work of the Lord, forasmuch as ye know that your labor is not in vain in the Lord."[3] That a similar sequence exists between eschatological reward and the endurance of persecution and affliction in the present life, is shown by 1 Thess. i. 4-7: "For your patience and faith in all your persecutions and in the afflictions which ye endure (is) a manifest token (*endeigma*) of the righteous judgment of God, to the end that ye may be counted worthy of the Kingdom of God for which ye also suffer; if so be that it is a righteous thing with God to recompense affliction to them that afflict you and to you that are afflicted rest (*relief*) with us at the revelation of the Lord Jesus from heaven," etc. The same axiom underlies the argument of Rom. ii. 6, 7: "Who will render every man according to his deeds: to them who by patient continuance in well-doing seek for glory and honor and immortality, eternal life," etc. The reasoning here is not dialectic, nor a species of *argumentum ad hominem,* employed to drive the Jews into a theological corner; it is a *hypothetical* argument, to be sure, but none the less, *e mente Pauli,* perfectly serious, and immutably valid from the standpoint of the divine procedure. Neither here nor elsewhere does the Apostle assert on principial grounds, that the bestowal of eternal life on the basis of fulfilment of the divine law would militate against the dignity of religion either from the side of God or from the side of man. It should be noticed that the terms in which the Apostle speaks to denote the reward are specifically-eschatological terms: glory, honor, immortality, eternal life. The passage proves that the eschatological principle is so deeply embedded in the structure of the biblical religion as to precede and underlie everything else. Even the procedure of

[3] That the phrase "in vain" does not admit of restriction to the promise of spiritual success in the labors of the present, appears from the connection with the foregoing by means of "wherefore." It is in and through the resurrection that the eternal fruition of the work will be obtained.

"grace" and "faith" on which the entire Pauline Gospel is staked, does not, when correctly apprehended, so far as the objective divine procedure is concerned, abrogate it; it only exempts man from its direct operation, and that for the twofold reason that when applied to sinful man it must prove futile, and moreover, that it must, when put into practice by the sinful subjectivity of man, inevitably carry with itself that mood of "boasting" and "self-glorying" which is not merely deficient in religious value, but pointedly anti-religious, the negation in principle of what is the core of religion itself.[4] The fact therefore remains, that Paul admits and retains the principle of reward within his eschatological scheme. As to the compatibility of this with the principle of a law-free gospel, the present connection is not the place for a thorough discussion of that problem. Our interest for the moment lies in the registering of the fact as such, not in the evaluation of it as something either to the discredit or the credit of the Pauline eschatology.

Attacks of still a different kind have been made upon the eschatological teaching of the Apostle. The difference from the foregoing lies in this that here not the injection of eschatology as such is on principle condemned, but the quality of

[4] Under the system of redemption the principle is simply transferred from man to Christ, in whom both the futility and temptation to "glorying" are unthinkable, cp. Phil. ii. 8, 9. Though sounding paradoxical, it would be quite correct to say, that the motive underlying Paul's championship of grace is at bottom not different from that binding him to the forensic principle of eschatological reward. The two are at one in this that they both aim at securing the revelation of the supreme glory of God, the one in the ethical sphere, the other in the soteric sphere. The eschatological reward-idea is simply one of the twin forms in which the Apostle gives expression to the absolute ascendancy of the divine glory in religion. The law of recompense for righteousness is intended to express that the ethical process (no less than the soteric process) exists for the sake of God. It is precisely in the recognition of this point that Calvinism proves itself the deepest interpretation of Paulinism, and in so far the purest expression of the spirit of Augustinianism and the Reformation. Cp. the author's article on *Alleged Legalism in Paul's Doctrine of Justification, P. R.*, 1903, pp. 161-80.

the Apostle's mental attitude in embracing its ideas and associations is subjected to sharp censure. The content of Paul's mode of thinking as to tone and coloring not merely but likewise as to moral and religious spirit is represented as an inferiority complex scarcely worth classifying under the head of religion at all. The charge is a charge against the *man* Paul; it is meant to cast a stigma upon his character. We are told that in his eschatology Paul was largely dominated by egotism to the serious injury of the altruistic element in his religious make-up. Seeing how prominent a place the eschatological strands of thought occupy in the teaching the seriousness of the charge lies on the surface. Altogether apart from the ethico-religious flaw, the abnormal proportion would interfere with the symmetry of the Apostle's faith. This, however, is by no means as yet the worst. Stunted and deformed characters have sometimes accomplished great things in the Kingdom of God. Nay even a sanctified egotism, provided it be intensely conscious of its vocation for the service of the truth, is not an uncommon phenomenon in the annals of religion. In the present case, however, the issue reaches out beyond such self-concentration of service. What is found fault with in Paul is egotism *per se*. It was something that sprang from a most intense desire for life, and that physical life. Nor was this purely negative, viz. the instinctive protest of human nature against death as a monstrous thing; it had assumed the character of an unquenchable thirst for bliss and glory. From this point of view the Apostle's entire eschatological "obsession" has been with great sharpness interpreted by Kabisch.[5] The Paul of Kabisch might be properly called the gluttonous man and wine-bibber among the eschatologists of the New Testament. Under this author's treatment almost all conceptions and processes are physicized. The fire by which the products of a man's work are destroyed, and from which he himself is narrowly saved at the last day (1 Cor. iii. 13-15), Paul is supposed to have understood as

[5] *The Eschatology of Paul,* 1893; cp. the review of this book by Dr. Purves in *The Presbyterian and Reformed Review,* 1894, p. 143.

literal physical fire; the insistence upon the value of his body and the eager longing for its preservation and restoration, so as to avoid an intervening period of nakedness between the moments of death and resurrection, are but symptoms of a vulgar interest in such delights as the possession of a future body alone could render possible. This would be the extreme form of the idea of reward viewed from its reprehensible subjective side. It goes without saying that such a type of belief did not, according to Kabisch, spring chiefly from the Old Testament but rather from the Rabbinical and Apocalyptic ideas of later Judaism. Notwithstanding the distorted and extravagant features of Kabisch's book, it may serve as a caution against certain hyper-"spiritualized" interpretations of New Testament religion, to which all occupation with the body as of religious interest has virtually become indifferent or even repellent. In the store set by the body Paul reveals himself, not in the first place, the pupil of Apocalyptic, but a true heir of the Old Testament tradition. That to the latter, so far as it had attained an outlook into the future life, the body could have in no wise appeared unimportant, hardly needs proof; the question would rather lie the other way, whether the idea of a purely spiritual, unembodied entity had, as concerns man, as yet entered within its purview. All that is related in the Messianic prophecies concerning the enjoyments of the future age is inseparable from the existence and functioning of the body. It is not otherwise with Jesus, who likewise associated with the resurrection the reëndowment of the heirs of the age to come with a true body.[6] The correct interpretation of the passage Matt. xxii. 30; Mk. xii. 25; Lk. xx. 30 leads to the same conclusion, for, although in the abstract the idea of a resurrection without a body is not unthinkable, and actually occurs in the Apocalyptic literature,[7]

[6] Cp. *The Bible Student,* Vol. III, 1901, pp. 189-97.

[7] Charles, *A Critical History of the Doctrine of a Future Life,* 2nd ed., 1913, pp. 295ff. finds the belief in a resurrection without the body in the two following writings of the First Century B.C. En. xci-civ and Psalt. Sol. Prior to this it occurs only in En. vi.-xxxvi, dated by Charles from the preceding century. In the First Century *after* Christ,

yet from the discourse of Jesus in the passages cited such an idea is plainly excluded. The being *"like unto angels"* (Lk. v. 36 ἰσάγγελοί εἰσι) does not express similarity to the angels in every respect, but only in regard to the absence of the faculty of procreation; for conveying the idea of bodiless existence not ἴσος but ὁμοῖος would have had to be employed. A comparison of the passage with other utterances of Jesus leads to the same result.[8] The two classical contexts 1 Cor. xv and 2 Cor. v are explainable only from the standpoint of one to whom a bodiless existence in the world to come would have fallen short of the ideal of supreme blessedness. There must have been some powerful motive underlying such a state of mind. Mere emotional shrinking from a condition of nakedness, while to some extent involved, will not completely account for it. But to say that the Apostle loved his body, and loved it for specific eschatological reasons, is by no means equivalent to saying that this love sprang from hedonistic desire. Other things might very well have come under consideration. For one thing the wish for redemptive consummation should be taken into account. Paul was not a man easily satisfied with half-way attainment in the redemptive sphere. He was governed by the absolutistic impulse, which is in the same manner characteristic of the teaching of our Lord. Nor should we dismiss in such a connection the ideal of a fuller measure of glorification of God through the completely restored organism of man than would be possible in a disembodied state.[9] Not the slightest evidence, however, can be produced of an anticipation of, far less of a legitimate, eschatological satisfaction cherished by Paul apart from God and the enjoyment of communion with Him. Had he been animated by an irreligious interest in the things of the future life, then the inevitable accompaniment of this would have

on the other hand, he finds it represented in the Book of Wisdom, the writings of Philo, and 4 Macc.

[8] Cp. Matt. viii. 11, and in general the realistic terms in which Jesus speaks of the life to come, a mode of speech inconceivable without belief in a body.

[9] Cp. 1 Cor. vi. 13, 19; Phil. iii. 21; 1 Thess. v. 23.

been a pronounced individualism. In reality the eschatological interest attaches with Paul to the large collective happenings rather than to the destiny of the individual, although, of course, the latter can never be wholly kept separated from the former. In 1 Cor. xv the center of gravity does not lie in vs. 58 but in vs. 28. The intense Christ-ward bent of the Apostle's piety also is irreconcilable with the type of hedonism laid to his charge. If hedonism be principially individualistic, then the inclusion of additional egos would be bound to break its force. The climacteric consolation extended to the Thessalonians in connection with their ultimate deliverance is that they shall "be forever with the Lord," 1. iv. 17. Where the note of joy and glory enters it is not seldom produced by the sense of pride arising from the presentation of believers in holiness and blamelessness at the parousia rather than from any hedonistic prospect opening up for the Apostle himself, 1 Thess. ii. 19, 20.[10]

A thorough discussion of the alternative of self-interestedness or altruism in the Apostle's eschatological consciousness can not be given except in the closest dependence on the two fundamental realities which make up for him the content of the eternal state. These two realities are that of "life" and of "glory." The investigation of these two, however, belongs to the concluding chapter of our treatise, that dealing with the future world. Before reaching that subject of "static" eschatology, we shall have to deal with the preceding dramatic developments. It is to the consideration of these that we now proceed.

[10] Of course, it is not intended to deny to Paul that transfigured spiritualized type of "hedonism," if one prefers so to call it, as distinct from the specific attitude towards life that went in the later Greek philosophy by that technical name. Nothing, not even a most refined Christian experience and cultivation of religion are possible without that. It is concreated with "the seed of religion" in man. Augustine speaks of this in his *Confessions* in these words: "For there exists a delight that is not given to the wicked, but to those honoring Thee, O God, without desiring recompense, the joy of whom Thou art Thyself! And this is the blessed life, to rejoice towards Thee, about Thee, for Thy sake." *Conf.* X, 32.

CHAPTER IV

THE COMING OF THE LORD AND ITS PRECURSORS

The two overtowering final events in the drama of eschatology are the Resurrection and the Judgment. As we shall presently see they are the points where the rivers of history issue into the ocean. There are numerous subsidiary streams, but, regarded from the standpoint of the ultimate basin as a whole, these are but minor affluents whose waters do not reach the sea except by way of the two principal outlets. That of the latter there are two, and only two, is due to the inherently religious, and partly remedial, character of the process of which eschatology is the consummation. The Judgment is, of course, the inevitable summing up of a world-process that has fallen subject to the moral abnormalcy of sin; the Resurrection, after a parallel manner, serves for restoring what has become the prey of decadence and death. Where both purposes have been accomplished, their accomplishment makes *ipso facto* provision for whatever else in detail is disordered in the present age. Only in regard to the resurrection an additional factor must be taken into account. What pertains to it can not be exhaustively deduced from the remedial necessity created by sin and death. For the eschatological process is intended not only to put man back at the point where he stood before the invasion of sin and death, but to carry him higher to a plane of life, not attained before the probation, nor, so far as we can see, attainable without it.

This double-faced aspect of the final issues of history and redemption is in itself conceivable without a specifically-Messianic complexion. Many a time in the Old Testament the conclusion of things, both by way of judgment and of transformation, is connected with the epiphany of Jehovah without Messianic assistance. In fact the characterization of the great double event as a "coming" of the Messianic figure is very rare in the Old Testament. Even at the first opening of New Testament revelation in the disclosures made to the family of John the Baptist, and subsequently through the latter himself, the other mode of representation, that of the Lord's (God's) coming still maintains itself. In the teaching of Jesus and particularly with Paul the terminology undergoes a deep change in this respect. While the description of the end-crisis as a signal interposition of God is never entirely in abeyance, we may say that on the whole it gives way to that of the coming of Christ. This is highly significant, because the term "coming" had in certain connections become practically a technical term for eschatological eventuation, just as we are accustomed to speak of the "parousia" meaning without explanation that of Jesus. Now this whole complex was bodily shifted from Jehovah-God to the Messianic circle of thought. The great and uniformly expected "coming" is henceforth a coming of the Messiah. Perhaps no more sweeping and in its effects more momentous transfer of a fundamental Old Testament concept and its reincarnation, as it were, in the New Testament frame of thought than this can be imagined.[1] It should not be forgotten, of course, that the

[1]In the O.T. "coming" of God in the eschatological sense: Ps. l. 3; lxxx. 2; lix. 20; Zech. xiv. 5; Mal. iii. 1; iv. 6; of the Messiah's advent: Gen. xlix. 10; Num. xxiv. 17 ("shall rise"); Dan. vii. 13; for the N.T. cp. Matt. xxiv. 3, 27, 37, 39; 1 Cor. xv. 23; 1 Thess. ii. 19; iii. 13; iv. 15; v. 23; 2 Thess. ii. 1, 8 (vs. 9 of "the Man of Sin"); Jas. v. 7, 8; 1 Pet. iii. 12 (of God); 2 Pet. i. 16; iii. 4, 12 (of "the day of God"). To these must be added the references to "the day of the Lord," so far as with certainty they mean by "Lord" Christ: Rom. xiii. 12; 1 Cor. 1, 8; iii. 13; v. 5; 2 Cor. 1, 14; Phil. i. 6, 10; ii. 16; 1 Thess. v. 2 (4); v. 5, 8; 2 Thess. ii. 2; 2 Tim. i. 18; iv. 8; 1 Pet. iii. 10. The term "ἐπιφανεία" likewise ought to be taken into account, because of its O.T. frequency with regard to Jehovah; it occurs connected with Jesus' future coming in 2 Thess. ii. 8 (joined to parousia); 1 Tim. vi. 14; 2 Tim. i. 10; iv. 1, 8; Tit. ii. 13; finally "ἀποκάλυψις" likewise comes under consideration as an example of transference from the O.T.: 1 Cor. i. 7; 2 Thess. i. 7; 1 Pet. i. 7, 13; iv. 13.

Cp. for the pervasiveness of the idea of "coming" in biblical eschatology, Sellin, *Der alttestamentliche Prophetismus,* p. 181.

transference was facilitated by the attribution of the Kyrios-title to Jesus, which made it almost unavoidable to identify the "coming" of Jehovah-Kurios with the advent of the Messiah. Nevertheless the significance of the phenomenon remains. It lies not so much in the frequency of the association of Jesus with the eschatological crisis, but rather in the simultaneous disappearance of more or less similar eschatological terms once connected with God.

First we deal with the Pauline use of the term "parousia." This occurs of Christ in the following passages: 1 Cor. xv. 23; 1 Thess. ii. 19; iii. 13; iv. 15; v. 23; 2 Thess. ii. 1, 8, (9). Being originally an appellative, in course of time the word tended to become a proper noun, the advent of Jesus at the end to such an extent monopolized its usage that other connections were lost sight of. This had for its further result, that in the later stage no determinative Genitive was required any longer, "the parousia" being in Christian parlance referable to one event only, and therefore not in need of closer specification. But such was not the original employment of the word; the specific de-genitivized use lies beyond the New Testament and the early Christian period. In the Pauline Epistles there are half a dozen passages where the Apostle speaks of his own parousia or of that of his own fellow-workers in the Gospel, in each case, of course, with the necessary personal determination: 1 Cor. xvi. 17 (of Stephanas); 2 Cor. vii. 6, 7 (of Titus); x. 10 (of the body of Paul); Phil. i. 26; ii. 12 (of Paul). It is true, even in such cases the word carries a certain stress of solemnity or importance, due to the consequences associated with the arrival of the person in question. Of the advent of the Messiah "parousia" does not occur in the Jewish literature. With an approach to eschatological meaning it appears in "The Testaments of the XII Patriarchs," where Test. Jud. xxiii. 3 we read of "the parousia of the God of Righteousness," which certainly sounds as if a degree of affinity between it and the eschatological manner of speech had begun to be felt.[2] In its secular as well as in its religious-eschatological use the word expresses the two closely connected ideas of arrival and presence. Parousia signifies "becoming present" and "being present" for a longer or shorter period. Somewhat of an analogy to this is furnished by the double sense of the English word "visit." It has been surmised that in parousia the static significance was the original one, out of which the other developed. This, however, is not certain. In the New Testament the idea of occurrence, arrival, plainly stand in the foreground.[3] Of chief importance to note is the absence of the notion "again" from the word considered by itself. The noun means "arrival," not "return."[4] It can not correctly be rendered by *"second coming."* When the Christians spoke of the parousia of their Lord, they were, of course, aware and mindful that the event spoken of was in point of fact a second arrival, duplicating in a certain respect that of the incarnation. Still there did not develop out of this consciousness the phrase "second parousia." That this did not happen is only explainable from the intensively prospective outlook of the early Church. So many things and such absolutely-consummating things had become associated with the parousia of the Messiah, that only the catastrophe of the

2 Occurrences in extra-biblical Greek: Soph. El. 1104; Eur. Alc. 209; in the later period: Pol. 23, 10, 14; Dion Hal. 1, 45, 4; Thuc. 1, 128, 2. In the Greek O.T. Neh. ii. 6 (variant reading **πορεία**); Jud. x. 18; 2 Macc. viii. 12; xv. 21; 3 Macc. iii. 17.

3 How close the two lie together can be estimated from the fact that the coming is not for bringing other things, but has for its chief purpose the bringing by the Lord of Himself to his own; cp. 1 Thess. iv. 17. On the background of the "parousia" lies the "apousia"; this naturally tends towards making the static sense a subject of attention; in the passages where the parousia of others is spoken of, the comforting note of abiding presence, at least for a time, is distinctly co-audible; cp. 1 Cor. xvi. 17; 2 Cor. viii. 6, 7; Phil. i. 26; ii. 12.

4 The English rendering is in regard to the point of time less explicit than the German "Zukunft" and the Dutch "toekomst," both of which are compound nouns in which the element of futurity is coexpressed. The English lacks such a word and has to content itself with "coming," which, to be sure, is a more correct rendering of "parousia." The futurity of the event can be supplied through joining the auxiliary to the verb: 1 Cor. xv. 23.

last days seemed capable of attracting and retaining the word for itself. This undoubtedly differs from the gravitation of present-day Christianity towards the historical life of Jesus in the past. The New Testament believer felt that while the Messiah had entered the world and been present in it, nevertheless the epochal coming, the one fully worthy of that name, the actual parousia of the Lord, belonged to the future. While the centering of Christian contemplation upon the nativity is both justified and understandable, yet it is more in the line of doctrinal perspective than in the line of instinctive, immediate apprehension of things.[5] Paul in this respect occupies the same standpoint as Peter and James, whilst in the Synoptics, if not the term "parousia," at least a past "coming" is predicated of Jesus, and that in words spoken by Jesus Himself.

The parousia taken as an event is with Paul catastrophic. Of a development within the limits of the concept, or a duplication or triplication of the event there is nowhere any trace. It is a point of eventuation, not a series of successive events. About the question, whether it ushers in the "millennium" or the eternal state, nothing can, of course, be decided by this in itself. Only, if it should be found to refer to an "interregnum," then this by stress of usage would be apt so closely to bind it to the chiliastic complex of hope, as to dim the eternity-prospect beyond. It designates *the momentous event,* and consequently that which it opens up must needs carry a supreme, absolute weight to the religious consciousness. To conceive of Paul as focusing his mind on any phase of relative consummation, and as tying up to this the term "parousia," inevitably would involve his relegating the eternal things to a rank of secondary importance. It would have meant a repetition, or perhaps a continuation, of the Judaistic scheme of thought.[6] Whether the evidence

[5] The fact stated should not be exploited to deny the Messianic complexion or consciousness of our Lord's earthly life. The joint-occurrence in Paul of the two ideas "has come" and "will come" proves that the one point of view need not exclude the other.

[6] A difference is observable here between the terminology in regard

bears out the conclusion here anticipated (and in a certain sense "prejudiced") the subsequent discussion of the chiliasm-problem in Paul's eschatology will have to determine. A chiliasm-parousia tends to make for a chiliasm-complexion of the final state as a whole. And this would be worse than the Judaism of *4 Ezra* and the *Ap. of Baruch.* What appears there as a compromise between the temporal and transcendental strands would with Paul have become a principial appraisal of the former above the latter. The vista of the transcendental world of heaven would have become all but effaced by the concrete shapes moving in the temporal foreground.

A second term descriptive with Paul of the eschatological coming of Christ is the term "revelation," ἀποκάλυψις. This occurs 2 Thess. i. 7; 1 Cor. 1,7; iii. 13; (Rom. ii. 5; viii. 18). The idea of a "revelation" of the Messiah is older than Christianity. It did not first grow out of the belief of the present hidden life of Jesus in heaven which began with his withdrawal at the ascension and will come to an end through an open reappearance in the last day. The older eschatology had already learned to conceive of a twofold sense of this revealing. In some cases the conception moves entirely within the terrestrial sphere, both the hiding and the unveiling (revelation) taking place on earth, whatever place or time of existence might be further put back of that. The belief existed in certain circles that the Messiah, after his birth into this lower world, would for some time be kept hidden in some unknown place on earth, and that not until the appointed moment He would leave this hiding-place, and show Himself in public to the people, to perform his specific task,

to the parousia and the kingdom. The latter is duplicable; it comes in instalments; so in the Gospels, where the present and the eschatological kingdom are clearly distinguished. Nevertheless this has not led to any duplication of the "parousia" of the Christ. The latter is one and indivisible. The nearest that (in terminology of the kingdom) comes to a twofold advent is such a saying as John xiv. 3, but the parousia-idea is foreign to the Johannine writings with the exceptions of 1 John ii. 28, where the word refers to the end and excludes a preliminary occurrence no less than in Paul. Cp. further Heb. ix. 27, 28.

cp. 1 Ap. Bar. xxix. 3; xxx. 1; 4 Ezr. vii. 28; Test. Lev. 18.[7] An instance of his Jewish belief is recorded in Jno. vii. 27: "When the Christ comes, no one knows whence He is," although the idea thus suggested is in no wise countenanced by Jesus or the Evangelist. Apart from this the Scriptural passages are all framed on the principle of a direct translation from the heavenly into the earthly regions, so as to impart to "apocalypsis" a technical (theological) sense, applied frequently to the transfer, or coming down, of great things, from the supernal to the terrestrial sphere. In this sense we meet with it already in the vision of Dan. vii. which depicts one like unto a son of man (= man) as coming with the clouds of heaven, words which certainly assume a previous existence, although giving as yet no information, how far the preëxistence was understood to reach back in time or into eternity. This general background, however, of a revelation from heaven, could not but assume a quite different complexion through becoming correlated with the visible disappearance of Jesus into heaven, and thus coupled with the promise of a likewise visible movement in the opposite direction, viz. his appearance in the future. That, rather than the incarnation, now become his "revelation" *par excellence*.[8]

The flavor attaching to the term "apocalypsis" differs somewhat from that carried by the term "parousia." The latter concerns believers chiefly, the former the enemies of God's people, though in neither case exclusively so. In 2

[7] The above statement does not, of course, exclude, that in the Apocalyptic writings (and sometimes in the same books), most transcendental representations of the Messianic introduction into the earthly world occur side by side with the other. Cp. the writings above cited.

[8] In the First Epistle of Peter, where the idea of the hidden invisible existence of Jesus and his salvation in heaven is stressed, the eschatological usage of "revelation" is likewise in evidence; cp. i. 13; v. 4. In i. 20 the word is φανεροῦν instead of ἀποκαλύπτειν. This passage is a striking proof for the eternal actual preëxistence of Christ. "Foreknown before the ages" and "manifested in these last times" yields an impossible contrast, unless "foreknown" be given the pregnant sense of "eternally beloved as an existing being."

Thess. i. 7, 8 the militant revelation is described in the following terms: "At the revelation of the Lord Jesus from heaven with the angels of his power, rendering vengeance to them that know not God, and to them that obey not the gospel of our Lord Jesus." To believers the appearance of Christ will partake of the character of a "revelation," inasmuch as his glory has not been visibly disclosed to them before. The idea is in all passages plainly implied, that Jesus' eschatological revelation will bear the features of a strictly momentary, miraculous act. While things preceding and preparing for it do not, of course, lack all gradual and orderly unfolding, yet the event itself is catastrophic in the absolute sense, nay this very idea of suddenness and unexpectedness seems to be intimately associated with the word. Hence of the "Anomos" of 2 Thess. ii. 3, 6, 8 an *ἀποκάλυψις* is predicted; many forces may after a hidden, mysterious manner work towards the ripeness of the time for his activity, none the less he is to be revealed "in his time."

A third term designating Christ's advent is *ἡ ἡμέρα.* 1 Thess. v. 4; 2 Cor. iii. 13; (Heb. x. 25). This is found in various forms, according to the complements added to it. In Paul's writings the following of these enlarged designations occur:

ἡ ἡμέρα τοῦ Κυρίου, 1 Thess. v. 2; 2 Thess. ii. 2; 1 Cor. v. 5 (Acts ii. 20; iii. 10);
ἡμέρα τοῦ Κυρίου ἡμῶν, 1 Cor. i. 8;
ἡ ἡμέρα τοῦ Κυρίου Ἰησοῦ, 2 Cor. i. 14;
ἡ ἡμέρα Ἰησοῦ Χριστοῦ, Phil. i. 6;
ἡ ἡμέρα Χριστοῦ, Phil. i. 10; ii, 16;

The first of these forms is a rendering of the O. T. phrase "the day of Jehovah." Hence, in regard to some passages there is doubt, whether "the Lord" in it be meant as the Greek translation "Lord" = "Adonaj" = "Jehovah," or signifies the Lord Jesus. Where the name "Jesus" is found in apposition, or the pronoun "our" is appended, there can be, of course, no doubt but Christ is meant. Absolutely certain of this we can not be, when the title simply reads "the Lord."

As to the import and bearing of the word "day," various theories are being held, of none of which absolute certainty can be affirmed. Some think the origin lies in the conception of Jehovah as a victorious warrior, who has *his day* in which He will be the center of the entire scene of battle and victory, the day thus being monopolized by Him and filled with the revelation of his glory. There are certain contexts in Paul which favor this association. According to 1 Thess. v. 2; ii. 8 the day brings with it destruction for the enemies of God's people. The O.T. usage is to a large extent in accord with this: Am. v. 18; Hos. i: 11; Isa. ii. 12; x. 3; xiii. 6, 13; xxxiv. 8; Jer. xlvi. 10; Ez. vii. 19; xiii. 5; xxx. 3; Joel i. 15; ii. 1, 11, 31; iii. 14; Ob. 15; Zeph. i. 14, 15; ii. 2, 3; Mal. iv. 5.[9]

Others think that the source of the idea must be sought in the terminology of judgment in the forensic sense. A judge or a court have their day on which they are in session. That such usage was not unfamiliar to Paul may be seen from 1 Cor. iv. 3: "But with me it is a very small thing that I should be judged of you, or of any man's *day*."[10] The idea of a judgment-day is plainly associated with the phrase "day of the Lord," wherever Paul by means of the idea urges the practice of holiness: Rom. ii. 16; 1 Cor. ii. 13; Phil. i. 6, 10; ii. 16. It should be remembered, however, that the punitive-realistic and the purely-forensic conceptions cannot in all cases be cleanly separated, as little as this can be done in the Old Testament.[11]

In a couple of passages Paul seems to have colored the

[9] Isa. ix. 4 has been quoted as furnishing an analogy through the phrase "the day of Midian"; cp. W. Robertson Smith, *Prophets of Israel,* p. 397. The comparison is not exact, because Midian, after whom the day is named, appears in it as the conquered, not as the victor, as Jesus does in the interpretation suggested in "the day of Jehovah." Wellhausen calls attention to the Arabic phrase "the day of some tribe" for the day of its great victory.

[10] Cf. Acts xix. 38, "**ἀγοραῖοι**" (i.e. ἡμέραι) are being held; it was easy for the adjective to drop out of the phrase.

[11] The "visitation" in Isa. x. 3 is a visitation for judgment; in the same ominous sense the word occurs in 1 Pet. ii. 12; Jude 6.

word "day" forming part of the phrase with the (not-purely chronological), but likewise physical-pictorial association of the element of "light." "Light" belongs to the day as its characteristic, the opposite of the darkness that pertains to the night. Hence "the day of the Lord" can be visualized as a day of deliverance, joy and blessedness. There is perhaps no figure more pregnant in its religious associations than the figure of "light." In the sphere of the emotions (no less than in that of the intellect for knowledge) it is made to render service as a physical analogon for spiritual rejoicing. The two main passages inviting to this, as at least a partial interpretation interwoven with the preceding usage, are Rom. xiii. 11-14 and 2 Thess. v. 1-8. According to the former the world-night is a time of wickedness, characterized, as the night-time in the pagan world usually is, by such things as revelling, drunkenness, chambering, wantonness, strife, jealousy, because the publicity inseparated from daylight holds these and other things under restraint. vs. 13. Moreover, for the wicked as well as the good, the night is the period of sleep, vs. 11. Of this world-night the Apostle further affirms the nearness of the end: it is far spent; the emergency, therefore, demands watchfulness ("waking out of sleep") and abstinence from all forms of pagan immorality, through the consciousness of the imminence of the crisis: it is high time; salvation, eschatological salvation, is relatively at hand.[12] Believers must put on the "armor of light," vs. 12. Besides the usual warning attached to the thought of the approaching moment of the judgment, there is here an allusion to the ushering in of the future state as a state of light, and salvation, a day in the literal (not

[12] Grossheide, *De Verwachting der Toekomst van Jesus Christus,* would apply vs. 29: "The time is short" to the nearness of death for individuals, and reveals in general a tendency to remove the strong sub-eschatological consciousness from the record through unrealistic exegesis. To confine ourselves to Paul, he interprets Phil. iv. 5 "The Lord is near," of the Lord's omnipresence. In Rom. xiii. 11 "now is salvation nearer" he puts upon "salvation" the otherwise quite permissible but here impossible sense of "the sum total of what the Christian obtains through faith, while of "nearer" he gives no satisfactory explanation. These and some other passages are grouped together under the

merely chronological) sense; the day has become a qualitative conception, by reason of its association with light; the word has received ethico-religious import *bono sensu,* it is a *day* and not a *night.* And, through its contrast with "the night which is far spent," it has also ceased to be the mere marking of a *point* in the eschatological process; this day so quickly to ensue is quantitatively stretched out to a *period* of extended duration. As the night had a course of which a "being far spent" could be predicated, so the day has its extension and means more, to speak in terms of the same figure, than the break of day, or the morning.

In 1 Thess. v. 1-8 the contrast is in the first place one between the ominous surprise which the arrival of the day of the Lord involves for the wicked when it arrives as a thief in the night, or as travail comes upon a woman with child. Up to the third verse, it will be observed, the contrast of light-darkness is still absent. In vss. 4-8, however, this element enters. On the whole it is utilized to stress the contrast between the sobriety of the day and wantonness of the night; likewise between the heedlessness of the wicked and the watchful preparedness of believers. Still the statement in vs. 5: "Ye are all sons of the light and sons of the day" reminds of the same allusion observable in Rom. xiii. Throughout the terminology of the two passages is strikingly the same. The occurrence of "light" as a soteric term in other connections likewise adds force to the understanding here; cp. Eph. v. 8, 9, 13; Col. i. 12. Even in the O.T. there are points of contact, for the association of darkness, on the one hand, and light, on the other hand, with judgment and salvation. If one were to follow this lead, the proper paraphrase for "day of

heading, "Scripture passages wrongly brought into connection with our subject" (the Parousia). For the other class (where the Parousia is actually involved) he quotes from Paul, 1 Cor. vii. 29; xv. 51; 1 Thess. iv. 15, 17; 2 Thess: ii. 1ff. The treatise is exceedingly valuable on account of the detailed lists inserted with each passage of previous, or contemporary, writers and their various views on the exegesis at issue. It deals, of course, not with Paul's statements alone.

Jehovah" in the passages cited would be "the light-reign (day) of Jehovah" as well as "the dawn introducing it."[13]

A remarkable feature about these several terms is their detachment from the precedents, attendants and subsequents of the crisis they describe. They mark the mere event to come; of further eschatological speculation they are void. The Apostle handles the theme in a large, one might almost say abstract, manner. Yet this is not due to the terms themselves, which are fully capable of a rich filling-up with solid concrete material. The cause will have to be sought in the constructive, history-building rôle eschatology had come to play in the mind of Paul. In view of the outstanding summit the detailed and scattered features on the slopes of the mountain have, while not entirely effaced, at least lost their sharpness of contour. While this may less satisfy the interest of eschatological curiosity, it for this very reason greatly contributes to the outstanding of the chief structural elevations. The transparency of the atmosphere secures for the latter a clear vision of their unique importance.

It would be a mistake, however, to infer from this that for the Apostle the eschatological crisis bears no fixed organic relation to the preceding historical process. The very scheme of the two successive worlds renders it unthinkable that at any arbitrarily chosen point the world to come should supersede the world that is. The phrase *πλήρωμα τοῦ χρόνου*, Gal. iv. 4, implies an orderly unrolling of the preceding stages of world-history towards a fixed end. It is true, this statement refers to what we call "the first coming" of Christ, but we must not forget that the whole drama enclosed between the two "comings" is so much a unit for Paul, that orderly progression towards the close being characteristic of the former coming, a similar approach could not possibly be absent from the

[13] In Am. v. 18 the prophet warns the wicked, that "the day of Jehovah" is darkness and not light. Evidently it had been considered by the people largely in the latter aspect, for they are said to "desire" it. Cp. on this passage and the O.T. usage of the phrase in general, Gressman, *Der Ursprung der Israelitisch-jüdischen Eschatologie,* pp. 141-159.

climacteric termination of the whole. But also in certain concrete ways the Apostle has set definite limits to the continuance of the present aeon on its course, and thereby at the same time fixed the point of arrival for the world to come.[14] In Rom. viii. 19-23 the final stage appears as a painful birth-process: "The whole creation groans and travails in pain together until now." A clear analogy to this is furnished by the Jewish theology, where it speaks of the *"chebleihammashiah,"* "the birth-woes of the Messiah." While this explicitly refers only to the arrival of the Messiah himself, it undoubtedly carries with it the idea of great changes and new conditions to be ushered in by his momentous appearance. Still, a difference exists in this regard, that Paul has divested the idea of its limited form of expression, and made it expressive of the entire foregoing world-process as characterized by the universal prevalence of sin: "The *creature* was made subject to vanity"; it suffers from the bondage of corruption in an all-inclusive sense; it waits in eager expectation for the liberating end. That the *κτίσις "the creature"* is meant here in distinction from man, the context clearly shows; particularly the words "itself" and "ourselves also" (vss. 21, 23) preclude all doubt concerning this. How this grandiose conception was filled out in detail, and whether it involves the belief of a progressive, and in course of time accelerated, corruption of nature cannot with certainty be determined, al-

[14] The word ὠδῖνες, technically "birth-throes," does not occur in our passage; it *is* used by Paul figuratively of the destruction coming upon the wicked at the arrival of the day of the Lord, 1 Thess. v. 3. Being likewise found in our Lord's eschatological discourse, Mark xiii. 8; Matt. xxiv. 8, it would seem to have acquired its specific association with the pains of childbirth previously. In itself it can denote any violent pain, Ps. xviii. 5ff., but the eschatological reference, both in the saying of Jesus and here is not subject to doubt. The ktisis here in Romans seems to be the lower ktisis, whereas according to the Gospel-prophecy also astral bodies are involved. The usage goes back in general, and here with Paul in particular, to the curse upon the soil pronounced in the account of the fall. That Paul looked upon his own time as exhibiting an extreme intensity of the curse, and a correspondingly strong aspiration of nature towards deliverance, is not capable of proof. The thing dates from the beginning; cp. "until now" in vs. 22.

though this idea would fit well into the general scheme of Paul's thought. It should be noticed, however, that the representation reflects a genuinely sympathetic feeling towards the lot of subhuman nature. Paul is sometimes charged (in distinction from Jesus) with a lack of sensibility towards the natural, subhuman world, but here at least with a certain tenderness he sympathizes with the pitiable lot of the lower creation. Whether there lies back of this mere personification, or whether perhaps, as some would believe, it betrays the ascription of a degree of consciousness to the animal and vegetable, or even the astral, world, is a question at least worth considering. The terms used certainly are strong: the creature manifests an ἀποκαραδοκία for the manifestation of the sons of God. The contrast between willingness and unwillingness is introduced to describe the tenor of the creature's subjection. The creation follows in this not its own natural bent but finds itself implicated in the woeful destinies of mankind. In this fact lies, on the other hand, also the reason for its ultimate deliverance, which on account of such origin must coincide with the removal of the bondage of man to corruption and his endowment with the glorious liberty of the coming age. One almost gets the impression, as though this remarkable piece of the philosophy of nature were introduced as a foil to the wilfully wicked self-surrender of man to his enslavement by sin. It is scarcely subject to doubt that the participle ὑποτάξας does refer to *man,* not to God. The strain of pessimism in Paul with regard to the world in its sub-redemptive state is plainly traceable here. It is, however, no more *absolute* pessimism than is the Apostle's estimate of the ethico-religious condition of unredeemed mankind. The gloom of the one, no less than that of the other, is in anticipation dispersed by the assurance of the glorious deliverance at the end. The redemptive optimism lies deeper and by far outweighs the pessimism of the sense of sin and corruption, cp. Rom. viii. 18.

More particularly relating to social conditions in the circle of believers is the ἐνεστῶσα ἀναγκή spoken of in 1 Cor.

vii. 26, in view of which the Apostle inclines towards dissuading such as are single from entrance upon the state of marriage. The phrase in itself has no eschatological color; nevertheless, in view of the context evidently requires to be understood in that light. The average troubles connected with married life as such can scarcely be referred to. Nor is justice done to the language by thinking of marital troubles made more complex and burdensome for Christians through impending persecution. A quite particular aggravation of the distress referred to must have stood before the Apostle's mind according to the closing words of vs. 28: "Nevertheless such shall have trouble in the flesh, and I would spare you." In the decisiveness of these words "*shall* have trouble" the eschatological note clearly makes itself heard. A quite special tribulation is imminent. Explicitly this is affirmed by the opening clause of vs. 29: "The time is short." The manner in which this statement is introduced by: "This I say, brethren," shows that the expectation of the nearness of the end carries the emphasis. But the words "the time is short" certainly cannot have the rather banal sense, that it is no longer worth while to marry. The shortness or rather "contractedness" of the time serves simply as a reminder of the belief that the parousia may not be far distant, and that from the parousia all sorts of worldly distress are inseparable. Thus understood the idea of the present "anangke" and the statement "the time is short" fit perfectly into each other. But there appears in the context still a third motive pointing to the same conclusion. The counsel takes in view other relationships and occupations, vss. 30, 31: they that weep should be as though they wept not, and they that rejoice as though they rejoiced not, and they that buy as though they possessed not, and they that use this world, as not abusing it. And the reason for all this is given in vs. 31: "the fashion of this world passes away." But here again the readers are immediately reminded of the fact that the relevancy of the advice, so far from resting on a purely chronological opinion as to the nearness of the event, derives its main force from the state of mind in which the Christian ought to contemplate the end and make ready for it. The underlying idea is none other than that the times preceding the parousia require a unique concentration of the minds of believers upon the Lord and the manner in which they may best please Him. The last days are to be days of undivided and most assiduous interest in the Lord and the unparalleled mode in which He may soon come to reveal Himself: "He that is unmarried cares for the things that belong to the Lord, how he may please the Lord; but he that is married cares for the things that are of the world, how he may please his wife." There is difference also in regard to this between a wife and a virgin. The unmarried woman cares for the things of the Lord, that she may be holy both in body and in spirit: but she that is married cares for the things of the world, how she may please her husband" vss. 32-34.[15]

A further datum making the time of the parousia dependent on certain future developments is furnished by Rom. ix. 11-15; 25-32. Here Paul outlines in broad strokes the course determined for the extension of the Gospel to those to be saved through its effect. This outline has the peculiarity that it names not only the bare facts, but to some extent adds a psychological and soteric explanation, so that one might call it a philosophy of the history of the church in the widest sense. The close connection between it and eschatology lies in two statements: vs. 15, where the result of the "πρόσλημψις" i.e., the receiving back of the unbelieving majority of the Jews into favor brings with itself what is called "life from the dead." The climacteric nature of the event to be expected as the issue of the unfolding ways of God forbids to tone down this phrase to the purely-metaphorical, making it fall within the terms of mere spiritual revival. "Life from the

[15] The form of marriage in use among the Dutch Churches generalizes the idea of affliction as connected with marriage, so as to detach it from the eschatological background it has in our passage: "Inasmuch as ordinarily those that are married are subject to manifold adversities and crosses on account of sin," etc.

dead" must refer to the resurrection specifically so named, and so understood it presupposes the beginning of the closing act of the eschatological drama. The second statement, leading to the same conclusion, is found in vss. 25 and 26: "blindness in part is happened to Israel, until the fulness (πλήρωμα) of the Gentiles be come in and *so* (οὕτως) all Israel shall be saved, as it is written, There shall come out of Sion the Deliverer, and shall turn ungodliness away from Jacob." In this last statement, it is true, the immediate supervention of the eschatological crisis upon the preceding events is not directly affirmed, but it is clearly enough implied in this that the twofold great purpose of the Gospel-preaching will have at that point been attained, the bringing in of the fulness of both Gentiles and Jews. The motive effecting this stupendous reversal in the attitude towards the Gospel on the part of the Jews is described by Paul as a " παραζηλοῦν," or, in the passive, "παραζηλοῦσθαι." In vs. 14 Paul applies the principle involved even to the scattering results of his own Apostolic missionary activity among the Jews. There the "parazeloon" includes the indirect aim: "if by any means I may provoke to jealousy my flesh (the Jews), and so save *some of them.*" This subsidiary purpose the Apostle pursues alongside of and through the opportunities offered him in his evangelizing of the Gentiles, vss. 13, 14: "For I speak to you Gentiles, inasmuch as I am (specifically) the Apostle of the Gentiles, I magnify mine office (even so far as primarily it extends to the Gentiles), if by any means I may save some of them (the Jews)." Nevertheless such conversions remain for the present but sporadic examples, though at bottom expressive of a divine principle intended to work itself out on the largest of scales at the predetermined point in the future. And this is intimated in vs. 11: "Have they (the Jews) stumbled that they should fall? God forbid, but rather through their fall salvation is come unto the Gentiles, for to provoke them (the Jews) to jealousy." The "parazeloun" of x. 19 in a quotation from Deut. xxxii. 21 is of a somewhat different nature, for its proximate effect is "παροργιζοῦν," "to provoke to anger."

Paul, however, may have looked upon the anger aroused in the hearts of the Jews through the marvellous success of the Gentile mission as a sort of negative preparation for the "parazelousthai" in the nobler sense. It can only lead to confusion not to distinguish between the single conversions spoken of in such statements and this comprehensive eschatological recovering of the unbelieving Jews. The "pleroma" held in prospect for them stands in contrast to the "ἥττημα" and "παράπτωμα" of vs. 12. Both words, taken together with the question of vs. 11, leave no doubt but the general, national apostasy of Israel is referred to, and consequently the recovery from this must bear the same collective interpretation. Just as the "riches of the world," and the "riches of the Gentiles" take the pagan world in its organic, collective sense, so the other term in the antithesis requires the same understanding. It need scarcely be added, that "collective" is not identical with a "universalistically"-conceived extension of the two effects to all single men on either side. If it were, then the curious question could not have been so simply passed by as to what in Paul's view had become, or was to become, of the individuals who had died away or were to die away in the intervening time between the setting in of the hardening of Israel and the end. It is precisely characteristic of the passage that it abstains from the consideration, far more the solution, of such problems, and speaks in ethnic terms. Only with this in mind can we take the events as tending more or less directly to the eschatological consummation.[16] The phrase "πώρωσις ἀπὸ μέρους," "hardening in part,"

[16] "Πᾶς Ἰσραήλ" could, of course, when taken by itself, mean the joint-body of the people of God composed of Jews and Gentiles by race. Whether it can bear this meaning in the surrounding context is a different question. This we feel bound to deny.

As to "οὕτως" in the clause at the beginning of vs. 26, "And οὕτως all Israel shall be saved," this is sometimes rendered by "then" owing to the (involuntary) injection of *chronological* progression into the passage. When translated "thus," it cannot signify aught else than "in the working out of the principle stated," "after this manner"; cp. Zahn, *Komm. z N.T., Römer,* p. 523, note 66, who paraphrases, with appeal to Acts xvii. 33; xx. 11; xxviii. 17, "not until after this has

p. 25, bears strong witness to the necessity of the collective exegesis. On the other hand, a frank recognition of this state of facts ought not to be exploited, as it often is, in the interest of a total denial of the Pauline doctrine of sovereign election as an integral factor in the salvation of individuals. The evidence of Paul's firm belief in that and the supreme importance it bears for the whole construction of his soteriology and eschatology is superabundant. Even if Rom. ix-xi were entirely left out of account this would still hold absolutely true. The trouble arises from too much mechanical exegesis expended on these particular chapters without penetrating into the inner core of the doctrine and from overhasty disregard of the numerous statements where this core comes into view. Nor should it be overlooked that even in the very opening up of the problem as regards Israel in the present in Ch. ix several times an individualistic turn is given to the idea of election. Apart from its national application the principial significance of the doctrine in soterics shines through everywhere in the argument. The Apostle was not led first from the ethnic employment of the idea to the introduction of it in individual cases. It is from certain theological standpoints convenient to assert this, but the opposite order of emergence as between the two is just as conceivable.

happened"; this paraphrase of Zahn *does* introduce the time-element, through its "not until," but only retrospectively. As observed above, the close sequence between the conversion of Israel and the end is suspended on the words *"life from the dead."* Whether this consummation is to be construed chiliastically, or otherwise, is not indicated by our passage. To the question of "Chiliasm" as present or not present in the Pauline Eschatology as a whole we shall have to revert afterwards.

That the things foretold will happen in or to the then present generation is not affirmed by the Apostle. Some have even thought that the possibility of this not being so is indicated by the (intended) omission of the pronoun "αὐτῶν" after the noun "πρόσλημψιν" in xi. 15. On this view the *certainty* of the national "receiving" is the only thing affirmed. A whole generation, or more, might intervene, and still the statement would lose none of its literal fulfilment, when the epoch-making event took place. The causal significance of the latter for the coming of "life from the dead" would not be impaired by the chronological interval.

Paul, we believe, came to the discussion of this problem, the unbelief of the greater part of Israel, as antecedently a predestinarian; he was not first made a predestinarian through his weighing of that problem. There is abundant evidence of his application of the principle of predestination or election before the writing of Romans. Cp. 1 Thess. i. 4; 1 Cor. i. To say that Paul revolved or further worked out the problem in his mind does not imply that for this reason it ceased to be for him an object of divine revelation, lost divine sanction. On the contrary, in Ch. ix. 2 he explicitly affirms that at least avowal of the one aspect of it there mentioned (the presence of great sorrow in his heart) was made "in Christ," that is, with the concurrent witness-bearing of the Holy Ghost in his consciousness.

Still another statement implying a gradual and fixed approach towards the goal of the Parousia is found in 1 Cor. xv. 24, 25. Here it is declared that before the arrival of "the end" (τὸ τέλος), Christ must have previously put down all "rule" (ἀρχή) and "authority" (ἐξουσία) and "power" (δύναμις); that Christ's reign of conquest must last until He shall have put *all* enemies under his feet; further that "the last enemy" to be destroyed is "death." Plainly there is affirmed in these words a progressive subjugation of enemies leading up to the consummation. The fact that death is named "the last" points to the resurrection. All this, however, moves in the super-terrestrial sphere of the world of spirits, so that it can scarcely be counted among the prognostics of the approaching crisis; it consists of happenings unobservable by men. There is further involved the somewhat complicated question, as to where the beginning of the conquests named should chronologically be placed: does it belong from beginning to end of the "millennium," as postulated by some on the ground of this and other passages appearing as a fixed element in Paul's eschatology? Or does it form part of the present period, in which case it would date from Christ's resurrection and be conceived by the Apostle as going on at that very moment so as to cover the entire period between the resurrection and the final parousia of the Lord. So far as the plausibility or implausibility of such a "chiliastic" exegesis is concerned, we shall revert to that aspect of the question in its proper place, when the presence or non-presence of a millennarian strand of thought in Paul's teaching comes under review.

Still another problem, although of less direct bearing on the question in hand, concerns the exact nature of the enemies spoken of. Are the words used abstract designations for certain types of movements hostile to God and Christ, or do they refer to concrete demonic powers? As concerns the other terms ("rules," "authorities," "powers") the general demonological statements in other passages of the Epistles put beyond doubt, that concrete beings, or groups of such, are meant. It is somewhat more difficult to assume this for "death," although Jewish analogies for even that are not lacking. Certainly in Rom. v. 12-21 "death" is highly personalized, but so are "sin" and "life." In the Apocalypse especially death appears in vivid concreteness, and the juxtaposition of death with the other powers speaks in favor of an analogous interpretation in all four cases. The phrase "all enemies" (vs. 25) opens still farther, but scarcely more definite, prospects.[17] At any rate this much is sure, that the Apostle assumes an incessant, uninterrupted pressing on of the soteric movement towards its absolute conclusion determined in the divine plan. The end stands in fixed relation towards what precedes it. Be the compass of time within which all things occur longer or shorter, the simple fact of the designation of "death" as the *"last"* enemy proves that a well-ordered succession is contemplated.

To the foregoing may be added a couple of passages from the Pastoral Epistles. As is well known, these Epistles lay strong stress upon the invasion of the churches by godless, depraved elements, and draw, on the whole, a dismal picture of the condition of things, both morally and religiously, at their time of writing. In itself it would have been

[17] Cp. O. Everling, *Die Paulinische Angelologie und Daemonologie*, 1888.

easy to bring these symptoms of decadence into connection with the near approach of the eschatological crisis. As a matter of fact we actually observe such a connection dwelt upon in John's First Epistle. In the Pastorals, on the other hand, such an inference is drawn only twice: 1 Tim. iv. 1 and 2 Tim. iii. 1. "In later times (ἐν ὑστέροις καιροῖς) some shall fall away from the faith, giving heed to seducing spirits and doctrines of demons." This forecast is introduced by: "the Spirit says expressly" (ῥητῶς "in so many words"), a form of statement indicating that the low appraisal put upon the character of the times was by no means the opinion of single, pessimistically inclined, persons, but a piece of actual prophetic revelation once expressed with great emphasis. The other statement (iii. 1 of the Second Epistle reads: "But know this that in the last days (ἐν ἐσχάταις ἡμέραις) grievous times shall come. For men shall be lovers of self, lovers of money, boastful, haughty, railers, disobedient to parents, unthankful, unholy, without natural affection, implacable, slanderers, without self-control, fierce, no lovers of good, traitors, headstrong, puffed up, lovers of pleasure rather than lovers of God, holding a form of godliness, but having denied the power thereof." The enumeration resembles to some extent the catalogues of forms of sin found in the earlier Pauline Epistles.[18] The vices and excesses of sin there rehearsed lack, however (with the exception of Col. iii. 5-8), the explicit reference to the semi-eschatological character of the times, and this is precisely what is present here in the Pastorals. It would be a mistake to assume that Paul in these later Epistles represents that sort of thing as still lying entirely in the future. The enumeration is followed in 2 Tim. iii. 5 by the injunction "From these turn away." It is a matter of present concern and eminent importance.

[18] Cp. Rom. i. 29-32; iii. 10-18; 1 Cor. vi. 9, 10; Gal. v. 19-21.

CHAPTER V

THE MAN OF SIN

"The Man of Sin," also called "The Son of Perdition," "The Lawless One," is an eschatological person described by Paul in 2 Thess. ii. 1-12. In ordinary eschatological parlance he bears the name Antichrist, and in the First and Second Epistles of John this name occurs. So far as we are able to ascertain, Antichrist is not a Pauline term, although the possibility must be reckoned with, that Paul may have been acquainted with it and simply not used it. Even the Johannine Apocalypse, with all its abundance of eschatological imagery, does not employ it. What lies back of 2 Thess. in early Christian literature or tradition, whether written or unwritten, does not know "the Antichrist" as a formal title. Going back still farther to the pre-Christian literature of the apocryphal or pseudepigraphical kind or to the Old Testament, we still look in vain for the later so familiar technical term.

To say that the name Antichrist is scarce in or absent from early documents by no means implies that the real person or the real thing called by other names but resembling to a larger or smaller extent the conception, is equally nonexistent in that period. Paul himself is a striking example for the fact that a reality-complex of great religious or historical moment can exist for considerable time prior to its finding significant, unifying designation in the theological and eschatological vocabulary. The time-distance between Thessalonians and the Johannine Epistles is scarcely long enough to permit the working out of such an extra-important and far-reaching complex of ideas. Whatever may be true of the sudden emergence of names, whole blocks of religious thought with all their psychological associations are not so suddenly upheaved. John certainly deals with it as something not then first made known to his readers, but avowedly familiar, and the same manner of introducing it is seen in Thessalonians. The attention called to it was for an eminently practical purpose, viz. to warn against the delusion, as though the day of the Lord had already arrived.[1] But for correcting that the simplest reference to a well-established eschatological program would have been sufficient. When instead of this the Apostle launches out into a somewhat detailed exposition of the entire subject, it becomes difficult to escape from the impression that Paul took a certain personal delight in drawing the figure at full length. And what he says seems to be derived from a fixed fund of knowledge. In the pre-Pauline tradition of the N.T. there is but one thing that could throw light on this. We refer to the phrase of our Lord in the great eschatological discourse *βδέλυγμα τῆς ἐρημώσεως*, translated in the English text by "abomination of desolation": "When, therefore, ye see the abomination of desolation, spoken of through Daniel, the prophet, standing in the holy place (let him that reads understand)." The Daniel-context refers proximately to a desecration of the sanctuary in Jerusalem expected, it seems, from the sacrilegious hand of Antiochus Epiphanes. That Jesus shaped the matter in his mind after the same fashion is plain; only he projects the horrible event from the past in which it had once taken place into a future beyond his own point of speaking. The monstrous concept is neither by Daniel nor by Jesus clothed directly in the form of a personal antagonist to God; in this respect the technical terms of the Antichrist-tradition do not yet appear, but as ominous shades they hover already in the background.[2] In our later treatment of the prophecy we shall

[1] "Has already arrived," thus we shall have to understand the verb "enhesteke." The rendering "is at hand" seems a compromise due to doctrinal motives; "just at hand" (A.R.) is a half-compromise, betraying that the simple "at hand" did not quite satisfy.

[2] The participle "standing" has in Matt. the neuter form, in Mk. the masculine. The masculine makes the statement point beyond the crime of Antiochus, who had only put an idolatrous altar, not an idolatrous image, in the holy place. In the masculine appears a degree of

endeavor to make clear that the same phenomenon observable in Paul and with Jesus already characterizes the representation in Daniel. Already there things are spoken of and not explained; there lies a world of not unknowable, and yet only half-known mystery beyond what is disclosed. Thus we are enabled to draw through the line from Paul to Jesus and from Jesus to Daniel and from Daniel to something already an object of knowledge, be it as yet only vague, to an older generation. This continuity is of great value to all Christian scholars who seek to deal with the Antichrist-subject. At bottom it furnishes the main scriptural justification for dealing with the subject on a typical basis. The modern mind may scorn this as one more instance of the unscientific, "rabbinical" treatment of the Old Testament by the New. Whatever maltreatment may be charged, it is a comfort to know that the crime was committed before by both Jesus and Paul.

Some have thought that evidence of an older Antichrist-tradition could be discovered in the name Beliar[3] occurring repeatedly in the O.T. There is in itself nothing objectionable in tracing such connections. Were Beliar actually connected with the Antichrist-genealogy, this would prove his origins to be exceedingly ancient. In the only passage where Paul introduces the name, 2 Cor. vi. 15, Beliar is naught else but a duplicate name for Satan. The whole meaning centers in the ethical exhortation that righteousness and iniquity and light and darkness can have no more communion with each other than Christ can have with Beliar. Examining the Old Testament we find that Beliar nowhere appears as a name directly given to a person, but always in the company of prefixes for the purpose of attaching to the persons or things referred to an evil connotation. Thus we read of "sons," "children," "daughters," "men," even of "brooks" of

approach to the personal. Still it is only the quasi-personality of the statue not the living one of the tyrant as yet. It is scarcely necessary to add that the warning "let him that reads understand" refers not to the reading of Matthew but of the Daniel-prophecy.

[3] The name itself occurs in various forms, such as: Beliar, Belial, Belian, Beliab, Belias, Belier, Belchor.

Belial, Deut. xiii. 13; Judg. xix. 22; xx. 13; 1 Sam. i. 16; ii. 12; x. 27; xxv. 17, 25; xxx. 22; 2 Sam. xvi. 7; xxiii. 6; 1 Ki. xxi. 10, 13; 2 Chron. xiii. 7.

Surmises and speculations about this O.T. Beliar are somewhat precarious precisely because of his appearance in a composite indirect form. Undeniably there hides behind these phrases a real demonic name which largely must have gone out of use, being replaced by Satan or some such name. It had ceased to perform further service than that of a term of opprobrium, varying according to the intent with which it was hurled at somebody in mere desire to tease or with the more serious purpose of inflicting real harm through an assumed magical force inhering in it. It is plain that Beliar is not in canonical Scripture a precursor or duplication of Antichrist.

But Beliar has not been allowed to rest in his O.T. oblivion. His name reëmerges in the apocryphal and pseudepigraphical writings and through the methods applied by the *religionsgeschichtliche* school has from there been thrown back into the olden times and that with a much more pronounced Antichrist-physiognomy than was his before. This school makes its great principle the substantial identity and continuity of all Oriental, especially Babylonian, religion. Much material concerning Beliar in the non-Canonical literature and in the earlier unwritten tradition is freely dated back into hoary antiquity, and thus a quite novel Antichrist-tradition is constructed.

The modern writer who has done most in this line of throwing back the late post-Christian material into a large pre-Christian tradition-reservoir is Bousset.[4] Following the ideas of Gunkel a.o. Bousset assumes that the conception of a Great Adversary is very ancient.[5] Its ultimate origins

[4] Bousset, *Der Antichrist in der Überlieferung des Judenthums, des Neuen Testamentes, und der alten Kirche*, 1895.

[5] Gunkel, *Schöpfung und Chaos*, likewise published in 1895. It should be added that Bousset is somewhat more restrained and cautious in drawing upon the ancient Babylonian material than Gunkel. In regard to this point Jülicher observes, *Th. L.*, 1896, col. 397, that not much

are traced back to the ur-Babylonian myth of the contest between Marduk and the Chaos-dragon. Through anthropomorphisation of this primeval myth arose the figure of a human opponent of God, used by Satan as his instrument. Then this again was changed into the image of a Jewish pseudo-Messiah. At a still later point of development the pseudo-Messiah became a political oppressor arising from the sphere of paganism. This is an abnormally long development, but Bousset thinks this feature need not tell against the hypothesis, because tradition in the eschatological sphere, and particularly so in the Antichrist-sphere, has always borne a rigid character enduring like a once set block of concrete. Therefore, in his opinion, the existence of the much earlier can be proven from even its sporadic emergence in certain beliefs at later points. Another observation is supposed to lend help to the same effect. It is believed that the material was largely transmitted through secret oral tradition, not in written form such as would be accessible to a greater number of readers.

It does not lie within our plan to criticize these views in any large way. The Antichrist-complex, it is true, forms part of them, but they comprise much more that is not of our direct concern. As to the fixity of the tradition, a single glance at the series of transformations which Bousset believes it through the course of the ages to have undergone is certainly not adapted to impress us with its alleged rigidity. And, so far as the manipulation of the material by Bousset and his followers is concerned this bears all the bad features of extreme arbitrariness. There is constant unwarranted combination and equation of names and features lying not only decades but ages apart, and a persistent effort to supply the lacking intermediate links from unevidenced hidden strands of popular belief. Furthermore, denying to the patristic writers the capacity of producing such things, even through an overheated imagination, does injustice to their mentality, as

has survived in Bousset's work of Gunkel's mythological mixture of the material.

though they had been entirely sterile in the power of eschatological production. It hardly agrees with what we know of some of them. Papias certainly was not under-endowed with fecundity in this line. Nor should one overlook the stupendous proportions this hypothesis has assumed, covering with its wings almost the whole compass of what is called sacred history. Both Gunkel and Bousset are driven to assume that this sinister tradition of the Arch-enemy is older than the Messianic tradition. The Antichrist has here eaten the young Christ-child after some such fashion as the Christian Apocalypse depicts in one of its visions.

We must not, however, let such observations turn us aside from our proximate purpose, which is to examine the alleged precedents of the Antichrist-concept in the Apocalyptic writings and their backward projection from thence into the pre-Christian literature. The following may fairly illustrate the method by which the results are obtained. In the Ezra-Apocalypse (4 Ezr.), a work dating according to Schürer a.o. from about 81-96 A.D., a realistic description of a human monster is given, in connection with which, however, the name Beliar does not appear. It is different in the *Testaments of the XII Patriarchs,* usually dated from the first Christian century. Here Beliar is actually introduced. The references are as follows: Test. Rub., 4: "whoredom brings upon a man the derision of Beliar and of men"; Sim. 5: "whoredom separates from God and drives to Belial"; Lev. 19: "the choice lies between the darkness and the light, the works of God and the works of Beliar"; Dan. 4: "when the soul is continually worried, the Lord departs from it, and Beliar obtains dominion"; Napht. 2: "the alternative rule of conduct for man is either a law of the Lord or a law of Beliar"; Iss. 6: "his descendants will leave the commandments of the Lord and cleave to Beliar"; Zeb. 9: "God will deliver all captive men from Beliar"; Jos. 20: "after Joseph's bones have been brought up to Canaan, God will be in light with the Israelites, and Beliar will be in darkness with the Egyptians"; Benj. 3:

"the spirits of Beliar incite to every kind of wickedness and oppression."

It seems clear that there is nothing in the passages cited compelling to think of an Antichrist figure differentiated from Satan. All that is said admits of easy derivation from the influence of the latter. And negatively the absence of the eschatological element is difficult to account for, if Beliar in those former times passed as a technical name for Antichrist. Still another writing bearing on the problem is the so-called *Ascensio Isaiae,* particularly in its later part, Chaps. vi-xi, apparently of Christian origin, whilst the preceding Chaps. i-v seem to be of Jewish provenience. The Jewish section is somewhat indefinitely dated after the destruction of Jerusalem by Titus. In iv. 2 occur these words: "And after the consummation has arrived, the Angel Berial, that great King of the world, over which he rules since it exists, will descend from his firmament, in the form of a wicked human matricidal king; he is the king of this world . . . ; this angel Berial, in the form of the said kingdom, will come and together with him will come all the powers of this world, and they will obey him in whatsoever things he shall desire." This passage does not form part of the central section of the Jewish core of the book. As standing in the text, it contains clear references to the rôle played by Nero in the Antichrist-expectation, and consequently must be later than the time at which Nero could have been expected to return as a supernatural figure, either from the Orient, still alive, or from Hades through a resurrection. On the other hand, his being called a wicked angel, the ruler of this world, having his habitation in the air, and the chief of the powers of this world, all this closely identifies him in character with Satan. There are things here scarcely predicable of Nero. Bousset, recognizing this, suggests that the Nero-references are a later insertion. This, it must be admitted, makes the passage harmonious within itself, but at the same time dispenses of the necessity to think of an Antichrist-Beliar. What is said of

Beliar as to his being the king of this world is identical with what Paul affirms of Satan.

In the *Book of Jubilees* we find ourselves according to the best critical judgment, in the first century of the Christian era. Beliar appears in i. 20 under the strangely deformed name "Belchor." God is invoked, that He may create in his people a right mind, and that the spirit of Belchor may not dominate them, so as to enable him to accuse the people before God. The last-mentioned thought plainly reminds us of the O.T. conception of Satan as "the adversary," the one who slanders and opposes man in the judgment. The second place where the figure appears (here in the ordinary form "Beliar") is xv. 33; of the apostate, heretical, antinomian Israelites it is predicted that in the excess of their wickedness they will abandon the rite of circumcision, and leave their children such as they were born. It needs no pointing out that Beliar is here entirely void of eschatological associations. The statement would fit far better into the scheme of Friedländer, to be considered presently, according to whom Beliar is the head of a Jewish-Gnostic, antinomian heresy.

We now come to the one context in the Apocalyptic literature, where the distinction between Satan and Beliar seems to be clearly drawn, each being invested with his own attributes and functions. This is the prophecy in *Orac. Sib.* iii. 46 ff. In this, according to Bousset one of the oldest ingredients of the document, the prophet (or quasi-prophetess) declares: "But when Rome shall rule over Egypt also . . . then the greatest kingdom of the Immortal King will appear to mankind . . . thereupon from among the Sebastēnoi will come Beliar and will cause high mountains to rise up, and will cause the sea to be silent, the fiery great sun and the shining moon, and also will cause the dead to be raised, and perform many signs among men. But no consummation will there be in him, only leading astray; and so he will cause many men to err, both believing and elect Hebrews and likewise other lawless men, which never yet heard the speech of God. But when thereupon the threatenings of the great God approach and a power of fire comes to the land through the water wave and burns Beliar and all overbearing men, who have yielded faith to him, then the entire world will be ruled under the hand of one woman and obey her in all things. . . when the ether-inhabiting God rolls up the heavens, as the scroll of a book is rolled up . . . when no longer will exist the shining balls of the lights of heaven, neither night, nor morning, no longer many days of care, no longer spring nor winter, likewise neither summer nor autumn. And then the judgment of the great God will appear in that momentous time when all this has come to pass." Not a few elements in this description remind of N.T. eschatological items, and the possibility cannot be *a priori* denied that these may be older than the N.T. both in their written form and in the tradition lying farther back. Absolutely complete and clear, to be sure, even here the distinction between Beliar and Satan is not: in fact Satan has no place in the whole prophecy: the conflict is purely between Beliar and the "great God." We are not told in so many words that Beliar is or will be a man; the fact of his being burnt with his human followers does not compel that assumption. His coming "from the Sebastēnoi" speaks somewhat in favor of human nature on either interpretation usually given to this strange phrase, which according to some designates the Samaritans (from the name of their city "Sebaste"), according to others is connected with "sebastos," a predicate of the Roman world-rulers. We must at this point agree with Bousset in his opinion that heterogeneous elements mingle in this strange composition. While the final stupendous world-upheaving events are ascribed to the intervention of the great ether-inhabiting God, yet certain preliminary things named in the line of nature-catastrophes scarcely fall within the power of a mere man however supernaturally endowed. The trait of the error-spreading activity of Beliar reminds vividly of the same element in the description of 2 Thess., although with Paul it is more stressed and elaborated. The idea of seduction in belief has some basis in the O.T. references to Belial. For the feature of the reign of the woman there is no point of contact in N.T. eschatology, for what the Apocalypse of John contains in this line is of a different nature. Here in the prophecy of the Sibyl an actual female ruler is meant.

This recurrence upon the Apocalyptic and Pseudepigraphical literature to discover the antecedents of the Antichrist figure does not carry much convincing force. Of course, it cannot *a priori* be denied that an amount of superstitious folklore was current in Jewish circles before the Pauline Epistles were written. Only that these current beliefs of such gross and rudimentary form were the source from which the N.T. Antichrist doctrine was drawn and from which it can be satisfactorily explained is hard to believe.[6] A writer like Cheyne seems to have felt this, when by the application of a far more radical method he seeks to identify Belial with the Babylonian "Belili." On the other hand Hommel asserts that the Babylonians borrowed their Belili from the Western Shemites.

A second, and widely different attempt to supply the Antichrist-concept with an extra-biblical origin is connected with the name of Friedländer. This scholar, a liberalizing Jew of wide learning, has worked out the hypothesis that there existed from comparatively early (pre-N.T.) times a specifically Jewish type of Gnosticism.[7] The days are past in which Gnosticism was supposed to be of heretical-Christian origin. Students find many references in ancient Jewish lore to a sect or party called *"Minim."* It was at one time customary to identify these Minim with Jewish-Christians. Friedländer gives the term a far wider and differently-oriented significance. He goes so far as to exclude the Jewish-Christians from its range altogether. The Minim are in Friedländer's

[6] *Expositor,* 1895, on 2 Sam. xx. 5: "The land whence no return is possible, Hades." Cp. Hepp, *De Antichrist,* 1st ed., 1919, note 34, p. 261; Cp. Jülicher's critique of Bousset's *Zur Entstehungsgeschichte des Christenthums,* 1894; *Der vorchristliche jüdische Gnostizisums,* 1898; in *Th. L.* 1896, coll. 375-379.

[7] Friedländer, *Der Antichrist in den vorchristlichen Jüdischen, Quellen,* 1901.

opinion a product of the Alexandrian-Jewish philosophy which had Philo for its chief exponent. Their tendency, religiously considered, lay in the direction of antinomianism. What Friedländer quotes from his sources as bearing out the equation Belial-Antichrist is of a decidedly legalistic complexion. It is this uniformizing point of view that enables the writer to give the figure of his Antichrist such a large and comprehensive range. But, and this is our chief criticism of the hypothesis,[8] into the figure of the Man-of-Sin drawn by Paul the construction will not fit. In Thessalonians the Antichrist appears far different and far worse than merely "antinomian." Even from an orthodox-Jewish point of view laxness in the legalistic mode of life or a degree of (conscious or only unconscious) infidelity to the law, tending through allegorizing to apostasy, could scarcely ever have produced the features of the Apostle's lurid description. It must be admitted, however, and in this respect Friedländer has called attention to a sometimes neglected element, that through the second half of Paul's prophecy in Thessalonians in what is predicted of the great error-produced and error-producing activity of the Enemy there runs an "antinomian" strain. In the first half the aggressive formidable traits are more in evidence. But on the whole Paul's relation to "antinomianism" as gatherable from his Epistles was of a far different, in certain respects even opposite, nature than that implied in Friedländer's construction. To the Judaizers Paul appeared as himself the great "antinomian"; had Paul had the sin of antinomianism specifically in mind when penning his great prophecy, he could hardly have been so entirely oblivious of the slanderous way in which it had been used by his enemies to defame himself as not to indicate by a single word his own interest in the matter.

Since then no clearly traceable and safe road leads back into the past to discover the Man-of-Sin except that via the

[8] The Talmudic sources upon which Friedländer has drawn for his evidence are not in their peculiar idiom usable for us, so that as to their adequacy as witnesses we may not allow ourselves a judgment.

prophecy of Daniel, we must now, in greater detail examine what are the points or features through which certain Danielic characterizations have become incorporated into the Pauline prophecy without meaning to suggest by this that the scattered elements in Daniel furnish a complete account, either as to substance or form, of all the outstanding features in Thessalonians. "The mouth speaking great things" Dan. vii. 8, 20, is a striking pre-analogy to all the blasphemy with which the Apostle in advance charges the Man-of-Sin. Thess. vs. 4 "he that opposes and exalts himself against all that is called God or is worshipped; so as to sit in the temple of God setting himself forth as God" reminds of vs. 24 in the same chapter of Daniel. The "doing according to his will" and "magnifying himself" Dan. viii. 4 finds its echo in the trait of anti-divine overbearing, which has so vividly set its impress upon the Pauline description. The "little horn," that came out of one of the four "notable horns," into which the "great horn" of the goat was broken, likewise proceeds to blasphemous acts, so far even as to take away from the Prince of the Host the most sacred religious apparatus, and to cast down the place of the sanctuary (Dan. viii. 14), and bears a striking likeness to the Apostle's description in Thessalonians. "The abomination that makes desolate" above commented upon (Dan. xi. 31), is entirely in line with the features named. Closely corresponding to Thess. vs. 4 is Dan. xi. 36, "he shall do according to his will and he shall exalt himself, and magnify himself above every god and speak marvellous things against the God of gods," anticipating the realistic description of Thess. It must be acknowledged, that the Danielic vision and the Pauline apocalypse cannot be so laid one over the other as a transparent paper is laid over a map in clear colors, so as to be able to trace for every detail a clear corresponding double underneath. With much likeness there is much unlikeness, or rather much lacking in close resemblance. There may be no exact resemblance in the behavior of the pagan tyrants to Antichrist's setting himself in the temple of God as a self-deifier, but as between type and antitype the correspondence is close enough. The only aspect in regard to which a somewhat pervasive difference remains lies in this that the element of perversion of revealed truth, so striking in Paul, remains in Daniel more or less in abeyance. But this is what one might *a priori* expect from an Old Testament visionary delineation.

In all these respects the latter part of Daniel is steeped in the colors not of the supernatural only, but the figures arising and walking across the scene of its visions are supernormal, gigantic, colossal shapes. The absolute, the unsurpassable, the excess of blasphemous behavior are written in large letters on the face of these exponents of unique wickedness to come. Nor need doubt be entertained as to the personal condensation which these bulks of evil receive in the process of forecasting the evil fortunes of the people of God. It is true, the complete unification imparted to the godless movement in Thessalonians, wherein Antichrist is made to stand out as a living sculptured personality, is in Daniel not yet attained. The storm-clouds have not that far opened their gaps to let him step forth as the personal spirit of the tempest. It should be remembered, however, that the ideas of the massal and of the individual, of the power in the abstract and its wielder in the concrete are not always sharply distinguished in such types of apocalyptic representation. This does not mean that the personal equation is ignored or ever entirely left in the background. That a wicked and oppressive and blasphemous world-power employs a king of the same characteristics is simply taken for granted. Let us notice, how, after the description of the beasts in Dan. vii. 1-8, which is adapted to make us think of kingdoms merely, the interpreter says (vs. 17): "These great beasts which are four, are four *Kings*." Hence also one is quite warranted to think in the theophany of the "One like unto a man (son-of-man)" of an actual single being and not merely, as nowadays so many would like to have us do, of a mere symbol of the kingdom of God. This interchange between power and head of the power regularly returns throughout the visions and their interpretations. In

viii. 10-12 things are predicated of "the little horn" conceivable of some individual only; the noun "horn" is feminine, and the feminine verbs of the sentences agree with this; in viii. 22-26 the first king of Greece is represented by the shaggy goat, and also by the great horn between his eyes; here at first the forms are feminine, but in vs. 23 "a king" is said to stand up, because, in accordance with this, the wickedness is brought to a climax through a concrete person. So it is represented in vii. 8 ff., where the fourth beast resolves itself into ten horns. Of the little horn, coming up from among these, it is said, that it had eyes like the eyes of a man, and a mouth speaking great things. Because of the supernatural coloring of this description it has been assumed that a vision of the personal Antichrist must be contained in it, the more so since the description immediately precedes the episode of the judgment, vss. 9-14. In the interpretation of the vision given by "one of them that stood by" the same close conjunction between the fierceness of the prosecution inflicted upon the saints and the judgment is noticeable; here likewise the picture given of the horn rising from the ten partakes of supernormal features: he speaks words against the Most High, vs. 25. To be sure, here this element is not so strongly stressed and by themselves the words might be understood of some human political force or its representative king. He "changes times and the law." But the vision of the judgment and the dominion of the saints following thereupon is again no less steeped in eschatological colors than the one standing at the close of the original revelation itself, vs. 14.

In Chap. viii. 10 similar phenomena present themselves. In some respects even stronger terms are used in the description of the doings of the "little horn" (here growing out of the four horns of the ram) as in the preceding account: "it waxed great, even to the host of heaven, and some of the host and of the stars it cast down to the ground and trampled upon them." Here, be it noted, we seem to be in the midst of the fortunes and afflictions of the Syrian war, and time-reckonings as to duration of the oppression are given; moreover, the account issues not into a scene of absolute consummation; the goal set is rather the cleansing of the sanctuary, which is in accordance with the fact that the wickedness of the tyrant had culminated in the sacrilege done to the holy places and things. None the less in the subjoined interpretation a king of fierce countenance appears, understanding dark riddles, mighty, but not by his own power, causing craft to prosper in his hand, magnifying himself in his heart, broken in the end without hand. In xi. 36 ff. the king is described as doing according to his will, exalting himself and magnifying himself above every god, speaking marvellous things against the God of gods, not even regarding the god of his fathers, nor the desire of women, nor any god, magnifying himself above all. In reading this we cannot help feeling strongly that such terms would not be naturally applied to any average human enemy, however much in the hysteria of excited religious patriotism the physiognomy of such a tyrant might tend to acquire a sort of supernatural monstrosity.[9] It has been assumed that where these phenomena emerge the Apocalypse makes a sudden leap of vision out of its forecasts of politico-historical setting, into the remoteness of the absolute end, so as to bring upon the scene the actual individual Antichrist. In order to make this to a certain extent intelligible we should have to fall back upon the law, not unfamiliar in the exposition of prophecy, of the foreshortening towards the end of the prophetic perspective. Even in regard to the most striking passages in Chap. xi and Chap. xii, where the injection of the idea of the resurrection proves that the seer deals with downright eschatological values there is no clean escape from this, because in xii. 1 the words "and at that time" mark, as it were, the hopping-off

[9] Perhaps the memory of what happened in this field of unrestrainable exaggeration during the World War may help somewhat towards making this psychologically intelligible. Only in the present case it was not impure human passion, but divine inspiration that enlarged the figures on the screen.

point for this flight out of the nearer present into the rarer atmosphere of the end. The view referred to is in some ways attractive. It yields a direct, realistic picture in the O.T. Scriptures of the veritable Antichrist without need of recurring upon the intermediate process of typical prefiguration. What is taught in literal terms about the Antichrist in the N.T. thus acquires a direct continuity with the O.T. predictions. This avoids abrupt, violent breaks in the development of the idea. True, it keeps the eschatological Antichrist closely entangled with personages or events of contemporary history. A suggestion has been offered to obviate at least part of this difficulty. Much has been theorized in the last decades concerning the ancient existence in several quarters of the ancient world of a fixed body of eschatological lore, in which, among other ingredients, also the figure of a personal supreme wicked power held its place. Revelation transferred the features of monstrosity that had gathered around this "Antichrist"-complex to any malign enemy of the nearer or more remote crisis, thus serving the double purpose of adding to what was previously known of this mysterious person and of rendering its central significance applicable to the practical needs of the time being.

But where are we to look within the Old Testament for a body of belief or revelation substantial enough to have created a fixed nomenclature of the character thus postulated? Were it a matter of eschatology in general, it might be more feasible to trace back the later beliefs to earlier beginnings, to which the later elaborations could attach themselves. But it is quite a different thing to assume such a process with regard to the figure of an individual Antichrist, even if discounting the etymology, we were to confine ourselves to the general idea of a supreme impersonation of malignity and hostility. In that field the stream of folklore derived from ancient sources flows but scantily, or even trickles down to nothing, so that at last we are driven back upon the dire dragon contending with Marduk in the ancient Babylonian cosmogony. From Daniel to these ur-Shemitic myths there is a far cry, and in the territory spanned there would remain little enough of continuity from span to span to be of much importance.

The "Gog (and Magog," or "from Magog"[10])-prophecy in Ezekiel might at first sight seem to afford some help here. Closely looked at, it presents rather a parallel of somewhat older date than, strictly speaking, a precedent of the Danielic vision. The prophecy of Ezekiel differs from the description in Daniel first through its warlike complexion and next through the absence of the directly Godward, blasphemic element; it also, however, falls out of the frame of the ordinary prophetic threatenings against the enemies of Israel, present or future, through the stupendousness of its proportions. Still this is a matter of degree rather than of principial difference. It has one feature not common to ordinary threatening prophecy: the attack of Gog and of his hordes is distinctly described as occurring after a period of rest and felicity enjoyed by the people of God subsequently to a previous redemption and return to their land, Chap. xxxviii. 7-12, 14. Even this also, however (the second attack on a world-wide scale and the gigantic victory over the assembled hordes), has its preformation in the earlier prophecy, notably so in Isaiah xxiv-xxvii and Micah iv. 2 and its context. In these earlier texts it proves more or less difficult to establish beyond doubt the particular point in question, viz. the time of succedence of the second all-comprehensive attack. Attention is called to such earlier utterances as Ezek. xxxviii. 17. The chronological definition of the great events as belonging to "the latter days," xxxviii. 16 is not of itself sufficient to mark the piece as consummatorily-eschatological, for, as observed in a previous connection, the phrase named has in the prophetic perspective a movable position. It is not

[10] Gen. x. 2, "Magog" as a "son" of Japhet; Ezek. xxx. 23; "Gog" of the land of "Magog," the Prince of Rosh, Meshag and Tubal; vs. 14, "Gog"; vs. 16, "o Gog"; "Gog," vs. 18, xxxix. 1; "Gog," "o Gog"; vs. 6 "a fire on Magog," as of a people or land; vss. 6, 11, "Gog," a people; vss. 11, 15, "the Valley of Hamoth," Gog; Rev. xx. 8, "Gog and Magog," as deceived by Satan with other nations to war against the holy city.

so much something in the content of the Ezekiel-prophecy, that secures it its prominence in O.T. eschatology, but rather something added to and brought into it from the New Testament, viz. the reproduction of it in Rev. xx. 7-10, where the context allows of no other than the reference to the absolute issue of events.[11]

After all, what we are chiefly concerned with are the antecedents in the earlier Scriptures of the Pauline Antichrist pericope. So far as this is concerned, it is plain at a single glance, that Paul is not to any large extent dependent upon the Ezekielian source, for in the one feature in which the latter might seem to go beyond Daniel, through the mention of a specific name, and the summing up in it of the entire complex of the final enmity, Paul has not availed himself of this, but confined himself to qualitatively descriptive designations, a trait entirely in keeping with the un-military, un-political tenor of the Pauline prophecy. And, on the other hand, it is in Daniel that the general tone and atmosphere of the pictures and visions are more unearthly and transcendental, so that no one need wonder at finding precisely in these respects the O.T. and N.T. epochal prophecies intentionally and intimately connected. Though Ezekiel may furnish us with the interesting names of Gog and Magog, it is Daniel who unrolls for us the scroll of the resurrection, something in the wake of which, with or without interval, the final consummation must ensue.

That Paul in 2 Thess. ii is dependent on Daniel hardly requires pointing out. The "falling away" (apparently a technical apocalyptic term) of vs. 3 reminds strongly of Dan. xi. 32 ff.; xi. 39; the predestinarian strain in Dan. xi, xii finds its reflection in 2 Thess. ii. 11-13. Particularly the anti-religious, blasphemous trait in the description of the enemy must have been copied after Daniel: "He opposes and exalts him-

[11] Particularly two concrete features have been in Ezekiel pointed out as marking an Antichrist connection: one is Chap. xxxviii. 4, "I will put hooks into thy jaws," comparing Gog to a wild beast; the other is that which speaks of the previous preparation of Gog, xxxviii. 7.

self above all that is called God, or that is worshipped; so that he sits in the temple of God setting himself forth as God"; cp. Dan. v. 20-23; vii. 20, 21; viii. 11; xi. 31; 36-40 with 2 Thess. ii. 4.

But, however striking these prophetic antecedents and literary dependencies may seem, the chief question remains how Paul for himself conceived of this mysterious power. First of all its personality, while not explicitly affirmed, is throughout assumed. It is true, the collective, abstract movement connected with his appearance, teaches that more than a single powerful person is involved. But most assuredly a personal *leader* of the movement, and that a human personality is suggested. The easiest way to prove this might at first sight seem to point to the phrases "the *man* of sin," "the *son* of perdition," were it not for the commonness of the idiom to prefix "son" or "man" to a certain attribute or characteristic in order to mark the person meant as the supreme manifestation or exponent of the quality spoken of. In such a case "son" would not necessarily determine the species of the person referred to; a superhuman, demonic leader of the forces of sin and the issues of perdition it could be properly called "man" or "son" of that with which he is identified, cp. Jno. xvii. 12 (of Judas) "the son of perdition." This idiomatic way of speaking does not even exclude Satan from the field of possibilities. And there are not a few features in the description reminding vividly of the nature and ways of Satan, that supreme antagonist of God. Nevertheless the whole tenor of the passage implies that a visible historically conditioned episode, playing in the clear light of human history, is thought of. Besides this, we are explicitly told in vs. 9 that his "coming is *according to the working of Satan.*" What is *according to* Satan's working cannot be identical with Satan himself. On the other hand, for an evil *superhuman* spirit under Satan, the stage set and the drama unrolled, if once placed in the historic sphere, would seem almost with necessity to require the visible interposition of him who is chief in the kingdom of evil, in association with that of the intermediate, be it superhuman, demonic agent. We may take for granted, then, that the Antichrist will be a human person. Into this view also best fit the developments and events connected with his appearance and activity. That his whole figure is steeped, as it were, in the atmosphere of the supernatural, cannot alter anything in this respect. He certainly stands at a far remove from the purely-naturalistically human; wonders and signs are attributed to him, vs. 9; the "*lying* wonders," are not characterized by the attribute "lying" as inherently false, spurious, of mere fictitious make-up; they are so called because they go with the propaganda of error as the revelation-miracles accompany the proclamation of the Gospel-truth. The supernatural environment is truly present; only it serves the sinister purpose of accrediting the Satanic instead of the Divine. This close conjunction between the supernatural and the Man-of-Sin has led certain writers to the extreme view, that the conjunction is of a hypostatic character, "Antichrist" appearing and acting as a veritable Messiah-Satan incarnate. Such a view is rendered impossible, not merely by its monstrous nature, but even antecedently through the inherent, subordinationistic function of the Messiahship as such. Who sets himself up as a Messiah, thereby, at least ostensibly, recognizes that there is One higher than himself. To the "Man-of-Sin" Paul ascribes the denial and abnegation of every other superior divine power. He deifies Himself in the most absolute sense; the Antichrist-idea and the Messianic idea are at this point mutually exclusive. Antichrist might choose to operate by means of a Messiah under him, as his instrument, himself he cannot pretend to be the Messiah, because that would involve abdication of his pretension to being God. When Jesus in the third temptation is offered a Satanically controlled Messiahship, through accepting which He would have to transfer His Messianic allegiance from God to the Tempter, the principle just stated is clearly brought out; the new relation proposed is instantly recognized as an idolatrous one, and for that, if for no other reason, repudiated. What Satan there suggested was nothing less than that he himself should figure as God and Jesus as *his* Messiah. One who receives worship and dispenses power over all the kingdoms of the world is, conceptually, equal to God; he who accepts such power in feof can be nothing else than inferior to God in office. Had Jesus reacted upon this truly blasphemous suggestion, He would have been an equally subordinated agent as He was in reality; only the relationship would have existed between Him and the false god, and thus partaken of illusoriness instead of reality from beginning to end. According to Paul's description the Man-of-Sin stands at the extreme opposite to this: he is one for whom to present himself as Messiah would have meant to disavow himself. If the two cases, that of the temptation and that in Thessalonians are perforce to be compared, we shall have to say that they agree in the extreme unholy pretensions displayed in both (exclusive claim to deity), but differ in the rôles postulated in each case for Jesus as Messiah-Apostate and the future Man-of-Sin. In both Satan subject to the true God aspires to deity; in the Gospel he endeavors to carry this out by means of the prostituted Messiahship (under himself) of Jesus; with this method, at least so far as the explicit statements of Paul lead us to infer, he will dispense in the future. His own claims will lie in the sphere of the divine, not of the Messianic.

On the grounds thus generally formulated we feel bound to reject the one concrete form in which the Messianic construction of the Antichrist-idea has been worked out. It has been suggested that the Apostle conceived of the coming Man-of-Sin as the pseudo-Messiah of the Jews, about to set himself up sooner or later as the abnegator and repudiator of Jesus, the Christian Messiah, and as on principle opposing the latter by his whole activity.[12] According to this view the Antichrist meant for Paul, at the date of 2 Thess., the person whom the Jews would recognize as their Messiah, and who would in

[12] Cp. Schneckenburger, *J. f.d. D. Th.*, 1859; *Weiss, St. u Kr.*, 1869; also Bousset, who, however, regards this only as one phase in the long evolution of the concept.

reality be the supreme embodiment of the spirit of disobedience and unbelief with regard to the true Christian Gospel as centered in the Messiahship of Jesus. The figure would stand for the Satanic corruption and prostitution of the Jewish Messianic hope. From the circumstances under which the Epistle was written, it is believed, the entire situation is easily explainable. Direct opposition and persecution the Apostle had, up to that time, experienced from the Jews only. Where the Gentile population had molested him, it had done so at the instigation of the Jewish populace. Precisely at Thessalonica the latter had happened during Paul's preaching in that city; likewise in Corinth, whence our Epistle was written, the same enmity had confronted him. Both First and Second Thess. speak of the Jews in the terms of strongest malediction. When "the mystery of iniquity" is said to be "already at work" (vs. 7), this, we are told, is most naturally understood of the enmity of the Jews even then plotting in secret for Paul's destruction. At bottom this enmity, while ostensibly confined to Jesus and his Apostle, was disobedience to God, and would therefore issue into downright apostasy with such open manifestations of godlessness and blasphemy as are subsequently depicted. It is even believed, that the blasphemous claims of the "Lawless One," opposing and exalting himself against all that is called God or that is worshipped, so as to sit in the temple of God, setting himself forth as God (vs. 4), can be explained on the principle of the Messiah's being the absolute representative of God, whence falsely claiming Messiahship amounts to falsely laying claim to divine honor and worship. The very fact of the enthronization in the temple at Jerusalem proves, we are told, that none other than a pseudo-Messiah of the Jews can be thought of, because by resorting to that place he recognizes the sanctuary as the habitation of God. The pseudo-prophecy mentioned in vs. 9 is likewise believed to favor this solution of the problem. The two features combined of usurped power and false prophecy are especially supposed to prove that the malign enemy must be a Jew, whilst elsewhere, when a pagan potentate impersonates the Antichrist (as in the Johannine Apocalypse) the false prophecy appears as a separate movement, working in connection with, but not identical with, the antichristian principle in its highest potency. Still further, on the view under discussion Paul anticipated that the Jewish pseudo-Messiah would attempt to overthrow the Roman Empire, and seek to establish a universal (not "universalistic") Jewish kingdom. Finally, on this interpretation the technical terms "the restrainer" (ὁ κατέχων masc.) and "the restraint" (τὸ κατέχον neut.) are supposed naturally to refer to the Roman power and the Emperor. By the Roman authority Paul had been more than once protected from the machinations and persecutions of the Jews, so that he could easily think of it as restraining for the present the fiercest and final flaring up of the Jews' hostility against the cause of Christ represented by himself.

When the Jewish-pseudo-Messiah-Antichrist theory is thus concretely put before us, we immediately begin to feel how impossible its implications are. It is not necessary now to dwell upon the fact that, if actually ascribed to Paul after such a bald fashion, it would most certainly fall under the rubric of mistaken and therefore unfulfilled (perhaps one should say unfulfillable) prophecy. What has most given popular support to it is the name "Antichrist" itself, reminding as it does of "the Christ," who is antagonized or opposed not only, but in very fact supplanted through usurpation of his office. But it ought to be remembered at the outset, that the word "Antichrist," or the predicate "Antichristian" do not belong to the Pauline vocabulary. They are Johannine terms within the New Testament.[13] And further, even where they occur in the Epistles of John, it is by no means certain that the preposition "anti" is meant to bear the pointed meaning of *"in the place of."* In the passages in John's Epistles the sense "Opponent of Christ" appears perfectly plain and natural. Still it is far from impossible that in the popular

[13] 1 John ii. 18, 22; iv. 3; 2 John 7.

mind the distinction between one who antagonizes Christ and one who seeks to supplant Christ was not always sharply felt. Of course, the supplanting involves the antagonizing, but the reverse does not hold true, because there are other modes of antagonizing than by ursurpation of the enemy's office. All we may attempt to affirm here is the larger generic conception, and then, proceeding from this, to seek to discover what elements, if any, and of what precise nature, enter of the more particularized conception, so as to ascertain whether the sense "in the place of" for "anti" unmistakably appears.

For the sake of precision a distinction should be drawn between the two concepts of a pseudo-Jewish Messiah, and that of an Arch-enemy of God, who, without meaning to exhibit himself as a Jewish Messiah, or professedly being recognized as such, none the less adopts or imitates certain methods put into practice by the genuine Christian Messiah, always, however, keeping his inner spiritual mentality and attitude, together with those of his followers, outside of the focus of the Messianic subordination to God. That the semblance of Messianic method and procedure will not be lacking may be safely affirmed *a priori*. After all, since we are here dealing with two supreme world-organizing forces, both operating on the same immense scale, there must needs be points and surfaces, where, formally considered, they will touch and in result of this to some extent resemble each other. The same wide folds of cosmical drapery are thrown over both; no wonder that, as they stride in gigantic shape over the field of prophecy and world-history, the impression is created that rivalry in the pursuit of the same supreme goal animates the onward march of each. There is a largeness in the construction of programme, that inevitably puts them in parallelism. Thus an *"apokalypsis"* is ascribed to the Man-of-Sin, vs. 6: "to the end that he may be *revealed* in his own season; vs. 8: "and then shall be *revealed* "the Lawless One"; in vs. 9 we read of his *"parousia"*: "whose parousia is according to the working of Satan with all powers and signs and lying wonders." His whole manner of working is described in terms that compel us to think of something parallel to the Gospel propaganda carried on by the servants of the true Christ. All these things, however, though apparently confirming the theory of pseudo-Jewish-Messiahship, fall short in the one vital respect: they neither imply, nor, taken together with vs. 4, permit of the consciousness or recognition or pretense of Messianic subordination to the supreme God. The Man-of-Sin is bent upon, and driven by Satan into reproducing and exploiting for his wicked ends certain grandiose concomitants of the Christ-epiphany, but is unable to sum these up under the supreme category of Messiahship, for the simple reason that such would defeat his innermost, and public, aim of absolute emancipation from all that is divine or quasi-divine. If a term be wanted to mark off sharply the one frame of mind and method of working from the other, it may be defined as that of "plagiarizing" certain exceedingly effective Messianic methods, and making the most of these, whilst all the time taking care lest they should be construed by his followers in such a way as would frustrate his un-Messianic, nay directly contra-Messianic intent. In reality no two things could be more opposite than this openly irreligious, antichristian state of mind, and the profoundly *religious* subordination, bordering upon self-effacement of Jesus to God. The plagiarisms adopted are in their very complexion but tools towards the setting up of an openly professed un-Messianic program, a program not only void objectively, but *meant* to be void of all Christian religious acknowledgments and aspirations. The Man-of-Sin is the irreligious and anti-religious and anti-Messianic subject *par excellence.*

It must be admitted, that among the patristic writers, from Irenaeus onward, the Antichrist appears not unfrequently as a Jew. The tracing back of his genealogy to the tribe of Dan is an instance of this. To Bousset this furnishes sufficient reason for declaring it part of the alleged ancient pre-Christian doctrine concerning the Man-of-Sin in Jewish writings or traditions, lost to us but still accessible to the

Church Fathers. The tribe of Dan came under consideration by reason of what is related concerning it in Gen. xlix. 16, 17: "Dan shall judge his people as one of the tribes of Israel; Dan shall be a serpent by the way, an adder in the path, biting the horse's heels so that his rider shall fall backward." According to Deut. xxxii. 22, "Dan is a lion's whelp, leaping from Bashan," viz., a rival or enemy of the Messianic tribe of Judah. Jer. viii. 16 depicts, how the snorting of the enemy's horses shall be heard from Dan, and the whole land tremble at the sound of the neighing of his strong ones. Lev. xxiv. 10, 11 was likewise called into requisition, because the man who blasphemed "the name" is there said to have been the son of a Danite woman. There was still further the fact, that, according to Jud. xviii. 30, 31, the Danites had from early times practised idolatry, and that, later on, Dan had become one of the two centers of bull-worship introduced by Jeroboam. But probably the main motive for this patristic judification of the Man-of-Sin lay (apart from the Apocalypse), in what Paul prophesies concerning his setting up his throne in the temple, which many could not conceive on any other basis than that of his affiliation with the Jewish religion. There is no reason to believe that for all this there was any other ground than allegorizing exegesis.

The above takes issue with the view that Paul, or as is asserted the author of 2 Thess., ascribed to the Man-of-Sin a Jewish provenience and modelled him after the image of the false Jewish Messiah. Another illustration of *"zeitgeschichtliche"* interpretation is afforded by the opposite view, that his is a pagan figure embodying in itself the wicked essence of paganism carried to its utmost intensity, and directed with intensest malignity against the true God and his people. Both Daniel and the Johannine Apocalypse contain much that, at least as a phase in the history of Antichristianism, seems to favor this. When, however, thus narrowed down to its *"zeitgeschichtliche"* interpretation, the process from which Paul expected the end of the world becomes no more than a piece of the drama of Roman imperial persecution inflicted upon

Jew and Christian and in its far-reaching import long since discredited. In its most popular form it is believed to have attached itself to the at one time current belief, that Nero, the arch-persecutor would, notwithstanding his disappearance from the scene by flight or death, soon return, and then, with the help of Satan, through supernatural influences and activities, set up a new phase of his wicked reign, conducted with an unparalleled virulence of Antichristian persecution. This view has been ascribed to the writer of 2 Thess. and the Apocalypse, both of which on that view being denied to the cononical writers under whose names they stand. Considering only the question of dating, it is plain that the Apostle Paul could have had on such a theory nothing to do with the writing of 2 Thess. The piece thus interpreted presupposes the death of Nero, which happened 68 A.D. And although the same charge of anachronism could not be brought against the (allegedly composite) Apocalypse, yet here the phantastic and in many respects conflicting scenes, derived, it is held, from the most various, to a large extent mythical, sources, would deprive the last book in our N.T. Canon, at least in its visionary part, of well-nigh all religious value. With the application of this hypothesis to the Book of Revelation we have here nothing to do, because we desire to keep strictly within the limits of the Pauline Eschatology. 2 Thess. particularly, as a unicum in the Pauline Epistles in its teaching on the last things, deserves to be treated by itself with undistracted attention. Only after the contents of it shall have been ascertained, so far as this is possible, does the law of the *"analogia fidei"* demand of the student that he shall endeavor to correlate and harmonize the one with the other.

Modern criticism has not always kept sufficiently in mind this methodical principle. Starting with the Neronian form of the Antichrist theory, too rashly forced upon the Apocalypse of John, it has caused the little prophecy of Paul to become darkened and dwarfed by the huge shadows of its larger companion. Under the obsession that the Nero story must be the chief source of ancient Christian occupation with and dread of the last things, it was regarded a self-understood maxim, that Paul's "Man-of-Sin" was cradled in the same circle of superstition. The Tübingen school lent to this Romanization (or rather Neronization) the aid of its prestige. Such champions of Hegelian N.T. Criticism as Kern, F. C. Baur, Hilgenfeld and many others strenuously advocated it from the first. The pictures of both Chaps. xiii and xvii of the Apocalypse were explained on this basis of the Nero-return-belief. In the former context it is related that one of the seven heads of "the beast" was smitten unto death, and his death-stroke healed, and that after this the beast received authority from the dragon, and acted and was worshipped after an Antichrist-fashion. The famous number of the beast is given as 666, and as lending support to the theory, the opinion arose that this number was the result of addition of the number-values of the Hebrew characters composing the name "Neron Kesar." In Chap. xvii it is related that the seven-headed and ten-horned beast upon which the woman sits: was, and is not, and is about to come up out of the abyss, and to go into perdition, and again, that he was and is not and shall come (πάρεσται). Further, that the seven heads are seven kings, of which the five are fallen, the one is, the other is not yet come, that the seventh, when come, must continue a little while, and that thereupon the beast will appear as the eighth, it being added that the beast is also of the seven. The seven kings are on this theory identified with the seven first Roman Emperors, among which Nero holds the fifth place. This piece, then, it is believed, was written after Nero's death, under the sixth Emperor, and it embodies the expectation that after a brief reign of his next two successors Nero will return from the dead in the rôle of Antichrist.

We have given a brief survey of these several attempts in order to make plain how unfeasible it is to fit into the lock of 2 Thess. ii the key of the Johannine Apocalypse. These are two, not one, prophecies, and each has the right to be exegeted on its own merits and within its own context. There is absolutely nothing in Paul's description of the Man-of-Sin to remind of Nero. True, the Man-of-Sin has his parousia, and, combining with this the idea of a double parousia ("second coming") of Christ, an intimation might be found in the introduction of this term to the effect that the Man-of-Sin will likewise appear twice, first in his historical emergence, and afterwards, having withdrawn from the scene, be it through death or through flight to the Orient, in a highly demonic, supernaturalized form, to play out his complete anti-Christian rôle. Surely a weak support to hang the over-rash identification of the happenings in 2 Thess. and in Revelation on. This formal distinction between "first advent" and "second advent," so familiar to us, had not at that time been drawn, at least it had not acquired any such fixed meaning as to become of itself suggestive of a duplication of the Neronic appearance. If Jesus' epiphany was one only, and that a future one, then the chronologically-innocent use of the term "parousia" could never suggest the idea of a Nero revenant, far less of a Nero redivivus. Moreover Nero had been the great persecutor of the Christians, and precisely to this character of persecutor he owed his eschatological reputation.[14] In Thessalonians his activity lies fundamentally in the

[14] Zahn, *Einleitung* I pp. 251 ff. presents a forcible argument against the injection of the Nero legend even into the Apocalypse. He argues from the chronology. The belief in the return of Nero ran through two successive stages. During the early stage it was supposed he had not been actually slain, but escaped into the Orient (the Parthians), from where, without previous death, he would return to resume his former sway. Later, when the lapse of time precluded his still being believed alive, the original expectation was changed into the more mysterious belief that he had, indeed, died, but would presently return from Hades. Now Zahn argues that the date of the Apocalypse is too early for finding in it the passing over, or the having passed over, of the earlier belief into the later one. Nero at the time of his disappearance was only 31 years old (68 A.D.). Consequently at or about the year 80 he would not have been more than 43. Thinking of him as at that stage of life, there was nothing implausible in the view that he would come back, or might come back at any time, as a living person. But the alleged Nero-figure of the Apocalypse is the figure of one previously dead up to the moment of his

sphere of religious and moral seduction. He proceeds, not by applying violence, but through estranging and leading astray his followers from the truth of the Gospel. Of political organization and activity, though in reality the antecedents of the Antichrist tradition made it difficult to dissociate him wholly from this, nothing is said by the Apostle in so many words. The theme is, as it were, lifted above this plane by the general tenor of Paul's teaching which was wont to seize upon large principles of religious development, either for good or for evil.

This latter feature of Paul's treatment of the great enemy is plainly reflected in the names "Man-of-Sin," or, according to a much adopted variant reading, "Man-of-Unrighteousness" and the "Lawless One." As has been observed above, these are Hebrew idioms; they designate one in whom sin and unrighteousness have become concentrated, yet not so as to make him entirely identical with Satan in Paul's conception. The words had acquired peculiar associations ever since the time of the Syrian crisis foretold in the prophecy of Daniel. It has been suggested, that "*ἀποστασία*," vs. 3 "the falling away" is likewise meant as a proper name to be coordinated with the others, so as to represent the Enemy as "Apostasy Incarnate."[15] That later patristic writers have made this for-

reappearance: he is healed from his death-wound and comes up from the abyss. Such a picture could not have been fitted into the at that time still generally current expectation of his return as a living man. Of course, this argument is dependent on Zahn's dating of the Apocalypse. As to 2 Thess., while fully reckoning with its nature as *prophecy,* we nevertheless think it highly improbable that, with Nero not yet on the throne and not yet having put into practice his malign and cruel designs, and not yet having disappeared, nor having been succeeded by another emperor, Paul should have simply taken for granted all these intermediate things, entirely unknown to his readers, and confronted the latter with an eschatological figure, for whose conception more or less familiarity with all these items of future happening was indispensable.

[15] Cp. Wohlenberg, *I u. II Thessalonicherbrief,*[2] p. 145, who refers to Nestle's article in *The Expository Times, On II Thessalonians,* Vol. XVI, pp. 472, 473. The feminine gender of "apostasia," and the use of the article, seem to us to tell against this view, especially since the other two names have prefixes indicating their reference to a person.

mal identification (so Chrys. and Thdt.) proves nothing for Paul's intent here. The change of the word into a proper name was probably favored by the occasional rendering of Belial by "Apostasis," and the consequent identification of Belial with Antichrist. While for Paul this usage cannot be substantiated, the immediate injection of the idea in the prophecy from the very outset proves the importance attached to it. The blasphemy against God constitutes to the Apostle the supreme wickedness. The self-deification, so elaborately set forth in vs. 4, is felt as the inmost sinfulness in the sin of the Man-of-Sin. The transition from vs. 3 to vs. 4, by means of the mere article strikingly brings out the nexus of thought: precisely because he goes to the *non plus ultra of sin,* he deserves fully the name "Man-of-Sin," and the doom announced by "Son-of-Perdition." Among the terrible things reserved for the proximity of the end, the most terrible to Paul's mind, is this negation of God in his very existence, this wilful insult to the divine majesty. In it the very foundations of religion are shaken. The "sitting in the temple of God" only sums up in one terse image that unholiest offense offered to the Holiest of Beings. Nor is this self-deification conceived as a purely passive attitude; it energetically asserts itself against all deity as such, pretended or true. The participle *ἀποδεικνύντα* implies the thought of intensified, positive assault upon God: deeds, not mere assertions, are meant by it. In this, as in every other strand of his teaching, Paul shows himself thoroughly theocentric.

In order still somewhat further to determine the character in which the Apostle represents this impersonation of wickedness, it will be conducive to raise the question, what inner connection there is between the "apostasy," this moral and religious débacle on the grandest of scales and the appearing and activity of the "Lawless One" up to its catastrophic finale at the end. The "Man-of-Sin" is not without more identical with the apostasy, which rather like an ominous cloud of blackest darkness, enwraps his appearance. The "falling away" is one of the attending phenomena in the infernal outbreak, but not entirely identical with the latter's explosion. It has, if only in a premonitory way, its sure connection with the arrival of the Enemy. The "Man-of-Sin" has his hand in fanning the flame to its fierceness as a world-conflagration. Such is the explicit affirmation of vss. 9-12. But the reverse relationship can be affirmed with equal warrant. In vs. 3, the sequence indicates that the apostasy comes first, and that on the waves of its tempest the Wicked One is lifted up and carried on to his ultimate destination. One might even infer, that not merely the falling in upon itself of the fabric of the world of evil, but likewise the first beginnings of its ominous origin, are due to him. The highly enigmatic words of vs. 7: "The mystery of lawlessness does already work," whatever in the concrete they refer to, certainly leave with us the impression of some preliminary, gradual, secret activity behind the scene, as it were, of what is impending. The "Lawless One" comes when the moment is ripe for placing himself at the head of a movement that has already gained impetus not without his initiative. Of course, such a movement stands from the outset under the influence of that same superhuman power, that will also bring the Man-of-Sin into the open. The two not merely follow each other in time, but are also internally connected through the Satanic influences working back of each. On the other hand, according to vss. 9-12 the appearance of the "Anomos" becomes the occasion for a more widely extended and systematically organized apostasy. He deceives those that are being lost (i.e. condemned to and on the way towards perdition). God through him sends them a working of error, so that they believe a lie. His deceptive and misleading methods lead to a culmination of that doom, which through the interaction of unbelief at the beginning, and the punitive hardening of God has been made inevitable. The whole representation reminds vividly of what is narrated in Exodus concerning Jehovah's dealing with Pharaoh. The phrase "not having received the love of the truth," seems to indicate, that not merely through neglect of the truth in the abstract, but that with a pointed antagonism to God the apostates have disdained his manifestation of love which formed the central substance of "the truth" revealed and offered to them in the Gospel, and which tended to their salvation. The excessive sinfulness of this attitude towards the gospel appears from the extreme reaction it provokes on God's part: "for this cause God sends them a working of error, that they should believe a lie." Vss. 10-12 show that the self-deification of the "Lawless One" is not something confined to his own conviction; through the spirit of error sent from God, they are made to believe "τὸ ψεῦδος" "the lie," that is the fundamental, all-comprehensive lie, that follows in its totality from the setting up of himself as God by the "Man-of-Sin," for as in God and his position of deity the entire world and system of truth are founded, even so from the self-deifying spurious God, the counterpart of this, a world of "lying," is inseparable.[16]

While thus sketching in broad strokes the immoral and irreligious character of this opponent of God and Christ, the Apostle has furnished neither the Thessalonians nor us with detailed, concrete information such as we, no less than they, might pardonably crave. Even the milieu from which all these terrible phenomena will in occurring detach themselves is not clearly designated. Besides this also stands unanswered the more concrete question, whence and how the personal head of this wickedness will enter upon the scene of his activities. Being a man, will he be born as a man, and at a point of ripeness assume his public rôle? Or are we perhaps to assume, that, like the whole manner of his activity, so the mode of his origin will be supernatural? If the latter, can we avoid the idea of a relative preëxistence spent in some mysterious hidden sphere, after some such manner as the Jews pictured to

[16] The passage is one of the most interesting statements in Paul binding the experience of true religion to a noëtic complex of verities, received through the mind. Even the false religion can not escape this law of intellect and belief in the primacy of religion because such a precedence is indispensable to the proper exercise of all religious functions. How different from the modern phantasy that a genuine type of Christianity can exist and flourish apart from every embrace of a substantial content of truth.

themselves the antecedent state of the Messiah previous to his public appearance? Will the termination of his career, described in words from Isaiah xi. 4, be after the manner of "slaying," preserving the personal identity of the enemy slain, or after the manner of annihilation. The words ἀναλίσκειν and καταργεῖσθαι do not necessarily carry the latter implication, but, at any rate, they emphasize both the instantaneousness and the finality of the act: "whom the Lord Jesus shall slay with the breath of his mouth, and bring to nought by the manifestation of his parousia."[17] The enquiry as to the proximate environment of his arising, whether Jewish or Gentile, savors overmuch of the narrowly-*zeitgeschichtlich* framing of the problem. It is, of course, easy to argue: if not Jewish, then Pagan. But this does not necessarily follow. In the foregoing discussion we have not aimed at the exclusion of *Jewish nationality* per se, but only argued against the possibility of *Jewish Messiahship*; these two are different things. In the same way we have not sought either to affirm or to deny the pagan provenience of the Man-of-Sin. His person is so closely wrapped up with the idea of "the apostasy," and the latter is so generally associated in the New Testament with the Christian Church, that naturally in this connection also our first thought would be of a birth from the womb of an unfaithful Church, profoundly alienated from the rectitude of the true faith. The milieu seems to be one to which the distinction between Jew and Gentile has become indifferent, a milieu dereligionized in principle. Still more interesting and to popular inquisitiveness more attractive, appears the enquiry as to how the Antichrist shall come into the world. It must be conceded that such an air of supernatural-

[17] Bengel finely defines the exact difference between the two terms "epiphaneia" and "parousia" in the following manner: "hic apparitio adventus ipso adventu prior est, vel certe prima ipsius adventus emicatio, ut ἐπιφανεία τῆς ἡμέρας". The joining of the two words with ἐπιφανεία perceptibly adds to the effect. In Isaiah, from whom the words are taken, the suddenness, instantaneousness of the working of the divine omnipotence is one of the most characteristic traits in the description of judgment.

ness, not to say superearthliness, envelopes the figure, that to think of a mysterious origin seems scarcely avoidable. Still his generic humanity remains beyond question, for, apart from the titles examined above, the very sharpness of the antithesis between him and God, the stress on the criminality of his pretense of being God, place him in the category of the creature beyond all shadow of doubt. It is not, however, plausible so to stress his historical emergence as to make him and his work a mere stage, by the side of other preceding stages, in the unfolding of the plan of God. As to a possible preëxistence, not merely as antedating the publicity of his appearance on the scene of activity, but likewise in regard to his entrance into the world, there is in the manner of his portraiture not a little that leads to thinking of this. Finally on the problem of his ultimate disposal it were presumptuous to risk a decisive conclusion. The Apocalypse itself tells nothing more of the Arch-deceiver, the devil, than that he was cast into the lake of fire and brimstone, where are also the beast and the false prophet, and eternal torment is inflicted upon them, the same lake of fire into which Death and Hades were cast, and which is called "the second death," xx. 6, 14. According to some exegetes this "second death" is equivalent to annihilation.[18]

But these problems, already sufficiently obscure to deter the exegete from framing any definite, positive answer, even do not yet constitute the most cryptic part of the prophecy. Strange to say, the latter is found in the practical momentary bearing of Paul's words on the needs of his readers. In vss. 5-7, to be sure, the main purport of the discourse is not quite so opaque as the significance of the single parts and their mutual relations to one another. Their obvious purpose is none other than still further to restrain the Thessalonians in their over-eagerness and excitability with regard to the imminent, or perhaps even in their opinion at that very moment transpiring, advent of the Lord, while yet at the same time

[18] Cp. Zahn's *Komm. z. N.T.* in loco.

detracting nothing from the central value and high seriousness attaching to the matter in itself. The words are intended to compose and lead back to patience the readers in envisaging the realities of the parousia, both in their terrifying and in their comforting aspect. There is still delay, before the supreme event transpires; a certain process of hidden preparation must run its course; this process is called the ἐνεργεῖσθαι. Together with the delay organically involved in this, there is also exercised a more positive κατέχειν "restraint," from which the person exercising it derives the semi-technical name ὁ κατέχων, "the restrainer," or τὸ κατέχον, that which restrains, in the neuter gender, vs. 6. The reason given for this is that the Man-of-Sin may be revealed in his own (proper) season, and not before that. Consequently the "restrainer" or "restraint" must be removed, "ἐκ μέσου γιγνέσθαι," whereupon straightway (τότε) the Lawless One shall be revealed, and whatever the prophecy has foretold concerning him go into fulfilment. Paul further ascribes to his readers a certain degree of knowledge formerly possessed concerning some of these things, partly derived from his previous presence with them, and a previous knowledge relating not to any peripheral matters, but to the very core of the Man-of-Sin's behavior. Now, at the time of his writing the second letter, he declares them possessed of *additional* knowledge as touching the "mystery of lawlessness" and the restraint retarding it. This, briefly stated, and with abstaining as much as possible from prejudicial exegesis, is the gist of what the crucial verses in question contain.

It will be observed that the several points named are not entirely independent from one another. That the "working" and the "restraining" mutually determine each other lies on the surface. But how is the mystery working? And where are we to look for the restraint that is being exercised? If the "νῦν," "now" in vs. 6 were to be construed, as is often done, with the increased knowledge of the readers, as differing from a previously relative ignorance, the inference would be plain, that at the time of writing the mystery was to a large extent solved for the Thessalonians. If they "knew" (οἴδατε) about the restraining power, then *a fortiori* they must have been likewise informed as regards the mystery of lawlessness held back by it. On this construction, however, the question inevitably obtrudes itself in which way such additional information had reached the Thessalonians. Not through the first letter, for in that no trace of it is to be discovered. Nor in the intervening time after the sending of I Thess., for Paul himself warns the readers against lending credence to communications concerning the presence of the day of the Lord, that reached them under the pretense of coming from him. It will be necessary, therefore, to abandon this construction, although the sequence of the words does not forbid it, and a natural contrast found between the words "when I was still with you," coupled with the verb "I told you these things" and the word νῦν lend a degree of plausibility to it: "*then* I told" and "*now* ye know." The other interpretation joins the "νῦν" to the participle κατέχον (in vs. 7 κατέχων). This would mean that they were informed about the power that was "now" holding back the outbreak of the ultimate wickedness, and, according to the γάρ at the opening of vs. 7, were informed likewise, through some initiation into secret happenings about the furtherance of the mystery of iniquity. The word "now," thus interpreted links the present knowledge of the Apostle and the Thessalonians to the absolute end of things, so far as the appearance of the Man-of-Sin can be said to precede the latter without further intervening developments at least on a large eschatological scale. Such a prospect overbridging ages is not an unknown thing in Biblical prophecy; the "now" of the reader and the "then" of the consummation not seldom stretch out hands towards one another over vast intermediate spaces. What causes unusual trouble lies not in that but in the fact that the point of departure for that long span is not for us determinable, although it was so for Paul and the readers of the Epistle. Still another difficulty should not be overlooked. The locating of the "restrainer" or "restraint," and the locating of the Antichristian center of wickedness are usually held to determine one the other on the principle of oppositeness. Where the Man-of-Sin is sought in Judaism, there the restraint or restrainer are sought within the pagan, particularly Roman, sphere. And the contrary view also has not been without advocates, viz. that the Enemy was expected from the Roman side, and the power of restraint somehow placed in Judaism. As to the latter view, the disproportionateness of the two factors is too obvious to deserve serious consideration. As to the former, the obstacles besetting the theory of Jewish provenience have been sufficiently brought out in an earlier connection. Where Judaism is entirely eliminated from the construction, and yet the "*zeitgeschichtliche*" principle upheld, as is the case with the Neronian hypothesis, it becomes necessary to place Antichrist and Restrainer within the same circle, one being e.g. one Emperor, the other his predecessor on the throne. The objection to this lies in the sharp antithetical character Paul seems to ascribe to the two principles. They are so diverse and antagonistic, that whence the one proceeds it is unnatural to look for the other. How could a relatively better Emperor restrain, or hold back the supremely iniquitous future Enemy, or even seriously hold back the increasing work of the "mystery of iniquity," when in the latter, as we are given to understand, the Satanic principles are making ready for their final assault upon the people of God? How could the temporary successor of Nero, with all the imperial might back of him, prevail for a moment against the onslaught of Nero returning, when the latter was being equipped and propelled by the Evil One himself? Truly, we move here among mysteries within mysteries!

A peculiar view worked out by Von Hofmann may lay claim to a brief notice. It is based on a representation in Daniel as to the successive powers contending against the people of Israel, and the relation of their activity one to the other. It need not be again pointed out, that in the vision of Daniel there is a higher super-terrestrial background to the contest the prophet is made to witness in the political devolutions of power. In Chap. x the supernatural person appearing to Daniel affirms to have been withstood by another supernatural power, called the Prince of the kingdom of Persia. This lasted for a certain length of time, after the lapse of which Michael, one of the chief Princes (also called "your Prince," i.e., the patron-Prince of Israel in vs. 21) came to help him, vs. 13, to confirm and strengthen him, xi. 1. According to this representation the world-power has its Prince, and Israel has its Prince in the world of superhuman Spirits, and between these fierce, protracted combats are going on for supremacy on an immense, though invisible, field of battle. Thus, besides the Prince of Israel, there is another, who declares, that, after having spoken to the prophet, he will return to the fight against the Prince of Persia. But, when abandoning this further encounter, he goes away, the Prince of Greece will appear on the scene to renew the attack. Von Hofmann thinks that here we have something resembling in general outlines the situation of 2 Thessalonians. The three features of a withstanding of the demonic head of the world-power, of a removal or departure of the one that withstands, and of the immediate appearance after this of a more godless Antagonist of Israel's cause, here meet together. In view of this coincidence between the two prophecies one might, at least hypothetically, be tempted to assume that Paul likewise understood by the κατέχον and κατέχων something supernatural and far superior to all the might of Rome. If this be tentatively accepted, it throws at least some light on one subject otherwise entirely veiled in darkness. None the less the fact remains, that it is impossible for us to form concrete conceptions of how the restraint of the mystery takes place, how its power is organized, whether there is a direct retarding influence brought to bear upon the "Lawless One," or perhaps he is only indirectly affected in his movements by means of the influences brought to bear upon his victims.

One of the objections raised against the genuineness (Pauline origin) of 2 Thess., is that the Apostle, who expected according to Rom. xi. 25 the coming in of the fulness of the

Gentiles and the salvation of all Israel, and regarded this momentous epoch as a precursor of the end, cannot, in direct contradiction to that, have made the end dependent on such an apostasy as is here predicted. The answer to this is that the coming in of the Gentiles does not preclude the falling away again from the Gentiles of considerable groups. The apostasy of the end had become too much a fixed factor in eschatology long before Paul, than that Paul could have simply ignored it or mapped out a program in which there was absolutely no room reserved for it. Even our Lord had distinctly predicted it. And in Rom. xi. 20 ff. it is hinted at as a possibility. In Daniel likewise it is an important ingredient closely interwoven with the typical Antichristian vision of the prophet. Dan. xi. 32.[19]

In what has been said in this concluding section of our enquiry there has entered much that of necessity remains highly problematical, and will only cease to be so in the same degree that the vision hastens on to the end. 2 Thess. belongs among the many prophecies, whose best and final exegete will be the eschatological fulfilment, and in regard to which it behooves the saints to exercise a peculiar kind of eschatological patience.[20]

[19] The standing article before the noun ἡ ἀποστασία bears witness to the technical meaning acquired by the term as a fixed element in the final unfolding of things.

[20] In view of the apparently insuperable difficulties of the exegesis of vss. 5-7 it might seem wise to content ourselves with a *non liquet*. Even Wohlenberg, otherwise so skilful in the solution of intricate exegetical problems, concedes, in regard to the *katechon* problem: "here the expositor finds himself hemmed in by difficulties"; *Komm.* p. 153, note. Perhaps more attention ought to have been given by exegetes to the not uncommon alternate significance of *katechein,* viz. "to occupy," "hold in possession." It is not unthinkable that through its over-ready acceptance of the meaning "to keep back" or "to restrain" the exposition may have been thrown upon a wrong track. Trying this other rendering we would obtain a reference to the world power, which at the time of writing enjoyed a wide international supremacy. This would lead back to the scheme of Daniel and Von Hoffmann's application of it to the program of 2 Thessalonians would in this way gain some additional support. It might appear easier to

The idea of the Antichrist in general and that of the apostasy in particular ought to warn us, although this may not have been the proximate purpose of Paul, not to take for

understand that the readers of the Epistle knew, and particularly knew then, what or who the "katechon" was. Even Augustine felt a sort of dissatisfaction with the traditional exegesis. Paul, he observes, could say to the Thessalonians, "ye know," whilst, as to ourselves, we do not know. Peculiar to the patristic writers is, that the rendering "to hold" carries with itself a rather favorable view of the Roman dominion. Whatever it might be in itself, it rendered the Church the good service of delaying, postponing something immeasurably worse. In a certain sense this is less an abandonment of the "restraint-*idea*," than a modification of the significance the word was usually supposed to express: it came now to mean "to hold the rule, and thereby to restrain the succession of the absolutely evil rule." In this line Tertullian does not hesitate to declare "*Romanae diuturnitati favemus.*" What a distance in eschatological appraisal between the picture of the fourth beast given by Daniel, and the rather mild, semi-benevolent estimate put upon it by these Fathers! For the Roman Empire has not ceased being "the fourth beast." Not until it is disposed of comes the acme of terror, with which for formidableness even Rome cannot be compared. The patristic writers, however, by no means are uniform and consistent in their translation and application of "katechein." Both Tertullian and Augustine employ the two senses "tenere" and "detinere" in various passages, and, curiously enough, sometimes with an ascription of one meaning to the masculine, of the other to the neuter participle. Augustine takes the term "apostasia" as signifying a person, rendering it by "Refuga," which is paraphrased by "*Refuga de Domino.*" It is likewise interesting to notice that Augustine resurrects the Nero-hypothesis, though cautiously stating that it is the view of some.

In the opinion of the Fathers named the realism of the eschatological substance and imagery are fully preserved. It was different with Origin, with whom the desubstantivation and spiritualization of this whole world of things plainly begins to play havoc with our passage. While not consistently abandoning the idea of a personal Enemy of God, he elsewhere seems to give countenance to the view that Antichrist signifies an impersonal, purely-spiritual principle. Taking the two usages together one might almost be made to feel that they yield a replica of the Antichrist teaching of the Epistles of John.

Finally attention may be called to Jülicher's words to the effect, that the disappearance of well-nigh all the apparatus of 2 Thess. is due to spiritualization arising from Rom. xi. *Th. LZ.* 1896 (Review of Bousset's book). For evidence to the contrary one need only consult Wohlenberg's instructive Excursus, at the close of the Commentary. The few facts culled from this Excursus, cited above, are sufficient to refute Bousset's opinion.

granted an uninterrupted progress of the cause of Christ through all ages on toward the end. As the reign of the truth will be gradually extended, so the power of evil will gather force towards the end. The making all things right and new in the world depend not on gradual amelioration but on the final interposition of God.

CHAPTER VI

THE RESURRECTION

The First Epistle to the Thessalonians, although less informative as to the nature of the resurrection itself, furnishes many details concerning the nature of the parousia. The instantaneous conjunction between the parousia and the resurrection is pointedly affirmed: "The Lord Himself shall descend from heaven . . . and the dead in Christ shall rise first," iv. 16. It is unwarranted, however, to appeal to the mention of "the clouds," and "the air" in vs. 18 for constructing the process in this way, that the Lord's descent will be provisionally suspended at some point on high before the earth's surface is reached, then subsequently, after certain preliminary actions have been performed from that higher station, to be continued earthward. It is true that the descent is *suspended,* only it is not *interrupted.* The place "in the air" is the nearest the Descending One comes to the earth. There is nothing unnatural or suggestive of mystery in this whole representation. A position of some remoteness from the surface of the earth is after all the most natural to assume in this connection. The far reach and universal scope of the tremendous event here set in motion are in better accord with some central elevated place in the air than a standpoint occupied on the flat surface of the ground. Of course, for the raised and the saints found living at the parousia, who are at first on the earth, a subsequent movement in the air is required, to meet the Lord at the point where He has taken his station. An element of mystery is injected into the situation through a certain exegesis of the statement "to the end He may establish your hearts . . . *at the coming of our Lord Jesus with all his saints,"* iii, 13. When here "the saints" with whom Jesus comes are understood of hitherto unembodied believers making together with Him this unique journey from heaven to earth, the difficulties, not to say inconceivabilities, are much increased. Various questions arise: how can these saints, who have hitherto lived in heaven without a body be suitable companions of the Lord at his embodied visible appearance? It is everywhere stressed by Paul as well as elsewhere in the New Testament (not to go back now to Dan. vii), that the feature of glorious visibility is the most outstanding feature of this supreme event. A large part of the resurrection, viz. that pertaining to the saints arrived from heaven, would then have to be anticipated, in order to endow this group with the appropriate radiant apparel in which they are to follow the Lord in his assumed further movement earthward. At the completion of this final descent the resurrection of all the believing dead would follow, and such believers as are found living would (after a change corresponding to the resurrection-change) join themselves to those having already brought the substance of the resurrection with them from the air, and thereupon this entire company would join the Lord to the place (or a place) previously selected for that purpose. With the Chiliastic associations of this construction we do not here deal; it will subsequently come under consideration in the chapter devoted to the problem of Chiliasm in Paul. For the present it may suffice to call attention to the phantastic ensemble created by such understanding of the term "saints" of men come from heaven. All this difficulty arising from accumulation of strange features disappears immediately when "saints" is taken to designate *angels* come with Christ from heaven. It is true, Paul does not in any passage call the angels "saints," and on the other hand, in Matt. xxvii. 52 we do read of the bodies of the saints that were asleep appearing in the holy city at the crucifixion of Christ. Over against this, however, may be placed the words of Jesus Himself, Mk. viii. 38: "the Son-of-Man also shall be ashamed of him, when He comes in the glory of his Father with the holy angels." From this saying it appears that the attribute "holy" could with a special fitness be given to the angels in eschatological connections. There is nothing whatever to contraindicate the angel-reference in a passage so steeped in eschatological atmosphere as 1 Thess. iii. 13. From vs. 14, "those who are asleep . . . God shall bring (ἄξει) with Him," no argument can be drawn in favor of the joint-coming of Christ and the risen saints at the parousia. Here "to bring" (ἄγειν) refers to the introduction of the saints, jointly with Christ, into the Kingdom of God, not to God's bringing them to earth in the movement of the parousia. The statement in iv. 17 can be interpreted in the same way, so as to make the meeting of believers with Christ in the air not preparatory to a further earthward descent for judgment, but introductory to an abode with Him in the supernal regions.

More explicit information as to the attending circumstances of the resurrection we obtain in iv. 16. Here we learn of the "shout," the "voice of the archangel," and the "trump of God" as accompanying the descent. The sounds thus described serve the purpose of summoning from afar, as it were, the dead to arise, in order to render them ready for their share in the event only a little later than Christ has begun his earthward movement.

The preposition used with these three descriptive phrases is ἐν. It describes the attending circumstances of the act. The following queries arise: (1) Who is the subject issuing the "shout" (κέλευσμα), and who are the objects receiving it? (2) What is the relation of the two subjoined terms, the "voice of the archangel," and the "trump of God," to the *keleusma*? The word *keleusma* is a forcible term used to describe the word of command given, for example, to soldiers, or to sailors rowing in a ship, or to dogs in the chase. Here, however, its meaning is not associated with any of these particular uses. Bringing in the military idea would represent Jesus as by a shout summoning his forces to the conflict with and final victory over the power of evil. But the power of evil remains entirely in the background in the whole representation. The shout is undoubtedly addressed to the dead as dead, that is, as in a state which would render them, figuratively speaking, deaf to every other impact of sound and require to rouse them all the authority and omnipotence of God. Both the immediateness and the irresistibleness of the power transmitted by such a sound to a sphere where otherwise no sound is able to penetrate are most strikingly expressed.

Now, who is the subject of the *keleusma,* the utterer of this tremendous command? Is it Christ or God? It has been urged that, since "the Lord" is the subject of the verb "shall come down," He must likewise be the subject of the act which attends his descent. But the second phrase, "with the voice of the archangel," shows that this argument has no force. If Christ can come down with the voice of the archangel, He can also descend with a *keleusma* proceeding from some one else, which would in this case be God. Still this, while possible, yields no more than a possibility, and falls short of convincing proof. The statement as a whole rather favors the other view, viz., that Christ is the One issuing the *keleusma.* Especially the emphasis thrown on the fact that Christ *Himself* will descend makes us expect the prominence of Christ in the whole transaction, and this would be secured through the issuing of the *keleusma* from Him. The direct ascription of this to Christ serves the further purpose of rendering the resurrection of believers undeniably certain: being "dead in Christ" they can not fail of participating in the effect of an act or process in which He is the princeps or center. At any rate, whether Christ be the subject of the *keleusma,* or not, it would yield an incongruous thought to regard Him as the object of the commanding voice. Such a loud summons to Christ who dwells in the immediate presence of God would be wholly out of place; whereas, when conceived as addressed to the dead, it is in entire harmony with the situation.[1]

Assuming then that the *keleusma* is uttered by Christ, the question next arises, What is the relation to it of the two other terms named, the "voice of the archangel" and the "trump of God"? Are these coördinated or subordinated con-

[1] Kabisch would have the *keleusma* addressed to Christ.

ceptions? Do they define what the *keleusma* consists in, or do they name two further and separate items? In the former case the construction would more likely have been that with the genitive (φωνῆς ἀρχαγγέλου), and similarly with the other member (σάλπιγγος θεοῦ). The repetition of ἐν favors the other interpretation. This, however, is not to be so understood as though the *keleusma* did not take effect until after the voice of the archangel and the trump of God had produced theirs, the latter two wakening the dead, the former summoning the dead already wakened. The three serve the same purpose and their force is cumulative. Who blows the trumpet is not stated; only the voice of the archangel should not be identified with the sound of the trumpet; against this the conjunction καί speaks. It must be granted, however, that the sounding of the eschatological trumpets is elsewhere assigned to the angels, cp. Apoc. x. 7; xi. 15, where, the number being seven, the seven archangels must be meant. Michael, one of the archangels, appears already significantly connected with the resurrection in Dan. xii. 12. The conception of Michael as having a special task in connection with the last things is found also in the Apocalyptic writings;[2] ancient Jewish traditions make him particularly the blower of the last trumpet.[3] The figure of the trumpet, however, has its root not there but in the Old Testament. Its origin seems to lie in what the Pentateuch relates of a trumpet blown at the giving of the Law: "There were thunders and lightnings, and a thick cloud upon the mount, and a voice of the trumpet exceeding loud" (Ex. xix. 16). According to Isa. xxviii. 13, a great trumpet will be blown to gather the scattered people of God from Assyria and Egypt and summon them to the holy mountain of Jerusalem, where they will worship Jehovah. From the standpoint of the Old Testament this is already eschatological. Full New Testament eschatological significance is given

[2] Cp. *Ass. Mos.* x. 2; *En.* x. 11; xxiv. 6; xxv. 4; xc. 14.

[3] Cp. *4 Esd.* vi. 23; *Or. Syb.* iv. 173.

the words from Exodus by the author of the Epistle to the Hebrews, who reminds the readers that they are come "not to a mountain that might be touched[4] and that burned with fire, and unto blackness, and darkness and tempest, and the sound of a trumpet, and the voice of words . . . but unto the heavenly Jerusalem" (xii. 19). Here the principle of typology is applied *via oppositionis*: the setting and the external apparatus are the same, but the significance and effects are opposite.[5] Our Lord, likewise, in eschatological discourse speaks of the great sound of a trumpet wherewith the angels shall gather the elect (Matt. xxiv. 31). Here also, it will be observed, the angels are the trumpet-blowers. Apart from the trumpets in the Apocalypse, the only other reference to the trumpet is found with Paul himself (I Cor. xv. 52). Here it is called "the last trump" (ἐσχάτη σάλπιγξ): "We shall all be changed . . . at the *last trump,* for the trumpet shall sound, and the dead shall be raised incorruptible." The adjective "last" in this phrase is usually misunderstood. The Apostle's meaning is not that during the ages of the world's history many trumpets have in succession been blown, but that this one, as marking the close of all history, will be the last one to sound. "Last" does not here signify "final" in a chronological sense. It is a technical eschatological term, which does not indicate plurality, but duality; there is one at the beginning, and there will be another, corresponding to it at the end; and between these two trumpets lies the whole content of historical eventuation. Finally the genitive ("of God") added to "trump," does not mean that God blows it, but simply characterizes it as belonging to the eschatological order of things.

[4] "Might be touched" is the expression of the material, tangible character of the mountain; it has nothing to do with the prohibition of touching the mount in Ex. xix. 12. Its opposite is not the accessibleness, but the spiritualness of the mountain of the New Jerusalem.

[5] Zech. ix. 14 is not meant eschatologically; here the trumpet is one of war: "And Jehovah shall be seen over them, and his arrow shall go forth as the lightning: and the Lord Jehovah will blow the trumpet, and will go with whirlwinds of the south."

By these colorful features Paul makes for us even more grandiose and impressive what under all circumstances can not help being a scene of intense realism. They furnish practically the only material on which our imagination can draw for filling out the large frame of the canvas. It were wrong undoubtedly to reduce all the things mentioned to the rubric of figurative language, in regard to which the author is aware of painting freely, rather than of copying the solid content of prophecy given him by the Spirit. On the other hand we should not overlook the equally obvious fact, that in painting by words, even with the fullest intent of accuracy, the Apostle had to avail himself of a fixed medium of language, which left room for a margin of over-literalism, and whose interpretation by others, while seemingly in full accord with the words recorded, nevertheless may introduce an ingredient of inadequacy when compared with the actual intent of Paul. We have here before us a striking example of the possibility of over-stressing the literalness of the language and imagery used, and yet, while thus seeming to do justice to the writer's speech, missing in reality the deeper and finer qualities and objectives of his true conception. The literalistic may appear to our human vision nearer the real, and yet, owing to our pardonable craving for the concrete, be more subjective than the spiritualized.

In view of the original literal, physical association of the words forming the resurrection-terminology with the notions of "sleep" or "causing to rise, or stand up," the question is asked whether Paul's idea of the state between death and resurrection is that of sleep or unconsciousness? If God wakes the dead, or if they are roused and made to stand on their feet, what other implication can this have than that they pass out from a sleeping into a waking condition? And, what seems stronger still, the representation of the dead as those who have been put to rest (bed), and consequently now are in that condition, appears inseparable from the phenomena of physical sleep. None the less it would be rash to draw even such theological, eschatological inferences from this as might seem to lie plainly on the surface. These are all words and modes of speech of most-ancient origin. Undoubtedly at the time of their first springing into usage they had clearly associated with themselves a feeling of their etymological significance, viz., that of a state dim consciousness or unconsciousness in the dead. But, like all words, especially like all words denoting universal common processes, they were subject to attrition. While, of course, continuing capable to describe the surface facts, they could not fail to lose part of the coloring and implications of the facts, whose apprehension had once asserted itself in their coinage. Except when particular occasion arose to reflect on their original force, they were handled as so many word-signs, into whose primordial picturesqueness the average language-user no longer enquired. Such was undoubtedly the case with words that had no specific revelation-function to perform, being common to the current speech of all. The words for "sleep" (*κοιμᾶν, κοιμᾶσθαι, κεκοιμᾶσθαι*) are words of this sort. These may have passed through more than one stage of primitive association, but inevitably they suffered the fate of becoming blind words. It is, of course, different with the class of terms that had to serve the purposes of revelation. True, while originally subject to this same attrition-process, Christian thought and feeling could bring back some of the old coloring. But the possibility must likewise be reckoned with that *κοιμᾶν* and *κοιμᾶσθαι* had come to mean little more than to be placed in the recumbent position of the grave. At the same time it is likely that among believers a special sense of tenderness accompanied the act, reminiscent of the ordinary act of putting a child to bed, with loving hands.

Nor need we doubt that, as the correlate of physical sleep is awakening, so this latter idea, never existing or at least long since obliterated in pagan language, might, as it were, acquire a new significance. Here a negative pagan concept came to meet the different sentiment of the Christian mind. For the pagan *κοιμᾶσθαι* is a sleep to which no waking is joined and in this quite important respect the two words were not by any means analogues. In the case of ἐγείρειν it is not merely a single association that differentiates the Christian from the pagan, in the latter the entire idea of a supernatural, miraculous "bringing back from the dead" is lacking, because the supernaturalistic background as a whole is in paganism absent. Consequently Scriptural usage had to translate the term into a totally new circle of belief and understanding: the ordinary, physical ἐγείρειν, has received a new, redemptive, superlative sense.

All this, and more, it is necessary to remember, before venturing to draw positive inferences from certain terms, and that sometimes even without assuring ourselves that in the later times of paganism a similar drawing of inferences was still a living process. When even pre-Christian paganism does not universally ascribe to the *koimomenos* or the *kekoimemenos* a sleep or rest, in the sense of *unconsciousness,* we may not assume that this ancient, imaginative corollary of the term was saved out of its semi-oblivion into a new literalness for the Christian faith. Though to the pagan poet there was nothing to look forward to but "nox una longa dormienda," a sleep without end, such a prospect was certainly never present to the early Christian; and if the ideas of "una" and "longa" were wholly eliminated for him, why should the notion of sleeping in the sense of unconsciousness have persisted? Moreover we have from Paul explicit statements concerning this "intermediate state," which positively exclude its having been to his mind a state of unconsciousness, such as, apart from dreams, physical sleep ordinarily induces. In 2 Cor. v the whole train of Paul's reasoning is based on the thought, that there will be a differentiation in feeling (that is, a perceptible difference in the self-reflexive consciousness) in the state after death. Whether he feels clothed with a body or feels naked will be an object of perception to him. To the unconscious dead there is not and can not be any distinction between the one state and the other: all things are alike to them. Even though only the minimum of what appears desirable to Paul, i.e., to die before the parousia, is in store for him, still he expresses the assurance that to be in an "unclothed" (naked) state at home with the Lord, will be a cause of contentment, and the looking forward to this provisional minimum becomes a reason for good courage, which it could not be without the expectation of consciousness in the post-mortem state. Similarly, in Phil. i. 23 the having departed and being with Christ is estimated as "very far better." To be sure, the estimate is formed in his present mind, but the whole contrast of "worse" or "better" loses its significance, if consciousness, the only organ of difference in appraisal, be denied. The Apostle, then, continues to make use of the common language of the day in teaching about these things, and there is hardly any perceptible effort on his part to correct or modify the latter. What he does is to fill with vital substance language that had so largely become voided of meaning.

It has been alleged, it is true, that Paul abstained from the use of the word "death" with reference to departing believers, and employed "to sleep" as a euphemism useful in enabling him to do this. This avoidance, it is held, was practised by him with reference to believers only, and not with reference to Christ, where the soteric necessities of the case almost compelled the use of "death." But, even with that restriction, the theory is not borne out by the facts, for in 1 Thess. iv. 16 he speaks of "the dead (*νεκροί*) in Christ"; and if he used "dead," he certainly could have used "death," which is no worse a term. Besides, it is one thing to prefer the use of one word to another on account of aesthetic reasons, and another thing to fill the form of a word with an entirely new content; the latter is what he would have done in forcing upon the then colorless term *κοιμᾶσθαι* the significance of death-sleep literally interpreted. The state of death is a state of consciousness, and, as already shown, capable of the sensation of comfort or discomfort, according to the presence or absence of the body, such as results from a garment one is accustomed to wear, and which one misses when it is not on him. It would, perhaps, be too much to assert, that, apart from this the death-state of believers is an undesirable experience. That it falls short of the acme of blessedness must be acknowledged, and it may be well to call attention to this fact as over against the error of death-sleep, for to the sleeper there is neither pain nor pleasure, a consideration which might incline minds, over-enamored with the idea of absolute quiescence, towards that erroneous theory and the erroneous exegesis on which it is based. The average terminology of burial customs is perhaps to some extent responsible for the error, though as a whole, no doubt, it is born out of a morbidly pessimistic appraisal of life, to which may be added the semi-poetic attraction of the language employed.

It has further been urged that I Cor. xi. 30 and I Thess. iv. 13 cast a reflection on the state of death even for believers. If this were correct it would furnish one more argument against the theory under criticism. It must remain doubtful, however, whether this is not putting too much into the words. To die is ordinarily a painful experience as such, irrespective of the state upon which it introduces. And possibly those who died in the Corinthian church died under special circumstances expressive of divine disapproval of their conduct, so that their departure was a chastisement in itself, leaving out of account altogether what their death might proximately lead them into. It should also be remembered, that, owing to the prevailing expectation of a speedy return of the Lord, Paul's teaching had not dwelt upon the intermediate state to any large extent, so that his converts in Corinth could more readily regard premature death as a chastisement than we would. In I Thess. iv. 13 the cause for the "sorrowing" which Paul deprecates does not lie in their regarding the state of death as an evil in itself, but in their apprehension of it as an interminable state. The Thessalonians, it appears, had not yet fully assimilated the resurrection truth. Paul's statements in this passage, with which we hope to deal more fully in another connection, confine themselves strictly to the one matter on which the Thessalonians were disquieted, viz., the presence at the parousia of their fellow-Christians who had died before. On the intermediate state this throws no light whatever.[6]

[6] It may be well at this point to subjoin a few linguistic remarks on

Having now the immediate precedents and the general terminology before us, we next attempt to obtain an insight into the religious and doctrinal principles underlying the resurrection. As a fact, and that a fact not lacking doctrinal explanation, it is, next to the cross, the outstanding event of redemptive history. But Paul has first made it a focus of *funda-*

the Pauline usage of speech concerning the resurrection. The largest place is occupied by ἐγείρειν, and that in the active voice, God the Father being the acting subject. Of Jesus Himself it is said that He "was raised" ("waked") implying the same relationship of activity on God's part. The creative aspect of the act standing in the foreground, this is what we should naturally expect. Nowhere is it said of Jesus that He contributed towards his own resurrection, far less that He raised Himself. His rôle is throughout that of the terminus upon whom God's resurrective action works, in order that through Him it may work upon others; cp. Rom. iv. 24, 25; vi. 4, 9; vii. 4; viii. 11, 34; x. 9; 1 Cor. vi. 14; xv. 12-17, 20; 2 Cor. iv. 14; v. 15; in these passages partly the active, partly the passive occurs, the former of God, the latter of Jesus. The verb ἀνιστάναι is much rarer in use than ἐγείρειν (cp. Rom. xiv. 9). As the figure allows more of response in the one that is raised, we find here the representation that Christ ἀνέστη (1 Thess. iv. 14), involving somewhat of the participative element on the part of Jesus in the transaction. But, apart from this slightly different turn in the application to Jesus, it will be seen at a glance that the verb ἀνιστάναι is much less in evidence with Paul than the companion-term ἐγείρειν. In the Pauline speech of Acts x both terms interchange (cp. Acts xvii. 18, 32; xxiii. 6; xxiv. 15, 21). In regard to the tenses employed the difference between the aorist and perfect in ἐγείρειν should be noticed. The peculiar force of the perfect can be most clearly felt in a passage like 2 Tim. ii. 8: "Remember Jesus Christ risen (ἐγηγερμένον) from the dead." The form "risen" here expresses that the experience of the resurrection constitutes Christ "a Risen One" *in perpetuum,* so that the act of remembering terminates not on his Person in general, but on that capacity of the Person that belongs to Him as "a raised, living One" (cp. 1 Cor. xv. 16, 17, 20); passages with the aor. pass. are frequent. In the sphere of the noun ἀνάστασις has the monopoly, because a corresponding noun ἔγερσις seems to have been in sporadic use only (cp. Matt. xxvii. 53, used of the resurrection of Jesus). A unicum in the New Testament is ἐξανάστασις (Phil. iii. 11, used of the resurrection of Paul), of which term more later on. The word *anastasis* is sometimes active, i.e., the act of producing the resurrection, but it may also be an abstract term, describing the event as such in its generality (Rom. i. 4; 1 Cor. xv. 12). Much less richly represented than the ἐγείρειν and ἀνιστάναι groups is the correlative term κοιμᾶσθαι, descriptive of the pre-ressurrection state; this is in the main confined to the two contexts of 1 Thess. iv and 1 Cor. xv. Here *mental* Christian teaching and built around it the entire conception of the faith advocated and propagated by him. In order to gain an insight into how this came about, we must first call to mind, that in the Apostle's construction of Christian truth, two distinct strands show themselves. The first we may call the *forensic* one. It revolves around the abnormal status of man in the objective sphere of guilt, and deals with all that is to be done outside of man, in order to its reversal, so that instead of an ἄδικος he may become in legal standing a δίκαιος before God. The other, while variously denominated, may here for convenience' sake be called the *transforming* one. It has to do with everything that pertains to the subjective inward condition of him to whom the grace of God is imparted. The former effects justification, the latter regeneration and sanctification.

The peculiarity of the Pauline system of truth consists in this, that these two complexes of doctrine do not exist side by side in such form as to yield by mere addition of the one to the other the complete body of Paulinism; the situation is rather this, that furnishing along each line a continuous conspect of the gospel, each after a fashion may lay claim to relative completeness. Hence the phenomenon that in the treatment of the Pauline teaching some writers from a sense of personal preference have chosen the one line, and tracing it out, have felt contented that they were offering the student a full-orbed compass of the Apostle's religious thought. All the time they were forgetting, or per-

νεκρός, though in itself a word of coarser associations, has come to occupy the field. We can not make the distinction, however, as though κοιμᾶσθαι were reserved for believers and νεκροί promiscuously applied to believers and unbelievers in the state of death. The phrase νεκροὶ ἐν χριστῷ (1 Thess. iv. 16) suffices to prove that the word, while reminding of the *nekrosis* which is the product of death, is not incapable of being joined to the most noble and intimate relationships of the Christian state. The corruptible is swallowed up by that mystical union with the Lord to which there is no suspension even in death. On the other hand, cp. for κοιμᾶσθαι in a dishonorable connection, 1 Cor. xi. 30. There is no difference in the use of the terms surveyed between the resurrection of Jesus and that of believers.

haps with some intentional partiality ignoring, that alongside of it, there runs the other twin strand making up the other semi-cycle of the teaching. Nor was this unfortunate only because it resulted in incompleteness of rendition, the more serious fact was that even in what thus obtained reproduction the proper balance was lacking. For it stands to reason that in a mind highly doctrinal and synthetic like Paul's a loose juxtaposition of two tracks of thinking without at least an attempt at logical correlation is inconceivable. In such a matter Paul's mind as a theological thinker was far more exacting than theirs who think that with their facile leaning over to one favored side they have done justice to the genius of the greatest constructive mind ever at work on the data of Christianity.

So far this is only looking at the question from the purely human standpoint of the religious thinker. But we dare not dismiss the point without reminding ourselves that the completeness and logical coherence of the truth taught through its organs is a preëminent postulate of revelation. It is for these reasons *a priori* to be expected that the two strands discoverable shall not be entirely equal in rank within the system of doctrine, for that would yield a dualism hard to put up with. And so soon as the question is raised, through the principial superiority of which of the two spheres the necessary balance and symmetry is safeguarded, the solution can be hardly other than that the forensic principle is supreme and keeps in subordination to itself the transforming principle. Justification and sanctification are not the same, and an endless amount of harm has been done by the short-sighted attempt to identify them. But neither are these two independent one of the other; the one sets the goal and fixes the direction, the other follows. What has darkened the vision of some in this matter was the taking for granted that for superiority in leading position all that is needed is greater bulk and outstanding prominence on either side. It was unavoidable that in practical communications directed to the building up of disciples in the faith, such as the Epistles, the viewpoint of sanctification could easily come to overshadow the more isolated and momentary problem of justification. This would undoubtedly have happened had not the latter principle found such emphatic and ineffacable testimony borne to it, as is the case, for example, in the Epistle to the Galatians and certain sections of Romans.

Coming now specifically to the resurrection, this before aught else would seem to be exempt from displacement out of the transforming into the forensic sphere. It signifies in fact the most radical and all-inclusive transforming event within the entire range of the believer's experience of salvation. It is equivalent to "becoming a new creation," and what could be excluded from such a sweep of renewal? The one in Christ is καινὴ κτίσις. In Him the old things have passed away, all things from that point on become new.[7] And what is true of the earthly prototype of the eschatological change must *ipso facto* hold true of the resurrection part of the supreme crisis at the end. There likewise in an absolutely unprecedented manner and to an unprecedented extent the idea of renewal furnishes the light in which all things are placed. And yet it were, from the point of view of Paul's teaching a mis-

[7] It is usually taken for granted, not merely in homiletical usage, but likewise in commentary-exposition, that καινὴ κτίσις describes the renovation in the subjective condition of the believer, if not entirely so, at least chiefly. The rendering "new *creature*" has promoted this partial misunderstanding. But *ktisis* signifies "creation" no less commonly than "creature." The context shows that Paul's real point of view is better rendered by "a new creation." Through the redemptive provision afforded by God in Christ, and specifically by one's εἶναι ἐν χριστῷ, the Christian has been transferred into a new world, a world which differs *toto genere* in all its characters, its whole environment, and (this could hardly remain unexpressed in such a sweeping statement) differs likewise principially as to the basis of objective righteousness on which the new man stands, from the present world. Nor is it necessary to reach this by inference; the context says it in so many words: "But all things are of God, who reconciled us through Christ to Himself . . . to wit, that God was in Christ reconciling the world unto Himself." And that this "reconciliation" is an objective process (atonement plus justification) appears plainly from the following words "not reckoning unto them their trespasses." For the sense of "creation" attaching to *ktisis* cp. Heb. ix. 11.

take to confound prominence here with undivided supremacy. To his view the resurrection with all that clusters around it, has behind it a still more potential principle, a principle from which in fact it springs, and in whose depths it lies anchored. And this deeper principle is that of the acquisition of righteousness, a forensic principle through and through, and yet no less than the resurrection a transforming principle also. It is especially by considering the nexus between Christ and the believer that this can be most clearly perceived: in the justification of Christ lies the certainty and the root of the Christian's resurrection. For the supreme fruit of Christ's justification, on the basis of passive and active obedience, is nothing else but the Spirit, and in turn the Spirit bears in Himself the efficacious principle of all transformation to come, the resurrection with its entire compass included. Resurrection thus comes out of justification, and justification comes, after a manner most carefully to be defined, out of the resurrection; not, be it noted, out of the spiritual resurrection of the believer himself, but out of the resurrection of Christ. On the basis of merit this is so. Christ's resurrection was the *de facto* declaration of God in regard to his being just. His quickening bears in itself the testimony of his justification. God, through suspending the forces of death operating on Him, declared that the ultimate, the supreme consequence of sin had reached its termination. In other words, resurrection had annulled the sentence of condemnation.

This is the simple meaning of Rom. iv. 25: "who was delivered up for our trespasses, and was raised for our justification." The preposition διά occurring in each of the two clauses, must have, of course, in each the same constructional force; what this force is the first clause shows beyond all possibility of doubt: Christ was delivered up to death "on account of our trespasses." Our trespasses were the ideally efficient cause of his death (διά c. acc.). If it is to correspond to this, the second clause must mean that He was raised "on account of our justification" (διά c. acc.). Because in his completed death our justification was virtually secured, it needed only the passing of death from off Him, and the consequent substitution of life for death to declare this. Not, therefore, to render our justification more easy to apply, nor even to release in Him forces working for its application, was He raised. There was in his coming to life something far more efficacious than a mere demonstration might have been.[8]

A passage with a similar trend of thought is Rom. viii. 23. Here the technical term *υἱοθεσία* ("adoption") is introduced in close connection with the "redemption of the body," i.e., the eschatological resurrection. It is not merely in the grace of this present life that the believer is given to taste the fruition of his release from the forensic power of sin, the same principle works through to the very end, so long as there shall still remain something to be set right, some sequela of sin even in the sphere of the body to be removed. Here it can be plainly observed how the one thought passes over into the other: "adoption" is by parentage a forensic concept; yet it fulfills itself in the bodily transforming change of the resurrection.

It has been not unplausibly held, that this forensic aspect of the resurrection as a declarative, vindicatory, justifying act, forms a very old, if not perhaps the oldest, element in Paul's doctrine on the subject. To Judaism the belief largely bore this meaning. Paul could later truthfully say, that in preaching the resurrection he defended the Pharisaic position, not merely through insistence upon the fact, but also so far as this fact amounted to a vindication of the people of God (Acts xxiii. 6). In 1 Cor. xv. 30-32 the resurrection is viewed as a reward for the incurring of danger and the daily dying undergone. In vss. 55-57 of the same context it is pictured as the swallowing up of death in victory, and death is here pointedly named as the penalty for sin imposed by the Law, so that the

[8] The idea here found in the verse has nothing to do with the doctrine of eternal justification. What is referred to is not an eternal, i.e., supra-temporal act, but an act in history. It was simply the ideal side in the mind of God to the visible, temporal occurrence of the suspension of the death of Christ.

resurrection is the final removal of the condemnation of sin. In vs. 58 it appears even as a recompense for the labor accomplished, hence as an incentive for the more intense prosecution of this labor: "Wherefore, my beloved brethren, be ye steadfast, unmovable, always abounding in the work of the Lord, forasmuch as ye know that your labor is not in vain in the Lord." After the long disquisition on the raising of the dead the "wherefore" can have no other meaning than that the motive of the exhortation lies in the sure prospect of the resurrection. The "forasmuch as ye know" relates in like manner to the unshakable assurance of this culminating event in which all rewards of the pious will be summed up.

Of course, all this must be understood in harmony with the Apostle's principle of salvation through grace, apart from works, as must his doctrine of reward in the judgment generally. Side by side, therefore, with the resemblance between it and the Jewish doctrine, the vital difference between meritorious and non-meritorious ground of bestowal should never be overlooked. Still it remains worth observing, that the Apostle has incorporated this idea of the resurrection in his forensic scheme. It seems a pity that in the more prominent associations of our Easter observance so little place has been left to it. The Pauline remembrance of the supreme fact, so significant for redemption from sin, and the modern-Christian celebration of the feast have gradually become two quite different things. Who at the present time thinks of Easter as intended and adapted to fill the soul with a new jubilant assurance of the forgiveness of sin as the guarantee of the inheritance of eternal life?[9]

[9] Much light falls on the forensic significance of the resurrection in believers from a comparison with the case of Christ's resurrection. The Spirit is in Christ the seal and fruit of his righteousness, and at the same time it is in Him through his exalted state, produced by the resurrection, the perpetual witness of the continuous status of righteousness in which He exists. In Him unintermittedly springs up that fountain of justification, from which all believers draw. To say that forgiveness of sin procured through the imputation of Christ's merit constitutes only the initial act in the Christian life, and that thereafter, the slate having been wiped clean, there is no further need for nor allowance of recourse to it, all being

We hasten on, however, to outline the other, more familiar aspect of the event. That it bears such an aspect so far as the body is concerned lies on the surface. That this is a transformation effected by Christ Himself is likewise plain; and still further that the transformation is analogous to that produced in the body of Christ Himself at his own resurrection. All this is implied in the classical passage Phil. iii. 21, where the expressive term μετασχηματίζειν is employed for describing it. The question, whether this transformation of the body takes place in the believing portion of the Church then living, or in all found alive at the parousia may be here left to one side. Nor can it make any difference for our present purpose, whether the change spoken of shall coincide with the raising of believers, or constitute a separate subsequent act.

A far more complicated problem is whether at the parousia this transformation will concern the somatic condition of believers only, or will include a corresponding psychical change, affecting more particularly that side of human nature where the body is most closely interrelated with the soul. *A priori* it seems difficult to deny this. The opposite would involve a kind of physical construction of the resurrection-principle, such as we may well hesitate to ascribe to Paul. Bodily the resurrection certainly is, and every attempt to de-physicize it, so often inspired by a dislike of the supernatural on its material side, amounts to an exegetical *tour de force*, so desperate as to be not worth losing many words over. Now, if there be a somatic resurrection, we can not otherwise conceive of it than as a somatic transformation. There is not a simple return of what was lost in death; the organism returned is returned endowed and equipped with new powers; it

thenceforth staked on sanctification, is, apart from all other criticism, wrong, because it ignores forensic righteousness as a vital factor in the exalted state of the Saviour. If this were not so, it would remain unexplainable why, in the matter of justification, Paul directs the gaze of faith not merely to the cross retrospectively, but likewise upward to the glorified existence of Christ in heaven, wherein all the merit of the cross is laid up and made available forever.

is richer, even apart from the removal of its sin-caused defects. The normal, to be sure, is restored, but to it there are added faculties and qualities which should be regarded supernormal from the standpoint of the present state of existence. To receive back a body, and to have a body at all is much (2 Cor. v. 1-9), but we may feel sure that it was not to Paul exhaustive of the grace of the resurrection, even considered from the somatic point of view. Nor do we lack information to that effect. According to 1 Cor. xv. 45-49 believers shall bear after Christ the image He Himself obtained in his own resurrection. And this is not a case of mere analogy as to radiancy of appearance through externally imposed glory, it is something deeper and farther-reaching, intensely real, although we may not be able to form a concrete conception of it any more perhaps than could Paul himself. With all the difference inevitably existing between the two cases the ὁρισθῆναι ἐν δυνάμει ἐξ ἀναστάσεως νεκρῶν of Rom. i. 4 must have its counterpart in the resurrection of believers; in their case likewise there must take place an investment with δύναμις.[10]

The resurrection-idea has been too much concentrated upon

[10] The analogy, and its bearing upon our problem become most clear when the passage, Rom. i. 3-4, is somewhat closely analyzed. Here we read that Jesus was ὁρισθεὶς υἱὸς θεοῦ ἐν δυνάμει κατὰ πνεῦμα ἁγιωσύνης ἐξ ἀναστάσεως νεκρῶν. The clause stands in parallelism to the one in vs. 3: τοῦ γενομένου ἐκ σπέρματος Δαυεὶδ κατὰ σάρκα. It will be noticed that the following members correspond to each other in the two clauses: γενόμενος ——— ὁρισθείς; κατὰ σάρκα ——— κατὰ πνεῦμα ἁγιωσύνης; ἐκ σπέρματος Δαυείδ ——— ἐξ ἀναστάσεως νεκρῶν. The reference is not to two coexisting states in the make-up of the Saviour but to two successive stages in his life. There was first a γένεσθαι κατὰ σάρκα, then a ὁρισθῆναι κατὰ πνεῦμα. The two prepositional phrases have adverbial force, yet so as to throw emphasis on the result no less than on the initial act: He became, as to his sarkic existence, and He was "of the seed of David." The ὁρισθῆναι Paul refers to is not an abstract determination, but an effectual installation, with bestowal of the requisite energy pertaining to the new state. Paul seems to avoid the repetition of γενόμενου, not so much for stylistic reasons, but because it might have suggested, even before the reading of the sentence to the end could correct this, that at the resurrection the *sonship* of Christ, as such, first originated, whereas his actual meaning is that the sonship κατὰ δύναμιν there began to enter into operation. By the twofold κατά the manner of each state of existence is contrasted, by the

its somatic aspect *per se*; it has been taken too much for granted that the bare body is all that is needed for the sake of restoring the completeness of human nature. If we may judge of the resurrection of believers *mutatis mutandis* after the analogy of that of Christ, we shall have to believe that the event will mark the entrance upon a new world constructed upon a new superabundantly dynamic plane. It is for the body, no less than for the soul a new birth. The resurrection constitutes, as it were, the womb of the new aeon, out of which believers issue as, in a new, altogether unprecedented, sense, sons of God: "They are sons of God, being sons of the resurrection," therefore they neither marry, nor are given in marriage (Lk. xx. 35-36). This whole idea of the ἀνάστασις as a genesis into a higher world opens up the largest conceivable perspective into a life of new structure and new potencies for the entire state of the Christian man. There exists a certain analogy at this point between the ἀνάστασις and the cosmical παλιγγενεσία of Matt. xix. 28.

Thus far, however, our discussion has confined itself to the resurrection of the body. A continuity has been established between this as it took place in Jesus, and what will take place at the parousia in them that are Christ's, and the securing of this continuity has been found to be due to no one else than to Christ Himself. When desiring to construct from Paul's statements an organic bond between the entire Christian life here upon earth and the resurrection at the end, we feel per-

twofold ἐκ the sphere of origin of each. As to the one He was "from the seed of David," as to the other He was "out of resurrection from the dead." The resurrection (both of Jesus and of believers) is therefore according to Paul the entering upon a new phase of sonship characterized by the possession and exercise of unique supernatural power. That this should apply to Christ's body alone, or to the exertion by Christ of somatic power on the bodies of believers alone, while not here expressly denied, is in itself highly implausible.

The above interpretation does not, of course, imply that Paul denied the supernatural conception of Jesus by the Spirit. Precisely, because speaking of the *pneuma-state* in the absolute eschatological sense, he could disregard here the previous Spirit-birth and the Spirit-endowment at the baptism.

haps that what has been said above renders us in a degree unsatisfied. The leap we had to make from Jesus' resurrection to the believer's leaves, as it were, the intermediate spaces unfilled, and thus threatens to destroy the true organic coherence. What we desire is to be able to show, that the believer's whole ethico-religious existence, the sum-total of his Christian experience and progress, all that is distinctive of his life and conduct demands being viewed as a preparation for the crowning grace of the resurrection. Only by showing this can the Apostle's teaching be fully cleared of the charge of incoherency between his religion and his eschatology. We believe it is possible to show this. The passages in which the entrance upon the Christian state is represented as a being raised with Christ come here under consideration. As shown before, they are semi-eschatological in import; they take for granted that in principle the believer has been translated into the higher world of the new aeon. Still for this very reason they establish a real, a vital relationship between what is enjoyed already, and what will be received at the end, for it is characteristic of the principle to lead on unto the final fulfilment. Thus, according to Rom. vi. 5, the likeness ("the image made like") of the Saviour's resurrection is to be reproduced in the Christian. Even now believers are to reckon themselves alive unto God in Christ Jesus, the Lord (vs. 11). Those who have the vision of the glorified Christ are through it "transformed into the same image from glory to glory." 2 Cor. iii. 18. Whatever may be the exact meaning of these mysterious words it is at any rate plain, that a transforming influence proceeds from Christ, such an influence as He could bring to bear upon us only in the capacity of the glorified, i.e., the risen Christ, and which has for its goal the acquisition of the same glory-image on the part of believers.

In a different form the same principle of continuity between the present spiritual life and the resurrection shows itself, where believers are exhorted to strive after sanctification with the thought and desire in mind that at the day of the Lord's coming they may be presented to Him in a sanctified condition, which will at the same time cause rejoicing in those who have labored for them and make the event objectively productive of greater grace and joy. On behalf of the Thessalonians Paul gives expression to the hope, that the Lord may make them to increase and abound to the end that He may establish their hearts unblamable in holiness at the coming of the Lord Jesus with all his saints (1 Thess. iii. 13; v. 23). Further, we shall have to add to these indications the complex of ideas gathering around the phrase "to be in Christ."[11] It is not Pauline to conceive of believers who are in Christ as enveloped by Him after a quietistic, unproductive fashion. The relation is one that has its intent determined by their destiny to share after their own degree in his glorified state. Even dead believers are in the intermediate period before the resurrection "dead in Christ" (1 Thess. iv. 16). The statement is made in order to assure those then living of their certitude of being themselves changed in due time. If Christ gathers to and envelopes in Himself all his own with such comprehensiveness that even the "dead" are never separated from Him, nor He from them, then the conclusion is surely justified, that the entire activity He directs towards them aims at raising them unto likeness with Himself. Their life and lot are so inwrought with Christ's that the general law of happening in the large phases of his experience must repeat itself in them: "If so be that we suffer with Him, that we may be also glorified with Him."

Finally, in a more un-Christological form the principle of continuity and causal nexus between the growth of the state in grace here and the inheritance of the resurrection has found

[11] It is not essential to assert that the two formulas ἐν χριστῷ and ἐν πνεύματι are entirely synonymous and coextensive, nor that the formula "in Christ" is coined after the analogy of "in the Spirit," as Deismann thinks (*Die neutestamentliche Formel in Christo-Jesu,* 1892). To the contrary, Walter (*Der religiöse Gehalt des Galaterbriefs,* 1904, pp. 122-144) has shown that the usage of the former considerably overlaps the limits within which the latter would be applicable; it has a large forensic connotation. But where "in Christ" pertains to the mystical sphere, the two formulas are practically interchangeable.

striking expression in the figure of sowing and harvesting: "Whatsoever a man soweth, shall he also reap. For he that soweth unto his own flesh shall of the flesh reap corruption, but he that soweth unto the Spirit shall of the Spirit reap eternal life. And let us not be weary in well-doing: for in due season we shall reap, if we faint not" (Gal. vi. 7-9). A connection and proportionateness between the future life of the Christian and his conduct here are affirmed in this no less than in the foregoing passages.[12]

The same problem thus far considered in terms of Christology admits of being studied likewise under the head of the doctrine and function of the Holy Spirit. In order to perceive this the reader should endeavor to make clear to himself how intimate a connection there exists between the Holy Spirit and Eschatology. The lack of recognition of this fact, so common among even doctrinally informed Christians is mostly due to the eclipse which the Spirit's eschatological task has suffered on account of his soteric work in the present life. The ubiquitousness and monergism of the Spirit's influence in the gracious processes we now experience have, as it were, unduly contracted our vision, so that after having emphasized the all-inclusiveness of this work, we forget that we have forgotten, or merely counted in *pro forma* the other hemisphere pertaining to the Spirit, that dealing with the introduction into and the abode in the life to come. Paul has not left us in uncertainty or unclearness in regard to this part of the Spirit's working. In I Cor. xv, and other classical contexts the subject is placed in such prominence and the light of revelation so superabundantly focussed upon it, that some have even felt, as though it outshone somewhat the Christ-

[12] It might seem almost unpardonable here to pass by the words of Phil. iii. 10, 11: "Becoming conformed unto his death, if by any means I may attain unto the resurrection from the dead." The thought here expressed, however, seems to go beyond the import of the above passage in so far as *the obtaining of the resurrection as such* would seem to be made dependent on Paul's Christian striving. The passage will be discussed in a subsequent connection.

glory ordinarily so inseparable from the things soteric. But soteriology so long had the priority in the Church's familiarizing herself with the Spirit, that the other part of the subject had little chance left of obtruding itself and so gaining the attention it is by nature entitled to. What makes this relative neglect all the more unexplainable, and up to a certain point inexcusable, is the fact that after all the Spirit's eschatological functions are simply the prolongation of his work in the soteriological sphere. But be this as it may, now that in more recent times the attention of Scripture students has been attracted to the facts, the intensity of occupation with them has more than made up for the shortcomings of former times.

The connection of the Spirit with Eschatology reaches back far into the Old Testament. The fundamental sense of רוח is in the Hebrew, and other Semitic languages, that of air in motion, whilst with the Greek πνεῦμα the notion of air at rest seems to have been chiefly associated. This rendered the Hebrew term fitted for describing the Spirit on his energizing, active side, which further falls in with his ultimate eschatological function of producing supernatural effects on the highest plane. Thus, the Spirit comes to be linked together with eschatology. We can observe this along several lines of thought.

There is first the idea that the Spirit through certain extraordinary manifestations of the supernatural, in certain prophetic signs, heralds the near approach of the future world. Thus in Joel iii. 1 ff.[13] the outpouring of the Spirit on all flesh is described as taking place "before the great and terrible day of Jehovah comes."[14] It is not excluded by this, that the

[13] ii. 28 ff. in the English versions.

[14] Volz (*Der Geist Gottes und die verwandten Erscheinungen im Alten Testament und im anschliessenden Judenthum*, 1910, p. 93) while explaining Joel as above, thinks that Peter in Acts ii. 16-21 follows a different exegesis, because representing the disciples as permanently possesseed of the Spirit. The contrary is true: Peter distinctly quotes the entire Joel-passage, including the words which put the phenomena named before the coming of the day of Jehovah (vs. 20), and which assume a period of some length during which opportunity is afforded to call upon the

Spirit will also have his place within the new era itself, but this is not indicated here. The Spirit works these signs, not because He stands for the eschatological as such, for the latter idea has not yet been reached.

Next, the Spirit is brought within the eschatological field itself as furnishing the official equipment of the Messiah. It will be noted that in the passages where this occurs (Isa. xi. 2; xxviii. 6; xlii. 1; lix. 21 (?); lxi. 1) the Messiah receives the Spirit as a permanent possession. In calling this equipment with the Spirit official we do not mean to imply that it is externally attached to the Messiah, not affecting his own subjective religious life, for He is not merely a Spirit of wisdom and understanding, of counsel and might, but also a "Spirit of knowledge and fear of Jehovah." Still the prophet does not mean to describe what the Spirit is for the Messiah Himself, but what through the Messiah He comes to be for the people.

Thirdly, the Spirit appears as the source of the future new life of Israel, especially of the ethico-religious renewal, and thus first becomes suggestive of the eschatological state itself. To this head belong the following passages: Isa. xxxii. 15-17; xliv. 3; lix. 21 (?); Ez. xxxvi. 27; xxxvii. 14; xxxix. 29. It will be observed that in these prophecies the sending of the Spirit is expected not from the Messiah but directly from Jehovah Himself, although the statements occur in prophecies containing the figure of the Messiah. The emphasis rests on the initial act as productive of new conditions; at the same time the terms used show that the presence and working of the Spirit are not restricted to the first introduction of the eschatological state, but characterize the latter in continuance. The land and the nation become permanent receptacles of the

name of Jehovah in order to ultimate salvation in the day of judgment (vs. 21). The Spirit's working is here no less *sub-eschatological* than it is in Joel. Peter is even more explicit than Joel in regard to this point, for he modifies the quotation by introducing into it the phrase "in the last days," a phrase which in the New Testament is everywhere sub-eschatological.

Spirit. The promise assumes in Ez. xxxvi. 26 an individualizing form.

Fourthly, we must take into account that in the Old Testament the word "Spirit" appears as the comprehensive formula for the transcendental, the supernatural. In all the manifestations of the Spirit a supernatural reality projects itself into the experience of man, and thus the sphere whence such manifestations come can be named after the power to which they are proximately traced. This is in harmony with the two-fold aspect of the wind, which is at the same time a concrete force, and a supernal element seeming to come from above. But the Spirit stands for the supernatural not merely in so far as the latter connotes the miraculous, but likewise in so far as it is sovereign over against the creature: it "blows where it listeth." In man the pneumatic awakes the awe pertaining to the supernatural, and exposes to the same danger. Even in his ordinary life the prophet is, on account of his pneumatic character, as it were concentrated upon a higher world, "he sits alone because of Jehovah's hand" (Jer. xv. 17).

The idea mentioned in the fourth place is the one which has undergone a somewhat further development in the Apocalyptic literature. Here at least the Spirit is explicitly described as a Spirit of eternal life (*Orac. Syb.* iii. 771), a Spirit of holiness pertaining to paradise, named in connection with the tree of life (*Test. Levi,* xviii. 11). Still further goes the Rabbinical Theology when it brings the Spirit specifically into connection with the resurrection: "Holiness leads to the Holy Spirit, the Holy Spirit leads to the resurrection."[15] The impression that the period of Judaism felt itself to be an unpneumatic period is sometimes due to an unwarranted comparison with the following Spirit-filled days of the early Christian Church. Both the wise men and the Apocalyptic writers of that period feel themselves men of a higher divine

[15] Cp. the author's article on "The Eschatological Aspect of the Pauline Conception of the Spirit" in *Princeton Biblical and Theological Studies* (1912), pp. 211-259.

rank. Sometimes the pneumatic state vaunted of assumed the form of a translation into the heavenly sphere.

Coming back to Paul we may adopt for guidance the twofold aspect in which the eschatological function of the Spirit appears in his teaching. On the one hand the Spirit is the resurrection-source, on the other He appears as the substratum of the resurrection-life, the element, as it were, in which, as in its circumambient atmosphere the life of the coming aeon shall be lived. He produces the event and in continuance underlies the state which is the result of it. He is Creator and Sustainer at once, the *Creator Spiritus* and the Sustainer of the supernatural state of the future life in one. As to the first, Rom. viii. 11 affirms that God *διὰ τοῦ ἐνοικοῦντος αὐτοῦ πνεύματος ἐν ὑμῖν* or *διὰ τὸ ἐνοικοῦν πνεῦμα* shall give life to the mortal bodies of the readers. *Πνεῦμα* is here not the human spirit, psychologically conceived, as vs. 10 at first sight might make us assume. It is the divine *Pneuma* that is referred to, to be sure, in its intimate union and close association with the believer's person. Hence in vs. 11 there is substituted for the simple *pneuma* the full definition "the Spirit of Him that raised Jesus from the dead." In this designation of God resides the force of the argument: what God did for Jesus He will do for the believer likewise.[16] It is presupposed by the Apostle, though not expressed in so many words, that God raised Jesus through the Spirit. Hence the argument from the analogy between Jesus and the believer is further strengthened by the observation, that the instrument through whom God effected this in Jesus is already present in the readers. The idea that the Spirit works instrumentally in the resurrection is plainly implied. This is altogether apart from the interesting divergence in the construction of *διά*

[16] It should be noticed how significantly Paul varies in this connection the name of Christ. First he speaks of the raising of *Jesus* from the dead. Here the Saviour comes under consideration as to Himself, his own human nature. Then he speaks of the raising of *Christ Jesus* from the dead. Here the Saviour comes under consideration as the Messiah in his representative capacity, which furnishes a guarantee that his resurrection must repeat itself in that of the others.

which occurs with the accusative in several important authorities. That would yield the paraphrase: If the Spirit of God who raised Jesus dwells in you, then God will create for that Spirit the same appropriate *habitat* as He created for Him in the resurrection-body of Jesus. This is a unique idea; it reverses the relation between Spirit and resurrection-body; usually the Spirit is for the sake of the new body, here the new body would be for the sake of adorning the Spirit. But, interesting though the thought may be, the other reading (διά *cum genitivo*) seems to have more textual weight in its favor. Adopting this, we paraphrase: If the Spirit of God who raised Jesus dwells in you, then God will make the indwelling Spirit accomplish for you what He accomplished for Jesus in the latter's resurrection. The idea of the "indwelling" of the Spirit in believers, occurring as it does in a train of thought prospective to the resurrection, can hardly help suggesting a process of preparation carried on with a view to that supreme eventual crisis. The Spirit is there as indwelling certainly not for *assuring* the Christian of his ultimate attainment to the resurrection alone. The indwelling must attest itself by activity also.

It might be said, however, that in statements of this kind the point of departure is the soteriological conception of the Spirit as a present factor in Christian life, and from there it moves forward to the future, so that the eschatological task of the Spirit would not be something peculiar, but only his general task applied to one particular situation. We therefore turn to another train of thought, which clearly starts from the eschatological end of the line, and from that looks backwards into the present life. This is the case in 2 Cor. i. 22; v. 5; Eph. i. 14. Here Paul derives the proof for God's having prepared him for the eternal state in a new heavenly body from the fact of God's having given him the ἀρραβὼν τοῦ πνεύματος. The "earnest" consists in the Spirit, the genitive being epexegetical, just as in Gal. iii. 14 the "promise of the

Spirit means the promised thing consisting in the Spirit.[17] Now the Spirit possesses this significance of "pledge" for no other reason than that He constitutes a provisional instalment of what in its fulness will be received hereafter. The quite analogous conception of the ἀπαρχὴ τοῦ πνεύματος (Rom. viii. 23) proves this. Ἀρραβών means money given in purchases as a pledge that the full amount will be subsequently paid. In this instance, therefore, the Spirit is viewed as pertaining specifically to the future life, nay as constituting the substantial make-up of this life, and the present possession of the Spirit is regarded in the light of an anticipation. The spirit's proper sphere is the future aeon; from thence He projects Himself into the present, and becomes a prophecy of Himself in his eschatological operations.

As indicated above, the Spirit is not only the author of the resurrection-act, but likewise the permanent substratum of the resurrection-life, to which He supplies the inner, basic element and the outer atmosphere. It is this second aspect of his function we must now look into. A difficulty meeting us at the outset may be briefly referred to. It concerns the two-fold aspect in which the Scriptures present to us the character of the Holy Spirit. Owing to the task He performs in the work of individual salvation, together with the other two members of the Holy Trinity, it is most familiar to us to conceive of Him as a Person, and not only this: the task has become so thoroughly personalized, as to leave almost no room for aught else in our practical contemplation of the Spirit. When, alongside of this, operations and functions are ascribed to Him, for the expression of which we need figures clothed in impersonal terms, we must not over-rashly conclude that in this matter, taken as a whole, two disjointed, differently oriented conceptions of the Spirit confront us, such as it would be absolutely impossible to reduce to common terms. We may not be able to make a construction that shall

[17] A third conception, that of the σφραγίς ("seal") lacks the outstanding element in the ἀρραβών and the ἀπαρχή, viz. the identity of the pledge and the thing pledged, cp. 2 Cor. i. 22; Eph. i. 13; iv. 30.

reconcile what seems to our minds incombinable in the same subject, but this does not prove that actual coexistence between these two aspects is in the Deity impossible. A Christological parallel can easily disabuse us of the necessity of such a negative conclusion. Nothing can be more personal than the intimate relation which the Christ (particularly the Risen Christ) sustains to the believer. And yet the background or underlying basis of this personal relationship is largely expressed in terms, that, did we not know better, might make us think of an elementally distributed Christ-atmosphere, in which, at least from the Saviour's side the personal is submerged, and of which the imagination fails to supply us with an adequate idea of what it consists in, inwardly considered. If to be "in Christ," and at the same time to live in conscious intercourse and fellowship with Him are not logically identical, and are yet to our common Christian faith joined in the same believing subject without endangering the recognition of the one aspect by that of the other, then why should an analogous double relation of the Holy Spirit to our persons be deemed incongruous? This parallel between the two cases, that of Christ and of the Holy Spirit is all the more convincing, since in the Pauline soteriology the two phrases ἐν πνεύματι and ἐν χριστῷ, at least so far as the latter is not meant forensically, are equivalent as to purport. The Holy Spirit is, comparatively speaking, even more *elemental* than the Risen Christ. Still less is there need for wondering that the Spirit plays in Eschatology this, as it were, semi-personal rôle.

Let us now briefly survey the evidence found for this representation in the Epistles. 1 Cor. xv. 42-49 contrasts the two bodies that belong to the preëschatological and the eschatological states successively. The former is characterized as ψυχικόν, the latter as πνευματικόν. This adjective *Pneumatikon* expresses the quality of the body in the eschatological state. Every thought of immaterialness, or etherealness or absence of physical density ought to be kept carefully removed from the term. Whatever in regard to such qualifications may or may not be involved; it is certain that such traits, if existing, are not described here by the adjective in question. In order to keep far such misunderstandings the capitalizing of the word ought to be carefully guarded both in translation and otherwise: πνευματικόν almost certainly leads on the wrong track, whereas Πνευματικόν, not only sounds a note of warning, but in addition points in the right direction positively. Paul means to characterize the resurrection-state as the state in which the *Pneuma* rules. That it rules signifies more particularly, that it impresses upon the body its three-fold characteristic of ἀφθαρσία, δόξα and δύναμις (vss. 42, 43). Over against this stands the *psychical* body, which in order of time precedes the *soma Pneumatikon*. The former for its part is characterized by φθορά, ἀτιμία and ἀσθενεία. The passage is unique even in the long register of the high mysteries of the faith with Paul, in that it contrasts not the body affected by sin, not the body as it came to exist as a result of the entrance of evil into the world, with the future body, but the primordial body of Adam ("the First Adam") and the body of the consummation. The proximate reference is to the contrast between the two *bodies* only; but in vs. 46 the representation widens out to a far more general, indeed a cosmical one. In the all-comprehensive antithesis there established by the principle: "that is not first which is τὸ Πνευματικόν, but that is first which is τὸ ψυχικόν, then that which is τὸ Πνευματικόν", this is expressed by the contrast ἐκ γῆς and ἐξ οὐρανοῦ. When it is affirmed that the Second Man is from heaven, this has nothing to do with the original provenience of Christ from heaven; the "from heaven" does not necessarily imply a "coming from heaven," any more than the opposite "from earth" implies a coming of Adam from the earth at the first creation.[18] To refer

[18] Cp. for this use of ἐξ οὐρανοῦ 2 Cor. v. 2, "our habitation which is from heaven"; likewise Mk. viii. 11; xi. 30; Jno. iii. 27; vi. 31; Apoc. xxi. 2. The test of this interpretation of the phrase lies in the use of ἐπουράνιος in vss. 48, 49; this adjective is applied to believers no less than to Christ, and in the case of believers it can not mean that they are

"from heaven" to the coming of Christ out of the state of preëxistence at his incarnation would make Paul contradict himself, for it would reverse the order insisted upon in vs. 46; not the "Pneumatic" is first, but the "psychical." Besides this it would make the Pneumatic the constituent principle of the human nature in Christ before the resurrection, of which there is no trace elsewhere with Paul. The phrase "from heaven" simply expresses that Christ after a *supernatural* fashion became the Second Man at the point marked by ἔπειτα. A "becoming" is affirmed of both Adams, the second as well as the first, for the verb ἐγένετο in vs. 45 belongs to both clauses. How far in either case the subject of which this is affirmed existed before in a different condition is not reflected upon. The whole tenor of the argument (for such it actually is) compels us to think of the resurrection as the moment at which τὸ Πνευματικόν entered. Christ appeared then and there in the form of a Πνευματικός and as such inaugurated the eschatological era. But, besides identifying the eschatological and the pneumatic, our passage is peculiar in that it most closely identifies the Spirit with Christ. Up to this point the Spirit, who works and sustains the future life was the Spirit of God. Here it begins to be, not so much the Spirit of Christ, but the Spirit which Christ *became*. And, being thus closely and subjectively identified with the Risen Christ, the Spirit imparts to Christ the life-giving power which is peculiarly the Spirit's own: the Second Adam be-

at the time of writing "from heaven" or "in heaven." The absence of the word σαρκικός from 1 Cor. xv. 45-49 affords in itself the strongest conceivable proof that the contrast is between the creation-body and the resurrection-body, not between the body invaded by sin and the body restored by redemption. The partial transformation is, of course, included in the larger one. It is like a transaction, if such a one there could be in the sphere of therapy, wherein the physician, while administering medicine for healing, should mix with it an elixir of eternal life. The patient at the end of the treatment would then find himself, not merely healed, but a new man, not figuratively as we sometimes say after a complete recovery, but in the literal sense of the phrase. This, apart from its philosophical background, is the element of truth in the φαρμακὸν ἀθανασίας of the Greek Fathers.

came not only Πνεῦμα but πνεῦμα ζωοποιοῦν. This is of great importance for determining the relation to eschatology of the Christ-worked life in believers.[19]

We have found that the Spirit is both the instrumental cause of the resurrection-act and the permanent substratum of the resurrection-life. The question here arises which of the two is the primary idea, either in order of thought or in point of chronological emergence. It might seem plausible to put the *pneuma*-provenience of the resurrection-act first, and to explain this feature from what the Old Testament teaches concerning the Spirit of God as the source of natural life in the world and in man, especially since in the allegory of Ezek. xxxvii this had already been applied to the national resurrection of Israel. If the Spirit worked physical life in its present form, what was more reasonable than to assume that He would likewise be the author of physical life restored in the resurrection. As a matter of fact, however, we find

[19] The question why Paul, after having up to vs. 43 (incl.) conducted his whole argument on the basis of a comparison between the body of sin and the body of the resurrection, substitutes from vs. 44 on for the body of sin the normal body of creation is an interesting one, though very difficult to answer. The answer should not be sought in the direction of ascribing to him the view that the creation-body and the body of sin are qualitatively identical, in other words that the evil predicates of φθορά, ἀτιμία, ἀσθενεία, enumerated in vs. 42 belong to the body in virtue of creation. Paul teaches too plainly elsewhere that these things came into the world through sin. The proper solution seems to be as follows: the Apostle was intent upon showing that in the plan of God from the outset provision was made for a higher kind of body (as pertaining to a higher state of existence generally). From the abnormal body of sin no inference could be drawn as to that effect. The abnormal and the eschatological are not so logically correlated that the one can be postulated from the other. But the world of creation and the world to come *are* thus correlated, the one pointing forward to the other; on the principle of typology the first Adam prefigures the last Adam, the psychical body the pneumatic body (cp. Rom. v. 14). The statement of vs. 44b is not meant as an apodictic assertion, but as an argument: if there *exists* one kind of body, there *exists* the other kind also. This explains why the quotation (Gen. ii. 7), which relates proximately to the psychical state only, is yet treated by Paul as proving both, and as therefore warranting the subjoined proposition: "the last Adam became a life-giving Spirit." The quotation proves this, because the "psychical" as such is typical of the

that the operation of the Spirit in connection with the natural world recedes into the background already in the inter-canonical literature, and remains so even in the New Testament writings themselves. It is more plausible to assume that the thought of the resurrection-life was the first in order, and that, in partial dependence on this at least, the idea emerges of the Spirit as the Author of the miracle of the resurrection. For the pneumatic character of the age to come there existed a solid Old Testament basis in trains of thought, which had fully held their own and even found richer development in the early New Testament period. And, quite apart from eschatological contexts, the thought that the heavenly world is the pneumatic world meets us in Paul, 1 Cor. x. 3, 4; Eph. i. 3. From this the transition is not difficult to the idea that the eschatological state is preëminently a pneumatic state, since the highest form of life known, that of the world of heaven, must impart to it its special character.

A second problem on which the eschatological evaluation of the Spirit may perhaps be expected to throw some light concerns the ubiquitousness of the Spirit in the entire Christian life on earth, his equal distribution over all its spheres and activities. In Paul first from the subjective side Christianity and the possession of and action through the Pneuma become interchangeable, and with strong emphasis the center of the Spirit's operations is fōund in the ethico-religious

pneumatic, the first creation of the second, the world that now is (if conceived without sin) of the aeon to come. This exegesis also disposes of the view that Paul meant to include vs. 45[c] in the quotation, the latter being taken from Gen. i. 27 (man's creation in the image of God). On such a supposition Paul's manner of handling the record would have to rest on the Philonic (and older) speculation of a two-fold creation, first of the ideal, then of the empirical man. According to this speculation the ideal man is created first, the empirical man afterwards, since Gen. i comes before Gen. ii. But Paul affirms the very opposite: not the pneumatic is first, the psychical is first. If there is reference at all in vs. 46 to this Philonic philosophoumenon, it must be by way of pointed correction. Paul would mean to substitute for the sequence of the idealistic philosophy the sequence of historic unfolding; the categories of his thought are Jewish, not Hellenic: he reasons in forms of time, not of space.

sphere. With such thoroughness and emphasis this had not been done before Paul. Gunkel has no doubt exaggerated somewhat the originality of the Apostle in this respect and underrated the preparation made for this development by the Old Testament prophetic and earlier New Testament teaching.[20] Still a simple comparison between the Petrine speeches in Acts and the Pauline statements abundantly shows, that Paul was the first to ascribe to the Spirit that dominating place and that pervasive uniform activity, which secure to Him, alongside of the Father and the Son, a necessary divine relation to the Christian state at every point.

[20] Gunkel, *Die Wirkungen des Heiligen Geistes nach der populären Anschauung der apostolischen Zeit und nach der Lehre des Apostels Paulus.*

CHAPTER VII

ALLEGED DEVELOPMENT IN PAUL'S TEACHING ON THE RESURRECTION

The recent intense occupation with the significance of the Spirit for the structure of the Pauline eschatology has in many respects enriched our knowledge of the subject. At the same time, and offsetting as it were this benefit, it has given rise to certain efforts from the critical side to work out a scheme of development for the Apostle's convictions and expectations as to the resurrection. The resulting views are so radical and deep-cutting, as to have modified in the mind of their supporters not only this one important point but the entire organism of the Pauline teaching. Into these theories and their supposed basis this chapter proceeds briefly to look.

As just intimated, the idea of the Spirit is made the starting-point and the propelling power of this evolution both in its particular and in its general aspect. Once adopted it is then turned into a search-light throwing its luminous beams on all the high mountain tops of the Apostle's world-view. It de-Judaizes and to not a small extent Hellenizes his Christian thought. The development thus assumed is not, however, like the normal progress that might have been expected in one who once testified concerning himself: "When I was a child I spake as a child . . . now that I have become a man, I have put away childish things" (1 Cor. xiii. 11). It is rather welcomed as a development consisting in the elimination of error, each successive stage of belief contradicting the preceding stage, and in turn being superseded by the following one. The stages in this evolutionary construction and the forces back of them are counted as follows:

The *first* stage of the development is found by these critics in the First Epistle to the Thessalonians.[1] It contains an as yet

[1] 2 Thess. is not taken account of in this theory on account of its assumed unauthenticity.

purely-Jewish form of eschatological belief, differing from the Jewish only in being centered around the Person of Jesus. Like *Apoc. Bar.* l. 2 it assumes that God will raise the dead, *nihil immutans in figura eorum*. Paul, we are told, at the time of writing this Epistle, and during his previous preaching, believed that the bodies would be brought up from the grave in the same condition as when laid therein. The main purpose of his preaching this doctrine to the Thessalonians was to reassure them that those who had recently died would be on the same footing with themselves at the moment of the parousia. Hence nothing is said about the change in those living at that point. The fact of the decomposition of the body in the grave did not trouble Paul, because he took for granted that the time until the parousia would be very short!

The *second* form of the development is represented by the First Epistle to the Corinthians. If the Thessalonians-stage can be called pre-pneumatic, this next one is characterized by the influence exerted by the pneuma-idea. Here the pneumatic eschatology begins. Paul now expects the resurrection to bring about a vast change in the rising body, and expects its occurrence at the very moment of rising. The pneumatic-transformation-idea virtually becomes a part of the resurrection-idea itself. Nor was this conception made possible only by the introduction of the *Pneuma*-factor; it became inevitable so soon as the *Pneuma,* whose very function consists in transformation, was closely joined to the event of the resurrection. The Spirit would have denied his own nature, as in very essence a transforming agent, had He been contented with the purely objective task of bringing forth the dead, without effecting a creative change in the somatic substance, which in the resurrection He operates upon. Further, the new man consisting as to his essence in spirit, and the *sarx,* the very opposite of spirit, having its seat in the body, the prime necessity for such a fundamental act as the resurrection can from the nature of the case consist in nothing else than the elimination of the "sarkic" body. This, of course, means the cutting off in reality of all connection between the present body and the body of the resurrection, although it is admitted that this last consequence of the modified view is not in so many words drawn by Paul. Although on such a view the real continuity lies in the *Pneuma,* and no longer in the body, the Apostle nevertheless continues to assign the resurrection to the moment of the parousia. This, we are told, was an instance of inconsistency. It fitted only into the mechanical system of Judaism as exhibited in his own previous position of 1 Thessalonians. The inconsistency necessarily led on to the development of the third position.

This *third* position is based on the observation on the part of Paul, that the Spirit being present in the believer from the beginning of his Christian life, there existed in reality no reason, why his crowning work should be postponed till the moment of the parousia, which, no matter whether Paul thought it distant or near, involved an element of objectionable retardation. The moment of resurrection was now placed at the believer's death. Be it noted, however, that the resurrection placed at that moment savored in no respect of the diluted modern spiritualization so largely favored in certain circles. It was not to his mind the mere entrance upon a superior incorporeal state, but the entrance upon a better *embodied* state, as refined and spiritualized as that expected during his second period, only no longer postponed till a later point, but immediately accorded in *articulo mortis*. There is, then, no discarding of the resurrection-idea here, but only the remodelling of it on a new basis. This third conviction is found reflected in the remarkable passage, 2 Cor. v. 1-8. It also finds recognition in certain statements of Romans and Colossians. Apart from the logical motivation above stated, the impulse towards embracing it arose from the Apostle's experience of the danger of death he had repeatedly incurred in his missionary labors. Hitherto he had believed in such a close nearness of the Lord's coming as to cherish reasonable hope for a life prolonged to that point. Now reckoning seriously with a previous death, he had to reconsider his resurrection-belief in adjustment to it. And it was under the emotion aroused by the thought of a pre-parousia-death, and particularly the inevitably ensuing interval of "nakedness," i.e., the existence of the soul without a covering body, that he found refuge within this new construction of things. Nakedness could be prevented, if at the very moment wherein the old body slipped off a new somatic garment were produced and put on in order to take its place. It seemed even possible to add to this view the belief in the preëxistence of the new body, as held ready antecedently in heaven, and put to its predestined use at the very moment of the believer's death. In accordance with this new construction he speaks, we are told, in Rom. viii. 19, not of the glorification of the sons of God, but of the *revelation* of the sons of God, an expression adapted to suggest that the glory of God's children already exists and waits only to be manifested. Similarly in Col. iii. 4 the statement occurs that when Christ, who is our life, shall be manifested, the Colossians also shall be *manifested in glory.*

Still a *fourth* standpoint is attributed to Paul, according to which in certain connections he implies the genesis and development of a somatic organism *within the believer* during the course of the *present* life, whilst the earthly body is still upon him. This, however, differs from the preceding stages enumerated in that it does not follow them as something attained in chronological sequence replacing a belief held before. It occurs in Epistles which at the same time reflect one or the other of the previous standpoints. According to 2 Cor. iv. 17 the "weight of glory" is wrought for the believer while he is still in the present state, and according to iii. 18, in the same context, the "transformation into the image of the Lord from glory to glory" takes place gradually here and now as the words themselves suggest. Consistently carried out this would, of course, have led to a considerable modification of what the new exegesis fiinds in 2 Cor. v. 1ff., as above formulated. Not even at death would the draping with a new body have, on such a theory, been rendered necessary. The new body having been already formed within the old body previously to death, all that remained to happen was the slipping off of the old which had hitherto hid the new from view, so that it might be manifested from within.

It will not be necessary to review this scheme of development in each of its steps. Only in so far as it involves a deviation from the traditionally accepted doctrine of the resurrection, so largely received from Paul, need we enter into the questions involved. The alleged second stage, that found in I Cor. xv, agrees in its broad outlines with the common Christian faith. It is different with the remaining three phases. To these we therefore address some critical remarks.

As regards the first stage the point in question is the absence of the pneumatic factor. It is true that the Spirit is not here explicitly named either as the author of the resurrection-act or as the substratum of the resurrection-life. Does this reveal non-acquaintance on Paul's part with such a circle of ideas? We must not overlook that the absent features did not bear directly upon the purpose of Paul's exhortation. Not the nature, but the fact of the resurrection required stressing. The point that the living should not anticipate the previously dead on this joyful occasion was the point in need of emphatic affirmation. Such Paul affords explicitly. It were, however, foolish to infer from this, that he could not have told his readers much more about the nature of the event, had it been expedient. Indirectly the Epistle shows clearly enough that the idea of the pneumatic character of the resurrection was not unknown to the author, whatever might be the case with his hearers. In iv. 14 the certainty of the readers' resurrection is based on the fact that Jesus "died and rose again." The ground of the certainty can not lie in this, that Christ is now alive, and therefore able to serve as the instrument of resurrection for the others. For in that case there would have been no reason to emphasize that Christ not only rose but "*died* and rose again." The real nerve of the argument is that because in his life their experience had been prefigured, the phase in question must be likewise reproduced in them. Now everywhere in the Pauline teaching the Spirit is the mediating factor, whereby the reproduction of the experience of Christ in believers takes place, and there is no reason to assume that the idea has any other than this same pneumatic background here. We meet even with the phrase "dead in Christ." This does not apply to any particular class of "dead," e.g. to such alone as had died for Christ's sake; the words do not suggest this, and there is no evidence of early cases of martyrdom in Thessalonica. The phrase "in Christ" can have no other meaning than belongs to it elsewhere. It describes the fundamental, mystical union between the dead and Christ. The phrase "in the Spirit" undoubtedly lies back of it.

In regard to the *second* stage a few brief words may suffice. The main point to take issue with here relates to the assertion that on the view developed by Paul, and taken over from him into the Church's creed, the real continuity between the original body and the resurrection-body is broken off. To be sure, this is more in the nature of a dogmatic contention than of an exegetical finding; it means that to Paul's modified standpoint and for his unspiritual followers the trend of belief in this direction was leading to that. They were on the point of losing something that had always been precious to their imagination, to wit, the recovery of the identical body here possessed. Not now enquiring into the metaphysical or physical or biological elements of the issue but confining ourselves to the purely-exegetical question what Paul's words about the subject may mean, the answer need not be over-difficult nor dubious. To be sure, the figure of "sowing" (σπείρειν), which plays so large a rôle in the argument, does not suffice of itself to vouch for Paul's belief in a real continuity (which is still different from complete identity) between what is deposited in the ground and what is raised. Nevertheless by way of implication this idea seems to underlie the word and figures used. Only a mistake has often been made through over-estimating the purport of the representation. Paul did not adopt or frame the figure for the *sole* or even *main* end of stressing the continuity between the two bodies. The argument, in which it lies enclosed, is an argument for the truth of the resurrection in general, and not for this one special point. The idea of "sowing" forms, within the argument as a whole, a means to an end; it is not the end in itself. Hence it gives no information as to the *modus quo* of the intermediate process between the figurative "sowing" and "harvesting." Its meaning is confined to the twin poles of the mysterious process, its beginning and end. We are sure Paul could and would have felt like the man in the parable, who *knew not* how the growth was brought about. What the actual purpose of the use of the figure was we can only ascertain by carefully considering the course of Paul's argument. It is necessary to go back to vs. 35. Here Paul formulates the two principal objections raised in Corinth, probably first by pagans, but later likewise by Christians, on whom the cavillings of the others had not failed to make some impression. The formulation is as follows: "But somebody will say: how are the dead raised, and with what kind of body do they come?" This, be it observed, is not one question presented in two forms for the sake of emphasis or clearness. Two *distinct* grounds for scepticism are plainly distinguished. The first, "How are the dead raised," ridicules the phantastic folly of believing in the return to life of a dead body. The whole thing was considered as lying beyond the sphere of arguable possibilities. The second objection is contained in the second part of the verse: "With what kind of body do they come?" This second question relates to the indeterminableness or unimaginableness of the form. The Apostle proceeds to deal with these two questions in due order of sequence.[2] The answer to the former is given in vs. 36; to think that what is "dead" (*νεκρόν*) cannot be raised is in flagrant contradiction to the facts of experience: "what thou sowest is not made alive except it have died." Death, so far from being an ob-

[2] The two questions, while logically distinct and recognized as such by Paul in the order of treatment, are not entirely independent, and therefore merged somewhat in the double interrogative sentence: the unimaginableness was in reality a part of the more largely conceived impossibility.

stacle to quickening, is its very prerequisite. Here the figure of "sowing" is already present; it serves the purpose of pointing to a common law of nature. Quite different is the use to which Paul turns it from vs. 37 onwards. Here the second (or secondary) objection, "With what kind of body do they come?" is met. The objectors found it impossible to frame a concrete conception of the nature of the resurrection-body, that is of its form and appearance. It is important to note that the question of *substance* does not seem to enter into either of the two stages of the argument. What the doubters felt perplexed about, concerned the *quality* of the new bodies, viz. their *external* quality. Perhaps it is not irrelevant here to remember the peculiar mentality of the average Greek (not now including the philosophers). The Greek would want above all in such things the convincing force of vision and imagination. To be unable to form a concrete image of something was of itself an invitation to doubt. In accordance with this Paul speaks throughout the sequel of the discourse (up to vs. 50) of the present and future bodies in terms of quality and appearance. The way of introduction of the substance-question in vs. 50 indicates of itself, that there a new aspect of the mystery is for the first time touched upon.[3] Previously to that point the figure of "sowing" served merely to answer the second objection raised, viz. that no concrete visualisation of the body to come could be formed. Paul meets this with an appeal to the richness of God's resources in the bestowal of form, and to his sovereignty in choosing from the available forms in each individual case what seems fitting to Him: "And that which thou sowest thou sowest not the body that shall be, but a bare grain, it may chance of wheat, or some other kind; but God gives it a body even as it has pleased Him, and to every seed a body of its own."[4] The form, the

[3] "Now this I say, brethren, that *flesh and blood* can not inherit the kingdom of God."

[4] The Past Tense in the Greek "as it pleased Him," might seem to suggest a reference to the creative appointment of the "bodies" of things. But in connection with the Present Tense "gives" this is little likely.

appearance, that characterizes what comes out of the ground, is not to be limited to a replica of what was put into the soil. The grain, the seed-kernel, is "naked," that is unclothed with foliage or flowers. The dress, the envelope, are given by God. No observation of a seed-grain could have taught, without previous experience, what the appearance of the sprout or plant issuing would be like. What right then has a man to argue from the impossibility of pre-vision and pre-imagination, to the presumptuous conclusion that the forthcoming of a new differently-shaped and differently-appareled body is *a priori* an absurdity?

It is evident that this feature, the intent of bringing out the non-resemblance between seed and plant governs Paul's entire treatment of the comparison. That in this explanation we have correctly diagnosed the Apostle's intent, is borne out likewise by the subjoined argument of vss. 39-41. Here Paul elucidates the principle at stake from two other spheres, passing over from vegetable to animal and astral existence. This, of course, excludes the possibility of every attempt at genetic explanation, which in the foregoing, where sowing and reaping came under review, might still have seemed to be possible. What here remains of the argument is solely the variety of somatic condition in the groups named as a *static* fact. Naturally the group of animal creatures as standing nearest to man is first drawn upon for illustration. After that the astral world comes under review. The point at issue, however, remains the identical one dwelt upon before. The variety, existing *de facto* as a constant phenomenon, though differentiated in its multiplicity, removes the right of doubting the possibility of the resurrection on the sole ground of a differently complexioned body being inconceivable. Let us briefly follow the progress in the reasoning. Its structure is carefully and skilfully framed through the alternate employment of the two adjectives ἄλλος and ἕτερος. Unfortuntely the precise difference between these two, and, in consequence, the full force of the argumentation, are lost to the English reader. The clearness of contrast could have been retained only through a pedantic alteration between the philosophic phrases "generically different" and "specifically different." Paul calls attention to the differences appearing both in the sub-human and in the superhuman realms between single species. He likewise calls attention to the generic, fundamental difference between the realms taken comprehensively. Ἄλλος marks the difference among the species included in one and the same genus, whilst ἕτερος marks the difference between the genera. Between the flesh of mankind and beasts and birds there is specific difference only; as to genus they belong in common to the same animal world; hence in vs. 39 ἄλλος is used: "there is one flesh of men, *another* of beasts" (κτηνῶν), etc. When, however, all these are taken together, and the heavenly bodies placed over against them a heterogeneity results: "the glory of the celestial and the glory of the terrestrial are ἕτεραι." But among the heavenly there is again a specific difference: "another (ἄλλη) is the glory of the sun and another is the glory of the moon, and another is the glory of the stars, for star differs from star in glory." Here again it is at once seen that the reasoning revolves not about the substantial make-up of these bodies, but about their kind, their quality, their appearance. This follows further from the fact that the close of vs. 38 links on closely to vss. 39-41, and there, as shown above, the reference to plant-clothing in foliage and flowerage is unmistakable. The same observation can be made by noting carefully the word here chosen by the Apostle to express the aspect in regard to which the variety exists. It is a variegation in "glory" (δόξα), and "glory" is primarily a term of outward manifestation. Again, the same conclusion may be drawn from the manner in which Paul, returning to the figure of sowing, immediately resumes the terminology of the qualitative. He contrasts the two bodies ("sown" and "rising") as possessed of corruption (*vs.* incorruption), dishonor (*vs.* glory), weakness (*vs.* power). In keeping with all this we shall have to understand the word *sarx* in vs. 39 not of "flesh" as so much animal matter, but of the ordinary somatic instrument for revealing certain traits or a complex of appearances. *Sarx* is simply in this connection a synecdochical designation of *soma* from this qualitative point of view (cp. vss. 38, 40). When Paul says: "another is the *sarx* of men, another is the *sarx* of beasts, another the *sarx* of birds, another the *sarx* of fishes," he means nothing else than that a cognate somatic organization in each case defines the limits of the species. Earthly bodies can be thus differentiated by the term *sarx,* because *sarx* is in them the most conspicuous feature, one of these elements after which the language is wont to give names to things. But, coming to "celestial things," the difficulty arises that such celestial entities possess no *sarx,* after which they could be synecdochically denominated. Yet, although *sarx* was excluded, the word *soma* in the sense of medium of appearance, above defined, continued to admit of use. It is somewhat difficult to determine, when Paul speaks of σώματα ἐπουράνια, whether the word "body" is used in the sense of physics or of biology. That sun, moon and stars are named as instances of heavenly bodies would seem to favor the former. This is held by others to be non-decisive, because, following a prevailing belief, both Jewish and pagan, Paul might have looked upon these celestial balls as inhabited by angels. In that case their glorious outward appearances might have been considered as a radiance of angelic inhabitants. Whatever one's exegetical choice between these two opinions may be, the conclusion to be drawn is, in this instance as before, that the resurrection-body will differ greatly from the kind of body we now possess in its eradiation of glory. It will be a case of *heteros* and not merely of *allos.* What will be the attributes from which this difference in manifestation results is stated in vss. 42, 43. Four contrasts are distinguished. These four, however, are not simply coördinated. On either side the three first named are thought of as the product of the last and fourth. That the earthly body consists in corruption, dishonor, weakness is in some way connected with its being a σῶμα ψυχικόν. In the same manner the heavenly body is characterized by incorruptibleness, glory, power, all three of which result from its being a σῶμα Πνευματικόν. The only difficulty thus remaining unsolved is how Paul could connect as inevitable consequences with the psychical body, which is according to the following context the body of creation, the unfallen body, these three ugly predicates of corruption, dishonor, weakness. One might suggest that what he connects with creation is not the actual existence of these qualities, but the contingency of their emergence: the "psychical body" would then be a body, not infected by, but nevertheless not immune either from corruption, dishonor, weakness, whereas the Pneumatic body is lifted above all invasion of these. It must be admitted, however, that this is dogmatic construction, so far as our passage is concerned. Taking into account Paul's teaching as a whole, we believe it to be a quite justifiable construction; only the principle is not here expressed in so many words. Still there is even here one phenomenon lending favor to the view suggested: Paul seems intentionally, in characterizing the body of the First Man, to avoid the adjective *sarkic* and the noun *sarx* to which it belongs. From both words in the ordinary Pauline vocabulary the notion of sinfulness, moral corruption, is inseparable. The introduction of such words as ἐκ γῆς χοϊκός, χοϊκός, vss. 47-49, where on the ordinary terminology *sarx, sarkic* would have been indicated, proves to our minds that the avoidance was intentional, and not for the sake of stylistic variation only. In vs. 50, on the other hand, where the body of man's sinful estate is indisputably spoken of, the term *sarx* immediately emerges.[5]

We now have the facts with sufficient completeness before us. The question is in order, whether in this context, so full of mysteries, there is actually present, as the evolutionary pneumatology would have it, such a powerful influx of the pneuma-principle as would overbear everything else, and even exclude the factor of the erstwhile earthly body from the process described. The answer must be in the negative. Let it be observed that so far as the act of raising is concerned, the Spirit does not receive the prominence we should expect Him on the new theory to acquire or possess. It is God, as else-

[5] "*Flesh and blood* can not inherit the kingdom of God."

where, who raises. No doubt He does it through the Spirit, but pointedly stressed this is not. Where it does come to expression the form is Christological, that of the Lord having become a Πνεῦμα ζωοποιοῦν (vs. 45). This concerns the *act* of the resurrection, strictly so taken. It does only through inference teach that in the subsequent resurrection-*state* we shall bear the Spirit-image, or live in the Spirit-atmosphere (vs. 49). As to the presence and operation of the Spirit in the intermediate state, preparing the dead for the issue of the resurrection, nothing whatever is stated; we are here thrown back on the scanty phrase "dead in Christ" from 1 Thessalonians. If the last-mentioned idea could be legitimately drawn from the passage, then, the importance of the Spirit would be greatly enhanced; but even then, with the mystery thus increased, it would contribute nothing to the problem of how the body buried can retain continuity with the body raised. The Spirit were in that case no more than the preparatory agent for bringing about gradually the event of the resurrection. On one view only could a measure of light seem to fall on this mystery of all mysteries, viz. if in any way the Spirit could be conceived as so identified with the body sown as no longer to form the Actor but the object acted upon, no longer the Sower, but in some sense the seed sown. For in that case the continuity and identity of what is sown and what rises at the end would be absolutely assured, since the Spirit is according to the judgment of Paul the absolutely Unchangeable One. This suggested solution brings us face to face with the unsolved, and perhaps unsolvable problem of the relation between the Holy Spirit *ad extra* and the Holy Spirit *immanently* considered as part in the make-up of the believer's person. Whether solvable or not, the problem, even if it promised elucidation in general, would from the terms employed in the context here be plainly eliminated as a true solvent. This will appear straightway, if once more the several elements entering into the figuratively formulated transaction be recalled. The term "naked grain" is assumed as the starting-point for this construction. This "naked grain" is explained as carrying in itself a germ, a nucleus of life, and on the same principle the body buried would have within itself the Holy Spirit as the principle or potentiality of a requickened life. Unfortunately Paul in working out the figure makes no distinction between *germ* and *seed* in such a way that the presence of the former could serve as a guarantee of the identity of the rising with the buried body. On the contrary he affirms that that which is *sown* is quickened, and precisely what is *sown* dies. The subject is the same in both propositions. And moreover, in vs. 37, instead of picturing the connection between seed and plant in terms suggested by the interpretation offered, he passes over to a totally-different train of thought. After stressing the necessity of dying previously to the possibility of quickening, the argument turns to the variegated exhibition of external clothing in the plant-world. On the theory advocated attention ought to have been immediately called to the fact that the dying is but a partial one in which the Spirit-kernel is not actually involved. Nothing of the kind is done. Neither do the terms subsequently employed fit into the theory under discussion. If the Spirit is sown as residing within the seed, then it can no longer be affirmed that what is sown is naked, for on such a view the Spirit-kernel is precisely clothed upon with the seed. Of what is sown it is emphatically affirmed that it undergoes this process in corruption, dishonor, weakness. All these and such-like things are utterly unpredicable of the Spirit, no matter, whether He be taken objectively as a divine entity, or subjectively as immanent in man. Thus, whichever way one turns, the proposed explanation proves impossible and futile. It is better to leave the matter where it is and to commit the working out of the mystery to God, who can bring about things unsearchable to the mind of man. The resurrection belongs with many other objects of eschatological faith to the region "which eye saw not, and ear heard not, and which ascended not into the heart of man."

We proceed to the discussion of the alleged third stage in the evolution of Paul's resurrection-belief. This is the stage in which the Apostle is supposed to have moved forward the endowment with a new body to the moment of *death* in case the death of his earthly body occurred before the parousia. This view is not ascribed to Paul as a firmly established conviction, but as a more or less contingent eventuality, which none the less he seriously reckoned with. The passage on which it is chiefly based is 2 Cor. v. 1-8, a context extremely difficult of interpretation, partly as a result of some uncertainties in the text, which, however, may themselves have arisen from a desire through emendation to remove exegetical or doctrinal obstacles. The best method of dealing with the passage seems to be to give first a cursory exegesis of the successive clauses, paying particular heed to their syntactical coherence, and then to sum up the results obtained in a brief paraphrase. In order that the exegesis may be conducted with the greatest degree of discrimination, it will be desirable to place clearly before our minds the traditional understanding of the words, which was common up to the time when the modern exegesis took hold of them. This old view interpreted as follows:—Paul felt himself in uncertainty as to whether he was destined to survive till the parousia or die previously to that point. If the former happened the eagerly desired heavenly body would become his immediately, and that without any strange, fearsome process of first stripping off the earthly body now clothing him. In both respects this mode of transformation appeared to him the more desirable. There would be no delay, and there would be nothing of the dread ordinarily associated with death. But in case the other alternative happened through his dying before the coming of the Lord, both of these advantages would not only be lost, there would in addition ensue the far more serious detriment of having to spend the interval between his death and the parousia in a disembodied state, a state of "nakedness" as he calls it. Confronted with these two possibilities and their differing implications, he gives voice to a strong desire for obtaining the former and escaping the latter. With the idea of a *tertium quid,* viz. that the new body could possibly become his immediately upon death, he did according to the old exegesis in no wise reckon. That which on the modern exegesis formed the very pivot of the movement of his hope, did according to the ancient exegesis never enter his mind. He had before him a maximum and a minimum; the former he preferred, but with true Christian resignation expressed himself contented with the latter, should the Lord have that in store for his servant. He could be thus contented with fulfilment of the lesser hope, because after all it had in common with the higher desire the assurance of being with Christ immediately after death, even if the supreme satisfaction of *entering* upon that blessedness *in the body* were denied him.

Proceeding now to our cursory exegesis of the complex of thought, we observe that the opening statement in vs. 1, when read in the A.V. has perhaps more than aught else in the passage given rise and encouragement to the modern interpretation: "For we know that if our earthly house of this tabernacle *were dissolved* (καταλυθῇ), we have a building from God," etc. This subjunctive "were" injects into the statement the thought of the improbability of its happening after the manner the sentence describes: *Even* if it *were,*—but it is *not likely* to happen. This rendering at the outset prejudges the Apostle's state of mind as to the outcome, and is in no wise required by the Greek text. The conjunction "if" (ἐάν) with the Aorist Subjunctive not infrequently has the force of a Future Perfect. The correct rendering accordingly would be: "We know that *in case* our earthly tent-house *shall have been* dissolved, we have a building from God," etc. The inaccuracy has been corrected by the R.V., which reads: "For we know that if the earthly house of our tabernacle *be* dissolved" ("be" instead of "were"), etc. Through this correction of the rendering the impression is made less obtrusive, as if Paul in these words reflected upon the availableness of a new body for himself in the very moment that the less desirable event of his pre-parousia death should occur. All that the words, strictly taken, mean is that the loss of the earthly body will be made up for (sooner or later) by the supervening of a wholly-differently complexioned body pertaining to another sphere, but of the time-point when this certainty shall enter into actuality, nothing is said. Nor do the words, taken by themselves, contain an intimation as to whether the "dissolution" is near or not. But, it will be asked, does not the Present Tense "we *have*" (ἔχομεν), when joined to the foregoing, imply that the new body must be in possession of the Apostle, *when* he dies; how otherwise could he declare that at the extreme moment of his earthly life he *has* it? There is more than one way to meet this difficulty. The verb "we have" can be given the sense of *assured possession,* carrying a title *de jure* to something that may or may not as yet be in existence. Or "we have" might be a case of imaginative projection into the world to come. The closing words of the verse (ἐν οὐρανοῖς) favor the latter, for they do not, of course, describe where the body now is or has been from the first. That would be a formal avowal of the preëxistence of souls, and could hardly in the Apostle's view have been confined to souls, when once embraced with regard to them. What the phrase really means is that heaven is the place in which the body, when received, will be permanently possessed, in which it will exist and move and live; that such is the correct interpretation can be verified from the corresponding phrase "earthly" (ἐπίγειος), applied by way of contrast to "tent-house" (οἰκία τοῦ σκήνους). Further, that the term "house" (οἰκία) which is the object of "we have" is used from the standpoint of the actual and permanent possession in the heavenly life, appears from the difference between it and the term "building" (οἰκοδομή) used just before. In the latter the emphasis rests on the origin of the body: it is a *building,* something constructed, hence the added words ἐκ θεοῦ; it is a building provided by God, of his own making. In the former the emphasis rests on the existence of the body as a finished product, a "house." Vs. 1, therefore, leaves it undecided when this body will be received, and in no way implies its preëxistence. The characterization of the new body as "eternal" only intends to set it off against the frail and collapsible "tent-house," serving as a figure for the earthly body. A contact for the idea of preëexistence has further been sought in the closing words of vs. 2, "our habitation from heaven." But this "from heaven" is simply another form of statement for what is called in vs. 1 "from God." The resurrection-body is from heaven because it is in a special supernatural sense from God. Heaven is the seat and source of the Pneuma by which the resurrection-body is formed.[6] On the other hand the word ἐπενδύσασθαι in this second verse is distinctly unfavorable to the view that Paul looked forward to or weighed the possibility of receiving the new body at or immediately after death. 'Ενδύσασθαι means "to put on," and ἐπενδύσασθαι signifies "to put on one garment over another garment"; it is the preposition ἐπί, that effects this plus in the meaning. The latter word expresses the same thing which in 1 Cor. xv. 53 Paul calls ἐνδύσασθαι, because there the subject of the act is the present earthly body: "this corruptible must put on incorruption, and this mortal must put on immortality." Here in 2 Cor. v, on the other hand, the subject is the *self*, the incorporeal part of the believer, conceived as already clothed upon with its present body-garment, and desiring to put on over this, as some over-garment, the eschatological body. Now, how did or could Paul conceive of the realization of this desire? The answer seems plain. He could hardly conceive of it as taking place at death, for death is precisely the putting off of the first garment hitherto worn. On such a supposition room would remain for an ἐνδύσασθαι only, no longer for an ἐπενδύσασθαι. It yields an utterly fantastic thought to assume that the Apostle expected at death to carry over, were it only for a moment, the earthly body, and then to slip on over it the new body. In such a case there would have been no real death, nothing would have remained for burial. The only way in which we can intelligibly construe for ourselves this ἐπενδύσασθαι is that it takes place at the parousia, and then, in those to whom the parousia takes place before death. Under

[6] Cp. 1 Cor. xv. 47: "the Second man is (by virtue of the resurrection) from heaven." Notice also the difference between ἐξ οὐρανοῦ (*singular*) relating to origin and ἐν τοῖς οὐρανοῖς (*plural*) of locality in vs. 1.

these circumstances alone Paul would still be wearing the old body, and therefore able to put on over it the habitation from heaven. Vs. 2, therefore, is utterly irreconcilable with the modern exegesis of a reception of the new body at death.

Vs. 3 we wish to pass by without comment for the moment, because it is exceedingly obscure, owing in part to the uncertain reading of two words, and thereby incapable of yielding any definite conclusions on the question before us. We shall revert to it presently, when endeavoring to paraphrase the passage as a whole.

Coming to vs. 4, we notice several points entirely inconsistent with the idea that Paul is thinking of something to happen at death. He declares: "We that are in the tent do groan being burdened, because we would not be unclothed, but be clothed upon, that what is mortal may be swallowed up of life." Here an alternative is formulated by Paul and a preference expressed. The alternative is between the two experiences, *first* of being unclothed, and *then* being clothed anew, and *second* of being clothed upon *immediately*. And he prefers the latter. The preference is a strong one. Under the influence of the uncertainty of its decision Paul groans. Now the question arises: Does this situation fit the case of the bestowal of a new body at the moment of death or the case of the bestowal of it at the parousia? In answer let us make clear to ourselves that the groaning and the strong preference become entirely unintelligible, if we conceive Paul thinking of both members of this alternative as attached to the moment of death. For, how could the resolution of such an alternative *in articulo mortis* become to him a matter of burdensome uncertainty? It would have certainly been regarded by him as pertaining to the formalities of getting into the proper apparel for a solemn occasion; in both cases the outcome would have been precisely the same. If once it were fixed that the new body comes immediately, it certainly, in comparison with that tremendous fact, must have appeared a matter of slight importance, whether it immediately (with the smallest of intervals between) shall succeed the old body, or shall, casting a veil over all that goes on beneath, swallow up the old body, absorbing it, as it were, into itself. For one who was assured that death without fail would bring with itself the new body, it would seem pusillanimous to groan on account of the trifling question whether the instantaneous occurrence should take place one way or the other. Paul was, with his entire periculous and painful life-experience behind him, hardly the man to let his mind be distracted to the point of groaning fear over such matters. All this vexing uncertainty and painful weighing of a small issue must have lacked real importance for a man of his temperament. The fear of death *per se,* as a momentary experience we have no reason to ascribe to him. It follows, therefore, that the strong sense of uneasiness and the strong preference expressed must have revolved around another, far more serious and solemn question, viz. would there be or would there not be awaiting him in the near future a *protracted* state of being unclothed, that is "naked" between his possible death and the arrival of the parousia? The uncertainty, therefore, arising from this can not stand in direct contradiction to the "we know" in vs. 1; in other words "we know" can not, consistently with what follows, carry the meaning: we know that we receive a new body *at the time of death.* Such a conviction would from the outset have rendered all subsequent burdensomeness and groaning out of place. The simple sense of the verse is, as above intimated: in a general way Paul affirms that instead of the tent dissolved a new structure will be received, but he does not indicate here when or how it will be given.

It is said that vs. 5 proves the "being clothed upon" to be in Paul's view the common lot of all believers, because of the statement "He that wrought us for this very thing is God." The plural "us" is on this view understood of all Christians. Likewise the further words "who gave us the earnest of the Spirit" are taken to bear out this exegesis, since all Christians are recipients of the Spirit and must consequently share in what this gift is the pledge of. He could not have affirmed these things, had he confined the "being clothed upon" to those found alive at the parousia. To this our answer is that from the "us" and the statement concerning the gift of the Spirit as an earnest, no such conclusion can be legitimately drawn. Even if Paul does not use "us" here as a rhetorical plural, but actually includes all believers, this simply shows how he lived in the expectation, that the parousia might still find the great majority of the Christians of his day alive, and looked upon the cases of those who died in the interval as exceptions. After all, he could just as well say of believers in general, that they had been prepared by God to be "clothed upon," at the last day, as he could on the hypothesis under review affirm of his readers collectively, using the word "us," that they had been prepared of God for investment with a new body *at death,* for on every view he must have been aware that some would be found alive at the parousia, whom God could not have prepared for that peculiar experience, and to whom He could not have given the Spirit as an earnest for such experience. We have answered this argument on the assumption, that "this very thing" (αὐτὸ τοῦτο) in vs. 5 actually refers to the "being clothed upon," as excluding the "being clothed" of vs. 4. Of course, the affirmative answer brings us face to face with the difficult question, how Paul could so positively affirm that God had prepared the majority of the then living believers to survive till the parousia, then to be changed in the way indicated by "being clothed upon." For this reason we feel inclined to give to "this very thing" another reference. For the present, however, it suffices to have shown, that the usual interpretation of vs. 5 does not compel us to place the "clothing upon" at death.

Finally, vss. 6-8 are said to demand the modern exegesis. Here Paul declares himself of good courage, because immediately after death he will be with the Lord: to be at home in the body is to be absent from the Lord, whilst to be absent from the body is to be at home with the Lord. And this goal of his desire which he expects to reach at death is taken as identical with what is described in vss. 2 and 4 as the "being clothed upon," because by means of "therefore" it is connected with the foregoing: "Being *therefore* always of good courage," etc. Hence the conclusion drawn runs as follows: the being at home with the Lord is effected through the "being clothed upon" at death. To this we reply as follows: Paul's good courage in view of the fact that to die means to be at home with the Lord attaches itself to the preceding context in the *general import* of the latter, a general import that found clearest expression in iv. 17, 18 and v. 1. The *general* proposition, in regard to which Paul felt absolute assurance, was that after the present affliction, or in reward for it, there is eternal glory in store for the believer, and more specifically that, after this earthly tent-body shall have been dissolved, the believer will be put in possession of an eternal heavenly body. As to the *secondary* question, whether this consummate state of glory would be reached with or without an intervening period of nakedness of death, as to this Paul felt no conviction, either one way or the other, but only a desire and a preference. Hence he contents himself with expressing this preferential desire as growing out of a strong dislike of the state of nakedness. Now, inasmuch as his assurance on the general question far outweighed the uncertainty on that one particular point, Paul could, notwithstanding the unresolved doubt of vss. 2, 4, proceed in vs. 6 with the declaration, that he was always of good courage. Of course, he had to put the ground of his good courage under the circumstances in the form of the *minimum* of what he felt sure about; he could not say: we are always of good courage, because to be absent from the earthly body means to be put immediately in possession of the heavenly body. His uncertainty as to whether he would survive till the parousia forbade him that. Therefore he says only as much as he could with full certainty profess: to be absent from the body is to be at home with the Lord. Even in case that happened which appeared to him the less desirable, he would still be contented, because in this being with the Lord everything else was potentially given. Looking at it closely, the words of vss. 6-8 even seem to disparage the idea of the new body being given at death. He speaks here of death as meaning absence from the body. Of course, he means *the earthly body*; yet he would scarcely have expressed himself precisely thus, had he meant that immediately another body would be substituted, for the state in such a new body would hardly be describable as the state of one absent from the body. And likewise the phrase "to be present with the Lord" is so general that Paul, had he had in mind the presence with Christ in the new glorified body, would in all probability have chosen a more definite mode of expression in contrast to that of "being absent from the body." Our conclusion, therefore, is that vss. 6-8 do not favor the exegesis under review.

We must now look for a moment at the passage as a whole, and in connection with this at the difficult vs. 3, in order to grasp the import of the entire section, and thus to gather in the fruit of our somewhat laborious exegesis. The passage connects with iv. 17, 18 by means of "for" (γάρ): "*For* we know that in case our earthly tent-house shall have been dissolved, we have a building from God," etc. Chapter iv. 17, 18 affirm that the "affliction" in the body works out an eternal weight of glory, likewise to be enjoyed in the body, since there, in the body, the "affliction" was borne. The future body thus appears from the outset as the bearer of an eternal weight of glory. The knowledge that such a new body shall be ours is basic for the hope of possessing and enjoying the certainty of this eternal glory. Without such a center the glory could not exist. Especially the description of this new body as a "house" admirably fits into this train of thought, because a house is not a mere place of shelter, but has attached to it the aesthetic conception of a center of manifestation for the glory of its inhabitant. The next verse joins to this, by means of "*καὶ γάρ*," as a further basis of the conviction expressed in the "we know" of vs. 1, the circumstance that "we groan desiring to be clothed upon with our habitation from heaven.[7] Such an ardent, groaning longing affords a particularly strong

[7] **Καὶ** γάρ is stronger than the simple γάρ: "for verily."

ground for the assurance that a heavenly body must be appointed for us. This would not follow, of course, if the longing were of the nature of a purely-subjective sentiment or aspiration. In the present case it *does* follow, because, being worked in the believer by the Spirit, it becomes divinely prophetic of what is actually in store for him. The idea is that the Christian is so eagerly desirous of the succedence of the heavenly body, if possible, without the intervening of any period of bodiless existence, as to justify the conclusion that the Spirit's hand is discernible in this. The ardency and eagerness of the desire are guarantees of its divine origination. Paul continues, "in this we groan." Some render by "in this (tent)" referring back to vs. 1. This construction is somewhat favored by vs. 4 where the same thought is expressed as follows: "for we that are in this tent do groan." It is quite possible, however, to render: "*in this respect* we groan, that we long to be clothed upon."

The foregoing brings us to the difficult vs. 3. There are two points of uncertainty in the reading of this verse: (1) the conjunction introducing the sentence is in some MSS. εἴ γε (or εἴ γε καί), in others εἴ περ; (2) the participle following this conjunction is read in some authorities ἐνδυσάμενοι, in others ἐκδυσάμενοι. The evidence seems to be in favor of εἴ γε καὶ ἐνδυσάμενοι οὐ γυμνοὶ εὑρεθησόμεθα. But it is extremely difficult, on any view taken of the passage as a whole, to fit these words into the context with an intelligible result. The modern exegesis above criticized would take it as follows: the verse assigns the reason for the longing to be clothed upon at death: having put the (new) body on we shall not then be found naked. For in that case there will be no interval of disembodied existence. So far as thought is concerned, and taken by itself, this would yield appropriate sense. The fatal objection to it is that it takes ἐνδύσασθαι in the same sense as belongs specifically to ἐπενδύσασθαι. Now the latter is used vss. 2 and 4 with pointed emphasis upon the ἐπί, so as to compel the express understanding that it is not identical with ἐνδύσασθαι, but rather its opposite, if not in result, yet surely in method of procedure. This being so, we may say that Paul, in order to express the thought attributed to him by this new exegesis, would in all likelihood have repeated the word ἐπενδύσασθαι in its participial form; he would have said "we long to be clothed upon, since *having been clothed upon* we shall not be found naked." The verb which has but one prepositional prefix is distinguished from the doubly compound one in this very vital respect, that it does not imply the guarantee for the avoidance of "nakedness," inasmuch as it does not fix the point for the "putting on" as coinciding with the moment of death. We are bound, therefore, to take ἐνδυσάμενοι as different from ἐπενδυσάμενοι. But what the clause means, if the distinction be insisted upon, as we believe it must, appears difficult to tell. Under these circumstances we prefer, instead of wrestling with the text in order to extract from it some sort of meaning, such as will at best induce half-acceptance, to try how far the difficulty admits of relief by adopting the other reading with ἐκδυσάμενοι instead of ἐνδυσάμενοι.[8] With this combined with either εἴ γε καί or εἴ περ ("although"), we can reach comparative clearness. The sole warrant always for changing the text, either by pure emendation, or through adoption of some other, perhaps less-strongly attested, reading, is the discovery that the adopted modifica-

[8] Of course, it is not impossible for a skillful exegete, who finds himself in an impasse of this kind, to extort from the text some tolerable sense, sacrificing all naturalness of expression to the one desire of making the words say anything at all. As an example of this sort of exegesis the following might be offered: We long to be clothed upon through reaching the parousia alive, thus avoiding the interval of nakedness, since also, after having "put on" at that point, we shall not henceforth be found naked at our entrance upon the eternal state. In other words, since such is our ultimate destiny in any event, even though we may have to attain unto it through death, and subsequent nakedness and ultimate putting on of the body, rather than by instantaneous putting on of the new over the old, nevertheless we can not help continue longing for the *ante mortem* parousia-investment, because that reaches the eventual goal in the shortest and easiest manner. This exegesis, it will be perceived, separates the καί from the εἴ γε and joins καί closely to ἐνδυσάμενοι. It certainly is ingenious; but is it not too ingenious to invite confident acceptance?

tion suddenly lets in light where before darkness prevailed. Such is the case here. Ἔι γε καὶ ἐκδυσάμενοι yields "if so be that *also*, having put off this body (i.e., having died), we shall not *in the end* be found naked, our "being clothed upon" taking place at the general resurrection. Taking the other conjunction εἴ περ we obtain the following rendering: "although even having put off this body (died) we shall not ultimately be found naked."[9]

Vs. 4 takes up vs. 2 again, elaborating further the same thought there expressed, whence in the same manner the verse is introduced by καὶ γάρ. The groaning, though it be a groaning caused by uncertainty as to the how or when, nevertheless conveys assurance so far as the simple fact of ultimate attainment is concerned. The "being burdened" here by no means excludes the "we know" of vs. 1, as it would do on the modern interpretation.

In connection with vs. 5 we encountered a difficulty, left for the time to one side. Here is the place to consider it. It consisted in the problem, how the "this very thing" could be referred to the immediately preceding "clothed upon"?[10] How could Paul so objectively affirm that God had purposed and prepared him and his readers for "being clothed upon," if at the same time he continued in uncertainty, as to whether he was to attain it or not? That for which God prepares believers can scarcely be considered a matter of doubt, and conversely, if the point was subject to doubt, Paul could scarcely affirm that God had prepared him and the others for it. We suggested at the previous point a removal of the difficulty by making "this very thing" refer back not to the immediately preceding "clothed upon," but to the general thought dominating the whole preceding context, viz. that *in one way or*

[9] The conjunctival combination εἴ περ has in older Greek (Homer) not infrequently the sense of "although." Occasionally it retains this force in later Greek also.

[10] The difficulty here considered is, it will be observed, a difficulty which the old and the new exegesis equally encounter. Both must admit that in vs. 4 Paul expresses a *doubt,* and seek some reconciliation with the "we know" of vs. 1.

another the Christian is sure to obtain a new body. The question remains, however, whether "this very thing" is not too pointed and emphatic for reference to this general idea. For this reason we now offer for consideration the reference of these words not to the "being clothed upon," but to "we groan." The "groaning" is on this view taken as the very thing for which God has prepared the believer, which He causes to issue from his heart, whence also it has a prophetic significance, becomes a confirmation of the assurance that he shall obtain the heavenly body.

We have now at some length discussed the chief passage supposed to contain the proof that Paul had undergone a change in his eschatological outlook, and have found it inadequate, nay implausible at many a point. The other passages to which appeal is made for the same purpose are less involved and consequently more easily disposed of. In Rom. viii. 19 Paul declares: "the earnest expectation of the creation waiteth for the revealing (ἀποκάλυψις) of the sons of God." What will happen at the end is here called a "revealing" of the sons of God, not because their somatic glory preëxisted, and hence needed no more than a momentary flashing forth into light. The reason is a quite different one. It is none other than that their status as sons of God with all privileges attached, such as freedom and heirship, existed before, but had not been openly demonstrated. Not their celestial body, but their supreme sonship was in hiding. It is this *status* that will be revealed, and this revelation will be accomplished, by laying upon them the glory, the medium for whose manifestation, to be sure, is the body of the resurrection. For doing this, however, the body needed no previous existence. Paul does not even say that the glorious body will be revealed, but that the sons of God will be revealed, or, what amounts to the same thing, that the glory will be revealed "to us" (vs. 18).[11] Because the resurrection is a revelation of sonship (not of a hitherto hidden body), it can be also called the "adoption of sons"

[11] Notice the preposition εἰς ἡμᾶς, not ἐν ἡμῖν.

(υἱοθεσία). That not merely the bringing to light of an already existing body, but its real formation is referred to follows from the coincidence of the redemption of the body with the deliverance of the whole creation from the bondage of corruption. Still another passage appealed to (Col. iii. 3, 4) speaks of the life hid with Christ in God, and of the manifestation of believers with Christ in glory at the time of Christ's own manifestation. "Life" does not here necessarily imply somatic existence so that the hidden presence of a body for each believer in Christ would be affirmed. It is true the manifestation of believers together with the manifestation of Christ Himself in glory presupposes that they will, when manifested, possess a body to make them manifest *as Christ will be manifest through his body.* But it by no means follows from this that they possessed this body previously, simply because Christ possessed his previously to the joint-manifestation. The contrast between the hidden state and the manifested state has not the body for its subject, but the life of the believer. This life is first hid with Christ, because it is a disembodied life; at the last day it will become manifest through union with the eschatological body. For in the world to come all things are manifest and provided with the proper organs for being so.

In addition to the foregoing we note that the advocates of the modified resurrection-doctrine are compelled to admit an inconsistency on Paul's part even during the stage of development assumed for this third period. In this very chapter the Apostle speaks of the fact that all believers must be made manifest before the judgment-seat of Christ. The manner in which this is referred to shows that it contemplates a collective manifestation. We have already seen that in the preceding context the Apostle speaks of his conviction, that God, who raised up the Lord Jesus, will also raise him (Paul) up with Jesus, and present him together with the Corinthians. We may further compare Phil. iii. 20, 21: "For our commonwealth is in heaven; whence also we wait for a Saviour, the Lord Jesus Christ, who shall fashion anew the body of our humiliation, that it may be conformed to the body of his glory, according to the working whereby He is able even to subject all things to Himself." This last passage also suggests an answer to the question, why, if the new body is a product of the Pneuma, the believer should have to wait for it until the parousia, whilst the Pneuma is his already during the present life. The Spirit's work in the renewal of things proceeds according to a fixed, systematic method, in certain distinct stages. First it takes effect in the sphere of the inner man. Its laying hold on the outward man has to wait till the bodily appearance of Christ on earth. The "working whereby He is able to subject all things to Himself" will then draw within the sphere of its operation that whole visible external realm to which the body belongs. Consequently there is nothing arbitrary in the postponement of the transformation of the body till the parousia, nothing that could be called inconsistent with the Pauline doctrine of the present possession by believers of the Spirit.

There still remains to be looked into the fourth and most revolutionary extreme supposed to have been reached by Paul in his concept of the resurrection. This is the stage in which he is claimed to have reached the idea of an actual preformation of the new body within the believer during the course of the latter's earthly life. This lies so much on the line of the construction built on 2 Cor. v, that it must create wonder that the Apostle did not, once having reached this novel concept, consistently adhere to it, but fixed soon after upon the moment of death as the proper point for bringing the new body into existence. For it is chiefly in Chap. iii of the same Epistle that this extreme view is found. There is surely a hysteron-proteron here. The words which in Chap. iii are believed to speak of the mystical process in question are found in vss. 17-18: "Now the Lord is the Spirit: and where the Spirit of the Lord is there is liberty. But we all with unveiled face beholding as in a mirror (or reflecting as a mirror) the glory of the Lord, are transformed into the same image from glory to glory, even as from the Lord the Spirit," with which are to be compared the words in vs. 16 of the next chapter: "Wherefore we faint not; but, though our outward man is decaying, yet our inward man is renewed day by day." In judging of the exegesis imposed upon these statements, it should not be forgotten that the uniform testimony on the time-question runs squarely athwart such an opinion as is thus ascribed to Paul, for everywhere he excludes the earthly life-course from the resurrection-process, even there where according to some he places it at the moment of death. His tenses in speaking of the supreme event are throughout future; cp. Rom. viii. 11; Gal. vi. 8; 1 Cor. xv (*passim*); 2 Cor. v. 1-10; Phil. iii. 20, 21. If now in the context of 2 Cor. iii and iv a different conception of such a radically reversional type actually confronted us, the utmost we could say would be that the Apostle in these isolated moments, in a fit of rapture, as it were, had been raised to such mystical heights, as in this case to be swept entirely out of the consistency of a uniform doctrine. But even to assume this involves considerable difficulty. The assumption would lead us to expect that Paul would have from this point onwards at least made consistent progress along the line indicated. If between First and Second Corinthians he advanced sufficiently to move the point of the resurrection backwards from the parousia to the death of individuals, and even at certain moments by a flash of pneumatic illumination was given to believe that the formation of a new body is now already imperceptibly going on within the Christian, then we would surely expect that between that date and Philippians he would have made still further progress, and attained the last result of this development as an assured possession. As a matter of fact we find the very opposite. Philippians would suffice to disillusion us in this respect for it proves that the Apostle did *ex hypothesi* not only halt in his development, but surrendered the newly-gained ground by most distinctly placing the transformation of the body at the parousia. For this reason it is unlikely that even as isolated extreme modes of statement the passages cited can bear the interpretation put upon them. 2 Cor. iii.

18 speaks of the glory into which believers are changed by beholding as in a mirror (or, according to another rendering, "reflecting as mirrors") the glory of the Lord. This glory into which they are transfigured is meant to be set in contrast to the glory that shone upon the face of Moses, when descending from the mount of God. Now, inasmuch as with Moses this was a visible, bodily glory, it might be thought that with reference to believers it must be of the same nature, the more so, since "glory" (δόξα) has in most cases eschatological associations relating to the body. None the less the context shows that in the present case Paul attached a different meaning to the word, viz. the idea of an inward glory of illumination by the Spirit of God. It was not the body of Moses as a whole that shone but his face, the organ of vision. Christians likewise receive this glory through beholding it; it is the face which is the organ of its absorption. This takes place "with uncovered face" (ἀνακεκαλυμμένῳ προσώπῳ). To speak more literally, it is the *Gospel* by which this mysterious process is mediated, whence the Apostle calls it in iv. 4 "the gospel of the glory of Christ." The Gospel corresponds to the veiled countenance of Moses, so far as the perishing are concerned, in whom the god of this world (Satan) has blinded the minds of the unbelieving. At his conversion God shined into Paul's heart" in order that *the Apostle by his preaching might impart to others the illumination of the knowledge of the glory of God* πρὸς φωτισμὸν τῆς γνώσεως τῆς δόξης τοῦ θεοῦ *in the face of Jesus Christ.*" This beholding of the glory through a mirror is something that belongs, dispensationally speaking, to the present state, for in 1 Cor. xiii. 12, Paul pointedly distinguishes between the vision "in a riddle" (ἐν αἰνίγματι) and the vision "face to face," which latter is reserved for the end, with which further agrees 2 Cor. v. 7, according to which believers walk through the land of faith, not as yet through the land of sight. All this points to the conclusion, that in the context of the passage under examination a peculiar turn is given to the concept of "glory," a turn by which it is placed in the sphere of "knowledge"

(γνῶσις). This is confirmed by the fact that iii. 7 names as one of the concomitants of the state in which the transfiguration takes place "liberty," which "liberty" also in Rom. viii. 21 appears connected with the "glory." If the above interpretation be correct, we may conclude that the "glory" spoken of in our passage has nothing to do with the body, but is an inward state, specifically belonging to the sphere of supernatural knowledge.

Even less ground is there to find in the verses 2 Cor. iv. 16-18 the idea of a present transformation of the body within, while the old earthly body still continues to drape the inner man. Here the resurrection is in the context explicitly placed at the end, vs. 14: "knowing that He who raised up the Lord Jesus shall raise up us also, and shall present us with you." What has misled many here is that in the preceding context Paul speaks of the manifestation of the life of Jesus in "his mortal flesh," i.e. his body. But his speaking in terms of *sarx* suffices to show that he can not have meant thereby the transformation of the body, since that could come about only through the putting aside of the mortal flesh, and could never be called a "manifestation of life in the flesh." What the Apostle hints at by these expressions is the preservation of his life in the midst of the deadly perils spoken of in vss. 8, 9. He describes these in vs. 10 as an "always bearing about in the body the dying (νέκρωσις) of Jesus. "But, while it would be a mistake to identify this sustaining operation of divine power with the body-forming operation of the Spirit, there appears, nevertheless, and this is the element of truth in the fantastic view propounded, a real connection between the death-entailing experiences of the Apostle's labors and the ultimate resurrection. In vs. 14, in the closest dependence on the register of persecution and affliction written in the foregoing, Paul declares: "Knowing that He that raised up the Lord Jesus shall raise up us also with Jesus." What is the mysterious connection here obviously implied? It must be sought on the negative, not on the positive side. The process of resurrection from its inherent nature has two sides, the stripping off of the flesh and the endowment of the believer with a pneumatic *soma.* From the negative point of view it could be truly affirmed that the resurrection-process was in operation: room was being made for the new body through the gradual removal of the old. But this is something far different from the assumption of the development of a new body within the old. On its negative side the disintegration of the old structure could also be interpreted as a prophecy of the rearing of the new building appointed to take its place. From the actual erection of the latter, however, this remains different. In this negative sense only the Apostle could say to his readers: "So then *death* works in us but *life* in you." The bodily life God sustained in Paul was the same life that enabled him to labor for the Corinthians. And he labored for them, certainly not by means of a mysterious invisible, embryonic corporeity built up within, but in no other way than by means of the present natural life of the body, in which he was undergoing hardships for their sake. Nor do the statements of vss. 16 and 17 compel us to think of a present bodily glory inwrought in Paul: the outward man, he declares, is decaying, the inward man is renewed day by day. For "the inward man" does not signify here a composite human person, consisting of the *Pneuma* plus a new body. It stands for the Spirit as distinguished from the present fleshly body. If the other view were correct, if ὁ ἔσω (or, ἔσωθεν) ἄνθρωπος meant spirit and body combined, then its opposite ὁ ἔξω ἄνθρωπος ought likewise to signify the natural spirit and body combined, whereas the context shows that it does stand for the bodily life alone. In the other two passages where ὁ ἔσω ἄνθρωπος is spoken of (Rom. vii. 22; Eph. iii. 16), there can be no doubt about Paul's referring to the inner spiritual part of man by itself and not including a new body. But this renewal of the inner man mentioned in vs. 16 is the beginning of the eschatological glory in its future sense. That here the future glory must be meant follows from the manner in which the light affliction is spoken of as lasting but for a moment; its momentariness is contrasted with the eternal character of the glory, and this contrast involves the contrast between present and future. On the principle of gracious recompense the affliction here endured works out for the eternal world, a superabundant weight of "glory." For the present, therefore, he speaks of the renewal of the inner man only. When speaking of the weight of glory comprehensively it is in contrast with the present, as of something that does not exist at the moment of speaking, but which is being laid up (not actually *in preparation*), something which the present tribulation creates the title for.[12]

[12] Along another line of approach the present preparation of the resurrection-body might be, and actually has been, postulated from what in two contexts the Apostle says concerning the "sowing" of the old body and the new body to be harvested from it (Gal. vi. 7, 8 and 1 Cor. xv. 36ff). It is plain that in Galatians the figure has nothing to do with internal bodily metamorphosis, but with ethico-religious conduct determining the eschatological issue on the principle of reward, not by physical nexus. As to 1 Cor. xv. 36ff., here the extreme end of earthly life (the burial) is spoken of, and for a previous extensive process of preparation there is no room. Only by making (like Calvin) the sowing cover the entire preceding life could the desired inference of an earlier fashioning of a new body within be drawn. The whole theory of present pre-eschatological formation of a body within a body savors of the fantastic. It reminds curiously of what was the primitive Greek conception of the soul, viz. not that of a spiritual entity within a material one, but that of a complete somatico-pneumatic interior entity within the exterior entity, a whole man within a whole man (cp. the description of primitive Greek psychology in Rhode's *Psyche*). From that to Paul's refined psychology, there is, of course, a far cry. It must be admitted, however, that, considering the question from the standpoint of pure exegesis, Calvin may claim support from the representation in 1 Cor. xv. The sowing precedes the dying in the plant: vs. 36, "is not quickened except it die." But it by no means follows from this that the inseparableness of the two involves in the corresponding spiritual process the same chronological sequence requiring a sowing on the part of man prior to his death. The correspondence, when put to such use, also halts in this point, that the requisite dying in the plant is not a momentary thing as the death of man is, but a gradual process of decomposition in the ground. Fixing the starting-point of *before* and *after* thus, it is no longer self-evident, that man must sow his resurrection-body before his death and burial. It must further be conceded that the qualities enumerated in vss. 42-44 favor somewhat a "sowing" during life. At least "dishonor" and "weakness" do. "Corruption" is more neutral because it can be said no less of the dead body than of the living body. What most favors Calvin's view is the phrase σῶμα ψυχικόν which can hardly apply to the dead body, but can be quite properly said of the living body before death.

CHAPTER VIII

THE RESURRECTION-CHANGE

So far as the Apostle's recorded teaching is concerned this subject of the resurrection-change relates to believers, both those whom the Lord's parousia will find living, and those whom at His advent He will raise from the dead. The changing is so intimately related to and connected with the agency of the Pneuma, that this of itself would exclude from its consideration the problem of what takes place in those raised not for an eternal Pneumatic state of blessedness, but for a subsequent state of punishment. It is true that the common earthly corporeity would as little fit in with a permanent destructive environment and its forces of perdition, as the same kind of corporeity would be adapted to the surroundings and powers of the eternal life that awaits believers. Leaving this question to one side because of its speculative and purely-inferential character through lack of exegetical data, the ulterior question may be raised, whether the change, as it affects believers, is substantially distinct from the process of the resurrection itself. The right of the distinction rests on the difference between the two situations in which those subject to the resurrection and those subject to the change find themselves. The former issue from a state of death, the latter, though already in possession of the Pneuma, nevertheless will exist as to their bodies in a condition of un-pneumatic life, and this postulates in their case the change as a distinct separate event. It is an event not mixed with any other process. On the other hand, the change in those raised does not partake of such separate, self-contained character: it is, as it were, swallowed up by the larger, more comprehensive event of the resurrection itself. We nowhere get the impression as though the believing dead were first in a purely negative manner restored to an as yet unchanged form of bodily life, and then through the superimposition of a second positive act made partakers of a transformed corporeal constitution. This would be a mechanical procedure. We may *a priori* expect that the Spirit will not in this respect deny his own nature, which loves organic procedure in all redemptive operations.

There are four passages which deal with the destiny and experience of believers *found living* at the parousia; these are 1 Thess. iv. 15-17; 1 Cor. xv. 51-53; 2 Cor. v. 1-5; Phil. iii. 20, 21. The first of these does not speak of any change; it simply affirms, that the living, after the previous raising of the dead, shall together with the latter be caught up in the clouds, to meet the Lord in the air. Without due warrant it has been inferred from this that at the time of writing Paul had not as yet developed his doctrine of a change in the resurrection-body, and consequently did not expect a corresponding change in the living either. But the question of change was altogether beside the point at issue in this connection, and the change for the dead is implied and guaranteed by the assumption of the presence of the Pneuma, which, as shown before, underlies their in-being in Christ even in the interval between death and resurrection. And, if the dead in being raised undergo a change, then we may count it certain that the same was believed by Paul as regards the living, who shared the same in-being and its cause, the activity of the Spirit. Of this change the other three passages speak explicitly. 2 Cor. v. 1-5 has already been discussed in detail. It contains the figure of the "ἐπενδύσασθαι" by the believer of the heavenly body over the earthly body, in result of which what is mortal (i.e. the earthly body) will be swallowed up of life.[1] The peculiarity of this representation is that it starts with the new body and makes the other body be absorbed by the former, but by the terms of the figure this particular mode of the process, is, of course, confined to such as are found living at the parousia; the others are only "clothed," not "clothed upon." That the several contrasts drawn in vss. 1 and 2 ascribe to the post-resurrection body a constitution wholly different from that

[1] **Καταποθῇ**, literally; "Drunk down so as to disappear."

possessed by the former body is plain at a glance. The former is no longer "earthly," has no longer the nature of a "tabernacle," but is a solid structure to be possessed and used in heaven forever, for this is what "eternal in the heavens" means. This radically altered condition, affirmed as a fact, involves that some change producing it must have taken place, and this applies to both classes here reckoned with by Paul, the living and the raised, since it is affirmed in its generality. In the other two passages, 1 Cor. xv. 51-53 and Phil. iii. 20, 21 the representation starts from the old body and makes this to be changed into the new body. There is no contradiction in this. Both are figurative and in so far, when each is taken by itself, inadequate representations. How little the two are mutually exclusive appears from the fact that in 2 Cor. v. 1-5 they appear side by side in "ἐπενδύσασθαι" and "καταλυθῇ."

Between 1 Cor. xv and Phil. iii. a disagreement has been discovered, and on the basis of this an argument constructed against the genuineness of Philippians.[2] It has been urged that according to Philippians the *identical body* of our humiliation is changed, whilst according to 1 Corinthians *we ourselves* are changed, and the earthly body is done away with. This also, however, amounts to nothing more than a verbal difference inseparable from the limitations of figurative expression. On the one hand the "μετασχηματισμός" of Phil. iii involves a doing away with the body of humiliation; on the other hand the doing away with the body of flesh and blood may not be understood in such a sense as to destroy the continuity between the old body and the new. Granting the point that Paul here says "*we* shall be changed," he likewise uses the alternate representation that "the corruptible must put on incorruption." Whether one says: the body of humiliation is transformed into a body of glory, or says, the corruptible puts on incorruption, the mortal immortality, makes no difference whatever as to the principle of continuity. In neither case is there any emphasis upon the perpetuation of

[2] Hoekstra in *Theol. Tydsch.* 1875, p. 443.

the substance which changes its σχῆμα or of the old garment which puts on over itself the new. When the Apostle says in 1 Cor. vii. 31 παράγει τὸ σχῆμα τοῦ κόσμου τούτου, he surely does not mean to affirm that the *substance* of the present world will abide. Even so in Philippians the point at issue is not the substance but the "σχῆμα," the contrast lying between "ταπείνωσις" and "δόξα."[3]

That a change will take place inherent in the resurrection-act for believers that are raised follows not only from explicit or more or less implicit statements, but rests besides on the stronger ground of the analogy between the resurrection of Jesus and that of believers which Paul throughout presupposes. According to Rom. i. 1-4, while the identical Jesus who had been buried rose from the grave, yet it was by no means the same Jesus in the endowment and equipment of his human nature. Not only a new status had been acquired through the resurrection: new qualities amounting to a reconstructed adjustment to the future heavenly environment had been wrought in Him by the omnipotent power of God: He had been determined (declared effectually) the Son of God with power according to the Spirit of Holiness, by the resurrection from the dead.[4] It is self-evident that these words do not refer to any religious or ethical transformation which Jesus in the resurrection had to undergo. Such a thought nowhere finds support in Paul's Christology, nor in his general teaching. Only, in the quite justifiable eagerness for excluding this, there is too narrow an interpretation put upon the sentence, as though it meant to affirm a purely bodily transformation. The other, psychical, side of our Lord's human nature was obviously affected no less than the physical side. This comprehensive change was inseparable from the resurrection itself; it was not an additional element, but an

[3] Cp. on the other hand 2 Cor. xi. 13-15, where the emphasis rests on the real character of Satan remaining the same, when he changes his σχῆμα into an angel of light.

[4] Cp. what is taught in 1 Cor. xv. 45-49 concerning the new constitution and image of the Second Adam, in terms which by no means are exhausted through a purely physical reference.

integral part of the first and only act required. Had this been lacking, then not the resurrection, but the subsequent transformation ought to have furnished the pattern upon which the soteric renewal of believers was fashioned. As it is the Pauline formula reads "raised with Christ," and of this generic designation of the renewal of the Christian the particular form "changed with Christ" could be only a specific variation.

As to how the mysterious process of this "change," where it appears by itself, apart from the resurrection, will take place we gain from the Apostle's figurative statements no more concrete information than we do on the corresponding problem of the mode of change in the resurrection. The question may, however, be put, as to whether Paul knows and uses a generic term descriptive of both, at any rate closely analogous, transactions. Does he designate both by the common term ἀλλάττεσθαι or μετασχηματίζεσθαι? The answer to this depends on the exegesis of 1 Cor. xv. 51-53 and Phil. iii. 20, 21. In 2 Cor. v. 1-5, as we have seen, the figure brings it about that both are formally distinguished, the one being named an ἐνδύσασθαι, the other an ἐπενδύσασθαι. But in the other two passages it is not uniformly recognized that such a distinctive way of speaking is actually present. Some interpreters understand the terminology used here comprehensively of all believers, those dead and those found living, others more narrowly apply it to the latter group only. The question is of some importance, because, if we adopt the former view, it would yield one more ground of assurance for the continuity of the new body with the old. For when Paul says—δεῖ τὸ φθαρτὸν τοῦτο ἐνδύσασθαι ἀφθαρσίαν καὶ τὸ θνητὸν τοῦτο . . . ἀθανασίαν, and we are warranted in applying this to the resurrection as well as to the change, then it will follow that in the resurrection the old body will play its part, that it will be there as an ἐνδυσάμενον, as something that "puts on for itself," in other words that we are not justified in thinking of it as simply the endowment of the soul with a new body, altogether without connection with the old body laid in the grave. The choice is, especially with reference to 1 Cor. xv. 51-53, a difficult one. It turns on the interpretation of the words: πάντες οὐ κοιμηθησόμεθα, πάντες δὲ ἀλλαγησόμεθα. If the more usual construction of οὐ be followed, the statement will mean: *it is true of all of us* that we shall not sleep, but be changed. This could mean nothing else than that Paul expected all his readers to survive till the parousia. On this view, further, the words οὐ κοιμηθησόμεθα may still have a twofold sense. They may affirm: we shall not fall asleep (die) between now and the parousia, but be changed at the parousia; the alternative view makes the clause mean: we all of us shall not at the parousia first have to fall asleep (die), but we shall all be changed directly at that time without such an intermediate experience. The difficulty in the way of this first exegesis, in either of its forms, is that the forecast has not been fulfilled. Neither Paul, nor any of those living when he wrote has reached the parousia in the body. He said of all: οὐ κοιμηθησόμεθα; in reality all ἐκοιμήθησαν. This difficulty is all the greater, since Paul does not seem to give expression here to a mere subjective hope or opinion, but explicitly characterizes the statement as a "μυστηριον," something received by revelation: ἰδοὺ μυστήριον ὑμῖν λέγω. In order to avoid this difficulty Meyer assumes Paul to have silently supplied with the subject πάντες the qualification "all who shall be left at the parousia," and understands the statement in the second sense indicated above, i.e., as a declaration to the effect that those left at the parousia will not then have first to die. If we adopt this view, the form in which Meyer presents it seems a fairly plausible one. The "μυστήριον" does not then refer to the fact that all shall survive, but only to the fact that those who do survive, more or less numerous or more or less soon, shall not have to die, but will be changed as living persons. And when Paul speaks in the first person plural, as though he himself and his readers were concerned in this, it is not necessary to ascribe this chiefly to individual curiosity, nor need the form of statement be considered a purely-rhetorical plural; it may be set down to the common hope of all Christians at that time of being perhaps permitted to survive till the parousia. The advantage of this view is that it enables us to take the verb ἀλλαγησόμεθα in the same sense in both vs. 51 and vs. 52, in each case with restricted reference to those found living. The loss in pregnancy of meaning lies in this that it ceases to throw light on the change of body involved in the resurrection from the dead. Plainly in vs. 53 the Apostle uses the word with this restricted application, for, distinguishing two groups, he says: *οἱ νεκροὶ ἐγερθήσονται . . . καὶ ἡμεῖς ἀλλαγησόμεθα.* On the other hand it must be confessed, that the silent supplementing of such a qualification as Meyer assumes leaves behind the impression of a degree of arbitrariness.

The other interpretation in its simplest form (for there are others) assumes a transposition of the negation οὐ. Πάντες οὐ is rendered as identical with οὐ πάντες.[5] This does not seem to be an impossible construction. While perhaps primarily inspired by dogmatic interest, it has not lacked advocates with whom this factor could scarcely count, but who felt linguistically justified in adopting it. The sense resulting is: it is not true of all but only of some that we shall sleep; it is true of all (both who sleep and who do not sleep) that we shall at the last day be changed. On this rendering Paul affirms the change for both groups. This suffers from the apparent implication that the resurrection of believers does not in itself as yet effect the necessary change, which takes place only a little later, in order that both raised and those found living may simultaneously partake of it as an identical experience; the real transforming aspect of the resurrection as such is lost sight of, a result which, as intimated before, ill agrees with the Pneumatic character of the act. It is likely that the Spirit, while performing his specific transforming task in the quickening of the dead, will as it were, refrain from carrying it to its logical completion through bringing the dead upon whom He operates to a state adapted to their henceforth eschatological, celestial life? The mere motive of guarding the simul-

[5] Cp., however, the phrase οὐ μὴ φθάσωμεν I Thess. iv. 15 and the interpretation put upon this in the Chapter on Chiliasm.

taneous occurrence of this final stage of the act may seem to some insufficient. Nor is this merely a question of appropriateness in the sequence of the process meant to form one continuous act. The adoption of a postponed change in those raised brings the idea into conflict with the explicit statement of vs. 52, where Paul does not simply affirm *οἱ νεκροὶ ἐγερθήσονται,* but *οἱ νεκροὶ ἐγερθήσονται ἄφθαρτοι.* According to these words the change for the raised does not *follow,* it *coincides,* and that not merely chronologically but substantially with the resurrection. The resurrection is in their case such a thing as to result *ipso facto* in "incorruptibleness." It is true, the verses from vs. 54 onwards speak of the victory over death in such general terms as render it difficult to believe that they attach themselves to but one particular aspect of this victory, viz. the change of the living. Still, perhaps even here the figure in *κατεπόθη* may, on account of its resemblance to 2 Cor. v. 4, seem to refer particularly to the change of the living. Overmuch weight, however, should not be attached to this, since the word in question forms part of a quotation here, being no more than a reminiscence from the passage in Hosea, whilst in 2 Cor. v it forms an independent figure.

The advantages and disadvantages of both views so nearly balance each other, that we do not feel competent to make a choice. The one thing certain is that Paul conceived of the resurrection as involving a pneumatic transformation. To that vs. 52, with its *ἐγερθήσονται ἄφθαρτοι* bears conclusive witness. But, whether he made the raised share in a still further change with the living, or, as a matter of language employed the word "change" sometimes generically to include both phases of the transaction, as to this we venture no positive decision.[6]

[6] How difficult the passage is, from the point of view of precise doctrinal construction may be judged from the several attempts appearing already in early authorities to alter the text. Besides the two variations above noted (*πάντες οὐ* and *πάντες μὲν οὐ*) we find: *πάντες μὲν ἐγερθησόμεθα, οὐ πάντες δὲ ἀλλαγησόμεθα,* and: *πάντες μὲν κοιμηθησόμεθα, οὐ πάντες δὲ ἀλλαγησόμεθα.* On these readings cf. Westcott and Hort in the Appendix.

As to Phil. iii. 20, 21, here the representation that the Christian "waits for a Saviour" seems to show that the Apostle speaks from the standpoint of such as look for the parousia during their lifetime, so that the μετασχηματισμός is not made to include the change in the resurrection. On the other hand, there is nothing in the conception of a μετασχηματισμός or in the phrase σῶμα τῆς ταπεινώσεως, that could have hindered Paul from applying these terms to the process of the resurrection itself.[7]

[7] Cp. Klöpper, *Der Brief des Apostels Paulus an die Philipper,* p. 224, note. Klöpper even thinks that the "ἐπενδύσασθαι" of 2 Cor. v. 3, 4 permits of a reference to those who are raised at the parousia, where it would mean the putting on of the new body over the old body just raised. This, it seems to us, is positively excluded by **οὐ θέλομεν ἐκδύσασθαι** of 2 Cor. v. 4, with **ἐπενδύσασθαι** as its opposite. The two categories exclude each other.

CHAPTER IX

THE EXTENT OF THE RESURRECTION

By the phrase "extent of the resurrection" we posit the question whether, according to Paul's teaching all dead men will be raised at the end, or only a limited section of those who shall have died previously to that time. The problem is, of course, to some extent bound up in part with that of Chiliasm, and in so far belongs to the following Chapter. The segment of the church set apart for an anticipated resurrection at the opening of the millennium, whether more or less narrowly counted, form part of the resurrection in any event, so that on the score of the chiliastic doctrine itself there is no objection to the comprehensive resurrection of all who have been, or are, or shall be believers, retrospectively, or at the moment, or prospectively during the interregnum to elapse before the absolute end. On the other hand, it stands to reason, that, when once the unitary and all-comprehensive scope of the transaction has at that point been broken in upon, the temptation may easily arise to affirm this partial aspect of the event likewise to the second and final act of the resurrection drama, confining this to believers so as to exclude from it all but the raising of Christians. The partialness of the idea is apt to fasten itself upon it, although originally proper to one application of it only. In logic, to be sure, this is by no means necessary: a partial resurrection at the opening of the millennium and an all-comprehensive raising of all the dead at the last day are by no means inherently contradictory. It is another question whether any limitation imposed upon the final resurrection is in line with the general trend of the Apostle's teaching, and if not, will not seem at the outset to be discredited, by the character of Paulinism as a whole.

Leaving these more or less *a priori* considerations to one side, we proceed to consider the direct data of Paul's deliverances on or allusions to the extent of the resurrection as such. The debate between limited and unlimited resurrection, distinguished by exclusion of non-believers or their inclusion, at first sight does not seem to leave the latter member of the alternative a fair chance for presenting the merits of its case. It has been plainly shown above that the resurrection of which Paul speaks in practically all the great contexts dealing with the subject, is viewed and treated by him as a *Pneumatic* event. But, the question immediately arises: how could a pneumatic occurrence, and that one in which the Spirit plays so prominent and intimate a part, fall within the sphere of the non-Christian? The same question, only presented from a different angle, arises where the close relation of the Spirit-*Christ* to the resurrection is considered. The raised are raised because of their being "*of Christ*" or "*asleep in Christ*," conditions inapplicable to such as do not possess the Spirit or are not possessed by the Spirit, for in this matter, no less than in regard to the Christian state as a whole appurtenance to Christ and appurtenance to the Spirit flow into one. Unbelievers having not the Spirit cannot undergo that part of his quickening activity that is productive of the resurrection, or, if they could, how could they be fit subjects for living the subsequent Spirit-life for which to all intents the agency of the Spirit in the act of the resurrection is but the necessary preparation. With regard to non-Christians the resurrection would come to appear as internally disrupted, inasmuch as in its better and eternal half it could never be expected to take place. So far as the pervasive tenor of the Pauline teaching is concerned, it must be freely conceded that the comprehensive interpretation is at a decided disadvantage. None the less too much weight may be easily attributed to this for the following reason: the Apostle is not *e mente sua* presenting in his letters a well-rounded, complete system of Christian truth, although more than any other New Testament complex of teaching it has come to be this for us. Paul writes to Christians and that for practical purposes largely. This fact reminds us that the phenomenon of his preoccupation with the resurrection of believers and his seeming neglect of the other side may easily be due to quite different causes than a logical disregard of systematic completeness. As a matter of fact the *loci* from which we draw our information of the thing as it lay in Paul's mind are in each case intra-redemptive in character; they are for comfort and, if for argument, than for such argument as the Christian readers stood in need of for comfort. It remains quite possible that in different situations, but scantily recorded for us, there may have been motives working in Paul's mind postulating a resurrection of non-believers, motives pertaining to a different than the strictly-soteric sphere. The pneumatic basis on which the resurrection is put only explains this one thing, viz. that Paul does not coördinate and mention together the two divisions of the resurrection, as otherwise would have seemed natural in an adherent of the doctrine of two-sided resurrection. For such joint-mention or coördination the significance of the event in the two classes of men had become too widely different in result of the thorough development of Paul's doctrine of the Pneuma. To the ordinary Jewish consciousness habituated to the belief that the resurrection would be the same thing in the case of all men, placing all in the same condition of a restored earthly corporeity before the judgment-seat of God, it was quite easy to speak after the well-known manner of a resurrection of the good and the evil. To Paul this must have been exceedingly difficult, for the simple reason that the term "resurrection" had to such an extent attracted to itself and begun to monopolize the habitual soteric associations, as to become after a fashion inapplicable to something in which these soteric concomitants had no place. Inevitably the term "resurrection" had lost somewhat of its neutral character, becoming graphically fit for use only *in sensu bono*. It is far from impossible in our opinion that Paul consciously refrained from speaking of the resurrection of the wicked. Still, and this requires strong emphasis, it would by no means follow from this, that such avoidance of the term could be justly construed as evidence of the principle, that the Apostle had thrown overboard the residue of content that had at one time been undividedly included in the term for evil and good alike, after discounting the specifically-Pneumatic elements. We must, therefore, proceed very cautiously here.[1]

An argument in favor of partial resurrection as the genuinely Pauline doctrine has been drawn from what is believed to have been the Pharisaic conception of the subject. For our information about the belief of the Pharisees in this respect we depend on Josephus. He states that according to them only the souls of the righteous have the power (faculty) of coming to life again, whilst the wicked remain forever imprisoned in the nether-world.[2] In another passage he records as the Pharisaic view that only the soul of the righteous man, in distinction from that of the wicked, passes into a new body.[3] If such was the Pharisaic position, it is argued, and if, as we know from elsewhere, Paul declared himself in essential harmony with the Pharisees on this issue, then the Apostle cannot have thought differently of the question under review than his former co-religionists. This argument, however, is not so conclusive as at first sight it might seem. We do not know to what extent one may rely on Josephus for exactness in formulating the Pharisaic doctrine on such a controversial, and somewhat esoteric point. That no complete reliance can be placed on his statements appears from the second passage above quoted, where he even credits the Pharisees with his own belief in the transmigration of souls, as expressed in the last-cited passage. Still it seems not improbable that what on two occasions Josephus ascribes to the Pharisees must have been a doctrine held at least by some among them. The Pharisaic leaders were hardly such expert and precise theologians as instinctively to extrude whatever

[1] According to Schwally, *Das Leben nach dem Tode,* pp. 168, 172, Josephus avoids the term **ἀνάστασις** even with reference to the righteous, for reasons of political prudence because **ἀνάστασις** can mean "revolt."

[2] *Antiquit.* XVIII, 14.

[3] *Bellum Jud.* III, 374.

ran contrary to the principles of their system. Paul in such matters had a much keener sensorium. We may be sure, however, that the view quoted by Josephus was not the only doctrine held in Pharisaic circles. In all probability more than one view was current. What all agreed on was the reality of the resurrection as such, apart from the question to whom exactly it was to extend. And possibly those Pharisees who did not deny the resurrection of all theoretically, yet for practical reasons threw so much more emphasis on its main aspect as a resurrection of the righteous, could by this alone lead Josephus to the mistaken inference expressed in his statements. But even, if feeling bound to take Josephus' account as substantially correct, this would not compel us to ascribe the same Pharisaic position, unmodified in any respect, to Paul after his conversion. Altogether apart now from the factor of revelation, Paul might through his contact with the earliest Christians have been led to alter his Pharisaic persuasion on the subject. The early Christians were, of course, not recruited from the Pharisees chiefly. Those converted from other circles may well have entertained varying opinions.

Leaving this matter of the Pharisees and Josephus to one side, it must be conceded that the doctrine of an all-inclusive resurrection was not before or at the time of Paul the firmly established doctrine of Judaism. In various quarters, in various forms, the range of the resurrection was limited. The Old Testament itself had approached the doctrine from the point of view of the people of God or of the pious among the people of God. Thus in Isa. xxvi. 19: "Thy dead shall live; my dead bodies shall arise"; the resurrection of the dead members of the holy nation is predicted, for assurance that they may share in the joys of the future. It is not clear how far back this promise is intended to apply, nor how comprehensive its range is conceived. In Dan. xii. 2 the prophecy confines itself to *many that shall awake,* although it is not limited here to such as are righteous, some being destined to everlasting life, some to shame and everlasting contempt.

Here probably the reference is not to all the righteous and wicked that have made up all generations of the people of Israel, but to those righteous and wicked who have played a prominent part in the crisis with which this prophecy deals. The idea that the martyrs of the people of God are sure of the resurrection, whilst nothing is said of the others, righteous or unrighteous, is found also elsewhere. For this Chap. xc of the *Book of Enoch* may be compared. In *2 Macc.* it cannot be determined with certainty, whether the resurrection of the evil is denied or not. Of Antiochus Epiphanes it is explicitly denied, but this relates not to the resurrection as such; the reference is to the ἀνάστασις εἰς ζωήν. It is said that Judas Maccabaeus made expiation for the slain in whose garments pagan idols had been found, ὑπὲρ ἀναστάσεως διαλογιζόμενος, "concerned about their resurrection." This, however, might relate to the punishment they might otherwise have to suffer in Sheol, previously to the resurrection, so that a resurrection with subsequent punishment is not necessarily implied.[4] Still another variation of the doctrine is that not only the martyrs of the last crisis, but all the righteous dead of Israel are to be raised. This is found in the *Psalms of Solomon,* iii. 10 ff. and in the section of the *Enoch Apocalypse* extending from xci to civ. A still somewhat wider extent the resurrection obtains in *Enoch* i-xxxvi. In this document besides the resurrection of the righteous from among Israel (in the body) a resurrection of some impious Israelites as disembodied spirits seems to be taught, viz. of those who have not been adequately punished in the present life; they are brought up from the nether-world, in order to be cast into Gehenna, the place of punishment, whilst the other wicked Israelites, already sufficiently punished in this life, appear to remain permanently in the more negative state of Sheol. Finally, the most inclusive view is that all the wicked as well as the righteous will be raised for judgment. Where this view is found two points are frequently left in obscurity, although the author in each case may have had a definite opinion on the subject: a) whether

[4] Schwally, *Das Leben nach dem Tode,* p. 171.

all the wicked and all the righteous from among Israel, or all the wicked and righteous composing the human race are meant; b) whether the wicked are simply to be brought up as disembodied spirits in order to be judged, after which they go to their final punishment in the same disembodied state, or whether they are put in possession again of their erstwhile bodies in order to receive punishment in these. The writings in which this doctrine of a universal resurrection is found are the following: the *Similitudes of the Book of Enoch,* li. 1: (here the two points just specified are left doubtful); *4 Ezra* v. 45; vii. 32; xiv. 35 (here the first two passages speak of a universal resurrection of the race: *Deus vivificabit creaturam,* whereas the last-mentioned passage might be limited to Israel); *Apoc. Bar.* xlii. 8; l. 2 (here the absolute universality is found by some writers, for instance Volz, but denied, among others, by Charles); the resurrection here is a resurrection in the same body, which is afterwards changed in bonum or malum; *Test. XII Patr.*: Benj. 10; Lev. 4; in the former passage it is said that after the fathers have been raised, all will be raised (whether this "all" relates to all Israelites or to all men is not plain); in the other passage the Greek text has that, when the Lord will hold judgment on all mankind, Hades will be depleted; the Armenian text contains the quite different words "the nether-world will make prisoners through the plagues of the Most High"; the fourth book of the *Sibylline Oracles,* vss. 180 ff. (here there exists some uncertainty as to whether the wicked to be raised are the wicked of all generations of history, or only those wicked just perished in the great world-conflagration); the *Life of Adam*: Chap. x, "the sinners shall be there"; xli, "the whole seed of Adam."

Especially this last class of writings teaching a universal resurrection, is of interest for our present purpose. For, while here the universality is explicitly affirmed, we nevertheless find certain other statements which speak of the resurrection of the righteous, and that in such a way as to make it appear as though no other aspect of the resurrection were known to the authors. Such varying representations appear side by side not only in writings which criticism believes to be composite, but likewise in documents or sections of documents whose unity is not subject to doubt. Thus e.g. in the *Similitudes* of the *Book of Enoch,* apart from the passage cited above (li. 1), there are several other contexts in which only the resurrection of the just is reflected upon, cp. xl. 3; lxi. 5; lxii. 8. In *4 Ezra,* side by side with the universalistic passages (v. 45; vii. 32; xiv. 35), we find the particularistic statements of iv. 35; vii. 28. In *Apoc. Bar.,* side by side with the universal resurrection of xlii. 8 and l. 2, the resurrection of the righteous is mentioned, as though it were the only one, xxvi, (21), 24; xxx. 1 ff. In *Test. XII Patr.* we have not so much two classes of statements, but at least statements of more or less doubtful interpretation. In the *Life of Adam* occurs the most striking juxtaposition of both forms of statement: Chap. xli, as just stated, contains the doctrine of the resurrection of the whole human race which is of the seed of Adam; Chap. xiii contains the words: "Then all flesh from Adam onward shall be raised, all those which are holy people." The point which, in view of these facts, we desire to make is the following: if in the case of the writers of these Apocalyptic books the one-sided emphasis thrown upon the resurrection of the righteous did not exclude a conjoined belief, be it of a more theoretical nature, in a universal resurrection of good and evil alike, then there is ample reason for hesitating to say that Paul must have restricted the resurrection to believers, on no other ground than that prevailingly he speaks of it as a Pneumatic transaction. To introduce the same double-facedness in his various references must have been more easy for him than for the Apocalyptists, because the constant emphasis on the Pneuma led of itself to relegating the other side to a sort of semi-oblivion, a feature not equally present in Apocalyptic literature, although its relative absence even there did not prevent the one-sided focussing of the attention on the saving side of the transaction. It so happens that *Apoc. Bar.* and *4 Ezra,* are the books in which the apparent contradiction is most conspicuous, and these are precisely the writings standing nearest to Paul.

The only explicit witness we have for Paul's belief in a comprehensive resurrection of the wicked as well as of the righteous is found in his speech to Felix, Acts xxiv. 15. The Apostle here declares that he believes all things which are according to the law, and which are written in the prophets. Probably he makes this double affirmation in order distinctly to align himself with the Pharisees over against the Sadducaic unbelief, which was based on a one-sided adherence to the explicit testimony of the Thora, and on refusal to take into account the prophetic statements. As the main content of this belief, based on both prophets and law, he names the hope he has towards God, which hope the (Pharisaic) Jews also themselves look for, that there shall be a resurrection both of the just and unjust. It will be observed that, though the two-sided character of the resurrection is here affirmed, nevertheless the main emphasis lies on its hopeful aspect, i.e., as a resurrection of the righteous. The whole doctrine is a "*hope* held towards God."[5] And this hope he declares to have in common with the (Pharisaic) Jews, which shows that in the Pharisaic doctrine likewise, while the resurrection of the wicked was not denied, yet the main interest attached to the hope which the doctrine afforded for the righteous. This may help to explain how Josephus came to believe that the Pharisees expected a resurrection of the righteous only. There is no ground for calling into question the accuracy of this speech of Paul to Felix, far less to deny its historicity altogether. The author of Acts proves himself in other points thoroughly acquainted with the differences in belief between Pharisees and Sadducees and with the prevailing Jewish be-

[5] It is perhaps not necessary to exclude altogether from the aspect of "hopefulness" the resurrection of the wicked from the Jewish standpoint. As shown before there attached to the Jewish expectation of the resurrection an element of triumph over the wicked opponents of the cause of Judaism: these had to see the vindication of the righteous for the satisfaction of the latter. In the background of the resurrection looms the coveted judgment.

liefs in general. Even if one were to assume that he had freely composed the speech, we might nevertheless expect it to be true in so much of its theological coloring as is of importance for the matter under review. The author could not have made the mistake of representing Paul as at one with the orthodox Jewish doctrine on this point, if neither the Jewish orthodoxy, nor the Apostle had actually entertained the belief imputed to them.

This testimony from Acts would be corroborated by direct testimony from two of the Epistles, if we could adopt the interpretation given by some to I Cor. xv. 22-28 and to Phil. iii. 11. If in the former passage the words "then comes the end" could be understood of the end of the resurrection, there would for this succeeding act of the resurrection be none others left than the wicked, at least supposing that those "of Christ," raised in the preceding act, included all believers. In another chapter, however, we will endeavor to show that "the end" spoken of is not "the end of the resurrection" with which negative conclusion the argument presented falls to the ground. As to Phil. iii, inasmuch as the personal privilege of resurrection striven after, would on the new interpretation have to be considered the martyr's privilege, it would leave open the field of any subsequent resurrection-stage for the non-martyr Christians, and the question of resurrection for the wicked would not be touched thereby.

An indirect proof for the resurrection of the wicked has been found in Paul's supposition of the presence of unbelievers at the judgment by which the resurrection is succeeded. The inconclusiveness of this argument is due to the circumstance that a judgment passed on disembodied souls is not an impossible conception, and actually occurs elsewhere in the Jewish sources, as has been shown above. Hence, so long as the question under debate is not entirely settled, one must reckon with the possibility that both the resurrection and the judgment will deal with the wicked in an uncorporeal state. To be sure, positively considered, there is nothing in Paul that would suggest such an idea. It amounts to no more than a mere abstract possibility. And there is, on the other hand, that which, while not amounting to absolute proof, at least tends towards favoring the opposite view. This will appear presently, when we shall have occasion to deal with the Apostle's doctrine on the Judgment. Finally, attention may be called to I Tim. vi. 13: "I charge thee in the sight of God "τοῦ ζωογονοῦντος τὰ πάντα." This, placed in comparison with 2 Tim. iv. 1: "I charge thee in the sight of God and of Christ Jesus who shall judge the quick and the dead, and by his appearing and his kingdom," seems to require an eschatological interpretation for the word "quickeneth," and the object of this being "all things" (or in view of the article prefixed "the universe") the all-comprehensiveness of the resurrection might seem to be affirmed. In classical Greek the word ζωογονεῖν actually has the sense of "to bring to life," "to quicken." In the two other N.T. passages, however, where this same verb occurs, Lk. xvii. 33 and Acts vii. 19, the sense is "to preserve alive," which does not suit the interpretation of the resurrection. If the correct reading were "ζωοποιοῦντος," instead of "ζωογονοῦντος," this objection would fall away, since "ζωοποιεῖν" is used elsewhere (by Paul and Peter and John) in the sense of "to quicken." As it is, the uncertainty of reading and rendering do not permit a sure conclusion. The issue of the discussion remains that for explicit proof of Paul's belief in the universality of the resurrection we are dependent on the testimony of Acts xxiv. 15.

CHAPTER X

THE QUESTION OF CHILIASM, IN PAUL

"Chiliasm," more commonly called "Pre-millennarianism," occupies a peculiar place in the scheme of Biblical Eschatology. It is difficult to form a deliberate judgment upon it, either by way of decisive rejection or enthusiastic approval. The question is, of course, a question of evidence, to be considered and settled on the basis of Scriptural testimony and of calm, sober, dogmatically-unprejudiced exegesis. Were it confined to the elucidation of the Pauline eschatology alone, the settlement should not appear overdifficult. Unfortunately, where one undertakes to do this, he must expect to have the scheme outlined in Rev. xx. 4 ff. brought to his attention with the insistent demand, that a laborious effort at harmonizing shall be forthwith undertaken in which the large mould of the Pauline eschatological teaching shall be reduced to the narrower, pictorial measures of the Apocalyptic vision. With all due respect to the authoritativeness of biblical prophecy, it is difficult to escape the feeling that this is an unmethodical procedure. The minor deliverances ought in the harmonizing process be made to give way to the far-sweeping, age-dominating program of the theology of Paul. After the latter has been interpreted to a satisfactory degree of clearness and certainty, then, and not until then, will come the time to look the Apocalypse in the face, and to endeavor to bring it into consonance with the Pauline deliverances. The law of proportion cannot be entirely waived in so far-reaching a matter as this. On the other hand, if we are urged to settle the problem not quite so objectively, but more on the basis of a theological imitation of philosophical behaviorism, putting to ourselves the question, which of the two, pre-millennarianism or post-millennarianism, has done or bids to do more good to practical Christianity, or which of the twain can be trusted to do less injury to the cause of religion, even then the answer is by no means so readily forthcoming. Chiliasm has to its credit the astounding readiness it evinces of taking the O.T. Scriptures in a realistic manner, with simple faith, not asking whether the fulfilment of these things is even logically conceivable, offering as its sole basis the conviction that to God all things are possible. This attitude is, of course, not attained except through a reckless abuse of the fundamental principles of O.T. exegesis, a perversion invading inevitably the precincts of N.T. exegesis likewise, heedless of the fact that already the O.T. itself points to the spiritualizing of most of the things in question. Apart from accidental features, and broadly speaking, Chiliasm is a daring literalizing and concretizing of the substance of ancient revelation. Due credit should be given for the naïve type of faith such a mentality involves. It is a great pity that from this very point of view pre-millennarianism has not been psychologically studied, so as to ascertain, whence in its long, tortuous course through the ages it has acquired such characteristics. Although pre-millennarianism is by no means a local phenomenon, there are evidently certain milieus in which it has found a more fertile soil than elsewhere. In certain countries it comes to meet an eccentric interest in the superficial, visible, curiosity-attracting events in eschatological perspective. The evil is not so much an evil in itself: it is a malformation or over-rank outgrowth drawing to itself a surplusage of religious interest, at the expense of what is more essential and vital in the eschatological sphere. The resulting evil lies largely in the deficit thus caused in the appraisal of other eschatological processes far overshadowing in importance this one feature, at least to the normally-constituted Christian mind. Its tendency towards eclipsing views more important than itself has done much harm. It is not an uncommon experience at the present day for one who expresses dissent from Chiliasm to be met with the question, Are you then, an unbeliever in "the second coming?" In other words the subject of eschatology in its broad and tremendous significance has vanished from the field of vision, the delusion has been created that eschatology and Chiliasm are interchangeable, the species has usurped the place of the genus, which is to be regretted, altogether apart from the question whether acceptance of the species is in accordance with the biblical data or not.

"Chiliasm" is so named from the numeral "χίλιοι," "a thousand." The name is more or less unaptly chosen, because the duration of the interval which is placed between the two successive resurrections, or the point of the departure of the two successive eras, is by various adherents of the scheme variously fixed. It might have been six hundred or four hundred, in neither case would this have affected the essence of the belief in the least. Since, however, in common usage the number "one thousand" is laid at the basis, the designation may be allowed to stand by reason of the preference of the vast majority of adherents. It is true another term, that of "pre-millennarianism," would deserve the preference if a more informing nomenclature be sought after. But this terminology is less perspicuous for the noun "pre-millennarianism" does not make it plain to what the preposition "pre" in it has reference, and the Latin "millennium" is no more free than the Greek name from prejudicially fixing the duration. The point of departure is in both cases the parousia; the number of years fixed upon begins with it; *pre-millennarian* is an adjective before the implied noun parousia, expressing the assumption that the return of Christ will take place before the millennium. The substance of the matter is that Chiliasm divides the eschatological future following upon the parousia into two distinct stages, the one of a temporary provisional, the other of an eternal, absolute character. The old traditional view of orthodox theology, and the current interpretation of Paul know of no such dualism in the eschatological prospect; they make the eternal state, strictly so called, begin with the return of the Lord.

This "chiliastic" division of the eschatological future into two distinct stages is probably of pre-Christian origin. It seems to be first met with in the *Book of Enoch,* Chaps. xci and xciii, in the "Vision of Weeks," so called, because it divides the entire course of the world's duration into ten weeks. The eighth of these stands for the Messianic period, the ninth and the tenth bring the final judgment, and it is not until the close of the tenth week that the new creation appears. In the third book of the Jewish Sibyl (vss. 652-660) the Messianic kingdom is represented as subject to attack and destruction by the assembled nations, and after in turn these are destroyed, the kingdom of God begins. The dating of these two apocalyptic documents is somewhat uncertain, but not a few authorities place them in the pre-Christian period.[1] The same distinction between a preliminary Messianic and a final kingdom has been found in the *Psalms of Solomon.* Here in Psalms xvii and xviii the Messianic reign seems to be described as something transitory, for the writer speaks not only of "his (i.e., the Messiah's) days," "those days" (xvii. 32; xviii. 6), but also of his (the Messiah's) lifetime (xvii. 37). On the other hand, in Psalm iii. 12 we read of a resurrection to eternal life. It is not absolutely certain, however, that all the Psalms in this collection are of one author. If we were sure of this unity in authorship, the succession of two differently-complexioned kingdoms would offer the only explanation of the two varying descriptions of the future. Were the authorship diverse such a conclusion would not be necessary, since the outlook of one author might be entirely confined to the Messianic era *sub specie temporis,* whilst another might contemplate the same era as of eternal duration.[2] Coming down into the Christian period, we meet the twofold kingdom in the Slavic Enoch and the two great Apocalypses of *Ezra* and *Baruch,* and here a definite number of years is fixed for the duration of the provisional Messianic reign.

1 So Bousset, *Die Religion des Judenthums,* p. 331, note 1.

2 It does not, of course, follow that the author of Ps. iii made such a distinction. He might have conceived the Messianic reign as eternal, or his conception of "eternal life" might have been un-Messianic. Only if we identify him with the author of Psalms xvii and xviii can we affirm that the eschatology of the latter was also his.

According to *4 Ezra* vii. 28 ff. the Christ reigns four hundred years, then He, together with all other earthly creatures, dies, after which the dead awake and the eternal judgment occurs. Similarly in xii. 34, where the reign of the Messiah lasts till the end of the world and the day of judgment. In the *Slavic Enoch* and *Apoc. Bar.* the limited duration of the Messianic era is connected with the system of world-periods. In the latter apocalypse, after the description of the Messianic kingdom in Chap. xxix, the opening verse of the following chapter states that, when the period of the arrival of the Messiah has been completed, He will return in glory into heaven, which return will be the signal for the resurrection of those who are fallen asleep hoping for Him. While Chap. xli. 3 represents the reign of the Messiah as "permanent forever," this is immediately qualified by the subjoined clause "until the world devoted to destruction comes to a close, and the things named above fulfil themselves." Finally, according to Chap. lxxiv. 2 the Messianic age is that which is transitory, and the preceding that which is non-transitory.

In regard to the motive underlying this conception of a provisional Messianic kingdom it has been suggested by recent writers that it should be looked upon as a compromise between two heterogeneous eschatological ideals, the ancient national-political, terrestrial scheme, revolving around the destiny of Israel, and the later transcendental-cosmical scheme, which has in view the transformation of the kosmos, and the introduction of altogether new conditions on a super-mundane plane. At first the ideas and expectations connected with these two schemes formed an orderless mass, a conglomerate without adjustment or correlation. The most diverse elements lay unreconciled and unreconcilable in close proximity to one another, as in the older parts of the *Book of Enoch* and in the *Book of Jubilees*. Or, the semblance of coherence was saved by bringing into the foreground only one of these two aspects of the eschatological hopes, leaving the other in eclipse, while not theoretically denying its right of existence. Thus in the *Similitudes* of the *Book of Enoch* and in the

Testaments of the XII Patriarchs the prevailing atmosphere is of the transcendental, super-terrestrial kind, although not to the entire exclusion of earthly national prospects. On the other hand in such writings as the *Psalms of Solomon* and the *Assumption of Moses* the eschatological drama plays mainly on the stage of this world and under temporal conditions, the interest being centered on Israel. Rarely, as in the *Slavic Book of Enoch,* does the spirit of other-worldliness become so dominant as to expel all the heterogeneous elements belonging to the other and lower plane. In most cases the contradictions were not actually removed, but only covered up by the distribution of emphasis. And for this reason it was inevitable, it is thought, that a more systematic attempt should in course of time be made to bring not only apparent but real order into the confusion. This was done through the distribution of the various elements over two successive periods. The older national, political, earthly hopes, it was now believed, would first go into fulfilment, and thus have full justice done to them. But this would last for a time only. Then, after this tribute had been paid, the new order of things could assume its eternal, cosmical sway, no longer hindered in the unfolding of its transcendental character by the intrusion of motives of a lower type.

Sometimes, as notably in the case of Bousset, the view sketched is coupled with the hypothesis that the entire higher eschatology of Judaism is not a native growth on the soil of the Old Testament, but an importation from Babylonian (ultimately Persian) sources. This peculiar assumption, however, so grave and far-reaching in its consequences, is by no means essential to the theory.[3] The cleavage and heterogeneity which mark the Jewish eschatology would invite reduction to a system quite as much if the

[3] The theory carries with it the inference that the basis and background of the entire Christian idea of salvation are of pagan origin. The question about the origin of the Apocalyptic eschatology resolves itself into a question of the antecedents of the specifically soteric element in Christianity. For the soteriology rests throughout on the eschatology.

disharmony were due to indigenous development, as if due to the intrusion of foreign influence. But apart from this, and considering the problem altogether by itself, we are not convinced that the solution, attractive though it may seem, is borne out by the facts. The origin of a scheme does not always coincide with the uses to which it may be subsequently put. When so far back as the period of canonical prophetism we find the twofold representation, on the one hand that the final order of things will be called into being by the appearance of a Messianic King, and on the other hand that it will come through the appearance and interposition of God Himself, so that the two conceptions of a Messianic Kingdom and a Kingdom of God appear at this early stage side by side without any attempt at harmonizing, then it would seem, that in this ancient prophetic diversity, we have a fully adequate explanation of the origin of the two successive kingdoms, without having to go to Babylonia and Persia, or deriving the whole from Apocalyptic dissatisfaction with the world. When once the problem inherent in this twofold perspective had made itself felt, it required no profound insight to perceive that the easiest way of solving it lay in making the two forms of the future state follow each other, in which case the first in order would naturally be the Kingdom of the Messiah, to be followed by the Kingdom of God as the absolute consummation of all things. Chiliasts resenting the charge of the dependence of their favorite idea on the streaming in of pagan elements of thought into the Old Testament, can make a good case for themselves on the ground indicated. Whether the New Testament stamps with its approval the solution by which on the theory stated the early Jewish Theology sought to solve the problem, or has a different solution of its own, may for the present remain an open question. But a charge of being rooted in paganism, rather than in statements of the Old Testament need not lie against Chiliasm.

From this possible origin of the distinction we must, however, keep separated the use to which in course of time it came to be put.[4] In itself the distinction between a preliminary Messianic and a subsequent divine Kingdom is indifferent to eschatological tone or atmosphere. In the earlier sources the Messianic kingdom is not depicted in particularly glowing sensualistic colors, as though any conscious effort had been made to save in it realistic hopes and dreams for which, it was felt, the more modern outlook left no room. Nor, on the other hand, is the final state described in such super-sensual terms as to convey the impression that an order of things so constituted is utterly incommensurable with the substance of the old earth-bound expectations. It is not in *Enoch,* not in the well-known verses of the third book of the *Jewish Sibyl,* nor in the *Psalms of Solomon* that the picture of the provisional Messianic kingdom assumes the complexion usually called "chiliastic" in the specific sense of the word. This happens first in the great Apocalypses of *Ezra* and *Baruch.* According to *4 Ezra* vii. 28, God's son, the Christ, when revealed "will dispense joy for four hundred years to those that remain." The same prospect of "joy" for those left in the land recurs in xii. 24. The most typical passage is *Apoc. Bar.* xxix. 1-8: "When the Messiah begins to reveal Himself, Behemoth and Leviathan likewise appear, and are given as food to the remnant; the earth produces ten-thousandfold; a vine will have one thousand branches, every branch one thousand clusters, every cluster one thousand grapes, and every grape will yield one kor of wine; winds will proceed from God and will carry to the people the fragrance of aromatic fruit, and at night clouds will distill healing dew; the heavenly supplies of manna will be let down and they will eat of them in those years, because they have reached the end of the ages.[5] Characteristic also is lxxiv. 1: "In these days the reapers will not

[4] This may be seen most clearly from the *Slavic Enoch,* in which, as Bousset observes, the atmosphere is pervasively transcendental, and which yet (for the first time) limits the Messianic kingdom to a thousand years.

[5] This is the passage from which Papias is believed to have borrowed his well-known description of the Chiliastic state, quoted by Irenaeus, v, 33, 3.

have to exert themselves, and those that build will not have to toil, for of themselves all works will have progress together with those who labor thereon with much rest." And it is precisely in these latest Apocalypses that the final state appears at the farthest remove from the conditions of earthly existence even in an idealized form. It is not a perfection of the present life, but a transposition of life into the supernatural key that is expected. There can be little doubt that some sense of the incompatibility of such glories with the Messianic joys, as ordinarily conceived, contributed to sharpen the distinction between the two successive states, and to make it one not merely of chronology, but likewise of antithetical character.

The Pauline eschatology in point of time lies between the older documents in which Chiliasm crops out and this later efflorescence of it in *4 Ezra* and the *Baruch-Apocalypse*. It is not surprising, therefore, that attempts should have been made to bring the Apostle in line with the general apocalyptic development in this matter. Effort is exerted to make him teach the future coming of some such temporal kingdom as the Jewish sources assume.[6] It is alleged that Paul expects a twofold resurrection, one of a certain class of dead at the parousia, and one of the remaining dead at the end of all, and that he places a glorious provisional reign of Christ between these two resurrections. Now it will be observed that the idea of Chiliasm, when introduced in this concrete form, which is, as a matter of fact, the only form for which any semblance of support can be found in the Pauline Epistles, does not particularly fit into the development of doctrine in Jewish Apocalyptic. It would represent a more advanced form of the idea than is met with in *4 Ezra* and *Apoc. Bar.*, inasmuch as

[6] Grimm, *Q. f. W. Th.*, 1873, pp. 380-411; Schmiedel in Holtzmann's *Handkommentar*² II, p. 196; Kabisch, *Die Paulinischen Vorstellungen von Anferstehung und Gericht und ihre Beziehung zur Jüdischen Apocalypse*, pp. 111-112; Bousset, *Die Religion des Judenthums*², p. 331. Among more recent writers the presence of Chiliasm in Paul is denied by Titius, *Die Neutestamentliche Lehre von der Seligkeit, Der Paulinismus*, p. 47; Charles, *A Critical History of the Doctrine of a Future Life in Israel, in Judaism, and in Christianity*, p. 386; Kennedy, *St. Paul's Conceptions of the Last Things*, pp. 322-324.

with Paul the differentiation between the two kingdoms would appear carried through to the point of a distinction between two resurrections. In the two above-named Apocalypses the resurrection is not yet divided, but remains fixed at its accustomed place immediately before the final judgment. The Pauline teaching then would in this respect be not in continuity with the apocalyptic development of doctrine, but overtake it and pass on beyond. Still it might be urged that this phenomenon can be explained from the specifically Christian feature, that the Messiah has already come, and that in Him, at a central point, the resurrection has already become an accomplished fact, so that naturally, when between this fundamental resurrection and the final resurrection the Chiliastic kingdom as a future stage is inserted, this intermediate stage must likewise have at its opening some kind of resurrection connected with itself. In this way at least somewhat of the strangeness of a departure from the ordinary scheme could be toned down, and the hypothesis of a real connection in the main point upheld.

It must be admitted, however, that the likelihood of finding Chiliasm in Paul is not favored by the trend of the Apostle's teaching as a whole. Not merely does his general concatenation of eschatological events, in which the parousia and the resurrection of believers are conjoined with the judgment exclude every intermediate stage of protracted duration, it is of even more importance that Paul conceives of the present Christian state, ideally considered, as lived on so high a plane that nothing less nor lower than the absolute state of the eternal consummate Kingdom appears worthy to be its sequel.[7] To represent it as followed by some intermediate

[7] Cp. 1 Thess. i. 10; ii. 17; iii. 13; v. 19, 23; 2 Thess. i. 10; ii. 12, 13. In point of fact, the Chiliastic scheme runs so contrary to the Apostle's teaching as a whole, that its assumed appearance in 1 Cor. xv. 4 and Phil. iii has been construed by some writers as *prima facie* evidence of the interpolation of the former passage (So Michelson, *Th. T.*, 1872, pp. 215-221, and Bruins, *ibid.*, pp. 381-415, and of the spuriousness of the Epistle to the Philippians as a whole (So Hoekstra, *Th. T.*, 1815, 442-450.

condition falling short of the perfect heavenly life would be in the nature of an anti-climax. It is, as shown before, of the very essence of salvation that it correlates the Christian's state with the great issues of the last day and the world to come. And in this connection it should be once more observed, that what the earthly Christian state anticipates is in each case something of an absolute nature, pertaining to the eternal life. No matter with what concrete elements or colors the assumed Chiliastic règime be filled out, nevertheless to a mind so nourished upon the very firstfruits of eternal life, it can for the very reason of its falling short of eternal life, have had little significance or attraction.

Still such general considerations do not absolve us from testing the exegetical basis on which adherents of the theory believe it to rest. There are not lacking those who fully agree with us as to the general structure of the Pauline eschatology, but who, on exegetical grounds, feel constrained to assume, that through lack of discrimination the Apostle let this heterogeneous strain of teaching, as a remnant from his Judaistic past, continue in his thought and work harm to his proclamation of the Gospel. The passages in which Chiliasm has been discovered are chiefly four: 1 Cor. xv. 23-28; 1 Thess. iv. 13-18; 2 Thess. i. 5-12; Phil. iii. 10-14. We shall examine these in succession. As to 1 Corinthians the argument for the Chiliastic interpretation may be briefly stated as follows. It is urged, first of all, that in the statement of vs. 22: "As in Adam all die, so also in Christ shall all men be made alive," the "*all*" must be taken without restriction. *All* men die, *all* are to be made alive. This necessitates, it is further said, since "*οἱ τοῦ χριστοῦ*" of vs. 23 does not exhaust the "*πάντες*," the assumption that vs. 24 speaks of a subsequent stage in the resurrection. The words "*εἶτα τὸ τέλος*" are therefore taken to mean: "Then comes the end," i.e., *the final stage of the resurrection*. And it is believed that with reference to these two successive stages thus obtained the Apostle writes in vs. 23: "Each in his own *order*." There are two orders, first the raising of those that are Christ's at his parousia, secondly the end of the resurrection (that is the raising of the remainder of men), when He delivers up the Kingdom to God, even the Father. And as in the first statement the phrase "at his parousia" is added to fix the time when this first act will occur, so in the second statement the words "when He delivers up the kingdom" are added to define the point for the second act.

The first resurrection, then, takes place at the parousia, the second when Christ abdicates his kingdom. This, of course, involves that the two do not coincide but are separated by an interval of shorter or longer duration. Just as between the "ἀπαρχὴ χριστός" and the ἐν τῇ παρουσίᾳ αὐτοῦ lies a period marked by "ἔπειτα," so between ἐν τῇ παρουσίᾳ and τὸ τέλος Paul places an interval and marks this by εἶτα. That there are two successive acts to be distinguished in the resurrection, follows also, it is believed, from the use of the term "τάγμα": "each in his own tagma." This distributive way of speaking implies that there is more than one *tagma,* and, since Christ in his resurrection *stands alone,* and cannot form a tagma by Himself, it is plain that there must be *two* tagmata besides Him. The one of these two is the tagma of those that are Christ's at his coming, the other is the tagma of those raised at the end. That the time elapsing between the resurrection of believers and the final resurrection must be a protracted period is said to be implied by the second ὅταν in vs. 24. The first ὅταν merely names in the Present Subjunctive the *point* of time, when the final resurrection takes place, ὅταν παραδιδῷ τὴν βασιλείαν τῷ θεῷ, "when He delivers up the kingdom to God"; the second ὅταν names in the Aorist Subjunctive the period *after* which the resurrection will occur, ὅταν κατηργήσῃ πᾶσαν ἀρχὴν, "when He shall have abolished all rule." Thus Paul not merely implies that there will be a period between the resurrection of believers and that of the others, but also conceives of this period as "the kingdom of Christ" specifically, in distinction from the kingdom of God, which is to follow after, and he moreover affirms that this specific inter-resurrection kingdom of Christ will have for its concrete content the progressive subjugation of the enemies designated ἀρχαί, ἐξουσίαι, δυνάμεις.

Having now the proposed exegesis before us, we perceive at a glance that it seems to commend itself by that most popular of credentials, surface simplicity. But, as is frequently the case, the difficulties lie beneath the surface. Let us begin with the argument derived from πάντες in vs. 22. There is an insurmountable obstacle to understanding this of "all men" in the fact that the ζωοποιεῖσθαι is represented as taking place ἐν Χριστῷ. How can this apply to the second resurrection at the end? Two answers are offered us, but they are both equally unacceptable on the basis of the general teaching of Paul. The first is that offered by Meyer and Godet. These propose to give to "ἐν χριστῷ" a weakened sense, so weakened indeed as to make it equally applicable to the resurrection of the lost as to that of believers. Thus Meyer interprets the phrase in question to mean that "*in Christ* lies the ground and cause, why at the final historical completion of the redemptive work death . . . shall be removed again and all shall be made alive." And Godet asks: "May it not be said of those who shall rise to condemnation, that they also shall rise ἐν χριστῷ? . . . The Saviour having once appeared, it is on their relation to Him that the lot of all depends for weal or woe; it is this relation consequently which determines their return to life, either to glory or to condemnation." We submit that all this rests on an utterly un-Pauline interpretation of the phrase "ἐν χριστῷ." Wherever this occurs in Paul it is always meant in the full sense of a soteric (though not necessarily "pneumatic") in-being in Christ. Especially a ζωοποιεῖσθαι taking place in Christ must needs be mediated by the Spirit; just as the ἀποθνήσκειν ἐν τῷ Ἀδάμ implies a real connection between Him and the all who die. This suggestion, therefore, is inacceptable. The second way of relieving the difficulty, that, after those who are Christ's have been raised, still others shall be raised ἐν τῷ χριστῷ is scarcely more plausible. It ventures to assume that the Apostle here rises to the height of belief in the so-called "ἀποκατάστασις πάντων," that is of absolute universalism. At the second resurrection those will be raised, who at the time of the first resurrection at the parousia were not yet "of Christ," but who in the meantime have been converted and thus become subjects of a saving resurrection.[8] Such an assumption, however, no less than the proposal of Meyer and Godet, is too palpably inconsistent with the Apostle's most explicit teaching elsewhere to deserve serious consideration. The eternal judgment of the wicked is taught not only in the earlier Epistles, but in this very same Epistle to the Corinthians, and in the later letters, so that the difference cannot be accounted for by any development in Paul's mind in the direction of universalism. Neither do the words "*ἵνα ᾖ ὁ θεὸς πάντα ἐν πᾶσιν*" in vs. 28 require an absolutely universalistic interpretation, so far as the ultimate salvation of all human and superhuman creatures is concerned. For these words refer to the bringing to nought of the enemies spoken of in vss. 24, 25 of whom the last is Death. These enemies are designated "*ἀρχαί, ἐξουσίαι, δυνάμεις, θάνατος*." They prevent until the end that God should become "*τὰ πάντα ἐν πᾶσιν*," that is they interfere with the complete victorious sway of God over the universe.[9] Full justice is done to these words when they are interpreted of the breaking of the power of these enemies in the world. To be sure, it may be replied, that, so long as any wicked men remain, the power of superhuman enemies is not wholly broken, because the very existence of moral evil among part of the human race would imply its continuance, and that, therefore, although the *ἐν πᾶσιν* be neuter, and does not directly affirm the conversion of all men, yet indirectly the unqualified subjection of the universe to God and the comprehensive *καταργεῖσθαι* of these powers warrant the same conclusion. In reply to this we would submit that if the phrase *πὰ πάντα ἐν πᾶσιν* is to be pressed to that extreme, then Paul must have meant to convey by it the idea of either the conversion or the annihi-

[8] This is the view of Grimm, *Z. W. Th.*, 1873, pp. 380-411. Also of Schmiedel, *Handkommentar*, II, p. 196.

[9] Probably *πᾶσιν* is neuter: "in all things," that is "in the universe."

lation of these spirit-forces likewise. If moral evil cannot continue to exist in man, no more can the theory of absolute universalism permit its continued existence outside of man. In the passage before us, however, the Apostle does not either speak of or hint at conversion or annihilation of these demonic powers, but simply affirms their future καταργεῖσθαι. This word does not, as a rule, mean to reduce to non-existence, but to render inoperative, to strip of power "ἀεργὸν ποιεῖσθαι."[10] And in the case of ὁ θανατός we have a concrete example of how it is meant. Death καταργεῖται when he is no longer permitted to slay men. This will happen no more after the resurrection. Assuming that ὁ θανατός is not a mere personification but a real demon-power, one of a genus divided into "rules" and "authorities" and "powers," and further assuming, that as such Death is assigned to eternal condemnation, there would be nothing inconsistent in all this with God's being all in all in the universe. And, assuming once more than the wicked of mankind are likewise given up by God to eternal perdition, there is nothing inconsistent in their continuing evil either with the καταργεῖσθαι of Death or with God's being all in all.

If these two proposals be unacceptable, the question remains what is the true interpretation of "all shall be made alive" in vs. 22? Again two possibilities offer themselves. The one is to assume that "all" is qualified by "in Adam" and "in Christ." Charles believes that this construction is indicated by the position of the words. According to him the rendering should be: "As all *who are in Adam* die, so all *who are in Christ* shall be made alive." This is a possible view; for analogies 1 Cor. xv. 18 ("those who fell asleep in Christ are perished"), 1 Thess. iv. 16 ("the dead in Christ shall rise first"), Col. i. 4 ("your faith in Christ Jesus"), Rom. ix. 3 ("accursed from Christ"), may be compared. On this view the whole succeeding context deals avowedly with the resurrection of believers only. It is, of course, quite possible to adopt this construction of vs. 22 and its

[10] Cp. 2 Thess. ii. 8; 1 Cor. i. 28; ii. 6; Heb. ii. 14.

corollary that the passage confines itself to the resurrection of believers, without endorsing Charles' further inference that Paul taught a resurrection of believers only. There is, however, still a second way, in which the same understanding of the passage may be had, and yet the more usual construction of "in Adam" and "in Christ" be retained. For even when construing these phrases with the verbs, we are quite at liberty to assume that Paul made the mental qualification: "all (who were in Adam)" and "all (who are in Christ)." We believe this to be the most plausible interpretation of the verse. What the Apostle means to say is not that there is no exception to the dying in Adam (although in point of fact this was actually his teaching), nor any exception to the being made alive in Christ, viz. so far as any making alive anywhere takes place. What he *does* mean to affirm is rather this that there is no variety of operation in the range of these two processes described as "in Adam," "in Christ." In other words not the *universality* of the law, but the universality of its *modus operandi* within the compass in which it works, this is what is affirmed. Vs. 22 serves to elucidate vs. 21, and in the latter verse the point of the statement is that both death and resurrection are through a man. Consequently in vs. 23 not "πάντες" by itself, but "πάντες" jointly with "in Adam" and "in Christ" has the emphasis; there is no dying outside of Adam, there is no quickening apart from Christ. With abstract, absolute universalism this has nothing to do whatsoever.

The next point raised was related to Paul's use of "τάγμα." This, it is maintained, implies two stages in the resurrection separated by an interval. And it will have to be conceded that there is no escape from this, if the primary meaning of "tagma" be insisted upon. Primarily the word stands for "division," "troup," "group," being used largely as a military term in tactics. "Each in his own tagma" would then imply, that there are two groups to be raised at least. Now, it is further urged, Christ could not possibly have been considered by the Apostle as forming a tagma by Himself; consequently the divisions (plural) referred to must exist and form a pair apart from Christ being reckoned in; in other words there must be two resurrections subsequent to that of Christ with the two necessary intervals. On this view the word ἕκαστος "each" in vs. 23 does not include Christ, but covers only the "all" of vs. 22, of whom it is said that they will be made alive *"in Christ,"* which latter affirmation could not, of course, apply to Christ Himself.

Against the validity of this argumentation we submit, that it is impossible to exclude Christ from the range covered by ἕκαστος. Christ is the ἀπαρχή and ἀπαρχή stands connected with ἔπειτα. No plausible reason can be assigned why Paul should have written the clause "Christ the firstfruits" at all, unless he meant to assign to Christ a clearly defined place in the order of the resurrection. On the other hand, by assuming that Christ forms a tagma by Himself, the reason why his resurrection is introduced here becomes immediately perspicuous. Probably the circumstance had been urged against the Apostle's doctrine of the resurrection, that the resurrection of believers ought to take place immediately after their death, at least with no longer delay than intervened between Christ's death and his resurrection. To this the Apostle may be conceived as replying: "each in his own order." Christ has a precedence, He is the ἀπαρχή, the source of the entire process, therefore his resurrection had to follow without delay, but it is only natural that that of the others should be postponed till His coming, precisely because He is the ἀπαρχή. The Apostle, it seems to us, does not use tagma with any conscious emphasis upon its primary military meaning; ἀπαρχή belongs to a totally different sphere of figurative representation, that of the firstfruits and the harvest. The only point of comparison in the use of tagma is that of order, sequence of occurrence. By so understanding it here we also meet the argument drawn from the difficulty that Christ cannot form a tagma by Himself. To adhere to the primary sense of "division," "troup," and yet include Christ would be possible only by throwing strong emphasis on the military meaning of the word, as if to suggest that He was, as it were, a host in Himself, an entire division by reason of His own strength. This might suit the rôle He plays in the eschatological process, and fit in with the representation of Him as the conqueror over all enemies in the sequel. But, as already observed, it is not favored by the characterization of Christ as "aparche," rather than as ἀρχηγός or some such term. And it certainly does not fit the case of those who form the other tagma, for believers in their resurrection do not appear in any military capacity.

If then tagma be given the sense of "order," "rank," and Christ comes in the first tagma, every necessity falls away for inferring from the mode of statement that there must be a further tagma beyond that of Christ and that of believers, and for finding here, in consequence of the other rendering, the doctrine of a twofold resurrection, one before and one after the millennium.

Much is made of the argument that εἶτα at the beginning of vs. 24 proves a substantial interval between the parousia and "the end." It must be granted that, had the Apostle meant to express such a thought, εἶτα would have been entirely appropriate for the purpose. But it is not true that εἶτα is out of place on the other view, viz. if Paul means to affirm mere succession without any protracted interval.[11] Εἶτα can be used just as well as τότε to express momentary sequence of events, as may be verified from a comparison with vss. 5,6,7 in this same chapter, and with Jno. xiii. 4, 5. Of course, a brief interval in logical conception at least, must be assumed: "τὸ τέλος" comes, speaking in terms of strict chronology, after the rising of οἱ τοῦ χριστοῦ. But that by no means opens the door to the intercalation of a rounded-off chiliad of years.

The absolute phrase "τὸ τέλος" does not favor the view that "the end of the resurrection may, or even must, be meant by

[11] The contention of Titius, *Der Paulinismus unter dem Gesichtspunkt der Seligkeit,* p. 47, to the effect that Paul, if he wanted to mark a protracted interval, was bound to repeat: ἔπειτα is not borne out by grammatical analogy.

it. In its absoluteness the simple "τὸ τέλος" is too weighty for this; it requires a more absolute force. To interpret it of the "end" of the present aeon is scarcely admissible, for that coincides with the parousia, and by means of εἶτα "the end" is represented as a step subsequent to the parousia. We have the choice between taking it in its strictly teleological signification as "the goal," i.e. the goal to which the entire process of redemption has been tending, or, if the time-element be retained, taking it as the close of the great eschatological finale, which leads over from this aeon into the coming one. The latter seems favored by the time-sense of ὅταν and the clauses which this conjunction introduces. That which forms, as it were, the concrete content of the "telos" is the giving up of the kingship to God, the Father. And this "giving up" is nothing else but the culminating result of the eschatological process of subduing the enemies, whence also the second ὅταν describes it as taking place after all these enemies have been reduced to subjection. Taking telos in this sense as marking the consummation-point of Christ's eschatological reign, we can no longer find in it the evidence for a millennium which it would contain, if taken to mean "the end of the resurrection."

The question remains, however, where Paul makes this eschatological reign of Christ, which comes to a close after the resurrection of believers, begin. It is on the answer to this question that the understanding of εἶτα, which in itself may mean sequence with or without chronological interval, in the present case depends. If Paul made this reign of Christ begin at the parousia, then there must lie a period between the parousia and the telos, because the beginning and the end of things cannot but be separated in time. If, on the other hand, the reign dates from a point back of the parousia, then the telos can follow closely united with the parousia. Here the second ὅταν-clause may help us to a decision. It affirms that the delivering up of the kingdom will happen after Christ has brought to nought the various powers enumerated. The question resolves itself into this: Is there anything in the conception of these hostile powers and of their subjection that compels us to think of Christ's warfare against and victory over them as *not antedating the parousia*? Plainly the conquest is of such a nature that it covers a period of some duration; this is implied in the ἄχρις οὗ and in the word "last" of the phrase "the last enemy." But the question is where we shall make the period begin: at the parousia or at some earlier point? Ὅταν is retrospective, but the point to which the retrospect extends is uncertain. All we can say is that there is nothing in the words of the passage itself, nor in Paul's general teaching, to hinder us in dating this period of eschatological conquest from the Saviour's death and resurrection. Paul regards these last-named events in an eschatological light. In Col. ii. 15 he speaks of the conquest of the ἀρχαί and ἐξουσίαι as having in principle been accomplished in the cross of Christ. In Rom. viii. 38, 39 he assumes that even now Christ so reigns over and controls death and life and principalities and powers as to preclude every separation of the Christian from the love of God in Him.

But, while the words of the second ὅταν-clause will fit into either view, nevertheless, when this clause is taken in connection with the statement of vs. 26, it will be felt decidedly to favor an earlier beginning of the kingdom of Christ than at the parousia. The last enemy that is brought to nought is Death. The conquering of the other enemies, and consequently the reign of Christ consisting in this, precedes the conquest of Death. Now Paul makes the conquest of Death coincide with the parousia and the resurrection of believers. According to vss. 50-58, when the dead are raised incorruptible, and the living are changed (i.e. according to vs. 23 at the parousia), Death is swallowed up in victory. And still further, apart from this specific argument, a more general argument can be built on vss. 50-58, because it is there implied that the resurrection of the righteous and the very last "end" fall together. The Apostle here speaks throughout in terms of absolute consummation. When the righteous dead are raised this is the moment of their inheriting "the kingdom of

God," vs. 50. Notice, the Apostle does not say "the kingdom of Christ," as he ought to have said according to the chiliastic exegesis of vss. 24-28, for this exegesis makes him distinguish between a kingdom of Christ and the kingdom of God in this way, that the former extends from the parousia till the "end," whilst the latter does not begin until the "end." Vs. 50 proves that the kingdom of God begins with the parousia and the resurrection of the righteous, therefore the kingdom of Christ must, so far as it is chronologically distinguished from the kingdom of God, lie before the parousia. It begins, as already stated, with Christ's own resurrection. This conclusion also follows from the equivalence of the *κυριότης* of Christ and the *βασιλεία* of Christ. The *κυριότης* begins with the resurrection of the Saviour, therefore his *βασιλεία* cannot begin at a later point. Phil. ii. 9-11 connects with Christ's exaltation to the *κυριότης* the same things that 1 Cor. xv. 24-28 connects with his reign as King. The trump blown for the resurrection of Christians is "the last trump," which excludes the prospect of any further crisis. Elsewhere also the Apostle joins together the resurrection of believers, the change of the living and the judgment of the world.[12] Finally, Paul expects that the renewal of the *κτίσις* will accompany the resurrection of the saints.[13] When the creation is delivered from the bondage of corruption into the liberty of the glory of the children of God, this of itself must mark the consummation of all things, and excludes the further activity of enemies, such as would still have to be reduced to subjection.

Two other passages usually quoted as carrying chiliastic implications are 1 Thess. iv. 13-18 and 2 Thess. i. 5-12. The argument from the former passage is not so much an argument from direct statements contained in it, but rather based on the observation that without the injection into the exegesis of the millennium-idea the passage yields no clear sense, whilst becoming lucid so soon as the factor of the millennium is

[12] Cp. 1 Thess. ii. 19; 2 Thess. i. 7; 1 Cor. i. 7, 8; 2 Tim. iv. 1.
[13] Cp. Rom. viii. 18-22.

reckoned with. It is argued that the Thessalonians appear to have been dubious as to whether those who had died from among them after the formation of their church would be raised from the dead at the coming of the Lord. But, it is further argued, they cannot possibly have been ignorant of or non-believers in the final resurrection of the saints as such, since this latter doctrine holds a central, prominent place in Paul's gospel, and he cannot but have preached it to them emphatically. They could not have been Christians without knowing and accepting it. The situation is supposed to become clear and conceivable only, if we understand the doubt or unbelief involved as relating not to the resurrection of believers in general, but to the question whether the already departed saints would obtain for themselves a resurrection at the parousia which would enable them to share in the provisional kingdom of Christ, together with those whom the Lord would find alive at His coming, or whether they would have to wait for their resurrection and glory until the end of this kingdom. It was for them not a question of resurrection or no-resurrection, but a question of earlier or later, the former meaning participation, the latter non-participation in the blessedness of the millennial kingdom. And that such was the real situation, it is urged, follows not merely from the impossibility of conceiving it otherwise, but also from the manner in which Paul meets the difficulty. He does not affirm in general that there is a resurrection of the dead, as he does in I Cor. xv, but says "those that are fallen asleep, God will through Jesus bring with Him." And "we that are alive, that are left unto the coming of the Lord, shall in no wise *precede* them that are fallen asleep." The use of the verb φθάνειν, "precede" is taken as proof that the question was a mere question of precedence. Paul denies the precedence in the particular form in which the Thessalonians had imagined it. There will be no later or earlier as regards believers, no discrimination between living and dead as to sharing in the provisional Messianic kingdom. All will be brought by God to be with Jesus at his coming. But, while denying this, and in the very act of denying this, Paul implies that the general scheme of the resurrection left room for the possibility of doubt on this point. If there is room for precedence in the abstract, there must be successive stages; there must be a double resurrection, one at the parousia, another at the close of Christ's millennial reign. The Apostle virtually assures the Thessalonians that their dead will be present at the first meeting of the saints with Christ, which distinctly presupposes that there will be a second meeting at a later point.

Here, even more than in the case of I Cor. xv, it must be conceded that the argument looks like a very plausible and convincing one. But, when we look more closely at the actual words of the passage, the matter becomes considerably more complicated and less certain. First of all, it should be observed that little can be built on the *a priori* assumption of the impossibility of the Thessalonians doubting the resurrection of the dead saints *in toto* after the preaching of Paul. To the Church of Corinth Paul had also preached the resurrection, still some of the members of that Church were disbelievers of the doctrine. To be sure, the doubt of the Thessalonians, if it existed, must have been of a somewhat different complexion, more naïve, less theoretical, that that of the Corinthians, otherwise Paul would have met it systematically as he does in I Cor. xv. But, if theoretical considerations made the *Corinthians* sceptical, notwithstanding the explicit preaching of Paul, then some more primitive or instinctive form of the same pagan unbelief may have kept the *Thessalonians* from assimilating this part of Paul's gospel, in a more innocent way, of course, for the Apostle does not blame, he simply comforts and reässures them. It is not *a priori* impossible, that there were those among the Thessalonians who believed the glory of the end to be restricted to those who would be found living at the parousia, and expected nothing for the dead, neither at the parousia nor thereafter, neither in the body nor as to the soul, in a word who judged of the dead after a pagan fashion, while taking a Christian view in regard to those whom Christ would find living in the body at his coming.

But the decisive question is: What does the passage itself imply? The very words in which the Apostle introduces the subject seem to make it plain that the Thessalonians did not take into account, as a reason for relative disappointment, or relative comfort, a resurrection of their dead later than the parousia at a point separated from the latter by an intervening reign of Christ. Vs. 13 indicates that the readers were given to sorrowing over their dead as the pagans do who have no hope. The question has been raised, whether this necessarily must mean their sorrowing for the same reason for which the pagans are wont to sorrow, or whether justice perhaps may be done to these words, by merely making them mean, that the Thessalonians sorrowed in the same excessive manner as the Gentiles do, only for a different reason, the Gentiles because they have no hope for the post-mortem state at all, the Thessalonians because they feared that their dead would not return to life until after the Messianic (provisional) reign of Christ with its possibilities for enjoyment was hopelessly past. It has been argued that Paul distinguishes the case of the Thessalonians from that of the λοιποί; the λοιποί are *οἱ μὴ ἔχοντες ἐλπίδα* ; they themselves, therefore, must be *ἔχοντες ἐλπίδα* ; consequently Paul does not class them with unbelievers concerning the resurrection; the *manner* or *excess* of their sorrow only was the same as that of the pagans; not the reason was the same. This argumentation, however, overlooks the fact that the *ἐλπίδα ἔχειν*, which certainly is implied with reference to the readers, is not an *ἐλπίδα ἔχειν* in their subjective consciousness, but in the objective conviction of Paul. The Apostle does not mean to say: You *need* not have sorrowed, because *you knew* you had hope. What he means to say is: You *need* not sorrow, because *I know* there is hope for you. These words, therefore, do not help us in any way to determine the subjective state of mind of the Thessalonians, whether they doubted merely the raising of their dead at the parousia or the raising of their dead at any time whatsoever. Decisive, however, it seems to us are the following considerations: (1) The *καί* **before** *οἱ* λοιποί indicates that the Thessalonians in their own mind *also* belonged to the class of those who had no hope; had the mere manner or degree of sorrowing formed the point of comparison, Paul would have written καθὼς οἱ λοιποί; (2) The way in which Paul explains himself in vs. 14 shows how he conceived of the subjective state of mind of the Thessalonians. It will be noticed how in this verse he really gives a double assurance: (a) that the κοιμηθέντες will be raised; (b) that they will be brought by God into the presence of Jesus at the parousia. This sounds as if both points had been in doubt. Had the *latter* only been in doubt, Paul would have said: the resurrection will take place not later than, but at the parousia. What he says is: *there will be a resurrection of the dead,* and *the dead will be present at the parousia.* Especially the protasis of vs. 14: "for if we believe that Jesus died and rose" makes this very clear, because logically it requires the apodosis: "then also those that are fallen asleep will rise in Christ." That Jesus rose Paul would not have mentioned at all, had there not been doubt concerning the fact of the resurrection generally. The apodosis which Paul actually wrote does not show our point so clearly, because it contracts into a single clause two distinct propositions: ὁ θεὸς τοὺς κοιμηθέντας ἐγερεῖ διὰ τοῦ Ἰησοῦ and ὁ θεὸς τοὺς κοιμηθέντας ἄξει σὺν αὐτῷ; (3) Had the Thessalonians been merely concerned about a belated participation of their dead in the blessings of the future, and had Paul wished to call attention to the relative hopefulness of even this state of mind in contrast with the utter hopelessness of the pagan unbelief, then the Apostle would as a matter of fact have given the Thessalonians two distinct grounds of comfort: in the *first* place that even so their doubt did not call for such excessive sorrow, since they themselves continued to feel assured of an ultimate resurrection embracing all Christians; in the *second* place that the actual situation was far better than they imagined, since they could count on an *immediate* resurrection coinciding with the parousia. But in reality there is no trace whatever that the Apostle had two such distinct thoughts in mind: vs. 14, by means of "for" attaches itself to vs. 13, yet it makes no reflection upon the main thought which would according to the Chiliastic exegesis find expression in vs. 13, viz. that the Thessalonians had at any rate the final resurrection to fall back upon.

On the ground of these three considerations it may be confidently affirmed that the sorrow of the Thessalonians had no Chiliastic background, but was caused by misconceptions of a more fundamental nature. It is true this yields no more than a *negative* result. It can *not be proven* from their state of mind, that they were Chiliasts, nor that Paul had taught them such doctrine. Notwithstanding this the possibility is not thereby precluded, that in the answer Paul gives in order to instruct or relieve them, there might have lain Chiliastic implications. The general doubt of the Thessalonians, as to whether their dead would be present at the parousia, Paul might have met in the more precise form of implying that they would not only participate in the resurrection, but would obtain a first resurrection restricted to believers. In other words the writing of this very passage might have been the first occasion on which Paul called the attention of the Thessalonian converts to the subject of the provisional kingdom. This brings us to the question how the *φθάσωμεν* in vs. 15 is to be understood. The verb expresses the thought of arriving earlier at a goal than somebody else. How is this to be understood in the present situation? Did Paul, when using this figure, have in mind that there were two distinct arrivals at the presence of the Lord and at the resurrection-crisis, one earlier and one later, and does he assure the Thessalonians that those who remained alive would not have the advantage of the earlier arrival and that the dead in Christ would not have to put up with the later one of these two arrivals? In that case the background is that of Chiliasm with its twofold resurrection. Or, did Paul simply employ the figure to assure the readers that in gaining the presence of the Lord the dead would not be *one moment behind* the living? In that case the representation has nothing to do with Chiliasm. It seems to us that everything speaks in favor of the latter exegesis. The Chiliastic scheme distinguishes between two resurrections, but not between two *resurrections to glory,* so that it fails to explain the mode of expression: those that are left will not anticipate the dead. Of an anticipation in glory the Chiliastic scheme knows only where the first resurrection is confined to the martyrs, and that could not be the case here, since Paul speaks of all the dead in Christ.[14]

In 2 Thess. i. 5-12 two expressions occur which have given rise to a Chiliastic explanation. In vss. 5 ff. the Apostle says that the persecutions and afflictions endured by the members of the church are a manifest token of the righteous judgment of God, to the end that they may be counted worthy of the kingdom of God for which they also suffer, since it is a righteous thing with God to recompense affliction to them that afflict the readers and to those that are afflicted rest with Paul at the revelation of the Lord Jesus from heaven. In vs. 11 we have the more general idea, that God may count the Thessalonians worthy of their calling κλῆσις here in the objective sense "that to which one is called," as ἐλπίς elsewhere, "that which is hoped for"). There is, however, nothing in these statements that would go beyond the general thought that suffering and glory, sanctification and the inheritance of the kingdom of God are inseparably linked together. The

[14] It is a question in dispute, which will probably never be settled to satisfaction, how much of vss. 15-17 belongs to the λόγος Κυρίου which the Apostle quotes, and with what degree of literalness it is quoted by him. If we could feel sure that the words in vs. 15 οἱ περιλειπόμενοι οὐ μὴ φθάσωμεν τοὺς κοιμηθέντας (with a change, of course, from the first to the third person) were literally Jesus' words, either orally transmitted or by revelation delivered to Paul, then it would be plain that to draw the inference of Chiliasm from φθάσωμεν would involve not merely the ascription of this doctrine to Paul but likewise to Jesus. But it is scarcely worth while for our present purpose to pursue this any further, because we have no data to determine the precise extent nor the exact literalness of the quotation. The words of Jesus might merely have affirmed the resurrection of the believing dead at the parousia, and Paul might have made use of this declaration in an argument with or without Chiliastic implications.

persecutions and afflictions of which the former passage speaks are not specifically those of martyrdom, and to think of a separate resurrection for all those that were persecuted and afflicted, would be without analogy. Besides this, the kingdom to which Paul refers is "the kingdom of God" (vs. 5), and this, according to 1 Cor. xv. 24, is the kingdom of the absolute end, not any intermediate kingdom preceding it.[15]

The last passage we must examine as to its bearings on the question of Chiliasm is Phil. iii. 10-14. The Apostle, it is said, here expresses the desire to become conformed unto the death of Christ, i.e., to suffer martyrdom. The motive for this desire is expressed in the words: "If by any means I may attain unto the resurrection from the dead." Paul, according to this interpretation, expected a preliminary resurrection in which those only would share who had died for Christ's sake, whereas the others would have to be content with the general resurrection at a much later point. This, it will be observed, would yield a conception far more analogous to what chiliastic exegetes find in the well-known passage of the Apocalypse, than to the chiliastically interpreted statements of 1 Cor. xv. 22 ff. Here in Philippians we should actually have the idea that the martyrs receive as a special reward a resurrection preceding that of the others, whereas, according to 1 Cor. xv, all those that are of Christ would share at his coming in the resurrection.[16]

[15] Cp. 1 Thess. ii. 12: "To the end that ye should walk worthily with God, who calleth you into His own kingdom and glory." It will be observed, that if the passage from 1 Thess. iv discussed above and the expressions in 2 Thess. i both teach Chiliasm, they pointedly disagree as to the type of Chiliasm taught, since the First Epistle implies that all believers, who have died, share in the resurrection at the parousia, whereas the Second Epistle would restrict this privilege to those who have endured persecution. This might easily be construed as a reflection on the genuineness of the Second Epistle.

[16] The difference between the Chiliasm found in 1 Cor. xv. 22 ff. and that of the Apocalypse relates to several other points: the Apocalypse makes the reign of Christ last one thousand years; Paul in 1 Cor. xv would speak of an indefinitely portracted period. According to the Apocalypse at the close of the one thousand years during which Satan is bound he is let loose again previously for his final defeat by Christ;

It so happens that in the Epistle to the Philippians it is more impossible than anywhere else to reconcile the alleged Chiliastic elements with the fundamental structure of the Pauline Eschatology. According to Chap. iii. 20, 21 Paul makes the parousia coincident with the change of body not merely for himself but for all: "for our commonwealth is in heaven, from whence also we wait for a Saviour, the Lord Jesus Christ, who shall fashion anew the body of our humiliation, that it may be conformed to the body of his glory, according to the working whereby He is able to subject all things unto Himself." If Paul expected any special privilege for himself and other martyrs as regards time and order of resurrection, it cannot have been in connection with the parousia. We should then have to assume that he looked forward to an earlier resurrection, perhaps immediately after death. On such a view it would perhaps be possible to explain the plural of vss. 20, 21 rhetorically so as not to include Paul himself, and confirmation might be found for that in the first chapter, where "to depart" is equivalent to "being with Christ." Thus at least a degree of consistency could be saved for the Epistle. But even such a modified form of the anticipated-resurrection theory would not be plausible enough to entitle it to serious consideration. On the one hand it is unnatural to exclude Paul from the ἡμεῖς of iii. 20, 21; on the other hand there is nothing in i. 20-24 to suggest the Apostle's conceiving the "being with Christ" to which his death would immediately introduce him, as an *embodied* life in heaven. It is true the phrase σὺν Κυρίῳ εἶναι designates in 1 Thess. iv. 17 the presence with Christ in the body after the

in 1 Cor. xv the close of the millennial period would signify the conquering of the last enemy. In the Apocalypse the conflict between Christ and the enemies is concentrated in the crisis at the end, whilst with Paul it would cover the whole period of Christ's kingdom. The millennial reign, which according to the Apocalypse would be a reign of peace, Satan being bound, would be a reign of war according to the interpretation put on Paul's words. It is usually assumed that the millennial reign of which the Apocalypse is believed to speak, is a reign to be exercised by Christ on earth; the process of which Paul speaks plays in the transcendental heavenly sphere.

resurrection, but in that passage it receives its special meaning from the context, as is indicated by the word οὕτως, "and *thus* we shall be forever with the Lord." In our passage the "being with Christ" does not have its meaning contextually determined in this way. The phrase in itself decides nothing as to the form which the presence with Christ will assume. Nothing hinders and everything favors giving it the same meaning as the ἐνδημῆσαι πρὸς τὸν Κύριον of 2 Cor. v. 8.

Another serious objection to the Chiliastic interpretation lies in the expressions of vs. 12. Here Paul speaks of that which would enable him to καταντᾶν εἰς τὴν ἐξανάστασιν τὴν ἐκ νεκρῶν as an "apprehending," a "having been made perfect," and denies having attained to this: "Not that I have already apprehended or am already made perfect, but I press on, if so be that I may apprehend that for which also I was apprehended by Christ Jesus." It is plain from this that the condition on which the Apostle suspends his attaining unto the resurrection cannot be martyrdom, for it would have had no sense for him to assure the readers that, that he had not yet obtained this, nor was yet in that way made perfect. Some *internal* process of attainment and perfecting must be referred to. So soon as we understand the words as speaking of attaining to the resurrection in that sense they appear to be identical in substance with other Pauline statements affirming the causal nexus between suffering here on earth with Christ and glorification with Him hereafter, and in which it is universally recognized that no special privilege granted to a class of believers can be meant but only the general grace of the resurrection-glory in store for all believers.[17]

But the difficulty arises that on this exegesis Paul seems to make his participation in the resurrection, which elsewhere appears as an assured predetermined hope of every Christian, contingent upon the issue of a process he is undergoing here

[17] Cp. Rom. viii. 17: "If so be that we suffer with Him, that we may also be glorified with Him"; 2 Tim. ii. 12: "If we suffer, we shall also reign with Him."

on earth. How could he speak, one unavoidably asks, of his resurrection with the dubiousness implied in the words: "If by any means I might attain unto the resurrection from the dead?" In order to relieve this difficulty Van Hengel in his Commentary on the Epistle proposes the following: the word ἐξανάστασις does not mean here Paul's own resurrection, but is a designation for the time when the parousia takes place, equivalent to "the hour of the resurrection." Paul then would, with a degree of dubiety, express the desire that, as a result of his striving after conformity to Christ, he might be permitted by God to attain unto, i.e., to survive until the day of the resurrection.[18] But this is an impossible exegesis for several reasons. Why should Paul call the day of the parousia by this name "the resurrection from the dead," if he himself wishes or hopes to survive, so that to himself personally it would not be a day of resurrection? Going outside of his usual terminology to employ a strange name, we should expect him to choose at least a name that had some application to his own personal case. And in the first chapter of the Epistle Paul shows very plainly that survival until the parousia did no longer at the time of writing appear to him so desirable a thing as to be the supreme goal of aspiration. He there declares to depart and be with Christ "very far better" than "to abide in the flesh.[19]

We are thus compelled to face the fact that ἐξανάστασις designates Paul's own resurrection at the parousia, and that the Apostle represents this as in some sense dependent on his whole Christian striving and living as this revolved around the apprehension of Christ and the conformation to his death. This may be an unusual representation, but we have no right to declare it impossible or rule it out *a priori*. If taking it at its full meaning should have to be done at the cost of embrac-

[18] *Commentarius Perpetuus in Epistolam Pauli ad Philippenses,* 1838, pp. 234 ff.

[19] Van Hengel thinks that the verb καταντᾶν demands the interpretation of "*pervenire ad tempus hujus eventi.*" But he overlooks the fact that the choice of the verb is determined by the figure of "striving," as in the sequel is the verb διώκειν. Both are obviously metaphorical.

ing the pre-millennarian scheme, we should not over-dogmatically shrink from the issue. Still, with all openness of mind, we cannot bring ourselves to the conclusion that such is the absolutely necessary exegesis. The protests raised by the Epistle as a whole seem to be too emphatic for this. From one point of view, of course, the resurrection belonged to the province of the Apostle's absolute certitudes, viz. as viewed from the standpoint of the divine purpose reflected in the believer's assurance of salvation. But, from another point of view, the resurrection could appear none the less as the ethically and religiously conditioned acme of his progress in grace and conformity to Christ. The best way to make this believable is to place side by side Paul's strong sense of accountability towards the judgment-day, and his absolute conviction about the all-comprehensiveness and certainty of the verdict of justification. The sanctification of the believer is to him in practical life the *sine qua non* of the divine approval in the last day. This may throw light upon the analogous representation of the resurrection as the goal of a process of ever-growing apprehension and reproduction of Christ. As no one can expect to stand in the last day who has not practised holiness in the fear of God, so no one can hope to attain unto the resurrection of life who has not learned to know Christ and the power of his resurrection and the fellowship of his sufferings, being conformed unto his death. Such a mode of viewing the resurrection need not do away with the other mode of viewing it as a gift of free grace bestowed for the sake of the merit of Christ. The first relation in which Paul stands to Christ is expressed in vss. 8, 9: "That I may win Christ and be found in Him, not having my own righteousness, which is of the law, but that which is through the faith of Christ, the righteousness which is of God by faith." This is the forensic relation of justification and it is fundamental. But this is followed by a second, that of the apprehension of Christ subjectively in sanctification. And that it is not impossible for Paul to hold up the resurrection as a goal to be striven after, appears from the fact that he here plainly so represents the spiritual resurrection, which elsewhere he views quite as much as the bodily resurrection under the aspect of an absolute act or gift of God. The process of "knowing Christ," more particularly of knowing "the power of his resurrection" is, in some sense, subject to a διώκειν. It is at one and the same time a divine grace and a Christian attainment. It is a γνῶσις in which Paul takes an active part, in which there is place for a καταλαβεῖν, just as there is a καταντᾶν with reference to the eschatological resurrection. It may not be easy to explain in the concrete how precisely the Apostle conceived of this. The only point we desire to make is that, if the terms of effort be appropriate terms to be used in connection with the spiritual resurrection, then we lack the right to say that καταντᾶν εἰς used with εἴ πως involves an impossible representation from Paul's point of view as regards the resurrection of the body at the last day. Possibly in vs. 14 "the prize of the high-calling of God in Christ Jesus" likewise designates the resurrection-experience or the resurrection-state as something to which God will call at the end, or as something lying ready in heaven as the goal to which the believer has been called. Now of this prize Paul declares that he presses on towards it as towards a goal, and he expects of all mature Christians (τέλειοι) that they will be "thus minded," that is assume the same attitude of pursuit.

We have completed our exegetical survey, and the conclusion is that in none of the passages where Chiliasm was supposed to have been discovered, the discovery is borne out by the facts, while in not a few contexts it is positively irreconcilable with the Apostle's representation. It ought to be remembered, however, that this result of our investigation concerns only the idea of a provisional Messianic Kingdom as *future,* i.e., strictly eschatological from Paul's own standpoint, beginning with the parousia of the Lord. The argument in no wise precludes Paul's having regarded the present reign of Christ, with its semi-eschatological character in the light of a provisional kingdom to be succeeded by an absolute kingdom at the parousia. In point of fact such a conception is found in the passage of 1 Cor. xv. Here we are told in so many words that at "the end" Christ will deliver up the kingdom to God, even the Father. This implies plainly a distinction between the kingdom of Christ as a *present* and the kingdom of God as a *future* reality. In this place then Paul has plainly incorporated into his eschatology the idea of a twofold kingdom, just as in the teaching of our Lord there appears the same distinction between the present kingdom and the eschatological kingdom. In this form, and in this form only, is the distinction exempt from the objection that it must involve the anticlimax and interpose something different where the whole tenor of the Pauline teaching requires unbroken continuity. On our interpretation the Messianic provisional kingdom and the present σωτηρία are identical and coëxtensive, so that what the Christian now possesses and enjoys is the firstfruits and pledge of the life eternal. Paul's aspiration everywhere fastens, without any intermediate resting-point, on the eternal state. This is immediately explained, if the blessings and joys of the Messianic reign have already arrived, so that the Christian hope can with undistracted intensity project itself into the world to come.

It cannot be maintained, however, that Paul carries through this distinction between the kingdom of Christ and the kingdom of God with uniformity. Although to a larger extent an eschatological conception with Paul than with Jesus, the kingdom of God is not exclusively so in the Pauline teaching. The Apostle speaks of "inheriting the kingdom of God," 1 Cor. vi. 9; xv. 50; Gal. v. 21; Eph. v. 5; believers are "called to God's kingdom and glory," 1 Thess. ii. 12; they suffer "that they may be counted worthy of the kingdom of God," 2 Thess. i. 5. But the kingdom of God also appears as a present reality. According to Rom. xiv. 17 it consists not in eating and drinking, but in righteousness and peace and joy in the Holy Spirit, and acording to 1 Cor.

iv. 20 its essence is not in word but in power.[20] In these passages the kingdom of God and the present reign of Christ are identified. And if the present kingdom can be called the kingdom of God, it is also worthy of notice that the future kingdom can be called the kingdom of Christ. This occurs in Eph. v. 5, where Paul speaks of an "inheritance in the kingdom of Christ and of God." In 2 Tim. iv. 1 we read of "the ἐπιφανεία and βασιλεία of the Lord Jesus Christ" as coinciding with the judgment. This has been brought into connection with the advanced doctrine of the later Epistles, where Christ is represented as *the goal* of the world-movement.[21]

The above observations show that a hard and fast distinction between a Messianic kingdom and the ultimate kingdom of God cannot be carried through in Paul. Obviously what has invited the distinction in 1 Cor. xv is the fact, that there the reign of Christ appears in one specific aspect, viz. as a reign of conquest. The βασιλεύειν of Christ here virtually consists in subduing one enemy after the other. As such it naturally enters into contrast with the absolute eternal reign of God at the end, of which it is characteristic that from it all enemies and warfare shall have been banished. Confirmation to this may be found in Col. i. 13, the one passage besides 1 Cor. xv. 24, where the kingdom of Christ has a somewhat militant setting: "God has delivered us out of the power of darkness and translated us into the kingdom of the Son of his love." To be sure, here the conqueror, who rescues us from the enemy, is rather God than Christ.

[20] Cp. also 1 Cor. iv. 8 and Col. iv. 11.
[21] Cp. *Enc. Bibl.* II, 1386.

CHAPTER XI

THE JUDGMENT

Resurrection and Judgment are the two correlated acts of the final consummation of things. They are like twin-woes in the travail by which the age to come is brought to birth. But they are not cleanly separated even at their eschatological emergence. In the resurrection there is already wrapped up a judging-process, at least for believers: the raising act in their case, together with the attending change, plainly involves a pronouncement of vindication. The resurrection does more than prepare its object for undergoing the judgment; it sets in motion and to a certain extent anticipates the issue of the judgment for the Christian. And it were not incorrect to offset this by saying that the judgment places the seal on what the believer has received in the resurrection. Broadly speaking, and keeping the whole trend of revelation in mind, the two processes cover between themselves the entire religious destiny and status of man. The physis and the ethos appear here in their interdependence. Ethically man must be set right, physically, or rather soterically, he must be healed and transfigured. To these two ideas nothing of equal fundamental importance could be added: they are in principle exhaustive of what takes place at the end.

The eschatological judgment appears in two widely varying forms of description, which, respectively, may be named the realistic and the forensic one. In regard to the former it is not necessary that the technical term "judgment" should be employed, or where this appears it is in a less formal half-metaphorical sense. The substance, however, is always there, viz. that God brings about an effectual termination to the preceding process and puts in the place of it something *toto genere* different of final significance. From the nature of the setting given to this it relates chiefly to the judgment of

God's enemies. The setting is martial; the background that of a fierce battle and a decisive victory. In the Old Testament this is for a long time the prevailing mode of representation, though from Daniel and the Psalms onward the formal forensic picture becomes increasingly in evidence, without, however, entirely superseding the other. In the martial judgment there is no apparatus of records kept and examined, and no verdict solemnly pronounced on the basis of these. The mode is theophanic, that is through an appearance of Jehovah, but the theophany assumes such dimensions and produces such absolute effects, that there can be no question as to its belonging to the sphere of eschatology proper. Through the subsumption of the apparently physical process under the category of judgment its basally-eschatological character is assured. What seems at first sight blind and unexplainable is placed in the light of supreme purpose.

The two terms in which this survival of the one, and that the earlier, of the Old Testament representations finds expression are ὀργή and ὄλεθρος. It is chiefly the merit of Ritschl to have once more placed in its proper eschatological setting the idea of the divine "wrath."[1] The term is not, of course, exclusively eschatological in its use; cp. Mk. iii. 5; Rom. xii. 19; xiii. 4, 5. But the overgrowing of the generally-ethical by the specifically-eschatological is clearly traceable. The ὀργὴ μέλλουσα of John the Baptist, the "ὀργή that abides" of Jno. iii. 36, the "coming ὀργή" of 1 Thess. i. 10 clearly indicate its ancient eschatological affinities long after the period of the Old Testament. Then there is also the figure of its "being stored up," which presupposes a final

[1] The seemingly obvious reference of "wrath" to the *present* in Rom. i. 18 has had an obscuring effect on its more specific eschatological application. The Present tense "is revealed," as well as the effects described in the immediate sequel, belonging to the perverseness of the Pagan ethico-religious life of the time, have rashly led to the conclusion that the context relates to the purely providential retribution of God. But the better version of the Present is "is *being* revealed." These religious and moral monstrosities are characteristic of the end, as may be seen from the Pastorals.

epochal terminus to its outworking. This reference is plainly required where the "orge" appears as something from which even believers need yet to be saved through the life of Christ, Rom. v. 9; for the present it would be absolutely impossible to conceive of believers as subject to the divine wrath, so that on that account alone reference of the "wrath" to the eschatological crisis appears inevitable. The objects of reprobation are designated as "σκεύη ὀργῆς" i.e. vessels in which wrath has been stored up for manifestation in the future, Rom. ix. 22.

Less frequent is the term "ὄλεθρος," perhaps a specifically-Pauline word in eschatological usage. It occurs four times: 1 Cor. v. 5; 1 Thess. v. 3; 2 Thess. i. 9; 1 Tim. vi. 9. With "orge" it has in common the unforensic setting. The root from which "olethros" is derived is the same as in "ἀπόλλυμι" and in the latter's correlative noun "ἀπώλεια." All these forms are pointedly eschatological. The "Man-of-Sin" in 2 Thess. iv. bears the name "son of perdition" ("apōleia"). I Tim. vi. 9 "olethros" and "apōleia" occur together. Whether the verb "apollumi" means, eschatologically, "to annihilate," and the noun "apōleia" "annihilation" is a question to be looked into presently.

There is one peculiar feature about this execution of judgment in act, viz. the immediateness of its effect. This is best illustrated by the description of the disposal of the "Man-of-Sin" in Thessalonians; it is brought about by the breath of the mouth of the Christ, by the mere manifestation of His coming. Plainly this feature was borrowed from Isa. xi. 5. In Isaiah it is simply one of the illustrations of the prophet's conception of the instantaneousness of Jehovah's supernatural working particularly in judgment.

It were a mistake to understand these realistic descriptions of the judgment as, to the mind of Paul, depicting God in a passionate state of non-reflecting self-assertion. Even in the Old Testament this is not so. Back of the bursting forth of the "wrath" and of the surrender to "olethros," there is always assumed to lie a decision taken deliberately and based on righteous grounds. What is so often alleged and so thoughtlessly repeated concerning the unethical nature of the God of a large part of the Old Testament finds no support in such representations. The terminology does not favor it, for the process is of old called a "Shaphat," a "judgment, and a "judgment" as such has intelligent discrimination in it. Else the term and its derivatives could never have been drawn into the service of certain current delineations of Jehovah's O.T. character, either eschatologically or otherwise. The peculiar term "zedakah" for "victory" in certain contexts of the Old Testament bears witness to the same principle.[2]

It would be no less a mistake, however, to identify these unforensic forms of judgment-execution with purely physical processes. Realistic they are, to be sure, but realistic is not to be equated to the sensual-physical. The breath of the mouth of the appearing Christ is not to be understood as a withering blast, although some of the Apocalyptic writers may have actually formed this conception of the Messiah's mode of action. But neither is all this material to be diluted into the purely ethico-spiritual, as though it were a species of psychological procedure, only on a higher plane. The divine realism is more than thought- or will-tissue. But the greater of these two misconceptions is, perhaps, that of solidifying what happens into elements of physics. Kabisch, who out-apocalypses the Apocalyptics, has gone farthest in the direction of the latter extreme. He handles the conception of "fire," not only after a realistic-substantial but after a materialistic fashion, particularly in connection with 1 Cor. iii. 13-15. To the physical nature of the fire here spoken of he attributes, first of all, the illuminating character of the judgment: "every man's work shall be made manifest: for the day" (i.e. the day of Jehovah) as a complex of light-producing fire. But fire is also a destructive, consuming principle, so that, if the process be once physically conceived, the literal

[2] It ought not to be overlooked that "orge" is objective; it designates the product, the issue in act of a state of mind; the corresponding state of mind giving vent to "orge" is "θυμός."

fire will furnish the unitary element in which these two effects are naturally combined. The fire spoken of is assumed to be, with the same literal understanding, the elemental fire of which the Spirit consists. This pneumatic fire, according to Kabisch, preserves in Paul's conception that which is similar to its nature, whilst destroying all the dissimilar, viz. the sarcical.[3]).

All this rests on an over-literal interpretation of what wishes to be understood as figurative language, although it can not be denied that by an unusually felicitous interweaving of a figurative woof with a literal-realistic warp a remarkably-impressive texture has been obtained. The figures are undoubtedly suggested by belief in the phenomenon of an actual, eschatological fire having a real function in the judgment-day. But this by no means suffices to render the entire representation physico-eschatological. It may even be doubted, whether in the Apocalyptic passages quoted much more than figures are intended, because in other passages the figurative meaning lies on the surface. Thus Test. Abr. we read: "He tests the works of man by fire, and if any man's work is consumed by the fire, straightway the angel of judgment takes him and carries him into the place of sinners . . . but if the fire shall test any man's work and shall

[3] For the Apocalyptic source of this Kabisch refer to the following passages: *4 Ezra* xiii. 9, 10, where the Messiah in combat with the enemies neither raises his hand, nor carries a sword nor any other weapon, but causes to proceed from his mouth a fiery stream and from his lips a flaming breath, and stormy sparks to fly from his tongue, all of which, mingling together, set the attacking host of the enemy on fire and annihilate them; then, in Chap. xxxviii, this fire is further, in the mind of the Apocalyptic writer (as interpreted by Kabisch) identified with the Law, alleged to have been understood by the Jewish Rabbis as a fiery substance, which would add one more element of possible literalness to the meaning of the representation; further, in *4 Ezra* xiv. 39 Ezra is made to drink the Law in the form of a chalice full of water with the color of fire; in *Apoc. Bar.* xlviii. 39 it is said that fire will eat the designs of the wicked and that in flames the cogitations of their reins will be tested. If all this in the Apocalypses is to be taken literally, then we shall have to say at the least that it goes far beyond the Old Testament realism. Cp. Isa. xi. 4; Mal. iv. 1.

not touch it, he is justified." The argument taken from the Jewish representation of the Law as a fiery substance, operating as such in the judgment-day, rests on a very slender basis, for in *4 Ezra* xiii. 38 it is only the Syriac Version that reads: "by his Law which resembles a flame"; the better reading seems to be: "by his word of command which resembles a flame."[4] In Chap. xiv. 39 the water which Ezra is given to drink resembles fire not because the substance of the law is of fire, but to depict the seer's inspiration.[5] But if some, or even all of such statements bore in the mind of these visionary writers a grossly-physical sense, it would by no means follow from this, that the images called up by the Apostle, simply because the same terms appear in them, require or allow the same interpretation. The fact alone that Paul in the passage of 1 Cor. iii turns the figure into three different directions suffices to prove that to him it is actually a figure.[6] Nor does Paul believe that any such fire will be needed to destroy that product of work which is compared to hay, wood, stubble. With as much right might one insist upon the literalness of these terms: wood, hay, stubble, in their application to the work- product as upon the literalness of the combustion-process when applied to the destruction of the things named. Were the destruction to be understood realistically as a destruction through chemical fire, then it would be unavoidable to assume the presence of the work-product in some realistic sense in the day of judgment, a consideration which, to be sure, does not deter Kabisch, for he asserts that according to the Jewish, and therefore likewise Paul's conception, the substance of works done is bodily preserved and bodily brought forward to undergo judgment. Support has been sought for this in the representation, that, when Christians are made manifest before the judgment-seat of Christ, each will

[4] Cp. Gunkel in loco in Kautzsch, *Die Apokryphen und Pseudepigraphen.*

[5] Gunkel, *ibid.*

[6] The three directions are: (a) the day will reveal it by fire; (b) the day will test by fire; (c) the fire will consume.

receive the things done in the body, whether it be good or bad, 2 Cor. v. 10. Within this statement, however, the phrase "done in the body" serves no other purpose than to specify the state of life, that in the judgment will pass under review, viz. the period spent in the body. It is impossible to conceive that Paul meant to restrict the judgment to corporeal sins, excepting from it all non-somatic wrongdoings. Even, when enumerating the works of "the flesh," he subsumes under this category several forms of sin that lie outside the sphere of the body, Gal. v. 19.

Passing over into the strictly-forensic field we find a technical terminology employed. The verb κρίνειν, κρίνεσθαι is the regular medium for describing the judging act of God or Christ. The noun for the passing of the judgment is κρίσις that for the resulting verdict κρῖμα; cp. Rom. v. 16. These terms are not, of course, confined to eschatological use, although in the majority of cases such is their actual reference. In its etymological origins the term "krinein" is an entirely neutral term meaning "to place or keep apart." The central idea is that of discrimination. In the basic natural, physical associations there is no technical judicial element present. "To judge" simply means to form an opinion, which, while it cannot help being to the credit or discredit of the one on whom the opinion is passed, is not even reminiscent of either law or law-court. How purely-ideal the mental action is becomes specially clear from its forming the main element in the concept of "to answer," ἀποκριθῆναι. A certain opinion is placed before the mind of one spoken to; this evokes a correlative opinion, and the act of "answering" is strikingly conceived as the result of the reaction of one opinion upon another. We meet this, ethically or juridically as yet uncolored, use in such passages as Lk. vii. 43; xii. 57; Jas. ii. 12. In Pauline statements it occurs Act. xiii. 46; xv. 19 ("my opinion is"); xx. 1; ("had determined"); 1 Cor. x. 15; 2 Cor. v. 14; Tit. iii. 12. Easily, however, there enters into this the formulation of a more or less official approval or disapproval. Thus the definitions brought from the council of Acts xv. to the diaspora Christians are called δόγματα κεκριμένα in xiv. 4. This is a court-terminology, although as a matter of fact it describes not an enforceable decision, but partakes of the nature of advice from the Apostles.

Within the province of divine jurisdiction, on the other hand, we plainly are in such statements as the following: Rom. xii. 2; iii. 6; vi. 2; 1 Cor. 1, 5; v. 13; xi. 32; 2 Thess. 11, 12; 2 Tim. iv. 1. In most instances of this forensic turn given to the word it contracts an unfavorable meaning implying divine disapprobation. The neutral "krinein" tends to change into an unfavorable "krinein," although this latter signification, notwithstanding its unfavorable import, still remains distinguishable from the absolutely unfavorable verdict of the last judgment.[7]

There is still a third group of terms relating to the judgment-procedure of God with its result of final, absolute determination. This group attaches itself to the "δίκαιος-δικαιοῦν-δικαίωσις"-idea which plays so large a rôle in the Apostle's soteriological, particularly his justification-vocabulary. It comes under consideration as to all three, adjective noun and verb, in a favorable sense only. The "dikaios" in result of justification cannot, of course, be condemned in the last judgment. Still of his positive final absolution and endowment with the supreme eschatological blessedness we read less than might be *a priori* expected in the judgment-contexts. And it is doubtless the relative absence of the element in question that reflects itself in the scarceness of the justification-terminology in such cases. The term "dikaios" (of God as Judge) occurs with undoubted reference to the final judgment in 2 Tim. iv. 8 only.[8] In 2 Thess. i. 5, 6 the

[7] The neuter sense of krinein (in the divine procedure) still appears in Rom. ii. 2; in Rom. v. 16 and 1 Cor. xi. 33 a sharp distinction is drawn between "*krinesthai*" and "*katakrinesthai*"; the Corinthian believers are "judged" on account of sinful conduct, but this is done through causing cases of sickness and deaths among them for the explicit purpose, that with the world in the last judgment they should not have to undergo the sharp verdict of κατάκρισις.

[8] In regard to the precise implicatons of the verse interpreters differ;

enduring of persecution by believers is called an "endeigma" of the "dikaia krisis" of God, to the end that the readers may be counted worthy of the kingdom of God; here both the entire context and particularly the term "kingdom" prove that the statement is meant eschatologically sensu stricto; there is no reflection here so much upon relative matters of degrees of blessedness; the inheritance of the kingdom of God is involved. The verb "dikaioon" "to justify" is found in the argument of Rom. ii. 13; while this argument is hypothetical, as explained above, it is none the less fundamental; it connects the principle ennunciated with the final judgment, which is explicitly named in vs. 16: the day when "God shall judge the secrets of men . . . by Jesus Christ." The noun "dikaiōsis" occurs with probably eschatological reference once only, Rom. v. 18; "(the free gift) came unto all men to justification of life"; here the reference to "life" certainly includes the consummate life of the eternal state, although it is not necessarily restricted to that. The synonym "dikaiokrisia" appears in Rom. ii. 5 with specific eschatological reference: "the day of wrath and of revelation of the righteous judgment of God." On the future tenses in certain passages no absolute reliance can be placed, because the tense may be logical and not chronologically-prospective.[9] The fact remains that the justification-terminology is somewhat in abeyance in Paul's references to the judgment. This in a measure confirms the conclusion reached before, viz. that in one important sense is to Paul virtually a judgment by way of anticipation.

By no means, however, does this mean that Christians have no further interest in or concern about the judgment

the reference to the last day is beyond doubt, and in connection with it God is called "the righteous Judge"; uncertain is the construction of the phrase "the crown of righteousness"; is the Genitive explicative or possessive? The former would yield "the crown consisting in righteousness" that is in the absolute eternal righteousness flowing from the final judgment. The latter yields: the consummation (crown) of that righteousness, which is the believer's possession already in this life; cp. the incorruptible crown of 1 Cor. ix. 25.

[9] Cp. Rom. ii. 13, 20; iv. 2; v. 17, 19.

still to come. How little this would be correct may be seen from the fact that by far the majority of instances where the last-judgment-idea occurs speak of believers. Of course, the first and most obvious reason for this is, that the letters are addressed to Christians, and that in consequence the judgment idea is brought to bear upon such. As God alone judges those that are "without," even so the Apostle might quite properly speak no more than was absolutely unavoidable of the judgment to be passed upon the world of unbelievers. The restraint in this respect could not help bringing about a certain abeyance of the sharp antithesis between believers acquitted and non-Christians condemned in the last day. [10] It were quite unwarranted to infer from this that the sharp contrast named was not familiar to or even was indifferent to the Apostle. Proof for the opposite is by no means lacking. Instances in which the act of "krinein" revolves around the salvation or non-salvation of persons are the following: Rom. ii. 2, 3, 8, 12, 16; iii. 6, 8; v. 16; 1 Cor. v. 13; vi. 2; 2 Cor. ii. 9; 2 Thess. ii. 12; 1 Tim. iii. 6; 2 Tim. iv. 1.

Giving full weight to these passages and not drawing any unwarranted generalizing conclusions from them, we still cannot help noticing that, broadly speaking, with Paul the judgment is an event that will make discrimination as to the future rank and enjoyment in the life to come between individual Christians. The differences established may and will be great, but the range covered by them lies within the realm of salvation. The Corinthian transgressors are "judged," that is disciplined by God through the infliction within their circle of sickness or death, but this happens not to the detriment of their final salvation, rather to the furtherance of it, 1 Cor. xi. 30-32. Particularly this principle is brought to bear upon those who are dispensers of the Gospel to others. All the work performed by one of this

[10] Cp. the words of Jesus, Matt. xxv. 32, 33. To the instances of condemnation of the evil may be added the affirmation that "the world" (that is "the world" in its evil complexion) is and will be subject to condemnation: Rom. iii. 6 (purely quantitative?); 1 Cor. vi. 2; xi. 32.

class may in the last day be destroyed as by fire, nevertheless the workman himself will issue from the judgment as a firebrand plucked out of the combustion that destroys his work, I Cor. iii. 14. At the same time the destruction of his work-product will be reckoned to him and by him as a real loss which he suffers. Paul, although only hypothetically, yet with real seriousness and a perceptible degree of fear, contemplates the contingency of becoming a castaway in his own person after all the labor expended by him towards the salvation of others.[11]

It might easily seem as if through the partial shifting of the emphasis from the personal issue to the question of degrees in the allotment of eternal benefits somewhat of the solemnity of the judgment-prospect were apt to be lost. The actual tone and tenor of the Apostle's deliverances on this subject do not verify such an impression. There remains hanging over the consciousness of approaching judgment a veil of disturbed apprehension, which even the most advanced in sanctification is unable to throw off. It forms in a certain sense the balancing counterpart to the pervasive and fundamental joyfulness of the first recipients of the new-born faith. And this tremor that runs as an undercurrent beneath and mingles even with the surface waves of the stream of primitive Christian experience is so real that it shows its presence in the mind of the Apostle himself to whom an ascent to the highest summits of Christian exultation was not unfamiliar. The supreme joy engendered by this was not able to render him immune to the fear and depression inseparable from the contemplation of the ultimate crisis with all it bears within itself of eternal issues. In the conscious presence of this thought he became acquainted with what he calls "the dread of the Lord," 2 Cor. v. 11.[12]

[11] I Cor. ix. 27.

[12] It is not quite certain that the statement, "Knowing therefore the terror of the Lord, we persuade men" should be understood of the particular fear Paul feels towards the judgment in the capacity of a dispenser of the Gospel, or of the fear he seeks to instil into his hearers through reminding them of their future exposure to the judgment. Vs. 10, urging that all must enter the judgment, favors the latter.

And in the case of the common believer likewise this sentiment is a constant ingredient. All the teaching on the fatherhood and love of God as connected with the experience of justification did not eradicate it. It yields no satisfactory explanation to say that this element in Paul's and the early Christians' mind represents but a lingering remnant of Paul's erstwhile religious way of thinking and feeling. It is far too deep-seated for that. Much more to the point would it be to recognize in it the thoroughly matured fruit of the age-long culture of the moral aspect of revealed religion among the Old Testament people of God fostered by the Law and the Prophets. In this respect also Paul was a genuine son of Israel, and through upholding the principle involved he took pains to make his converts spiritual heirs of what was finest and noblest in the Mosaic dispensation. Besides, nothing is more certain than that any depreciating judgment passed upon this strain in Paulinism affects with equal pertinence the teaching of Jesus.

The clear recognition of this aspect of the judgment brings us face to face with the problem of the legitimate or non-legitimate rôle played in the Pauline teaching (and in Biblical teaching generally) with the conception of reward. The question has been touched upon in our third chapter, but a closer examination at this point need not prove superfluous. The modern stress laid upon the autonomy and spontaneity of religion, even to the point of strict exclusion of every form of external authority, here plainly runs athwart what constitutes a main strand in the religion of the Scriptures. To propose any rule at all and to introduce any motives whatsoever *ab extra* is held to vitiate the religious process at its very root. The general answer to this radical position is, of course, that it puts man on an equal plane with God in the matter of religious converse, and that this in itself is an irreligious attitude to assume. Such autonomy and spontaneity as are thus insisted upon belong to God and to Him alone. If the objection to *forcing* religion upon man were to be taken in a strictly-literal sense the position taken might be readily allowed; there is no need of saying that with God no *such* gross violation of the nature of piety is conceivable. But the modern critique of the principle of authority in religion strikes far deeper than the view thus defined. It voices at bottom a protest against every non-volitional introduction of religious forces into the soul; the entire system of efficient, subconsciously communicated, grace is negated by it, so that to take one's stand on that ground would by one fell stroke annihilate the entire redemptive substance of the Christianity of the New Testament, and charge Paul with the incongenial rôle of unconsciously playing the Pelagian. What here we are more immediately concerned with embodies the obnoxious criticism in a much subtler and apparently less subversive form. The contention is that making use of the reward-motif in religion injures the delicacy of a relationship that by its very nature should be conducted on the high plane of absolute altruism. In other words it is the *commercial* aspect of the notion of reward, the *quid pro quo* method that provokes protest. Hence the name attached to it is "legalism" and its parentage is derived from the perverse system of Judaism, particularly as this system existed in post-Old-Testament times. The psychological root of this opinion lies not very far removed from the root of the preceding error: it is again the self-sufficient man thinking too highly of himself to suffer the dignity of his human nature to be encroached upon by God. No more than the psychic spontaneity of his religion can he permit the delicate texture of its fine spiritual disinterestedness to be interfered with from any quarter whatsoever.

Putting the question not now on the basis of the ethics or psychology of religion, but on the basis of the available evidence alone there can be no doubt as to the presence and vital significance of the reward-idea in the Pauline eschatology. The classical statement is that of Rom. ii. 6-10. We have explained before why owing to the intrusion of sin, the rule here formulated never attains to realization in practice, and what are the particular obstacles to its successful operation. The general cause lies in the refusal of the flesh (sinful human nature) to be subject to the will of God, Rom. vii. 5, 18; viii. 7; Gal. v. 17. But, while this belongs to the subconscious disposition of man, Paul goes further and points out to us the conscious channel which this inner opposition to God delves for itself to reach the open of surface manifestation. The general sinfulness of the heart might perhaps be mistaken for a negatively-disabling factor, something dooming all human efforts towards eschatological attainment to sheer futility. As a matter of fact Paul puts the failure of the law-method, if not on a more fundamental, yet religiously considered, on a more ugly basis. In its extreme form it assumes the character of enmity against God, such enmity to which the mere approach of and contact with God acts as a stimulus to hostile reaction. Still more specifically the Apostle teaches that the method formulated breaks down at one particular point, viz. its inevitable lapse into the sin of "boasting" before God. We can clearly observe that in his hamartological appraisal of the degrees of sin this constituted for Paul an extreme point of the fatal course traversed by sin in the human consciousness. It occupies this place for the simple reason of its being a profoundly irreligious attitude towards God as the rightful possessor and sole legitimate recipient of religious glory. The fact alone that the legalistic type of religion solicits and fosters this type of sin is in the Apostle's judgment sufficient to put it out of all consideration as a feasible method for arrival at the eschatological goal; cp. Rom. iii. 27.

Still this principial exclusion of the compensation-idea is enforced only in the sub-redemptive stage. Redemption reconstructs the relation of man to God. It does so not only in general, but also in this very respect, that room is again created for the introduction of the reward-complex. First of all in its ancient, immutable form it is incorporated and remains firmly embedded in the objective vicarious task of

Christ on behalf of man. Christ, according to Paul, does precisely what fallen man could no longer do in result of the insuperable obstacles thrown in his pathway by sin. For in Christ's case these obstacles do not exist; subjectively He is exempt from the disabling influence of sin. His positive moral and religious perfection renders every invasion of the self-glorifying factor into his consciousness *a priori* impossible. Hence in Phil. ii. 9 the gracious bestowal of the name above every name upon the Saviour is placed by Paul without the slightest hesitation on the footing of work rendered and value received: "*Wherefore* also God highly exalted Him and gave unto Him the name which is above every name."[13] Further, through an extension of the same principle to believers, although in their case no "earning" in the strict sense is according to Paul's general teaching conceivable, they are nevertheless admitted into a status within the régime of grace where with strict maintenance of the denial of merit, they are permitted to lay up a store of recompense for themselves towards the day in which all accounts are to be settled. As John spoke of receiving out of the fulness of Christ grace for grace, so after a somewhat similar fashion it might be said that in this Pauline construction there is deep calling unto deep, grace lying underneath grace throughout the successive divine dispensations at every point and on every plane.

Apart from Rom. ii. 5-10 the passages that speak of the allotment to the individual believer of a degree of reward are the following: 1 Cor. i. 4-8; iii. 8; xv. 32, 58; 2 Cor. iv. 16; v. 10; ix. 6-8; Gal. vi. 5-10; Phil. i. 10, 26; ii. 16; Col. i. 5; iii. 24; 1 Thess. iii. 13; v. 23; 2 Thess. i. 7; 1 Tim. ii. 18; iv. 8; v. 25; vi. 18, 19; 2 Tim. ii. 11; iv. 4, 8, 14, 16. What strikes one most in these pages is not so much the

[13] The Greek original for "gave," "**ἐχαρίσατο**," should not be overlooked in this passage. The name which Jesus had rightfully earned *yet* was bestowed upon Him by manner of grace. Even when God enters into the recompense-relationship with man He does so in virtue of an unmerited act of favor, granting something that He was in no wise bound to give.

enunciation of the compensatory principle but rather the matter-of-fact manner of its expression. It is evident that the Paul who had passed through the storm and stress of the Judaistic controversy, and come off triumphant in that crisis through the vindication of the doctrine of salvation by free grace, without the works of the law, could not possibly have felt any detraction from that in the incentive offered to the increase of the measure of reward. There was evidently to the Apostle's mind no retreat from the former position in all this. The matter simply belonged to a different plane.[14]

It should not be overlooked that the prospect of reward just discussed reacts upon the envisagement of the judgment both by Paul and the common Christian. While the judgment as such can not be otherwise regarded than as a matter of solemnity and fear, yet to this has now been added the reverse side, that of a prospect of joy and hopefulness and there results a still more complex feeling such as might well baffle the most skilful attempt at psychological analysis. Even the factor of a prospective reward, can, owing to its uncertainty and its dependence on the progress in sanctification, not but add a constant element of anxiety to the Christian hope. The judgment is unlike the resurrection in that its canvas can never be entirely flooded with light and joy. But neither can it, in view of the subintroduction of the note of

[14] The charge of continued infection of Paul by Jewish legalism is according to the above comments unwarranted, as has been shown before in Chapter III. The differences between the Jewish and the Pauline standpoint may be briefly formulated as follows: according to the Jewish mind the matter rests on a *commercial* basis; consequently God has no choice but is bound to reward; Paul never loses out of sight the prerogative of the divine sovereignty. God is not under obligation to reward such as He is under to punish sin, except in so far as He has bound Himself by implicit or explicit promise. It further follows from this that the reward according to Paul is never meted out on the basis of strict equivalence; in this respect also God retains His full sovereignty. Finally, the filial relationship of the Christian to God inevitably imparts to the procedure an altogether new physiognomy: henceforth it is not only a reward *of grace,* but specifically a reward bestowed by *paternal love.*

reward, be ever entirely overspread henceforth by the aspect of gloom and trembling. The things to be received, it is true, are not things of small importance; they concern tremendous issues in the world of eternity, so that even a mere question of degree can never wholly become a matter of secondary importance, far less of indifference. The element of trepidadation can not be fully eliminated, because it is inherent in the situation itself. But after all it can no longer reign supreme. With pride and rejoicing the Apostle looks forward to the day that shall exhibit in its clear light the accumulated fruit of a life full of service of the Lord. And out of this prospect of intense personal and official satisfaction there springs again in turn the intensified urge of exhortation addressed to his converts not to disappoint either him or themselves in the attainment of this unique prize. Such, doubtless, is the meaning of passages like 1 Thess. ii. 19; 1 Cor. ix. 15; 2 Cor. i. 14; vii. 4; 2 Cor. iv. 17; Gal. vi. 9; Eph. vi. 9; 1 Thess. ii. 19.

There are still two other aspects of the judgment on which reflection is made by Paul. The one is its publicity and the other its character as a vindication of the ways of God. These two are not independent one of the other. The vindication requires the publicity, since it is not to limited groups of persons but to the world, entering into judgment without exception, that this final divine pronouncement must be made known. Only this is in keeping with the majesty of God and the solemnity of the transaction. Paul, however, has in mind, besides the interhuman publicity confronting God with man and man with man mutually, also that exploration of men from within which draws the hidden content of the hearts into the open of the light of day. For God, the Omniscient One, this might seem superfluous, but for men it is not so, and the judgment fulfills itself in no other way than through the participation of all concerned in its execution. To Paul it was not without form and void, no mere metaphorical tableau to shadow forth a supersensual occurrence. The mysteries with which it remained beset in every attempt at visualization, did not hinder his interest in nor insistence upon an essential feature like this, in spite of its sharing in the mysterious character of the whole in all its details. It is part of the evil that it seeks to hide itself in the heart, nay would fain hide itself from the inlooking of God. The bringing of it to the surface of observation on every hand is an instalment of the retribution visited upon it, the first step, as it were, of its conviction and condemnation. In this respect it is the opposite to the hidden man of the heart, whose natural home is in the mystic recesses where he dwells alone with God.[15] Of the necessity that the hidden sin must be exposed Paul speaks in Rom. ii. 16 and 1 Cor. iv. 5. In the former passage the readers are cautioned not to pass judgment on one another before the time, implying on the one hand that previously to that eventful time the necessary data for fair judgment are lacking, owing to the hidden nature of the evidence, and, on the other hand, that the time of judgment having arrived and the veil of secrecy having been drawn aside, the possibility and opportunity for due judgment will be afforded them by God.

The thought of the vindication of the divine justice emerges only rarely in a direct way where Paul is speaking of the judgment. In his treatment of the process of justification, on the other hand, he touches upon it once and again.[16] The judgment has frequently been represented as a theodicy. The thought of the necessity of a theodicy can not have appealed to the Apostle's mind over-strongly: he was too deeply impressed with the divine sovereignty for that. Still the approach to this point of view is not entirely absent. In the O.T. one of the branches into which the idea of the divine Zedaquah divides itself is that of righteousness of vindication. This is found especially in the latter part of the Book of Isaiah. It is, however, the vindication of the people in their controversy with the heathen that is referred to there and not the vindication of Jehovah in his judging procedure specifi-

[15] Cp. Rom. iii. 4, 19.
[16] Cp. Rom. ix. 14.

cally. At the same time Jehovah's cause is so closely bound up with the cause of Israel that the vindication of Israel can not well be thought of, nor is it actually conceived, without that of God. The only passage which in Paul actually contains the thought of a forensic vindication of God occurs in Rom. iii. 4. It is a quotation, not however from those Isaianic contexts but from Ps. li. Here by a bold metaphor God is introduced as Himself a party at the bar. The Psalmist in his profound penitence thirsts, as it were, for some extraordinary recognition of the fact, that God is in the right and he himself in the wrong as regards his sins and for that purpose makes the pointedly personal confession "Against Thee only have I sinned," as it were, desiring to see Jehovah put in the right through some formal action at law. Here, then, God is not, within the terms of the figure the Judge, but one upon whom judgment is passed; the purpose for which Paul reproduces the situation is, however, that in his own judicial procedure God may be found true, but every man a liar.

There are a couple of points at which Paul's eschatology comes in contact with his demonology. The larger and most important part of these concern the action proceeding from Christ against the great demonic powers, who, with Satan at their head, rule the present age, and still in a measure retain their influence after the enthronization of Christ through the resurrection. Satan is "the god of this aion." As such he blinds the mind of the unbelieving in order to prevent the dawning upon them of the light of the gospel, 2 Cor. iv. 4. To the readers of Romans he holds in prospect that "shortly God will bruise Satan under your feet." This can refer only to the fulfilment of the curse pronounced upon the serpent according to Gen. iii. 15, and therefore is of strictly eschatological import. But Paul likewise speaks of a judgment upon the sub-Satanic powers of the demon world, such as are enumerated in Rom. viii. 38. The implication that these powers might attempt to separate believers from the love of God marks them as out of harmony with the divine purpose.

The inclusion of "angels" is not at variance with this, for the Apostle distinguishes formally between "angels of light" and "angels of darkness," 2 Cor. xi. 14.[17] That no more reference is made to Satan and his cohorts as the prime rulers and movers of the evil side of the universe is partly due to the supplanting of this antithesis (Satan vs. God) by the contrast between the "First" and the "Second" "Adam," which has an even wider reach in its ultimate issues; partly perhaps also to the familiarity of at least Paul's Jewish readers with this province of his theology.[18] There is no doubt that according to the writer's mind such powers, so far as they are evil, will enter into the judgment of the last day. They are perhaps included in the, apparently exhaustive, enumeration of those whose knees shall bow in the name of Jesus, since the three spheres of the universe are explicitly named as contributing the participants in this act, Phil. ii. 9-11. A more detailed description of the judgment in this realm of evil spirits is furnished by 1 Cor. xv. 24; here the "bringing to impotence" of all rule, authority, power, comprehensively designated in vs. 25 as "all his enemies" is spoken of. This, however, as argued in a preceding chapter is not confined to the last crisis strictly so called; it belongs, with the exception of the abolishment of death, the last enemy, to the period intervening between the resurrection of Christ and the parousia. A different point of view, that of an anticipated, but more gradual judgment-disposal is observable in 1 Cor. i. 18; here those not saved by the cross are described in the present tense as "the perishing ones";

[17] The "angel of light" into which Satan "transfashions" himself is not metaphorically so called; while explaining the deceptive, ingratiating form of Satan's appearance to seduce, it rests on the fixed literal distinction between "angels of light" and "angels of darkness." Satan by nature belongs to the latter class, but can put on the "schema" of the former.

[18] Cp. Everling, *Die Paulinische Angelologie und Dämonologie*, 1888. This monograph opens up a large, and largely unknown, territory in the faith of Judaism and of Paul. In regard to Paul, however, it is over-inclined to assimilate the data to the fanciful Jewish beliefs recorded in the Apocalyptic literature.

whether this includes the evil spirits seeking to bring about such a failure of the gospel-preaching, must remain doubtful. Of a "coming to nought" or "being reduced to nought" of "the rulers of this world" we read in I Cor. ii. 6; here there can be no doubt but demonic spirits are referred to, because in vs. 8 ignorance is predicated of these same rulers in regard to the glory of Christ such as led them to crucify the Lord.[19] In so far as this act was a condemnable and self-condemnatory act, and in so far, moreover, as it set in motion the eschatological winding up of affairs through the cross, it would not be rash to discern in this a form of anticipated judgment. In the various passages dealing with this subject one gains the impression that the Apostle was conscious of a mysterious drama being enacted behind the scenes of this visible world in the world of spirits, and that not a drama bearing its significance in itself; it is something pregnant with the supreme solution of the world-drama at the close of history. There is one passage, however, in which this fact, only divinable elsewhere, finds explicit statement. This is Col. ii. 15. Paul here declares that in the cross God was "ἀπεκδυσάμενος" the principalities and the powers and made a show of them openly "εδειγμάτισεν," and (thus) triumphed "θριαμβεύσας" over them. The precise implications of the statement depend almost wholly on the figure involved in the participle "ἀπεκδυσάμενος." The English versions render this by "spoiled," "despoiled," but there is an alternative translation, viz. "put off from Himself." Both renderings are unobjectionable linguistically considered; the main respect in which they differ is that the former accentuates the hostile relation between God and the principalities and powers, which is in accord with such terms as "making a show" and "triumphing" which can hardly be understood of any other class than evil angels. The other view involves the assump-

[19] The ignorance of the (evil) world-spirits in regard to the intent of God's procedure seems to have been a not unfamiliar idea in Judaism; cp. Everling, op cit. p. 12 ff. The N.T. parallels are rare; Eph. iii. 10 and I Pet. i. 12 are of a different nature.

tion that the powers named stood in some connection with the pagan gods; these had, as it were, veiled and obscured as by a mask the face of the true God to the view of heathendom, and God now openly declared his fundamental difference from them. Still even so the phrases "making a show" and "triumphing" with their ominous import remain. Besides, a difficulty arises from the connection into which Paul brings these demonological ideas with the soteric significance of the cross (to which "in it" in vs. 15 points back) and the putting off by God from Himself, or despoiling, the principalities and powers; the act means not simply the removal of delusions on the part of paganism, but involved for Israel itself the forgiveness of trespasses on the basis of the blotting out of the bond written in ordinances that was against those living under the law.[20] But, whatever interpretation may be put upon the mys-

[20] Zahn, *Einleitung in das Neue Testament,* I, pp. 334, 335, adopts the second view outlined above, but does not succeed in making clear how the interdependence between the soteric abrogation of the law-debt and the triumph over the principalities and powers is to be conceived of. The problem of the passage comes near to touching that of the *στοιχεῖα τοῦ κόσμου,* the "rudiments" or the "elements" of the world, which appear in Gal. iv. 8 and Col. ii. 8, 20. Here likewise Zahn maintains the traditional conception of stoicheia as rudimentary elements of teaching (Heb. v. 12) over against the modern demonological view which would take them as spirits connected particularly with the astral bodies, and regulative as such of the physical, ceremonial apparatus of pagan religion. The peculiarity of the use to which Paul on the latter view puts the conception lies in this, that he charges the Galatians, originally pagans in their religion, with the folly of returning to a stoicheia-worship when they embrace the Judaistic form of religion. He assumes the presence of a common element in this respect between the ceremonialism of paganism and that of Judaism. What it consists in the sequel, Gal. iv. 9-11 explains: the observance of days, months, seasons, years, under the rule of astral movements. This does not necessarily involve, however, that the stoicheia in all religions in which they occur are of the same character. Paul may have thought that this class of religious observances was during the Old Testament subject to special regulation and supervision by God, whereas in the pagan world they were left to develop without restraint. The stoicheia would have acted as divine instruments until such time as the new régime abrogated them. So far as Galatians is concerned this represents a tenable view. Nothing in the line of condemnation is there said against them; the blame, and largely a blame of foolishness and futility, is placed upon those who,

terious words, it is plain on any view that the Apostle viewed the crucifixion of Christ as a real judgment visited upon superhuman spirits, something that, after a manner, might be put in parallelism with the anticipation of the final resurrection in that of Christ.

There is still one other aspect in which the angels appear subject to judgment, not this time of God, but to judgment on the part of believers. This representation occurs in I Cor. vi. 3. Immediately before (vs. 2) it takes the form "Or know ye not that the saints shall judge *the world?*" It is not quite certain that Paul meant these two objects "angels" and "the world" to be understood interchangeably. In that case only evil angels could come under consideration, for "kosmos" with Paul has as a rule evil associations, although not uniformly so. Where the subject of the judging is God the term might be taken quantitatively in the sense of *totum mundum,* Rom. iii. 6, still this is not probable, cp. the accumulation of evil aspects of the world in I Cor. i-iii. It will be noted that Paul speaks of this function of judging angels and judging the world as something familiar to the Corinthian readers, which indicates that it was a commonly accepted belief; otherwise the statement could not have been put in the form of a question: "Know ye not that, etc." In the Pauline writings there is no

after having passed from under their rule, seek to restore it; there is no reference to any divine judgment pronounced upon them. In Colossians it is different. While the stoicheia themselves are not characterized as hostile to God, yet contextually they seem to be identified with the principalities and powers whom God despoiled or shook off from Himself and triumphed over. The latter occur in vs. 15; immediately before stands the statement of the blotting out of the bond written in ordinances that was against the people; the same powers appear invested with authority to hold a bond for God, and to be the objects of the punitive divine procedure; in vs. 8 they are outright called "stoicheia" and placed in an unfavorable light: "of the world and not after Christ"; in the sequel also (vs. 20) they are, with a close backward reference to vs. 15, characterized as beings or things of which the readers have died with Christ. Cp. "therefore" in vs. 16. The subject remains doctrinally beset with much obscurity. It belongs to the discussion in hand only in so far as it involves a judgment passed by God on reprehensible spirits identified with the present age. For the modern literature on the stoicheia question cp. the Bibliography.

further reference or allusion to this matter. Everling, who relies much on parallels from the Apocalyptic literature, has little light to shed on the question here. All he is able to quote for comparison is the *Book of Enoch,* Chap. xiii. to the effect that Enoch was commissioned by God to deliver to the evil spirits who had intermarried with the daughters of men (Gen. vi.) the condemnatory sentence of God, passed by God after the accusation presented by the Archangels. This latter feature, viz. that precisely the accusers are found among the Archangels, whilst the "sons of God" are the small group of Azazel with his two hundred angels, does not fit well into the quite unrestricted statements of Paul that "the saints shall judge the world," or that "we shall judge angels." The only thing furnishing a parallel are the words of Jesus assuring the Apostles that they are to sit on twelve thrones judging the twelve tribes of Israel, Matt xix. 28; Lk. xxii. 30. Judging is in the Orient a regal function, the king being lawgiver and law-executor in one. But, whilst the saying of our Lord could be placed under the general rubric of the saints reigning with Him, the statement of Paul is too specific to permit of such exegesis. What the Apostle finds fault with in his readers is not their domineering attitude towards fellow-Christians but their litigosity: they go to law before the unrighteous (pagans) and not before the saints. And they do this in regard to "the smallest matters," things pertaining to this life. There are in this two points of disapprobation on Paul's part. First, it is beneath the dignity of believers, who formed, even in Corinth, an aristocracy of the Spirit, to submit their trivial bread-and-butter differences (biotika) to common pagans. Secondly, in seeking redress from pagans they contemptuously pass by fellow-believers as not wise or distinguished enough to settle points of difference, where such arose.[21] In both respects the reminder of

[21] The more principial point, viz. that such differences admissable into court should occur among the Corinthians at all, Paul reserves till vs. 7: "Nay, already it is altogether a defect in you, that ye have lawsuits one with another."

their destiny to judge angels is (not without a certain admixture of irony) made by Paul to serve as a corrective. From this we may gather that the future judging of angels was not to the Apostle's mind a negligible function; it required respectful recognition from Christian to Christian; a slight in connection with it deserved rebuke. And further, the things which the judgment of the angels to be held related to were not small matters but matters of the life to come and consequently of supreme importance. Now, while this gives us a glimpse of what lay in the Apostle's inner mind on this subject, it by no means satisfies our not illegitimate curosity, the less so since it is evident that the Corinthian Christians knew more, perhaps all, about it.[22]

There remains still one question that needs briefly to be considered. It is the question of the Judge who, according to Paul, will preside at this solemn function and render the supreme decision. It is God from whom all righteousness and judgment issue, and to whom all the, to men un-disentangible, threads of conduct, be it inward or outward, are clear, who as His divine right executes this conclusive judicial act and thus receives this part of the glory that must accrue to Him from all that has ever happened in the world. This indeed is the finest note in Paul's manifold pursuit of the idea of the righteousness of God. It is not enough to be righteous objectively, nor sufficient to carry the approval of one's conscience within one's self, the crown in the process is not put upon it until God by formal judgment has declared a man absolved *sub specie juris divini.* As an undertone this may be overheard even in such an occasional utterance as of 1 Cor. iv. 3-4: "But with me it is a very small thing that I should be judged of you or of man's day (i.e. in a human court): yea, I judge not mine own self. For I know nothing against myself; yet am I not hereby justified: he that judges me is the Lord." But this isolated note is not in principle different

[22] Cp. for the entire passage the instructive, finely discriminating exegesis of Bachmann, in Zahn's *Komm. z. N. T.*, Vol. VII, 2nd ed., pp. 224-238.

from the music of the full chorus of the doctrine of justification: "That He might Himself be just, and (none the less) the justifier of him that has faith in Jesus," Rom. iii. 26; or: "let God be found true, but every man a liar; as it is written, That thou mightest be justified in thy words, and mightest prevail when thou comest into judgment," vs. 4. At this high point the theocentric principle of God's judgment-procedure and of his soteric justification-method are clearly seen to spring from the same root.

Side by side with the judgment of God stands that of which Christ is the presiding figure, 2 Cor. v. 10. This, however, is not to be interpreted as a later accretion to the dignity and office of Christ, and therefore particularly quotable as evidence for the Saviour's deity. Evidence to that effect it no doubt is, but it is by no means a piece of the investiture of Jesus with divine attributes or functions on the part of the early Church. The roots lie much farther back, viz. in the Old Testament conception of the Messiah as the representative of God, who on that account also is the executor of and the participator in the divine judgment. And even this rests ultimately on the inseparable union upon which the reigning and the judging function had entered in the Shemitic world from times immemorial.

There is one instance in a Pauline discourse where the Apostle reflects upon the essentialness of the human nature of Christ as a qualification for his holding judgment. This occurs in the Areopagus discourse, Acts xvii. 31: "inasmuch as He has appointed a day in which He will judge the world in righteousness by a man whom He has ordained."[23] A similar statement occurs in the Fourth Gospel, v. 27: "And he gave him authority to execute judgment, because he is a son of man."[24] It is not clear in either passage what motive

[23] The English versions evade the point of difficulty by rendering, A. V. "by that man whom He has ordained, R. V. "by a man," with "that man" in the margin, A. R. V. "by the man," with "a man, in the margin."

[24] Some have been tempted to find in John v. 27 a substitution of "man" for "son of man." The latter would then be the formal title of

underlies this stressing of the participation of Jesus in human nature. The ability on his part to enter into the subjectivity of those whom He is to judge has been thought of; this would approximate the thought to that so prominent in the Epistle to the Hebrews, only that there a specific turn is given to the idea: Jesus' sympathy is chiefly concerned with the temptation that befalls believers through suffering; it is profoundly moral and not merely emotional sympathy with suffering as such.

the Messiah, who as such holds the judgment. The intimate connection between the name "Son-of-Man" and the judgment is in evidence in the latter part of the Synoptics. If, however, there is a substitution here, it would have originated in the Greek original, for both the article before "son" and that before "man" are lacking in the text.

CHAPTER XII

THE ETERNAL STATE

The main character of the state following the resurrection and the judgment is described by the adjective "*αἰώνιος*." As will be presently shown, the character so named does not exclusively express some relation to or severance from time; certain qualitative associations are bound up with it. Of the final issue of the eschatological succession of events it occurs in the Pauline Epistles fourteen times: Rom. ii. 7; v. 21; vi. 22, 23; 2 Cor. iv. 17, 18; v. 1; Gal. vi. 8; 2 Thess. i. 9; ii. 16; 1 Tim. ii. 10; Tit. i. 2; iii. 7; Phi. 15; to these must be added Acts xiii. 46, 48. Of these passages the only one explicitly joining the term to the destiny of those condemned in the judgment is 2 Thess. i. 9: "*ὄλεθρον αἰώνιον*." The Hebrew "ʿOlam" to which the noun "*αἰών*" in "*αἰώνιος*" must be traced back seems to be in its original significance what the philosophers call a *"Grenzbegriff,"* but conceived after a rather concrete fashion; it denotes what is "unreachable to the time-sense of man.[1] This seems first and chiefly to have related to the past when lying beyond the reach of remembrance; "the hills of eternity" are the immemorially existing hills, which, of course, does not imply that they had no beginning in fact, Gen. xlix. 26; Deut. xxxiii. 15. Doubled phrases such as "leʿloam waʿed" came into use to intensify the idea by means of repetition.[1] Duplication could also serve the purpose of distinguishing between eternity *"a parte post" and "a parte ante"*: "me-ʿolam ʿad ʿolam."[2] It has been held by some that

[1] Etymologists make the root "ʿalam" signify "to be hidden"; the ideas of eternity (heaven) and being hidden appear in close association, cp. 1 Cor. x. 7; Eph. iii. 9; Col. i. 26; "mysterion" and "revelation" are correlative terms by opposition; hence in the last-quoted passage "hidden from ages."

[2] Cp. Von Orelli, *Die Hebräischen Synonyme der Zeit und Ewigkeit*, 1871.

"αἰώνιος" is derived not from the Old Testament concept of eternity but from the formal eschatological distinction between "this aion" and "the aion to come." This is unlikely for more than one reason. The notion of perpetuity, unendingness, while perfectly applicable to the age to come, is obviously inherently opposed to the phrase "the present age." Besides, the entirely uneschatological Hellenic "aion" is doubtless related to the word "aiei," "always," so that every derivation from a technical eschatological system appears superfluous. The present age is precisely the opposite of aionios, for it has a "συντέλεια." As for Paul's usage in particular, the Apostle finds in the consummate state the antithesis to "chronos," "time," Gal. iv. 4.[3] There is not a single instance in Paul which compels us to restrict the adjective aionios to a relative duration; of the instances above cited no less than eleven join the adjective to the noun "life," "zoe aionios"; the inherent content of the phrase "eternal life" precludes limitation. Both the Rabbinical theology and Greek philosophy already found the specific difference of the word in its negation of any recognizable time-extent beyond. By the Rabbins "the future aion" is characterized as "perfectly long," Kiddush xxxix. 2. Aristotle speaks of aionios as that which by nature has nothing beyond itself, *De Coelo* i. 9, which, to be sure, relates to the lifetime of a person, but in the same sense can be applied to the cosmical span of time. But, when speaking of the philosophical "ἀπειρία," he admits that the transfer of the period-limitation to this is of the nature of an epinomy, that is metaphorical.[4] We see, therefore, that the word-forms, both Semitic and Hellenic, bear the seed of the concept non-cessation in themselves although in each of the two spheres it required a different

[3] As remarked before in another connection, "fulness" is not meant here in the first instance as "ripeness"; it signifies the completion of what was "time" and the succession of it by what is different from time through the mission of the Messiah into the world. For the Messiah is the introducer and beginner of the eschatological world.

[4] Cp. Cremer *Wörterbuch der Neutestamentlichen Gräcität*, sub voce aionios.

principle to mature the term to its predestined absoluteness.[5]

When the eternal character of the final state is put over against the time-character of the present state the distinction proximately bears a popular meaning. While in no wise denying the philosophico-theological conception of an existence outside of and above time attributed to the divine nature, for which, subjectively speaking, the categories of present, past and future do not exist, and to a certain degree even suggesting this, the suggestion, if such there be, could only apply to the divine nature, and transcends the state of the creature under all circumstances, the consummate eschatological state not excepted. Paul nowhere affirms that to the life of man, after the close of this aeon, no more duration, no more divisibility in time-units shall exist. Life so conceived is plainly the prerogative by nature of the Creator: to eternalize the inhabitants of the coming aeon in this sense would be equivalent to deifying them, a thought whose place is in a pagan type of speculation but not within the range of biblical religion.[6] Paul clearly makes a difference to his own mind, not only between dying before the parousia and surviving till then, for these contingencies involve, of course, a *prius* and a *post,* both subject to the law of time, but he likewise, in his conception of a possible *post-mortem* state of nakedness, longer or briefer, projects the idea of perceptible duration into the life beyond. The declaration of the angel in the Apocalypse, x. 6; "χρόνος οὐκέτι ἔσται," is not meant to infringe upon the principle just laid down; it may be translated with

[5] The animus of the ever-repeated attempt to de-eternalize the word "aionios" is of a doctrinal-theological nature. It desires not so much to limit the state of blessedness, but rather to find a linguistic and exegetical basis for the attack on the idea of "eternal punishment." There is no real relief to be obtained from this offense by diluting the term aionios. Relief could come only through weakening the sense of word for destruction to which aionios is joined. Attempts to that effect we shall consider in the immediate sequel.

[6] An instance of such pagan self-deification Reitzenstein finds in the Hermetic writings, and brings this to bear on 1 Cor. iii. 4, where "are ye not men" is taken to imply that as pneumatikoi men are divine. Cp. on this the author's *The Eschatological Aspect of the Pauline Conception of the Spirit* in Princeton Theological Studies, pp. 248-250.

A.R.V. "that there shall be *delay* no longer."[17] Nevertheless time in the present life is so inseparably connected with the great astral movements that, when the latter should cease to exist or to operate, it could be truly said that time in the old terrestrial form had with them ceased to be.[8] Apart from such statements the descriptions in the Apocalypse of the dramatic developments in the supernal sphere are full of the movement of time.[9]

If further inquiring into the characteristics of the aionion, still keeping its formal aspect rather than its substantial content in view, the first feature obtruding itself is that of the imperishableness, including the unchangeableness, of the things pertaining to it. Paul declares, almost after the manner of an axiomatic truth: "the things which are seen are temporal; but the things which are not seen are eternal," 2 Cor. iv. 17. At first this reads like a differentiating appraisal of the visible and the invisible, something reminding of the antithesis between the two worlds of the ideal and the sense-things with Plato. A closer examination of the words in their context will soon convince that this exegesis would convey only part of the meaning, and for the other part produce a wrong perspective. The emphasis does not rest on the seen versus the unseen, but on the fact that the former, under the present circumstances happens to consist of perishable things, whereas the other under the same circumstances possesses the nature of the eternal, of what from its very nature cannot perish, because it carries the principle of eternity in itself. A permissible paraphrase would be: the things that in this lower, preliminary, state engage our interest are transitory and corruptible; the things which in the present dispensation the believer cannot yet lay hold of by vision are the eternal,

7 A.R.V. has the old rendering "time" in the margin.

8 Cp. Rev. vii. 16; xxi. 23.

9 It is usually believed that even the Old Testament contains the representation of Jehovah as subjectively existing above all progression of time viz. in Isa. lvii. 15, "the Lofty One that inhabits eternity." It is probable, however, that the clause should be rendered "who sits enthroned forever" which would retain the time-form expression.

incorruptible realities. It goes without saying, that the distinction thus interpreted partakes not of the nature of a cool, disinterested diagnosis of metaphysical difference; there is a degree of pathos in the declaration, occurring as it does in a highly emotional context. Paul is conscious of σκοπεῖν "looking at," that is contemplating with interest the make-up of the invisible world. Only, this mode of contemplation is with the Apostle not induced by the invisibleness of the things in question; in the abstract he practises no cult of the invisible as partaking *per se* of a superior complexion: that would be a Hellenic thought, but he has learned to recognize in the things unseen to the present aion the enduring things of the world to come, a world already in principle present, the contemplation of which can consequently render solace and support in the affliction of the moment. That thus and thus only the stress is rightly divided will be perceived from the closely following word: "for we pilgrimage through a land of faith, not of sight," 2 Cor. v. 7. Here the unseen things of the other passage are precisely the things of future sight, deriving their supreme value from this prospective visibleness, whilst the walking through a region of faith is felt precisely as a matter of relative lack of importance. After essentially the same fashion Paul measures the superiority of the building from God above the present tent-abode by this one supreme characteristic that it is "aionion," to be possessed and inhabited in heaven, 2 Cor. v. 1. Here also the synonymity of the "ouranion" and the "aionion" is clearly observable.

The emphasis placed on the aionion should not mislead us into assuming that Paul was most stirred by the mere endlessness of the state hoped for. In any ordinary prospect of felicity mere endlessness as such could not fail to prove an attraction, almost a thought of compulsion. But it is necessary to remember that the object or the objects to the possession of which endlessness is ascribed are of an altogether unique kind, of such a nature in fact that the endlessness became a part of their adequate apprehension. Common things can be appropriated and assimilated in a finite succession of single moments and part by part. The fugitiveness of occupation or intercourse with them may cause that wistful regret that is inseparable from converse with the finite. With God it is different. He himself being aionios, there can be no thorough, no adequate reception of Him into our finite consciousness, unless there be some assurance of the unceasingness of our communion with Him. He is not a God of the dead but of the living. All temporal, partial experience of God inevitably leaves a sense of dissatisfaction behind. God remains the Eternal One but we can never be lifted out of the sphere opposite to this. None the less practically this problem can be met through God's imparting a reflection of his unique eternal existence to our life as creatures, through admitting us into the realm of the aionion. In this He not merely confers a boon upon man, but at the same time provides a true satisfaction for Himself. Although in the abstract being self-sufficient as God, He has freely chosen to carry his concern with us to the extreme of eternal mutual appurtenance of which the creature is capable. Paul affirms both, on the one hand that God is the only immortal Being I Tim. vi. 16 and, on the other hand, that He has appointed as the eschatological goal of religious fellowship with Himself, among other things, the prize of an incorruption, Rom. ii. 7 such as is equivalent to eternal life. And that this attribute, existing in Him alone in its highest potency, and in us in an ectypical form means in both cases more than mere endless existence, but has a content commensurable with its eternity, should not be overlooked. The biblical terminology does not in respect to believers employ, after the philosophic fashion, the word "immortality," but chooses as a larger, deeper receptacle the term "life."[10] We find that the aionion-concept, thus understood, belongs to the acme of religion, serving to express its absoluteness. Eschatology ceases for

[10] Yet compare I Cor. xv. 53, 54: the mortal puts on immortality; still the very form in which this is expressed is such that it could never have been applied to God, who is the Only One who *has* immortality, I Tim. vi. 16.

those who have learned, and in principle experienced this, to be an abstract speculation: it becomes the profoundest and most practical of all thought-complexes because they, like Paul, live and move and have their redemptively-religious treasures in God.

To the opposite state awaiting the condemned after the judgment aionios is applied by Paul only once, 2 Thess. i. 9. This is the statement most frequently depended upon to tone down the principle of two-sided eternal retribution traditionally ascribed to the Apostle. It not being feasible to modify the eschatologically-constant value of aionios, the attack has centered upon the noun or nouns to which the adjective is attached. "Olethros" and "apoleia" have been given the sense of "annihilation." The absolute universalism thus forced upon the Apostle has a weak basis to rest upon. It can appeal to one passage only besides the one under review from 2 Thess. i. 5-9, viz. to the statement in 1 Cor. xv. 22 where the promise is found that in Christ all shall be made alive with the same universality as all die in Adam. The latter passage has been examined by us at an earlier point in the chapter on the Extent of the Resurrection. At any rate it does not speak of annihilation. As concerns the statement in 2 Thess. no one can deny that it posits a strong contrast between the destiny of believers and the end of their persecutors. Only, the question arises, whether the thought of annihilation is fitted to serve as the evil opposite pole in a contrast so sharply stressed by Paul. It will have to be remembered at the outset that "annihilation" is an extremely abstract idea, too philosophical, in fact, to find a natural place within the limits of the realistic biblical eschatology, least of all, it would seem, in this outburst of vehement indignation against the enemies of the Gospel. Closely looked at it is not a stronger but a weaker concept than that of protracted retribution to threaten with, so that, instead of contributing to the sharpness of the opposition intended, it would to a certain extent obliterate the latter. Nor is there any need etymologically of foisting this absolute meaning upon "olethros" or "apoleia," a derivative of the same root. The idea of a "second death" occurring in Rev. xx. 6, 14; xxi. 8 has indeed suggested the thought of "annihilation" to commentators, but in the Pauline contexts no such idea appears. In point of etymological import "apoleia," stands at a sufficiently far remove from even the milder sense of destruction, not to say from its extreme force found in annihilation. The verb originally means "to lose" and out of this first develops the signification "to ruin," "to destroy." In English idiom "to destroy" without difficulty passes over into the meaning "to annihilate," as when the philosophical physicists assert that matter cannot be destroyed, but this is deceptive, because it is a technical adaptation of a more general term to a specific usage for which, on account of the very strangeness of the idea, it is hard to find a proper English equivalent, so that the Latin "annihilare" for precision of speech would have been preferable. In Greek "apollunai," even when involving violent death, does not go beyond the limit of ruining, destroying. The exclamation "olola," "I am ruined," presupposes that the person using it has not ceased to exist. Interesting for the point in question is from the classical language Sophocles, Oedipus Coloneus, vs. 399: "Now the gods are setting thee up, formerly they destroyed thee." The upshot of the matter is that apollunai is but a stronger synonym for apokteinein, cp. Matt. x. 28, where the contrast lies between "killing the body" and "destroying both soul and body in Gehenna," the verb in the former clause being apokteinein in the latter apollunai. Instances elsewhere in the New Testament, e.g. Jno. vi. 27; 1 Pet. i. 7 do not allow the rendering "annihilatio." The same question that is here raised in regard to "apollunai" arises also in regard to the verb "katargeisthai" as used by the apostle in 1 Cor. xv. 24, 26; whether this signifies "to annihilate" or "to render inoperative" has been discussed in the chapter relating to the Question of "Chiliasm in Paul."[11]

[11] Nearest approach to the idea of "reduction to non-existence" within

The problem of the relation of "olethros" and "apoleia" to existence or non-existence could be solved without much difficulty, were writers willing to test the Pauline statements by reference to the words of Jesus, because the latter on the one hand uses "apoleia" of the state and Gehenna of the place of eternal destruction and on the other hand combines with these the strongest predicates of unceasing retribution; cp. Matt. v. 29; vii. 13; Mk. v. 29, 30; ix. 43, 44, 46, 48; Lk. xii. 5. But the argument would mean little to those who are bent upon deëschatologizing the teaching of Jesus, to the extent of declaring unauthentic what is called the "small apocalypse" in the closing part of the Synoptics. Even the Fourth Gospel in what it says about Jesus does not differ in this matter from the united testimony of the Synoptical Gospels Jno. xvii. 12. Could Paul in a matter like this have shown less severity than Jesus?[12]

The eschatological process, then, on its evil no less than on its favorable side, issues into a state that is literally eternal. The attribute "aionion," however does not remain entirely within the quantitative sphere. It attracts to itself certain associations of quality. The circumstance that the word had become so intimately and consistently attached to the realm of future blessedness has made it strongly suggestive of richness and nobility of content. In so far as this is the case it cannot be denied, that the reverse, sinister significance suffers a partial eclipse. The fact of its restricted occurrence, in that ominous sense, bears out this feature. It would nevertheless be a mistake to infer that the Apostle's conviction regarding the tremendous reality of the punitive side of the subject had received any impairment. The terms considered could never have been joined to the predicate of "aionios" at

Scripture is, perhaps, found in Job xxviii. 22: "Destruction and death say, We have heard the fame thereof with our ears," but this is a poetic hyperbole. It means to represent the most remote and non-accessible things as still unable to point out the dwelling-place of "wisdom."

12 The Pauline passages where ἀπώλεια occurs are: Rom. ix. 22; Phil. i. 28; iii. 19; 2 Thess. ii. 3. In none of these is there noticeable a lack of pathos, rather the opposite.

all, if the sharp edge of the Apostle's eschatological "dualism" had been actually worn off to any degree. The relative scarcity of usage is naturally explained from the fact that Paul was before aught else a minister of the grace of eternal life, an Apostle rather than a doom-foretelling prophet. We have already met the same phenomenon of unequal division of stress in discussing the doctrines of the resurrection and the judgment. In that connection no one would be so foolish as to infer a tendency on Paul's part towards detracting from the importance of these central topics of all biblical eschatology.

Passing on now from the more formal to the material make-up of the future state, we must endeavor to analyze the elements entering into its content. The Apostle has not left us without guidance in this endeavor. The category of time is exchanged for that of space when the final state is located in or identified with heaven. The "aionion" and the "ouranion" belong together and evince mutual attraction. It has already been noticed in a previous connection that the conjuncture was naturally brought about through the entrance of Christ into heaven in the course of historical development. There remains to be added, however, that the ultimate ground for this historical event lies far deeper. The primacy of the celestial sphere in the eschatological universe antedates as a constitutive principle every other reason. The structure of the two strata placed one above the other, with the higher stratum made regulative for the lower one in its laws and ideals, is, of course, older than Paul. It underlies the parabolic teaching of our Lord in the Synoptics, and more abstractly and principially reveals itself both in the setting and in the discourses of the Fourth Gospel. And this scheme, far from being a purely speculative construction, is of eminently practical import. It is the basis of what in devotional language we call other-worldliness. Other-worldliness neither with Paul nor elsewhere in Scripture is a negative state; it does not involve any morbid or distorted religious habit of mind. Every tendency or attempt to replace it by an earthly-oriented type of religion is productive or symptomatic of a basic disturbance in the very groundwork of the Christian mind. The Christian religion was born under the auspices of this primordial and irreducible contrast of the two worlds involving the trend of the pious from below to on high and their destiny to arrive at the goal of their deepest aspiration. Nothing can so ill afford a disavowal of its native milieu as historic Christianity. How easily to the mind of Paul the eternal and the heavenly melt into one may be gathered from such passages as 1 Cor. xv. 47; 2 Cor. v. 5; Col. i. 5. "Heaven" is to our feeling, possibly even more than to the Apostle's, a definition of what locally surrounds and encloses the realities and delights of the eternal state rather than a description of the content of these.

The actual elements into which the eternal and heavenly unfold themselves are chiefly four: the Spirit, life, glory, the kingdom of God. The first of these four underlies and produces the second and the third, so that the whole might be reduced to the Spirit and the kingdom of God. The Spirit is the fundamental creative factor as regards life and glory in the saints. It is a pity that the word "spiritual" has through the devotional usage become so wedded to the ideas of fineness and supersensuousness of religious texture as to lose some of its power for conveying to us the deeper core of its significance. It is easier to regret than to correct this, all the more so, since the states called "spiritual" in popular parlance *are* actually, the product of the Spirit's inworking. Another cause interfering with a clear solution of the problem of the Spirit's eschatological operation lies in the fixed antithesis between the "σάρξ" and the "Πνεῦμα" in the Pauline teaching. The flesh "lusteth" against the "Pneuma" and vice versa, Gal. v. 17. If we knew for certain what is the background of the evil associations of the flesh which are so much in evidence as to render "sarx" with Paul practically the synonym of sin, we should likewise be able, on the principle of opposites, to discover why the Spirit is the Antagonist and Conqueror of the flesh, and that not in virtue of some function given to Him as a mere matter of fact, but so as to be able to tell what there is in the nature of the Spirit to make Him the executive of the Godhead in this particular respect. The anthropological or psychological theory scarcely helps us on with the problem as regards the history of revelation. For on the one hand there seems to be no Old Testament passage associating the "flesh"with sin after the characteristic manner of Paul, nor, on the other hand does the Old Testament particularly place the Spirit's function in the ethico-religious sphere so as to make Him the Exterminator of sin par excellence as Paul does. The "flesh" is in the Hebrew Scriptures no less than in Paul a mystery. In the somatic constitution of man, as contrasted with his psychical make-up, no principle of sin is sought by the Old Testament. Nor can this have been the belief of Paul. The source of sin according to the Apostle does not lie in the flesh as a product of creation, but in the act of the First Adam imputed to all. Notwithstanding the present-day unpopularness of this exegesis of Rom. v, it is our conviction that a doctrinally unprejudiced scrutiny of the famous passage will compel a return to it, whether it agree with the doctrine or not. No more than a glance at Gal. v. 13 ff. is needed to prove that Paul reckoned among the works of the sarx things that have from an ethical standpoint nothing whatever to do with the body. Now it is quite true that the same Paul means to characterize *sinful human nature* by the name sarx. Only the very point at issue is, whether this can be wholly due to the notorious fact that many sins actually take their point of departure from the body. That would be denominating a *group* of phenomena from one peculiar feature which would be unappropriate to the larger remainder of the group. To say, therefore, sarx is not human nature as such, but *sinful* human nature, does not bring one step nearer the solution of the problem. It amounts to a matter-of-fact observation where explanation is desired so far as possibly attainable. And the explanation should cover not merely the ordinary soteric operation of the Spirit in the Christian subject during this life, but likewise cast light upon his eschatological presence and operation in the world to come. To our mind there is but one, at least halfway satisfactory explanation of this. It amounts to this that the central significance in all manifestations of the Spirit, both those that we are accustomed to call ordinary or those called extraordinary, consisted for Paul in the tremendous irresistible power with which the Spirit makes his impact and produces his results in every sphere of operation. This was something inherent in the nature of the Spirit. All the phenomena revealing his presence and working bore witness to this. The fundamental note in his activity was that of divine, unique forth-putting of energy. In the Old Testament this can be tested easily; one passage for many may suffice: "Now the Egyptians are men, and not God; and their horses flesh, and not Spirit," Isa. xxxi. 3. But, according to this statement "flesh" is the direct opposite of "Spirit" for no other reason than that *its* characteristic is inertia, lack of power, such as can only be removed by the Spirit of God. The two terms are not only correlatives but are mutually exclusive: where the one is the other is not. We can understand from this that in early times of the Christian faith the factor of the Pneuma was most easily associated with the manifold and variegated supernatural forms of miraculous expressions which marked the life of the Church. Paul did not put as high an estimate in point of edification upon this wonder-world of young Christian growth and the vigorous stirring of sap revealed in it. He knew full well and told his converts with great frankness that these were the things intended to pass away, and that there were other more distinctively ethico-religious things characterized as "abiding." Unfortunately in recognizing this state of facts a twofold mistake has but too often been made. The first is that the Apostle is represented as denying the provenience of these extraordinary gifts and modes of expression from the Spirit. There is no evidence to that effect. The second mistake is so to represent it that to his mind the relatively quieter and more equable impulses and habits of life among his converts were somehow detached from the Spirit, or that perhaps a somewhat modified and toned-down conception of the Spirit was substituted for the original one. For this there is no evidence either. We must, in order to understand the Apostle, first of all rectify the somewhat misapprehended antithesis in question. It is an antithesis expressive of a comparative judgment on the usefulness of these two different groups of phenomena for edification, not an antithesis between a non-Spirit-caused and a Spirit-caused group of things. The Spirit is in both. The, originally perhaps slight, shift in perspective might easily in the future course of thought give rise to the serious error, that Paul meant to desupernaturalize the quiet and in part unobservable processes, that, delighting more in the triad of faith, hope and love, he therefore conceived of these three as having no particular impulse or impact of the Spirit underlying them. Modern less enthusiastic and more self-restrained habits of religion easily favored this, even where there was no conscious intent to that effect. We must refamiliarize ourselves with connecting these quiet virtues and graces with the constant powerful urge and influence of the Spirit. The cultivation of faith and hope and love was perhaps not entirely confined for Paul to "the hidden man of the heart," nor need it have been overmuch governed by the desire to escape the charge of demonstrativeness. By remembering these things we shall better understand how the Spirit, in the center of whose operation stands out the feature of impulsive superhuman energy, can form the connecting link between the mode of the believer's life on earth and that in the age to come in heaven. Thus it may also become clearer to us how the firstfruits and the harvest can be identical in character. The Apostle's teaching may at least negatively supply a caution not to empoverish our eschatological hope to the unruffled surface of the waters of Shiloah. There may enter into it more than we suspect of the mighty rushing of the Pentecostal wind.[13]

The three other remaining conceptions conveying to us the contents of the eternal state are those of "life," "glory" and "the Kingdom of God." They sustain to the Spirit the relation of products to the Producer. Further they possess this in common that they set forth the eternal state in the most comprehensive manner conceivable. Herein also the Apostle shows himself as at one and the same time sensitively receptive to the influx of revelation and capable of the firm grasp of the theological thinker. His utterances reflect less of the charm of the pictorial than of the luminosity radiating from the core of condensed ideas. Where with Paul the concretely-pictorial does appear, it seldom fails to bring with it the impression of a mysteriousness incapable of being translated into terms of the reproductive imagination. It is what ear has not heard, what eye has not seen and what has not ascended into the heart of man, 1 Cor. ii. 9, 10. Even where the transcendental is anticipated in the concreteness of a visionary experience, and avails itself for expression of the forms of number and space combined, the inherent difficulty of speaking about such things, and the doubt about the "lawfulness" of doing so, show how thoroughly the Apostle remained convinced of the strangeness to an earthly creature of the concrete forms having their habitation above.

In view of this humble reticence, based in part on the consciousness of ignorance, we ought to be all the more grateful that, though not in detail, yet the Apostle has most positively named the great outstanding categories of heavenly

13 The above attempt at framing some doctrinal and historical substructure to the predominance of the Spirit in the eternal state does not lay claim to have thrown light on all difficulties. If the common denominator of what is "Spiritual" is power, are we not compelled, since the sarx, its opposite, is the comprehensive term for sin, to assume that the ubiquity of sin in the world is somehow connected with the latter's character as "inertia" springing from the lack of the Spirit in the things of God? Upon this we neither dare nor desire to enter further here. A few remarks about it will be found in Princeton Theological Studies, p. 255, note 61.

experience as destined to fill the vast spaces above. The most intimate and highly spiritualized relation of the believer to Christ as the focus of heaven points the way in this respect. In regard to what further belongs to this as its proper accompaniment and needful environment we may cherish the same conviction. And still further particular stress among this is laid upon the affectional attitude towards Christ which rounds off heaven in itself. Only we must not let the unavoidable stress thrown on this obscure to us the reference of all beatitude to God. The deepest-sounding notes in Paul's melodies of heaven find their point of unison in God the Father through His Son. Of a Jesu-latry such as would have forced the First Person of the Trinity into the unknown, uncultivated background Paul knows nothing. The deity of Christ surely needs not any repression of fact to prove its apostolic provenience. Paul's religion was from the very outset of his Christian life "theocentric," and it could never have become so "Christocentric" as it actually is, had not the rich, religious occupation with the Saviour secured for the latter the indisputable place wherein He appears in the closest unity with the Father. This was to Paul not so much a matter of doctrinal necessity as of devotional indispensableness. Though the ordinary prepositions are "ἐκ" and "εἰς" with reference to the Father, and the corresponding preposition for the Son is "διά," yet Paul does not fall short in his highest doctrinal flight from declaring that the universe was created "εἰς" Christ.[14] All this harmoniously existing inter-communion, as it existed before the aeons, could not possibly cease to exist in the transcendental aeons of the world to come.

The second and most frequent mould into which the content of the coming age is cast is that of "ζωή" or "ζωὴ αἰώνιος." The mere fact of the frequency of the conjunction of "life" with "aionios" shows how eminently eschatological the conception of life grew to be from the simplest beginnings.

[14] Cp. Rom. xi. 36; 1 Cor. viii. 6; Col. i. 16.

There are two distinct strands in Paul by means of which "life" attains, this eschatological completion. The first springs from the ancient antithesis in which life stands opposite to death since the very beginnings of the race. We may not let ourselves be drawn aside from the biblical emphasis thrown on this point by any findings or dogmas of evolutionary science; for here our sole purpose is to ascertain what was Paul's view on the subject, and in which respect it has influenced his doctrine of life. Two things are certain: whatever the modernly conceived provenience of venerable opening narratives in Genesis may be, to Paul they stand for real occurrences recorded as facts in an inspired record. But, one will ask, what have they to do with eschatology? "Much every way." For no matter whether the account involved is preëxilic or postexilic or harks back, as Gunkel and many others believe, to an ancient Babylonian soil, pregnant with eschatological mythology, the subject-matter after which we are enquiring is most certainly there. The tree of life and the other tree and the primeval paradise and the fall and death and the expulsion from the garden on account of the sin committed, all these are present in the scriptural narrative, and a single glance at Rom. v is sufficient to convince of the fact, that in the most fundamental manner they support (qua history) the entire eschatology of Paul. And the Apostle's eyes were centrally focussed on life and death in their forever interacting force. The only reasonable interpretation of the Genesis-account (*e mente Pauli*) is this, that provision was made and probation was instituted for a still higher state, both ethico-religiously and physically complexioned, than was at that time in the possession of man. In other words the eschatological complex and prospect were there in the purpose of God from the beginning. This, then, represents the first two of the eschatological strands spoken of above. Its eminent significance arises from connection with the individual's part in eschatology. The collective interpretation of the genesis of Biblical eschatology, while not untrue or out of place, has yet, together with critical aspersions cast on Genesis, had the result of obscuring the supreme importance of this great primordial event for the unfolding of Paul's doctrine. Probably it was not even necessary to contribute much *de novo* to this circle of ideas, for here, if anywhere, Jewish or Jewish Apocalyptic literature had, on the basis of the Old Testament, prepared the way for the Apostolic doctrine. The momentous sentence, "through one man death came into the world" itself is as to its substance derived from the *Book of Wisdom* ii. 24, although there "the devil's envy" has the place of what Paul simply calls "one man," evidently for the sake of a clearer parallelism between the First and Second Adam, vss. 12, 15. This original conception of life with its antithesis to death bore in itself, however, the seed of the collective conception, because the terms in which it is spoken of in the ancient narrative are not applying to our first parents alone, but mean to be taken generically; on Adam's son and on his son and similarly on successive generations the same curse and punishment fell that overtook him. Death and Life having been in this manner become collective ideas, there was only one step further required to *objectivize* them, and in particular to make out of the many living ones to be restored in the subsequent course of redemption the inhabitants of a comprehensive realm of life. Over against the nation that is subject to death revelation posits the nation that shall come to life again, and through the contact of this idea with the ultimate future hope and its projection on a large scale the appropriate issue of this development is reached; the future blessedness emerges as "the life" par excellence. Still one more consideration must be taken into account: so soon, and in the proportion that the promise of the resurrection began to stand out clearly on the horizon of religious hope, nothing else could fill the content of a state thus projected but the pregnant conception of "life." It is remarkable how deeply rooted in past religious experience, how compact and at the same time rich in content from an eschatological point of view this revelation-product has become. It is not possible here to trace the history in detail, but the point of departure and the point of arrival of its course lie clear before our eyes. It is needful in endeavoring to construe what lay between to distinguish carefully between "long life," i.e. a gift of divine favor for the single Israelite or the nation on earth, and the great prospective gift reserved for "the latter days," and no longer confined to the earthen vessels in which it had so long through the ages been carried. In Deuteronomy and in the Psalter there are some data helpful for this, but unfortunately in the latter book uncertainty concerning the date in which the single Psalms were written renders it hard to draw definite conclusions. If the "tree of life" spoken of in Prov. iii. 18 consciously and directly refers back to the original tree of paradise, the ultimate eschatological import admits of no doubt; there must have attached to this ancient concept some clear, more or less widespread, remembrance of an objective sphere of life once potentially realized, and beckoning again for the future. Deut. xxx. 15 represents Jehovah as setting before Israel "life and good" with, as opposites, "death and evil"; at first sight one is inclined to connect with such an absolute antithesis some outlook into the future world. Where, however, in vs. 19 the thought is repeated in slightly different form, the prospect draws back again into the present: "Therefore choose life that both thou and thy seed may live." Nearly the identical phraseology in Jer. xxi. 8 plainly speaks of the God-appointed and pre-determined issues of national destiny in the earthly sphere. The Psalter makes more frequent reference to the paradisical *rivers* of life than to the condensation of the idea in the *one tree of life,* and the former have fully retained their eschatological associations: Psa. xxxv. 9; xlvi. 4, 5. These waters must be intended to refer back to paradise, because they issue from (underneath) the throne of God, cp. Gen. ii. 10, and, as the counterpart of this, we learn in the vision of the Apocalypse of the same waters with undoubted eschatological perspective: ii. 7; xxi. 6; xxii. 1-17. What lends confirmation to thus joining the earliest and the later is the emphasis placed upon the divine favor as an indispensable concomitant of the eschatological life. The concept of life would never have obtained in the Old Testament its comprehensive and pregnant significance, had it not from the outset been wedded to the profoundly-religious thought of prospering in the favor of God.[15]

"Life bears the stamp of its eschatological nature upon itself through frequent combination with the attribute "aionios." The Pauline instances where this is found are Acts xiii. 46; Rom. ii. 7; v. 21; vi. 22; Gal. vi. 8; I Tim. i. 16; vi. 12; Tit. i. 2; iii. 7; a dozen passages altogether. The phrase is, however, by no means original with Paul. Our Lord accepts it as a phrase in common use, when asked by the rich young ruler, regarding the condition of entering "eternal life," and suspends its attainment after the orthodox Jewish fashion on the fulfilment of the law: Mk. x. 17; Lk. x. 25; xviii. 18. When the disciples feel perplexed about the hardness of the task, Jesus gives an answer in which "eternal life" is equated to "the Kingdom of Heaven." The latter is meant in precisely the same sense in which the enquirer spoke of "entering eternal life." The difference between "inheriting" and "entering" is in this connection of no further significance than its adjustment to the two terms. The mode of our Lord's dealing with the terminology proves that it had been in use considerable time before Him. In fact He Himself makes use of it on other occasions: Matt. xix. 29; Mk. x. 30; Lk. xviii. 30. We must go back as far as Dan. xii. 2 to find the antecedents of the phrase; it occurs in Ps. Solom. iii. 16; En. xxxvii. 4; 2 Macc. vii. 9, 26; 4 Macc. xv. 3.[16] By way of antithesis it receives its full meaning from the contrast with "death," and it is in part through this contrast with a comprehensive sphere of life that "death" in its turn

[15] Cp. Job. x. 12: "Thou hast granted me life and favor and thy preservation has preserved my spirit; Psa. xxxvi. 9: "For with thee is the fountain of life: in thy light shall we see light."

[16] Cp. Dalman, *Die Worte Jesu,* pp. 127-128.

likewise ceases to be an individual experience and becomes a realm with extension, as is clearly perceptible in 2 Cor. ii. 16: "the savor of death unto death . . . the savor of life unto life." There is, however, perceptible a difference here in that the conception of death, objectively taken, is more strongly personalized, whence some have inferred actual personal existence, whereas life being less the agent of aggression than the passive object of enjoyment tends more to remain a term of abstract comprehensiveness.

Life not only is pointedly opposite to "death" it likewise forms a sharp contrast to such precursors and concomitants of death as are destructive of life. Thus the category of "δύναμις," "power" obtains a place in the concept of life. It becomes a life not so much lived in quietness, but to a considerable extent a life asserting itself, a trait which again has its affinity with the attribute "aionios." The intimate relation between "life" and "Pneuma" could not fail bringing this about. Likewise the opposition of life to "φθορά," "corruption" Rom. viii. 21; 1 Cor. xv. 42, 50; Gal. vi. 8 proves it; corruption is a process that has in itself fatal power of increase and intensification. There is no reason to limit this, where the Spirit comes under consideration, to one only of the twin aspects of the latter's vivifying task. The Spirit cannot deny Himself in whatever sphere His energy is introduced, least of all where He works in the consummate state, where all God's works and ways run together to produce a perfect issue.

Of the soul transformation at death Paul speaks comparatively little in particulars. That sorrow, death, sin and all sin-born evils must make halt before entrance into the eternal state is self-evident. Such things as dishonor and weakness are incompatible with the life-state in heaven. But there also is joined to these a character of "humiliation" affecting even the body with its enveloping sphere, Phil. iii. 21. That the Spirit has again his part in effecting the necessary change requires no demonstration, it being included in the change wrought by the resurrection.

Such things should not be minimized in the interest of a hyper-spiritualizing of the content of the future life. Their incompatibility with the absolute perfection of God, with whom nothing of the frailness and corruption of the sinful can have fellowship is to be taken into account. It is noteworthy, however, that silence is observed on this aspect of the matter, so far as concerns the intermediate state. The great sin-extruding and evil-conquering processes are relegated, as it were, to the climacteric epoch at the end. It is there that Death and all that inevitably trails in his wake shall be swallowed up in victory, and the body of sin delivered from all that causes its bearer, or erstwhile bearer, to groan.

One more point is to be considered before dismissing the idea of "life" in its eschatological import. As it is strongly bound to God in its production, so it has a telic character directing it to God as its solitary goal. This is true of its earthly prototype, the life that believers live here below while still in the flesh. It is particularly at the height of his contemplation of it that the Apostle is reminded of this. No less than in the sphere of justification, the instinct of life tends to concentrate all its forces and aspirations upon God, and this law of existence is observable in the eschatological prolongation and consummation of the life of the world to come. This convergence upon and final arrival of life at the center of satisfaction in God, while inextricably interwoven with the fundamental texture of religion, receives with Paul an additional and intensified force from its connection with the life of the exalted Christ, and thus the deepest mystical verity in soteriology and Christology is found to join itself to the eschatological prospect. The reign in life promised to believers for the coming age is a dominion fulfilling itself through Jesus Christ, Rom. v. 17. When Abraham waxed strong through faith he in doing so gave glory to God, v. 21. The life lived by Christ is defined as "lived unto God," and this serves as a basis for the exhortation: "Present yourselves unto God, as alive from the dead," Rom. vi. 13. The conception of "sanctification," but too often restricted in practice to the soteric progress in assimilation to the ethical perfection of God, has for its irremovable core the idea of consecration to God and consequent appurtenance to Him. It cannot be too much emphasized that "holiness" is in the Pauline vocabulary never ethical perfection as such and without regard to its terminus in God. No construction of the idea losing this out of sight is from the Apostle's viewpoint a thoroughly Christianized idea. Whatever fruit it may cultivate, it can never produce the highest, which is in this case the only truly religious fruitage, its subserviency to the glory of God who is the absolute end of all ethical striving.

Among the constituent elements of the life-organism no mutilation of what properly is called "religion," is countenanced by the Apostle. The modern deplorable neglect, or even disavowal, of large normal and indispensable religious territories is unknown to Paul. In particular the noetic, or to speak in more popular language, the intellectual element in religion is recognized, and recognized in such terms that the primacy of doctrinal knowledge in all normal religious experience is on principle upheld. In Eph. iv. 17-20 the walk of the Gentiles in their pseudo-religion is from this point of view characterized as a walk in the vanity of their minds ("nous"); they are darkened in their "understanding" ("dianoia"); subject to "ignorance" ("agnoia"), which exists on account of the "hardening of their hearts," ("porosis tes kardias"). The salient point in this enumeration is the clause in vs. 18, obviously intended to explain the several abnormalities and perversions named as sprung from the basic religious ignorance in which paganism had become involved through sin. And it is in striking correspondence with this state of facts that the Apostle stresses the principle that, at their conversion they had "learned" (ἐμάθετε) Christ in a different way. It is true this peculiar noetic mode of approach to the Christ and the Christian world-view had probably something to do with the philosophic complexion of the problems it was by the Apostle intended to meet. Nevertheless it remains also true that Paul has, after a philosophico-religious manner contended with this untruth, and in doing so has diagnosed the entire complex of religious malformation, as it were, embryologically, from some ancient flaw in the thought-form of paganism. It was in its origin "alienation from the life of God" that gave birth to the ill-shapen product. Perhaps no more incisive criticism of the false modern slogan "religion is not doctrine but life" than these few verses from Ephesians can be conceived. What Paul says is not that perverted ideas concerning religion and Christ are unimportant and their correction negligible; what he maintains is that they are subversive of the true Christian religion, and ought to be resisted to the utmost. And the Apostle intimates by the phrase "life of God," that in the internal constitution of the divine life itself there exists a typical antecedence of mind upon which every religious reflex of the nature of God in the human subject ought to model itself. There cannot remain any reasonable doubt that what Paul considered essential for the present (in Ephesians particularly emphasized) semi-eschatological life on earth he regarded as in the highest degree normative for the heavenly life in the fully-attained state of eternity.

The question seems permissible, in view of what we have found, whether the Apostle regarded the state of life in the future aeon as in an absolute sense immune to further invasion of antagonistic forces from without. That he considered it unending has already been shown to sufficiency. It might be thought that therein lay irrefutable evidence in proof of its immunity to invasion from without. Still, strictly speaking, the two affirmations are by no means identical. Something might, as a matter of fact, continue indefinitely without termination, and yet the cause for this might not lie in any inherent essence of eternity. God Himself is "eternal" or "immortal" after this matter-of-fact fashion: metaphysically speaking He is immune to and incapable of death. The question can hardly be suppressed, how much of this essence of eternal life has been imparted as its inherent, inalienable character to the future aeon and everything that moves therein. And this leads us back once more to the deep unfathomable mysteries of the aionion-concept. The close assimilation and association between believers on the one hand and God and the divine Christ on the other hand seem to decide the question in favor of a principially and inherently uninvadable and unchangeable life-state. The supreme ideal of religion likewise would seem to postulate it. It is another question whether Paul has anywhere explicitly expresed himself to that effect. Nevertheless, in so far as he speaks of God as "the King immortal, invisible, the only God," I Tim. i. 17, and as "the One who alone has immortality," vi. 17, a distinction with regard to the presence of this attribute in God and in believers cannot be denied. God possesses this immunity to death *per essentiam*; to believers it comes *per gratiam,* yet so that an unceasing action on God's part secures its permanence. Like God possessing the fount of life in Himself, no creature even in the consummate state is permitted to be. Yet there is in each of them some reality vouchsafing continuity in the possession of what they have. The Second Adam dwells in them as a Quickening Spirit as undisplaceable as He lives in the human nature of the Lord Himself. In the discourses of the Fourth Gospel the presence of eternal life and the promise of its permanence forever are most unequivocally affirmed, cp. Jno. iii. 36; v. 26; vi. 53; xi. 25. And Paul is persuaded that neither death nor life, nor any of the demonic principalities, nor any creature will be able to separate him from the love of God which is in Christ. He who is united to Christ and lives within the circle of his love, to him the eternal retention of the supreme eschatological life is absolutely secure. Mortality is in every one made partaker of the resurrection swallowed up of life, 2 Cor. v. 4. The life of the Colossians is hid with Christ in God, so as to partake of the same security, notwithstanding its present invisibility, that pertains to the inward things of God and Christ. And the whole intimate life-union existing between the believer and Christ vouches for the certainty of the eternal persistence of this bond. Christ has abolished death and, brought life and immortality ("ἀφθαρσία") to light through the Gospel, 2 Tim. i. 10.[17]

With the second chief ingredient of the eternal state we can deal more briefly. In regard to it likewise Rom. ii. 7 lays down the fundamental rule: to seek after incorruption is equivalent to seeking after glory. Rom. iii. 23 names as the result of universal sin that all "ὑστεροῦνται τῆς δόξης τοῦ θεοῦ."[18] In Chap. v. 2 the glory of God is projected into the future and represented as an eschatological inheritance, the means of its apprehension being hope. The Aorist in Chap. viii. 30 "He has glorified" is anticipative: the act is as certain as if it had been already accomplished. Some questioning has arisen concerning the precise force of the Genitive in the phrase "the glory of God." Gramatically considered this could mean "the glory possessed by God." Parallel constructions are: "the life of God," "the peace of God," "the righteousness of God"; the peculiar feature of which is that they are pregnant constructions, in which the triple ideas of "original in God," "reflected from God" and "communicated in an ectypical sense to man" meet. The underlying principle is in each case that the inherent excel-

[17] The strongest affirmation in regard to the "immortality" of Christ is made by the writer of Hebrews, who attributes to Christ a "ζωὴ ἀκατάλυτος," a life incapable of dissolution. The statement is made with specific reference to the priestly work of Christ which could not be suspended by his death even for a moment, since its very execution consisted in his death. This was possible because all through death He remained in full possession of this undissolvable life, Heb. vii. 16.

[18] Some exegetes take "the glory of God" in vs. 23 as referring to the Shekhinah upon the mercy-seat; the verb on this view will have to be translated "are shut out" from the glory of God, as it appeared in the Old Testament sanctuary. This fits in well with the rendering "mercy-seat" for "ἱλαστήριον" in vs. 25. It is far from certain, however, that "hilasterion" has in that verse the meaning of "mercy-seat," which it has in LXX and in Heb. ix. 8. "Instrument of propitiation" has equal linguistic warrant, and suits the context fully as well. The verb "προέθετο" lends some support to the rendering "mercy-seat," since of a sacrifice, or any ritual act in general, it is less naturally affirmed that it is "set forth."

lence of God is reproduced and brought to revelation in his beatified creatures. No stronger witness than this to the God-centered character of the eternal world can be conceived. "Δόξα," glory, must be distinguished from "τιμή," honor, as appears from their occurring together in Rom. ii. 10. "τιμή" is good appraisal in the opinion of others; it is a judgment passed by others on somebody, something inward, therefore, not something substantially-outward. By right of etymology the two terms ought to exchange places, for it is precisely "doxa" that is derived from the verb "δοκεῖν," "to bear a certain reputation." But this rule was no longer of strict observance at the time of Paul's writing.[19] Glory is as closely connected with the Spirit as life is. The distinction lies in this, that what life is for the hidden side of the eschatological subject, that doxa is for the outward side in which the higher life comes to revelation. The doxa plays a large rôle in the interrelation between the risen Christ and the believer. The union of what is the personal possession in Christ (ἐκ τοῦ ἐμοῦ, Jno. xvi. 14) and the Spirit-endowment of the Christian is of the closest, so close in fact as to permit of the statement "the Lord is the Spirit," an equation not, of course, meant trinitarianly, but soteriologically. Because doxa pertains to the sphere of manifestation, Paul speaks of it as that "which shall be revealed to usward." The application of the general concept to the believer's state and condition works in two directions. There is a somatic and there is a doxa of the inner man. In both respects the Spirit is the Agent for its creation and bestowal. The body is raised "ἐν δόξῃ," 1 Cor. xv. 43. Doxa belongs to "ζωή" Col. iii. 4. In not a few instances, however, the idea is deepened so as to stand for religious excellence as such.

[19] The physical root-concept in the Shemitic languages seems to be that of "being heavy." Cp. von Gall, *Die Herrlichkeit Gottes,* 1900. This is easily associated with the metaphorically used idea of "weight," and next spring from this the ideas of "prestige" "renown." The glory of a king lies in the splendor of his retinue, since that most naturally expresses his majesty and power. It is curious to observe that thus derived the Hebrew "Kabod" stands nearer to τιμή in the Greek than to δόξα.

How solidly the endowment with doxa is conceived appears from 2 Cor. iv. 17: "an eternal weight of glory." The fundamental conception is aesthetic; doxa constitutes the beauty of the children of God. The "liberty" that comes at the end to the creation, now bound to the bondage of sin through the sin-bondage of man, forms part of it, because it draws into the light whatever change has taken place: for groaning there is substituted joy. By no means is doxa to be limited to somatic radiancy, although this forms an essential part of it; it was precisely from this (aesthetic) point of view, and not from purely-sentimental motives that Paul desired to be clothed, 2 Cor. v. 3. But doxa undoubtedly dwells also in the things that eye cannot for the present see, nor ear for the present hear, and that for the present do not come up in the hearts of men. For these things are not intrinsically incapable of the vesture of glory; they only require the proper eye, the proper ear, the proper heart, the proper milieu. And, since they are the Spirit's workmanship, the Spirit will impart to them that uniquely heightened intensity, which it is His nature and mode of working to produce. Whatever of anticipation there is of such things in this life is always viewed as a "Pneumatikon" par excellence, 2 Cor. iii. 18.

We close this discussion of the aionion-character of the world to come with the briefest of references to a question which sometimes unduly engages men's eschatological occupation with the future. It is the question concerning possible further progress for the inhabitants of the coming age beyond the point already attained by them when entering it. Strange to say, this question is not always predominantly concerned with inward ethico-religious growth, but not seldom relates to external increase in the visible embodiments of religion. Will there be worlds beyond this eschatologically-consummated world to conquer? It is not likely that from Paul we may expect information or encouragement in such a speculation. For, although Paul exhibited in all his labors for the Gospel the most intense zeal, and an outpouring of apparently exhaustless energy, yet, when it comes to the point of eschatology, there is to all this a sort of counterpoise, owing to which the Apostle never loses the desire of finding rest in the unnamable, unfathomable depths of a mystic satisfaction in God and Christ, such as craved no further out-venturing into realms beyond. All Paul's labor was a most strenuous endeavor to bring the restlessly-temporal to where it would lose itself in the forever-undisturbable aionion. There is no passage in the Epistles indicative of an opposite trend or desire. There may be heavens in the plural numerically or structurally, but there is no succession of ages or worlds to come. Eternity is not pregnant with other eternities.[20] We do not hear of further sowings nor further reaping in the fields of the blessed. It is useless to carry the spirit of time into the heart of eternity. There clings an earth and time-savor to this questioning what there will be to occupy one's self withal when arrived above. As if the Lord God Himself would not be there with his inexhaustible fulness! In his presence there can be neither surfeit nor teadium. The noblest distinction of the eschatological Church consists in this that thenceforth she will be able to lay aside the armor of her militancy, because she has become the *Ecclesia triumphans in aeternum.*[21]

[20] The phrase "ages to come," Eph. ii. 7 is a plural of immensity; it expresses itself in terms of time, whereas eternity marks the pleroma of time.

[21] Precisely of pagan eschatologies it is characteristic to look for incessantly recurring cycles after the world-year shall have been ended. The reason is that in paganism the concept of eschatology is a piece of naturalism, sprung from astral, zodiacal observation of circuits among the heavenly bodies. When the longest circuit has been completed and brought back to its point of departure, it inevitably proceeds to repeat itself along the immemorial selfsame courses. The "year of gold" has "come round" again. The future age of God, though made of the finest gold, does not "come round"; it simply comes and then abides.

BIBLIOGRAPHY

Baldensperger, W. Das Selbstbewusstsein Jesu im Lichte der Messianischen Hoffnungen seiner Zeit, 1903.

Blom, A. H. Th. Tijdschr., 1863, pp. 4 ff. (Stoicheia).

Bousset, W. Der Antichrist, 1895.

Die Religion des Judenthums im neutestamentlichen Zeitalter, 1906.

Die Jüdische Apokalyptik, 1903.

Kyrios Christos, 1921.

Nachträge und Auseinandersetzungen, 1916.

Box, G. M. The Ezra-Apocalypse, 1912.

Brückner, M. Die Entstehung der Paulinischen Christologie, 1903.

Bruston, E. La Vie future d'après St. Paul, 1895.

Burton, Ernest de Witt. Spirit, Soul and Flesh, A. J. Th., 1913-1916.

Charles, R. H. A critical History of the Doctrine of a future Life in Israel, Judaism and in Christianity, 1899; 2d ed., 1913.

The Apocalypse of Baruch, 1896.

Cremer, H. Über den Zustand nach dem Tode, 1892.

Dalman, G. Die Worte Jesu, Band I, 1898.

Deissman, A. Die neutestamentliche Formel "in Christo Jesu," 1892.

Paulus, 1911.

Dickson, W. P. St. Paul's use of the terms "flesh" and "Spirit," 1883.

Dieckmann, H. Die Parousie Christi, 1898.

Diels, H. Elementum, 1899 (Stoicheia).

Erbes, C. Der Antichrist nach den Schriften des Neuen Testaments, 1897.

Everling, O. Die Paulinische Angelologie und Dämonologie, 1888.

Ewald, H. Adam und Christus, J. Ch. W., 1849.

Feine, P. Jesus Christus und Paulus, 1902.

Friedländer, M. Der Antichrist in den vorchristlichen jüdischen Quellen, 1897.

Gall, Freiherr von. Die Herrlichkeit Gottes, 1900.

Giesebrecht, F. Beiträge zur Jesajakritik, Anhang, pp. 187-220.

Ginzburg, L. Jewish Encyclopaedia, Vol. I, Article, "Adam Kadmon."

Gloël, J. Der Heilige Geist in der Heilsverkündigung des Paulus, 1888.

Grafe, E. Die Paulinische Lehre vom Gesetz, 1884.

Gressmann, H. Die Entstehung der israelitisch-jüdischen Eschatologie, 1905.

Griethuyzen. N.J. f. W. Th. 1859, pp. 304-346. (On 2 Cor. v. 1-6.)

Grimm, W. Über die Stelle 1 Cor. xv. 20-28; Z. W. Th. 1873, pp. 380-411.

Grossheide, F. W. De Verwachting der Toekomst van Jesus Christus, 1907.

Gunkel, H. Die Wirkungen des Heiligen Geistes nach der populären Anschauung der apostolischen Zeit und der Lehre des Apostels Paulus, 1888.

Hepp, V. De Antichrist, 1st ed., 1919.

Holtzmann, H. J. Neutestamentliche Theologie (2nd ed. by Jülicher and Bauer), 2 Vols., 1911.

Kabisch, R. Die Eschatologie des Paulus in ihren Zusammenhängen mit dem Gesammtbegriff des Paulinismus, 1893.

Kennedy, H. A. A. St. Paul's Conceptions of the Last Things, 1904.

Klöpper, A. Die Bedeutung und der Zweck des Abschnittes Rom. v. 1-12. St. u. Kr., 1869.

Der Brief an die Colosser, 1882.

Der Brief des Apostels Paulus an die Philippenser, 1893.

Knopf, R. Paulus, 1909.

Oesterley, W. O. E. The Books of the Apocrypha, 1914.

Olschewsky, W. Die Wurzeln der Paulinischen Christologie, 1908.

Orelli, C. von. Die Hebräischen Synonyma der Zeit und der Ewigkeit, 1871.

Pfleiderer, O. Der Paulinismus, 2nd ed., 1890.

Philippi, F. Die biblisch-kirchliche Lehre vom Antichrist, 1877.

Rohde, E. Psyche, 1903.

Rinck, H. W. Vom Zustande nach dem Tode, 3rd ed., 1878.

Rothe, R. Neuer Versuch einer Auslegung der Stelle Rom. v. 12-21, 1836.

Salmond, C. H. The Christian Doctrine of Immortality, 1901.

Schlatter, A. Theologie des Neuen Testaments, 1910.

Schmiedel, P. W. in Handkommentar zum Neuen Testament (ad 2 Cor. v. 1. ff.).

Schneckenburger, M. Beiträge (Antichrist):
Theol. Jahrb. 1848.
J. D. Th., p. 405.

Schwally, J. Das Leben nach dem Tode, 1892.

Schweitzer, A. Paul and his Interpreters (tr. from the German), 1912.

Shoemaker, W. R. The use of "Ruach" in the O.T. and of "Pneuma" in the N.T., 1904.

Siebeck, H. Die Entwickelungslehre vom Geiste in den Wissenschaften des Alterthums; Z. f. Völker-psychologie und Sprachwissenschaft, 1880.

Simon, Th. De Psychologie des Apostels Paulus, 1897.

Slotemaker de Bruine, J. R. De eschatologische Voorstellingen in 1 and 2 Cor., 1894.

Sokolowski, E. Die Begriffe Geist und Leben bei Paulus in ihrer Beziehung zu einander, 1903.

Stähelin, R. Zur Paulinischen Eschatologie; J. D. Th., 1874.

Stark, W. Gebrauch der Wendung Beacherith Hajjamim im alttestamentlichen Kanon, Z. f. A. W., 1891.

Stegmann, B. A. Christ the "Man from Heaven," 1927.

Teichmann, E. Die Paulinischen Vorstellungen von Auferstehung und Gericht und ihre Beziehungen zur jüdischen Apokalyptik, 1896.

Thackeray, H. St. J. The Relations of St. Paul to Jewish Thought, 1900.

Tillman, F. Die Widerkunft Christi nach den Paulinischen Briefen, 1909.

Titius, A. Die neutestamentliche Lehre von der Seligkeit, II, Der Paulinismus unter dem Gesichtspunkt der Seligkeit, 1900.

Volz, P. Die jüdische Eschatologie von Daniel bis Akiba, 1903.

Vos, G. The Eschatological Aspect of the Pauline Conception of the Spirit; P.S.B.T.S., 1912.

Wadstein, E. Die eschatologische Ideengruppe: Antichrist, Weltsabbat, Weltende und Gericht, Q. W. Th., 1896.

Waitz, Th. Über 2 Cor. v. 1-4: J. f. P. Th., 1882.

Weber, F. Jüdische Theologie, 2nd ed., 1897.

Weiss, B. Apokalyptische Studien, St. u. Kr. 1869 (Antichrist).

Weiss, Johannes. "Himmlischer Mensch"; R.G.G., 1900.

Wendt, H. H. Die Begriffe Fleisch und Geist im biblischen Sprachgebrauch, 1878.

Wernle, P. Der Christ und die Sünde bei Paulus, 1897.

Windisch, H. Entsündigung des Christen nach Paulus, 1908.

Winstanly, E. W. Spirit in the New Testament, 1908.

Wrede, W. Paulus, 1904 (Religionsgeschichtliche Volksbücher).

APPENDIX

Eschatology of the Psalter

by Geerhardus Vos, Ph. D., D. D.

from

The Princeton Theological Review, January, 1920

ESCHATOLOGY OF THE PSALTER

There are certain editions of the New Testament which by way of appendix contain the Psalter, an arrangement obviously intended to serve the convenience of devotion. It has, however, the curious result of bringing the Apocalypse and the Psalms into immediate proximity. On first thought it might seem that scarcely two more diverse things could be put together. The storm-ridden landscape of the Apocalypse has little enough in common with the green pastures and still waters of which the Psalmist sings. For us the Psalter largely ministers to the needs of the devotional life withdrawn into its privacy with God. Such a life is not usually promotive of the tone and temper characteristic of the eschatological reaction. This will explain why the ear of both reader and interpreter has so often remained closed to strains of a quite different nature in this favorite book.

It requires something more strenuous than the even tenor of our devotional life to shake us out of this habit and force us to take a look at the Psalter's second face. It has happened more than once in the history of the Church, that some great conflict has carried the use of the Psalms out from the prayer-closet into the open places of a tumultuous world. The period of the Reformation affords a striking example of this. We ourselves, who are just emerging from a time of great world-upheaval, have perhaps discovered, that the Psalter adapted itself to still other situations than we were accustomed to imagine. To be sure, these last tremendous years have not detracted in the least from its familiar usefulness as an instrument of devotion. But we have also found that voices from the Psalter accompanied us, when forced into the open to face the world-tempest, and that they sprang to our lips on occasions when otherwise we should have had to remain dumb in the presence of God's judgments. This experience sufficiently proves that there is material in the Psalms which it requires the large impact of history to bring to our consciousness in its full significance. It goes without saying that what can be prayed and sung now *in theatro mundi* was never meant for exclusive use in the oratory of the pious soul. This other aspect of the Psalter has not been produced by liturgical accommodation; it was in its very origin a part of the life and prayer and song of the writers themselves.

After all, these two uses, the devotional and the historical, are not so divergent as one might imagine. We need only to catch the devotional at its proper angle to perceive how it forms part of a broader, more comprehensive piety uniting in itself with perfect naturalness the two different attitudes of withdrawal into the secrecy of God and of intense interest in the unfolding of the world-drama. The deeper fundamental character of the Psalter consists in this that it voices the subjective response to the objective doings of God for and among his people. Subjective responsiveness is the specific quality of these songs. As prophecy is objective, being the address of Jehovah to Israel in word and act, so the Psalter is subjective, being the answer of Israel to that divine speech. If once this peculiarity is apprehended, it will follow that there must be place, and considerable place, in the Psalms not merely for the historical interest in general, but particularly for that heightened interest which the normal religious mind brings to the last goal and issue of redemption. To the vision of faith that which Jehovah will do at the end, his conclusive, consummate action, must surpass everything else in importance. Faith will sing its supreme song when face to face, either in anticipation or reality, with the supreme act of God. Let Mary's case be witness from whose heart the great annunciation of Messianic fulfillment drew that Psalm of all Psalms, the *Magnificat*. The time when God gathers his fruit is the joyous vintage-feast of all high religion. The value of a work lies in its ultimate product. Consequently, where religion entwines itself around a progressive work of God, such as redemption, its general responsiveness becomes prospective, cumulative, climacteric; it gravitates with all its inherent weight toward the end. A redemptive religion without eschatological interest would be a contradiction in terms. The orthodox interpretation of Scripture has always recognized this. To it redemption and eschatology are co-eval in biblical history.[1] The case stands quite different with unorthodox criticism. By it the redemptive content and the teleological outlook of the ancient religion of Israel are denied. The ancient, that is the pre-prophetic, Israelite in this respect lived the life of a religious animal. Hence for the older period the absence of eschatology is characteristic. Still, even from the standpoint of this criticism, the eschatological aspect of the Psalms is not affected. For the Psalter is now commonly considered in these circles a product of the exilic and post-exilic times, that is of a period when through the prophetic channel and from foreign sources a flood of redemptive and eschatological ideas had streamed in upon Israel, so that the Psalm-singing Jew was bound to answer to its call in corresponding notes. Besides, the great influx of eschatological material is placed by many of these writers not in the early period of written prophecy, but in the later exilic and post-exilic times, most of the material of this kind now contained in the older prophets being treated as spurious in its present environment and brought down to a much later date. But this late dating brings it into close proximity to the time fixed by these same critics for the Psalter. Hence criticism has a direct and powerful stimulus to search the Psalms for the presence of that spirit with which the religious atmosphere is supposed to have been charged in that period. And, since under the control of God exegetical good not seldom comes

[1] In so far as the covenant of works posited for mankind an absolute goal and unchangeable future, the eschatological may be even said to have preceded the soteric religion.

out of critical evil, it has happened here also, that a criticism whose general methods and results we cannot but distrust, has brought to light from the Psalter valuable facts, whose existence had not been previously recognized with sufficient clearness. It cannot be denied that unorthodox criticism has done some valuable pioneer-work in exploring the eschatological views of the Psalter.[2] And what is true of the Wellhausen school may in a different sense be applied to its more modern competitor,—or shall we say successor? —the school of Gunkel and Gressmann.[3] Here it is not so much the inclination to fit the Psalter into the post-exilic world of thought, but rather the desire to assimilate it to Babylonian religious ideas that predisposes for the welcoming of eschatological material. For our purpose this is even better than the exegetical help received from the other quarter. It yields not only acceptable exegesis stimulated by perverse criticism, but has the additional advantage of in certain instances drawing the criticism of the Psalter back to a more conservative position from a chronological point of view. For, since according to this recent school there was an Oriental eschatology in very ancient times, there remains no longer any reason for disputing its early existence in Israel, nor for denying the pre-exilic date of any piece on the sole ground of its occurrence therein. On the contrary, other things being equal, the eschatalogical complexion of a document speaks rather in favor of the

---

[2] Cfr. especially Stade, *Die Messianische Hoffnung im Psalter* in *Zeitschrift für Theologie und Kirche,* 1892, pp. 369-412. The scope of the article is wider than the antiquated use of the term "Messianic" in the title would indicate. It covers the whole eschatological outlook of the Psalter, whether the Messiah occupies a place in it or not. Stade makes extensive use of a comparison between what he considers the later material in the older prophecies and the Psalms.

[3] Gunkel, *Schäpfung und Chaos, in Urzeit und Endzeit,* 1895; *Ausgewählte Psalmen,* 1911; Gressmann, *Der Ursprung der israelitisch-jüdischen Eschatologie,* 1905; Cfr. Sellin, Der alttestamentliche *Prophetismus;* Zweite Studie: *Alter, Wesen und Ursprung der alttestamentlichen Eschatologie,* 1912; Stärk, *Lyrik (Psalmen, Hoheslied und Verwandtes)* in *Die Schriften des Alten Testaments* edited by Gressmann, Gunkel, a. o. III, 1, 2, 1911.

older date than otherwise. As a matter of fact some Psalms have on this principle been again recognized as pre-exilic possibilities.[4]

As a third source, from which in recent criticism the eschatological interpretation of the Psalter has received encouragement, we may mention the widely-spread opinion, that the speaking subject in the Psalms is in many cases not a single person, but the collective mind of the congregation of Israel, into which the original composers have merged their religious individuality, nay, that many of the Psalms were written outright for liturgical use in the service of the second temple.[5] It is hard to tell whether this theory

[4] It should be remembered that critics of the type of Gunkel and Gressmann remain, so far as the broad literary issue of Old Testament criticism is concerned, Wellhausenians. They do not revise the verdict that the law is later than prophecy. In the reconstruction of the pre-prophetic religion of Israel they pursue the same backward-reasoning, divinatory method as the others. Only they apply this method to a subject to which the Wellhausen school had, on the whole, refrained from applying it, the question of pre-prophetic eschatology. The general structure of Wellhausenianism implies that there was no such early eschatology worth speaking of, that eschatology was a later product. Consequently no inducement exists for it to trace its origins in the ancient religion. Gunkel and Gressmann do not share in this prejudice. Convinced that the thing must have existed they are on the alert for every early indication of its presence.

[5] The more recent literature on this subject consists chiefly of: Smend, *Ueber das Ich der Psalmen,* in *Zeitschrift für die alttestamentliche Wissenschaft,* 1888, pp. 49-147; *Theol. Literaturzeitung* 1889, p. 547; Beer, *Individual-und Gemeindepsalmen,* 1894; Roy, *Die Volksgemeinde und die Gemeinde der Frommen im Psalter,* 1897; Coblenz, *Ueber das betende Ich in den Psalmen,* 1897. The collective view, however, is by no means a modern product. For its history in the earliest and latest exegesis, cfr. Coblenz, pp. 2-15; Cheyne, *The Origin and Religious Contents of the Psalter,* Bampton Lectures for 1889, 1891, pp. 259-266; Beer, pp. xiii-xvii. Early traces are found in lxx; it was applied by Theodor of Mopsuestia, by Raschi, Aben-Ezra and Kimchi among the mediaeval Jewish expositors, by Rudinger among the old-Protestant exegetes, in more recent times by Rosenmüller, de Wette, especially Olshausen, Graetz. After Smend's reintroduction of the subject, and in part independently of him, the same position has been taken by Cheyne, Stade, Baethgen. Criticising, and restricting Smend's ideas are Stekhoven in *Zeitschrift für die Alttestamentliche Wissenschaft* vol. 89, pp. 131-135; Stärk, ibid. vol. 92, p. 146; Sellin,

apart from its intrinsic merit or demerit, has in its actual working out done more good or evil to the cause of Psalter-exegesis. For one thing it is often too-closely bound up with belief in the post-exilic origin of the Psalms, because not until after the exile, it is believed, did a specifically religious congregation of Israel, a church-Israel, in whose name such songs could have been sung, exist. Of course, the intermarriage of these two views is not beyond the possibility of divorce. For one who recognizes a church-nation of Israel in much earlier times, it would be critically quite safe to assume early Psalms of a collective import. In the next place the theory, when one-sidedly and radically carried through, threatens to wipe out all the individual coloring which renders many of the Psalms so attractive to the Christian reader and so faithful a mirror of his own individual experience. All the concrete, plastic, lifelike self-portrayal by which the figure of David stands before our eyes as the most real of realities, and which plays such a role in the New Testament, is at one stroke swept aside, and figures like Asaph and Ethan likewise lose for us their value as sources of individual comfort and delight. The individual application made by our Lord to Himself of certain Psalter-passages has to be artifically justified, if it is justified at all, on the ground that He was entitled to make of what was originally meant for Israel a personal application, since in Him Israel was summed up. Still further, and this is perhaps the most serious element in the situation, the collectivistic exegesis now threatens to swallow up all the directly Messianic material hitherto found in the Psalter. It is seriously proposed that "the Anointed of Jehovah," "the King" in several places, where these titles occur, shall not be understood of an individual eschatological figure, but of the people of Israel as the collective heir of the Messianic promises, the writers of such Psalms being even credited with the clear consciousness of the abrogation of the hope of an individual, Davidic Messiah.

De Origine Carminum quae primus Psalterii liber continet, 1892, pp. 26 ff; Rahlfs, *עני und ענו in den Psalmen*, 1892, p. 82.

The nation of Israel then becomes the King set upon the holy hill of Zion, receiving the nations for his inheritance, the uttermost parts of the earth for his possession. Last of all, the collectivistic view has contributed toward eliminating from the Psalter the expectation of a life after death for the individual, the passages where this used to be found being now not infrequently interpreted of the immortality of the people of Israel. While undoubtedly in all these respects the view under consideration has wrought harm, it should be remembered that the several errors enumerated represent not necessary corollaries, but only abuses of an otherwise not implausible theory. The later liturgical use of the Psalms in the Jewish Church certainly supports it, for the liturgical is from its very nature collective. The instance where "I" and "we" alternate as the speaking subject, and where the context puts a national interpretation upon the "we," show how easily the self-personification of the people took place in the poet's mind, or at least how naturally the collective plural alternated with the individual singular. The sudden, abrupt changes in many Psalms from utter depression to the most jubilant assurance, which the individualizing exegesis has found it is so hard to explain, are perhaps more easily accounted for, if the personified genius of the people of God, with its indestructible, inexhaustible hope in Jehovah may be assumed to experience them. Even what may be called the pathological terminology of the Psalms, sometimes considered a serious obstacle to the collectivistic view, may be turned into an argument in its favor, for this reason that the symptoms of disease and distress enumerated could scarcely coexist in the state of an individual, whilst metaphorically explained, as details entering into the picture of the stricken nation, they cease to be subject to the same rigid test of consistency. That the nation of Israel should "water its couch with its tears" Ps. vi. 6, may seem an overbold figure to our restrained Western imagination, but we must remember the richer and different endowment of Israel's mentality. The prophets, especially Isaiah and other parts of the Old Testament, bear witness to the strongly developed habit of personification in the Hebrew mind and supply us with a sufficient basis of analogy. It is not necessary here to enter into the psychological aspect of the problem by enquiring, whether conscious and purposeful self-projection into the mind of Israel, or spontaneous lyrical expansion of the personality, or typical generalization of what was first felt as an individual experience, will best explain the phenomena.[6] Only one feature should be briefly touched upon: in certain cases the collective speaker is not the external, ethnical Israel, but the people conceived as to its ideal, spiritual vocation, or its pious nucleus, the church within the church, sharply distinguishing itself from the religiously disloyal majority. Such a cleavage of spirits would of itself facilitate the absorption of the individual into the ideal body.[7] Keeping these various reservations in mind, we shall have to acknowledge, I think, that to a greater or

[6] Beer would find the explanation in the general law of lyrical production deriving its themes from the common interests and feelings of mankind, love, religion, nature, historical happenings affecting the majority, pp. lxxix ff. But the collective spirit and sentiment of the Psalms are of too concrete and intimate a nature to rest on such a general natural basis. If the phenomenon is spontaneous, it will have to be explained from the unique cause of the special grace of God drawing all its objects into the circle of an experience, which is at once personal and alike in all individuals to whom it comes. The intenser homogeneity of redemption should be taken into account. This seems to us the truth underlying the early patristic efforts to account for the facts: Christ was in the Psalms and back of their writers, Christ and his mystical body are one, consequently the church spake in the Psalter. In Christian hymnology we can trace the effect of the same cause: hymns individual in their origin have become expressions of communal feeling, and liturgically intended pieces have been appropriated by the individual. The theory of lyrical expansion has also been brought to bear upon the problem of typical Messianism. Delitzsch identified the mystery of the consciousness of David with the mystery of all poetry: "The genuine lyric poet does not give a mere copy of the impressions of his empirical ego." Cheyne, *The Origin*, pp. 259, 260.

[7] Roy very carefully works out this side of the case. He, as well as Cheyne, makes much of the analogy between the "servant" in the Psalms and "the servant of Jehovah" in the second part of Isaiah.

lesser extent the mind of the congregation of Israel voices itself in the Psalter.

The sole purpose for which we are led to mention this fact lies in its bearing upon the question of eschatology in the Psalter. For, if the great change, the reversal of destiny, the deliverance, the victory so often spoken of in the Psalms, concern not individuals, but Israel, or even the pious nucleus of Israel, is it not plain that this whole complex of ideas moves on eschatological ground? What else could such a crisis, such a marvelous turn for the better, nay for the best, when predicated of Israel, mean but the eschatological transformation? What in the case of the individual could be kept within the limits of the present order of things and interpreted as a relative change, when understood of Israel, necessarily bursts through these bonds and opens us a totally new prospect, a wholly different mode of existence. It is true, the frequent description of the content of the hope in earthly, temporal forms, so characteristic of the Old Testament, might seem to imply a merely relative difference between present and future. But this is only apparently so. Notwithstanding the retention of this form there are two points which clearly mark off the one from the other. On the one hand, the truly eschatological expectation contemplates the fulfilment of all the promises of God. It has too large a sweep to be simply coördinated with any single good turn in the fortunes of Israel. And on the other hand, the coming state of affairs bears the stamp of unchangeableness, everlastingness: it is no longer, like the present, subject to the vicissitudes of history. Paradoxical though it may seem, revelation has not shunned here to wed the eternal in point of duration to the temporal in point of make-up. The inheriting of the earth, the eating and drinking before Jehovah, and what there is more of this description, is to be forevermore.

In the form of subjective responsiveness which the eschatological ideas assume in the Psalter lies for us the greater part of their value. So far as the content objectively considered is concerned, the difference from prophecy is not perhaps sufficiently pronounced to justify separate treatment. The general scheme is in both essentially the same. On the dynamic side we meet here as well as there such ideas as that of Jehovah's accession to the kingship, the judgment, the conquest of the nations, the cup of wrath, the recovery of territory, the vindication of Israel, the repulsion of the last great assault by the nations. On the static side we encounter the ideas of peace, universalism, paradise restored, the dwelling of Jehovah's presence in the land, the vision of God, the enjoyment of glory, light, satisfaction of all wants, the outlook beyond death towards an uninterrupted contact with God and a resurrection. Only in the Psalms all this is suffused with the genial warmth of religious feeling. We have here a great province of objectivity translated into terms of living religion, and that religion at the very acme of its functioning. The Psalter teaches us before all else what the proper, ideal attitude of the religious mind ought to be with reference to its vision of the absolute future. The trouble with eschatology in the experience of the church has frequently been that it was either dead or overmuch pathologically alive. In the Psalter we can observe what is its normal working. And through observing this we can learn the even more principial lesson, what is the heart and essence of all religion, because when eschatologically attuned the religious mind responds to the highest inworking and closest approach of God, and therefore operates up to the full potentialities of its own nature. To this must be added something else of almost equal value. Through the subjective, practical spirit in which these things are treated by the Psalter, we are most profoundly made aware of our vital unity with the church of the old dispensation. It is true, of course, that, just as we in the consciousness of the fulfilment of prophecy, make our faith reach back into the Old Testament, so the Old Testament, by means of prophecy, in advance lays its hand upon us: we are sons of the prophets and of the *diatheke* God made with Abraham. But this is a purely objective bond; it is the bond between a program and its execution; it does not directly enable us to feel our oneness with the Old Covenant people of God. No sooner, however, do we pass out from the region of prophecy into that of psalmody, than we come into touch with something that is internally akin to us, a preformation of our own living religious embrace of the realities of redemption. This must be so all the more, because our whole New Testament life and heritage was, from the Old Testament point of view, an eschatological thing. Here, therefore, we find ourselves and them occupied with identical fact; what they eschatologically contemplated we retrospectively enjoy, and the religious apprehension of it, while formally different, is in essence the same. In the eschatology of the Psalms we may trace the embryonic organism of our own full-grown state. We are enabled to see how our faith was made in secret and curiously wrought, when our substance was as yet imperfect and our members continually fashioned before the eyes of God.

When we say that the Psalter is more practically akin to us than prophecy, we must not be led by this to overlook another feature well worth our notice. Response to the work of God of necessity leads to a more or less reflective state of mind. There is a point where the devotional, the contemplative and the doctrinal, in its simplest form, touch one another. Underneath all the emotion that pulsates through the Psalter, there lies a deep water of serious thought and reflection. The feeling here is not the substitute for faith, it is the natural outcome of faith, the wave-swell of the sea, when the wind of the Lord has blown upon it. If one will only read and sing with the understanding, he shall perceive that the Psalmists pray and sing out of a rich knowledge of God. It is not for nothing that they have "meditated" upon Him and his works. Nor can it be accidental that so considerable a part of the New Testament faith-fabric is derived from this source. Paul over and over again quotes from the Psalter, and his appeal to it is not less apt and convincing than that to the Torah and the prophets.

Let us now endeavor briefly to review the outstanding characteristics of Psalter-eschatology. The first thing requiring notice is the historical background in the past of the Psalter's treatment of the future. True, in this it only proves itself a genuine Old Testament product, partaking of the specific difference that marks off the biblical eschatology from that of the pagan nations. The pagan eschatological beliefs have a mythical or astronomic basis; they bear no definite relation to any scheme of historical progress, and, with the exception of Parsism, know of no absolute final crisis, beyond which no further change is contemplated. These two defects are closely connected. Because the ideas have their origin within the present world-process, they cannot lead to anything beyond it. The world-cycle runs its course, obeys its stars, absolves its round, and then the end links on to a new beginning, ushering in a repetition of the same sequence. The golden age is bound to return, but it will be no more enduring than it was before. Old Testament teaching concerning the end is not born from myth and chaos and zodiacal "precession". Its origin lies in the realm of history, in the past creative and redemptive activity of God, ultimately in the theistic conception of the character of Jehovah Himself, as an intelligent, planning, building God, whose delight is ever in the product of his freely shaping hands. And consequently, what Israel expects is not a quasi-consummation, which would bear on its face the Sisyphus-expression of endless toil; it is an absolute goal, consisting in an age of more than gold, made of a finer metal beyond all rust and deterioration.[8]

[8] It is true, the Old Testament, and also the Psalter, know the thought of a correspondence of the end to the beginning, of the point of arrival to the point of departure. The river that makes glad the city of God is a reproduction of the streams of paradise. But this is not intended as a mere equation of the two. The past paradise is viewed as a

The Psalter is wide awake to the significance of history as leading up to the eschatological act of God. It knows that it deals with a God, who spake and speaks and shall speak, who wrought and works and shall work, who came and is coming and is about to come. To no small extent it is the dignity of Jehovah as Creator and Redeemer from which the eschatological necessity springs. As a Psalmist says, Jehovah cannot abandon the work of his own hands (cxxxviii. 8); He will perfect that which concerns his people. His work must appear unto his servants, his glory unto their children (xc. 16). The Psalms that engage in great historical retrospects were written with this thought in mind. A more concise illustration is offered by Ps. cxiv. Here we have first the retrospect: "When Israel went out of Egypt, the house of Jacob from a people of strange language, Judah was his sanctuary and Israel his dominion. The sea saw it and fled; Jordan was driven back," and then, as a corresponding prospect, the vision of the greater theophany at the end: "Tremble thou earth at the presence of the Lord, at the presence of the God of Jacob." The references also to the flood, as bound to repeat itself, must be interpreted on this principle. Jehovah's control for his own purpose of the primeval world-catastrophe is typical of his action in the final upheaval, when out of the last judgment a last world will be born. It is of importance to notice the sequence of the past and future tense-forms in Psalms xciii. and xxix. "The floods have (once) lifted up their voice . . . the floods will lift up their waves. Jehovah on high is mightier than the noise of many waters, the mighty breakers of the sea." And again: "Jehovah (once) sat (as King) at the flood, yea, Jehovah will sit as King forever."

There are certain phrases and figures in the Psalter, which are connected with the idea of plan and continuity in the work of God and of its destination to arrive at a final

beginning, that of the future stands in the sign of consummation; that it will inaugurate a new process is never reflected upon, far less that what it introduces will be a repetition of the ancient course of history.

goal. Most characteristic of these, because most Psalm-like, is the phrase "a new song," occurring five times.[9] It receives light from the idea of the "new things" found in prophecy, especially in the latter part of Isaiah. There the "new things" mean the great unparalleled events about to introduce the future state of Israel. The "new things" and the "new song" belong together, as may be clearly seen from Isa. xlii. 9, 10: "Behold the former things are come to pass and new things do I declare . . . Sing unto Jehovah a new song, his praise from the ends of the earth." This prediction of the "new things" culminates in the promise of the "new heavens and a new earth."[10] Here seems to lie the root of the later employment of the word "new" in eschatological connections, the new name, the new creature, the new *diatheke,* the new Jerusalem.[11] Further, the use made of the term "morning," again both in the prophets and in the Psalter, is significant. From Isaiah we are familiar with the figure of the watchman peering into the darkness of the world-night, to whom the prophet addresses the question, "Watchman, what of the night?", and from whom he received the answer, "The morning cometh, and also the night."[12] In the Psalter we find again this idea of "the morning" signifying the dawn of the new great day of Jehovah, and hence symbolic of all hope and deliverance: "God is in the midst of her; she shall not be moved, God will hear her and that in the morning." "Death shall be their shepherd, and the upright shall have dominion over them in the morning." "My soul waiteth for Jehovah, more than watchmen for the morning: O Israel, hope in Jehovah."[13] It is perhaps worth while asking, whether the phrase "the day of Jehovah" has not some connection with this eschatological use of the phrase

[9] xxxiii. 3; xcvi. 1; xcviii. 1; cxliv. 9; cxlix. 1.

[10] Isa. lxv. 17; lxvi. 22.

[11] Isa. lxii. 2; Jer. xxxi. 31; Mk. xiv. 24; 2 Cor. v. 17; Gal. vi. 15; Rev. ii. 17; iii, 12; v. 9; xiv. 3; xxi. 2, 5.

[12] Isa. xxi. 6 ff.

[13] Ps. xlvi. 6; xlix, 15; xc. 14; cxxx. 6. Cfr. also xvii. 15; xlviii. 15.

morning," so that it would mean the great light-filled day of the reign of Jehovah. It is hardly accidental that "the day of Jehovah" appears in some passages associated with the idea of light.[14]

Owing to this vivid consciousness of the historically-conditioned appointment of the end, the attitude of the Psalmists towards it is, on the whole, one of serene confidence and quiet expectation. Their soul is as a weaned child within them. There are Psalms that have as their keynote the question "How long?", but they are few, and even in them towards the end the trusting mood regains the upper hand.[15] There are only three Psalms which contain nothing but complaint.[16] Of the feverish impatience that is so apt to inflame the eschatological state of mind and of its usual correlate, the apocalyptic calculation of times and seasons, there is no trace in the Psalter. "True, with characteristic eschatological eagerness they continually suppose the end nearer than it actually is, but they do not attach their faith to a near parousia in such a way that it would be imperilled by disillusionment. . . . When doubting thoughts beset . . . they go into the sanctuary."[17]

The Psalmists know that the end is not flung upon the world out of the lap of chance, but that it proceeds with stately, unhastened, unretarded step from the council-chamber of God. The phrase "a set time" marks this conviction.[18] The connection between prophecy and the Psalms in this point may be observed in the statement "to execute the judgment written."[19] The "judgment written" is the judgment announced in the prophets; precisely because written it cannot fail to come. In a most striking way the dependence of the last great hope of redemption upon what

14 Am. v. 8, 18; Rom. xiii. 11 ff. 1 Thess. v. 5.

15 Ps. vi. 4; xiii. 1; lxxiv. 10; lxxvii. 8; lxxix. 5; lxxxv. 6; xxxix. 47; xc. 13; xciv. 3.

16 Ps. xxxviii (but cfr. v. 16); xxxix. (but cfr. v. 8); lxxxviii.

17 Cheyne, *Origin*, p. 373.

18 Ps. cii. 31.

19 Ps. cxlix. 9.

Jehovah has done before is expressed in Ps. lxxiv.: "God is my King of old, working salvation in the midst of the earth; thou didst divide the sea by thy strength; thou breakest the heads of the dragons in the waters: . . . thou didst cleave fountain and flood; . . . remember that the enemy has reproached O Lord; O deliver not the soul of thy turtle dove unto the multitude; forget not the congregation of thy poor forever; have respect unto the covenant; . . . arise O God."

A second striking feature of the eschatology of the Psalter consists in the central, dominating position it assigns to Jehovah in all that pertains to the coming change. The prospect of the future is God-centered in the highest degree. Of course, the Psalmists who could say "Whom have I in heaven but thee, and none upon earth I desire besides thee"; "God is the strength of my heart and my portion forever" and "Thou art my Lord, my welfare is naught without thee," might be confidently expected to carry this feeling with them, when projecting themselves into the future.[20] What is more characteristic of the Psalter is this, that, besides eschatology evoking worship, the opposite also takes place: The elemental urge of worship summons the last great realities to its aid, because it cannot be satisfied with aught short of this for expressing itself. The eschatology of the Psalter is in part begotten by the praises of Israel. No doubt the Psalter contains much of what is most humanly human in all religious occupation with God: the need and desire and prayer for help in distress. In their extremity of danger and affliction the Psalmists sustain and reassure themselves by the thought of the great deliverance which the end must bring. They lift up their heads, because their redemption draws nigh. They will not fear, though the earth be removed and the mountains be cast in the midst of the sea. The absoluteness of the assurance and the suddenness of attainment unto it are in many instances accounted for by the eschatological import. The appeal

[20] Pss. lxxiii. 25, 26; xvi. 2.

lies not to second causes or elements of hopefulness within the fabric of the present world, but to the great, crowning interposition of Jehovah *ab extra*. At this point especially we have occasion to remember, that often not an individual but Israel is the speaking subject. What within the limitations of the Old Testament the individual could scarcely hope for himself, that the people of God carried as a sure faith in its bosom through the ages. Ploughers might plough upon Israel's back and make long their furrows, the waters might overwhelm them, it could not extinguish the conviction, that the future and the end belonged to the chosen of Jehovah. Specifically the thirst for justice over against enemy and avenger quenched itself in anticipation at this deep fountain of judgment to be opened up at the last. But in the midst of all this soteric motivation the higher point of view of the subserviency of Israel's salvation to the glory of God is never lost sight of. When the Psalmists make eschatology the anchor of salvation, this is not done in a self-centered spirit. The very fact of the anchor being cast into such deep water implies a comparative estimate of human and divine help, which in itself cannot but be honoring to God.[21] The prayer for salvation inevitably embodies praise of the Saviour. That at least no individual selfishness underlies it, appears from the way in which clearly individualistic Psalms join together the deliverance of the suppliant and the salvation of Israel. The Psalmist succeeds in forgetting his own woes for the woes or for the hopes of the people as a whole. But it is even more important to notice that he is able to forget them for the overwhelming thought of the glory of Jehovah. The *gloria in excelsis* which the Psalter sings arises not seldom from a veritable *de profundis* and, leaving behind the storm-clouds of its own distress, mounts before Jehovah in the serenity of a perfect praise.[22] Nothing reveals more clearly the innate nobility of the Psalter's religion than this quality of its praise. But even where this highest altitude

[21] Pss. xx. 7; xliv. 6; xlix. 6; cxviii. 8, 9; cxlvi. 3, 4.

[22] Cfr. Roy, p. 25 note 2.

is not reached, where the thought of salvation remains consciously present to the end, the closing note of praise is seldom wanting.[23] Praise and prayer are inseparable, because God's very divinity is in his saving habit.[24] In the phrase "for thy name's sake" the recognition is expressed that the ultimate purpose of salvation lies in the glory of God.[25] Where the prayer assumes the form of a desire for vindication and deliverance through judgment and destruction of the enemy, it might seem as if the center were shifted from God to man. Still on closer examination this appears not to be so. When the praying subject is Israel and the opposing party the hostile pagan world, the conflict between these two, of course, coincides with that between Jehovah and the world, between light and darkness. And when the two parties belong both to Israel, their mutual opposition is again due to the fact that the party praying represents the cause of Jehovah and the true faith, whilst the party prayed against has aligned itself with the other side and becomes apostate from Jehovah and his people.[26] So that in either case the self-interest is identical with the interest of God. Of personal rancor or party-animosity not religiously motived there is no trace in the Psalter. While it is true, therefore, that the eschatological pressure is heightened, as it usually is, by fierce conflict and strife, this does not detract in the present case from its purity and God-centered character.[27]

Cheyne offers the suggestion that an unselfish religion was easier for the Psalmists than it is for us, because the sense of individuality was less developed at that time.[28]

---

[23] Pss. xxxii. 17; l. 15; lxxx. 18, 19.

[24] Cheyne, *Origin*, p. 344.

[25] Roy, p. 42.

[26] Ps. lxxiii. 15, 27, 28.

[27] Cfr. Roy, pp. 28, 29, 73; not nations but two *Weltanschauungen* stand over against each other; Cheyne, *Origin*, p. 293.

[28] *Origin*, p. 265; cfr. Cheyne's own striking statement at a later point: "that the people of Israel is to work out the divine purpose in the earth and do this with such utter self-forgetfulness, that each of its own successes shall but add a fresh jewel to Jehovah's crown," p. 340.

But this would apply only over against man and not over against God. And it is hardly in accordance with his own dating of the Psalms. The collectivism of the post-exilic Jews was not of the naïve, instinctive kind, a sort of primeval, semi-physical sense of solidarity; it partakes far more of the intelligent affectionate surrender to an ulterior object of devotion. Here collectivism is but another name for unselfishness. The awakening of the sense of individuality lies not beyond but back of it. It is spiritual loyalty, not ethnic coherence that binds the members of Israel together. The same is true of the still closer bond uniting the pious Israel within the larger body.

The acknowledgment that in the future salvation all is for the glory of God is not of the nature of a mere formal acknowledgment. Owing to the character of psalmody as the instrument of responsiveness, and owing to the uniqueness of the eschatological situation upon which it works, it develops a peculiar fervor and attains a degree of sympathetic projection into the interest of God scarcely equalled elsewhere. The Psalmists sometimes succeed in transporting themselves into the midst of the joy and blessedness, wherewith Jehovah himself contemplates the consummate perfection of his work. This faculty for entering into the inner spirit of God's own share in the religious process represents the highest and finest in worship; it closes the ring of religion, and in Scripture, as we might expect, it is peculiarly the Psalter that illustrates it. If even the Psalm of nature, after enumerating the wonders of creation, closes with the exquisite note, "The glory of Jehovah shall endure forever, the Lord shall rejoice in his works. . . . I will sing . . . as long as I live . . . my meditation of Him shall be sweet, I will be glad in Jehovah," could we expect less where the Psalmist's mind turns to the greater wonders in redemption?[29] "Sing unto Jehovah a new song, his praise in the congregation of saints, for Jehovah takes pleasure in his people, He will beautify the meek with sal-

[29] Ps. civ. 31-34.

vation." And again, "Jehovah takes pleasure in them that fear him, in them that hope in his mercy; Praise Jehovah, O Jerusalem, praise thy God, O Zion."[30] There is something deeper in this than the spontaneous welling up of gratitude from the heart that has received favor. It is the devotion of a mind able to lose itself in the very inward grace of God which is greater and more satisfying than even its greatest and final gift.[31]

The theocentric character of Psalter-eschatology appears also in this that it is prevailingly kingdom-eschatology. By this is meant a form of statement representing Jehovah as becoming, or revealing, Himself in the last crisis the victorious King of Israel. Certain Psalms may be called specific kingdom-Psalms. Pss. xciii, xcvii, xcix, open with the words "Jehovah is King." The context shows that this is declared from the standpoint of the eschatological future, when, after the judgment, his universal dominion shall be established. Into this future the Psalmist projects himself. The situation is the same in Ps. xcvi. 10, "Say among the nations, Jehovah is King; the world also is established, and it cannot be moved."[32] It will be remembered that the shout "Absalom is King" was the shout of acclaim at his assumption of the kingship.[33] Still in the Apocalypse this mode of

---

30 Pss. cxlix. 1, 4; cxlvii. 11, 12.

31 Cfr. Cheyne, *Origin,* p. 343. "Precious as is the sympathy of God for us, still higher is the ability put by Him into us to enter into his thoughts and feelings."

32 Cfr. Ex. xv. 17; Isa. xxiv. 23; lii. 7.

33 2 Sam. xv. 10. Cfr. Gunkel, *Ausgewählte Psalmen,* pp. 186-192; 324; Gressmann, *Ursprung,* pp. 294-301. According to Gunkel such accession-hymns might have been first sung for human rulers and afterwards transferred to the eschatological enthronement of Jehovah. Gressmann seeks to meet the difficulty that Jehovah's kingship is represented as purely future, by the suggestion, that the background is polytheistic, Jehovah's universal dominion being conceived as beginning with the conquest of the other gods, and that this mode of speaking was retained in the (no longer) polytheistic Psalms. The simple solution seems to lie in this that "kingship" is in the O. T. more a concept of action than of status. Jehovah becomes King=Jehovah works acts of deliverance.

speaking is employed with eschatological reference, xix. 6 "Hallelujah, for the Lord God, the Almighty reigneth." In other cases the act of enthronement is described and the accession is identified with an ascension. Thus Ps. xlvii. 5-8 "God is the King of all the earth . . . God reigneth over the nations. God sitteth upon his holy throne."[34] The ascension-feature might be explained from the elevation of the throne-seat, to which the king mounts by steps, or from the going up to the height of Zion, after a victorious return from war, in which Jehovah, as present in the ark, would participate and lead. Pss. lxviii. 18 and xxiv. 7-10 suggest the possibility of another explanation. In the former passage we read: "Thou hast ascended on high, thou hast led away captives." The Psalm is at its opening escatologically-prospective, but vss. 7-20 seem to be historically-retrospective, so that the statement about Jehovah's ascent is not directly eschatological. It does, however, describe a real ascent *into heaven*, and not a mere going up unto the earthly sanctuary.[35] In Ps. xxiv the language might more easily remind of the earthly dwelling-place of Jehovah (cfr. vs. 3), but even here in the second part of the Psalm the "everlasting doors" point to the higher habitation.[36] The idea of Jehovah's glorious return into heaven after accomplished victory, must have existed, and if so, would influence directly-eschatological representa-

[34] Besides the shout of acclaim the blowing of the trumpet and the clapping of hands accompanied the enthronement, Ps. xlvii. 1; 1 Kings i. 34-45; 2 Kings ix. 13; xi. 12.

[35] Cfr. Baethgen, *Die Psalmen*³, who observes that מרום is always used of the height of heaven. The N. T. adaptation to the ascension of Christ has, therefore, a good support, so far as the local conception is concerned. Gressmann also argues in favor of what he calls the "mythical-eschatological" view of Ps. xlvii. 6 from the use of the verb עָלָה, which according to him is not used of ordinary throne-ascension, the proper term for this being יָשַׁב. But the two acts of "ascending" and "sitting down" are obviously distinct, and the idea of ascent, might, as stated above, have arisen from the elevation of the throne.

[36] For the idea of the doors being opened by "lifting up" cfr. Gressmann, *Ursprung*, p, 295, note 1.

tions, like that of Ps. xlvii. 5-8. In Ps. xxiv. this seems to be actually the case.[37]

It is obvious that a representation which thus throws the emphasis on the future enthronement of Jehovah intends to magnify what the end means for God and for Israel in relation to its God. The core of the belief is that there must come and will come a time, when God will visibly take his place as the end and focus of all the glory of the world process. As the antique idea makes the state subserve the glory of the king, so the ripened ages will be made to yield their accumulated fruit to Him who is their King. Although the kingdom-idea has also its soteric aspect, the Psalter shows that side by side with this, and as even in a sense superior, the manifestation of the glory of Jehovah is expressed by it. The thought is not merely that Jehovah becomes King in order to save, but that through the salvation, as well as in other acts, He arrives at the acme of his royal splendor.

In still another way we can trace the same principle by observing the mode of Jehovah's activity in the coming crisis. The fundamental conception is that of the theophany. It may seem at first a trite thought, that Jehovah must appear on the scene before He can interpose. But the theophany does not occur as the mere prerequisite or precursor of the divine action, it is the vehicle of the action itself. This is facilitated by the realistic conception of the judgment, as a judgment of execution, rather than a formal forensic procedure. In a forensic procedure the bare appearance of Jehovah could figure only as the initial act, after which further steps would be indispensable. The realistic idea, putting sentence and execution in one, condenses the whole into a single act and this act is the supernatural arrival of God upon the field. While, however, fitting into this view of the judgment, the epiphanic character of Jehovah's action has not been exclusively produced by it. At the basis lies again the motive to exalt the majesty and power of Him, who by his mere entrance into the crisis

[37] Acording to Stade, *Zeitschrift f. Theol. u. Kirche,* II. p. 407, the scene of Ps. xxiv is eschatological.

decides the issue and thus centers all attention and interest upon Himself. Here lies the source of that technical eschatological phrase "the coming of the Lord," which like an unbroken thread runs through both testaments.[38] He comes, Jehovah comes, the Messiah comes, from Genesis to Revelation this is the import of the message in which ultimately the eschatological hope embodies itself. And the imagery of the theophanic representation is wholly in accord with this intent to make God the central figure. No matter whether Jehovah's coming be linked with or compared to the thunder-storm, or the tempest, or the flood or the volcanic eruption, in each case the sudden, inavertible, overwhelming nature of the event is emphasized.[39] Precisely for this reason the impression is sometimes most vivid where every attempt at the use of concrete imagery is abandoned, because the figures threaten to break down under the sheer weight of the reality signified. Nothing could be more effective than the studied avoidance of all intermediate apparatus, nay even of the mention of Jehovah Himself in a passage like Ps. xlvii. 4, 5, "For, lo the kings assembled themselves, they passed by together. They saw it, then they were amazed; they were dismayed, they hastened away." It need not so much as be said, that Jehovah appears; it suffices that He exists: his being God brings the crisis to its inevitable issue.[40]

---

38 Cfr. Sellin, *Der alttestamentliche Prophetismus,* p. 181.

39 For the reason stated the description of the eschatological scene has an inherent tendency to turn into a description of the theophany as such, even to the extent of the purpose of the latter being for the moment lost sight of. This is a feature observed also in prophecy, cfr. Isa. ii. The Psalm in Hab. iii. and also the opening part of Ps. xviii illustrate this. For an enunciation of the principle involved by Jehovah Himself, cfr. Ps. xlvi. 10 "Be still and know that I am God. I will be exalted among the nations, I will be exalted in the earth."

40 Stade, *Zeitschrift f. Theol. u. Kirche,* pp. 393-398 finds the eschatological theophany in a number of recurring phrases in the Psalter. He enumerates as such "to arise"; "to be exalted" or "lifted up"; "to awake"; "to be not silent"; "to hasten"; "to be not far"; "to stir up might"; "to restore"; "to heal"; "to quicken"; "to redeem"; to save";

One more observation may be made under this head. The profoundly religious state of mind with which the end is contemplated appears in this that it imparts the same coloring to the Psalmist's mood in view of its retardation as does the prospect of impending death by itself. As has been often remarked the attitude towards the latter furnishes a gauge for the depth of religious attachment to Jehovah. There is much in death to terrify the creature regardless of religious considerations. We find that with the Psalmists the chief cause of solicitude and perplexity is the problem of their future relation to Jehovah. Will there be in these strange shadowy regions remembrance of Jehovah, experience of his goodness, praise of his glory? "What profit is there in my blood, when I go down to the pit, shall the dust praise thee, shall it declare thy truth?"[41] What they most feared was not death as such, nor that they might lose themselves in death, but that they might lose contact with Jehovah. Now the same state of feeling asserts itself in regard to the great future coming of Jehovah. "How long, O Jehovah? Wilt thou hide thyself forever? . . . O remember how short my time is. For what vanity hast thou created all the children of men! What man is he that shall live and not see death? That shall deliver his soul from the power of Sheol? Lord, where are thy former loving kindnesses, which thou swarest unto David in thy faithfulness?"[42] Here the bitterness of death is measured by the danger that it may sweep out of reach the vision of Jehovah and the enjoyment of his glorious reign at the end. To lose touch with Him in Sheol would be painful, to miss Him at his final epiphany intolerable, it would be the supreme tragedy of religion. This is convincing proof that the eschatology of the Psalter seeks and loves nought above Jehovah Himself.

"to be gracious"; "to snatch out"; "to do justice." Although many or all of these terms find eschatological employment, it cannot be proven that all or any of them had become technical in that sense.

[41] Pss. xxx. 9; cfr. vi. 5; lxxx. 5.

[42] Ps. lxxxix. 46-49. A new Testament parallel is I Thess. iv. 13-18.

From a specific point of view we can observe the same principle in the universalistic statements of the Psalter. Here as in the prophets the subjection of the nations to Jehovah and their conversion form part of the great future change. In both cases this remains a hope and does not become a challenge to missionary activity. It is only through the gateway of eschatology that universalism and the missionary idea come in. More particularly it is the greatness and majesty of Jehovah from which they spring. Jehovah is so great that the nations must come and worship before Him. This is of itself a certainty. But when the idea is raised to the eschatological degree, when He is contemplated in the overpowering majesty of his final appearance, then a super-certainty results, that all the earth will be flooded with the knowledge of his glory.[43] While, however, with the prophets this remains, like so many other things, a matter of mere futurity, in the Psalter, owing to the entrance of the subjective element something more results. The mind of the Psalmist is not satisfied with holding the idea at the distance of objective contemplation, but translates it into an eager desire for witnessing the fulfilment of the prospect. Thus a real missionary urge is born out of the eschatological vision of Jehovah and his kingdom. This desire projects itself into the future and breaks out into a direct missionary appeal conceived as addressed to the Gentiles from that standpoint.[44] The world at large is summoned to acknowledge and praise Jehovah. Of course, this is not actual missionary propaganda.[45] Yet, at bottom, in its spiritual motivation, it is not different from the latter; perhaps one might even say that the impulse back of it is stronger than the fervor wherewith the Church seizes her present possibilities. The closest analogy to this is again

---

[43] Ps. ix. 19, 20; xviii. 47 ff.; xxii. 27, 28; xxiii. 8; xlvi. 10; xlvii. 1-3, 8, 9; lxxxvi. 8-10; xcvii. 1, 6; xcviii. 2, 3, 9; cii. 15, 21, 22.

[44] Ps. lvii. 8-11; lxvi. 1-4; lxvii. 2-5; xcvi. 3, 7-13; xcix. 3 (in the form of prayer); c. 1-3; cviii. 3; cxiii. 3, 4; cxvii. 1, 2; cxlv. 21.

[45] Rhetorically it may be put on a line with the prophetic summons to nature to "clap hands" and "sing."

found in the hymnodic portions of Isaiah. The remembrance of these things may afford us help in ever anew attuning the strain of our missionary-enthusiasm to its highest God-centered key. When we profess to missionarize, not in the last analysis, to improve the world, but to glorify God in the eternal salvation of sinners, this expresses not merely a theological conviction, but it is also eminently true to the principle inherent in the birth of the missionary idea itself. For this the missionary idea was born and for this cause came it into the world, that it should contribute to the glory of God. It was for Him and not for man alone that it was conceived in the womb of the Old Testament.

The question next claiming attention concerns the degree of spirituality in the eschatological outlook of the Psalter. This degree is often placed low, because for their descriptions of the future age the Psalms are dependent on earthly, material, time-bound forms. The future theocracy is a replica of the present one. The expected state is a state in which the eschatological people of Jehovah, dwelling in the holy land, with Jerusalem as its center, will forever enjoy without measure the blessedness afforded by Canaan, the paradise-garden of God. It would be difficult to prove, that all this was understood by the Psalmists with a clear consciousness of its symbolic, typical significance, as we, on the basis of the New Testament, believe it lay in the mind of God, the author of revelation. But, while this is true, and should not be covered up in the interest of unhistorical allegorizing, it should not, on the other hand, close our eyes to the profound spirituality with which in the Psalter even this ostensibly material content of the future is approached and apprehended. The main question is after all not what forms and colors enter into the picture, but what is the subtler atmosphere that pervades it to the eye of the pious Israelite, what with his finer religious sensibilities he sought and loved and admired in it. When the question is put in this way there can be no doubt as to the answer. The very fact of the intense concentration of the hope in God Himself supplies it in advance. The eschatological state is before all else a state in which the enjoyment of Jehovah, the beatific vision of his face, the pleasures at his right hand, the perpetual dwelling with Him in his sanctuary, form the supreme good. "Satisfy us in the morning with thy loving kindness, that we may rejoice and be glad all our days, . . . and let the beauty of Jehovah our God be upon us," these and other similar strains are characteristic of the future-music of the Psalter.[46] Whether the familiar passages in Pss. xvi., xvii., xlix., lxxiii, where the confidence of uninterrupted fellowship with Jehovah is expressed, are based on the belief in a future blessed life after death, as we think they are, or whether, on the ground of the collectivistic theory, the statements in question are interpreted of the imperishable life of Israel, on either view the underlying sentiment is clearly that of the supreme absorption of the religious life in the things of God.[47] And it will be noticed that this sentiment finds readiest expression in view of the future state. If only care be taken to exclude every idea obliterative of the sense of human personality, there is ground for speaking of a certain group of Psalms as mystical in their complexion, as in fact a mystically-inclined type of piety has shown a

[46] Ps. xc. 14, 16. Cheyne, perhaps, goes too far in spiritualizing the language of the Psalmists when he assumes the theophanic statements to have been meant as pure symbolism. This would hardly agree with the parallel drawn between the eschatological and the earlier, historic theophanies. The latter were certainly in part realistically understood. Another instance of the same nature is, where Cheyne credits the Psalmists who believed in spiritual sacrifice with the idea of a purely-spiritual sanctuary. But is there not some difference between these two? The spiritual sacrifice remains objective, the spiritual sanctuary would be a subjectivizing conception. Cfr. *Origin*, pp. 344, 387.

[47] Writers who deny the presence of the idea of personal blessedness after death in such passages, yet do not deny that the Psalmists expect participation in the Messianic era. Cfr. Beer, p. 70. Can this be entirely due to an acute sense of the nearness of the event?

marked preference for them in all ages.[48] But there is only a difference of degree between these and the Psalter in general. It is Jehovah's rest which the Psalmist desires Israel to enter, the city of his vision is the city of God.[49] How pervasively and intensely spiritual the atmosphere of the eschatology of the Psalter is, can best be appreciated by remembering to what an extent our Lord has reproduced it in his teaching. Most of the second clauses of the beatitudes are to all intent a description of the eschatological kingdom in Psalter-language. "The poor in spirit," "the pure in heart," "the meek," "the merciful," "the peacemakers," together with their respective predicates, the endowment with the kingdom, the inheritance of the earth, the obtaining of mercy, the vision of God, the adoption into sonship, these are all Psalter-types and Psalter-hopes, found fit to enter into a most highly spiritualized description of the future by the Psalter's greatest interpreter. The way in which the sanctuary is spoken of, the comparatively rare references to ceremonial sacrifice, the peculiar tenor of these references, where they do occur, which has led some to speak of a class of Puritanical psalms, the deritualisation of heaven, the emphasis on the nearness of Jehovah in the sanctuary, all these plainly show where the center of the interest lies.[50] Add to this the total absence of the weird apocalyptic element, and the predominance of a truly spiritual atmosphere, can not fail to be recognized.[51] Here also, however, we should note how this fine spirituality is closely interwoven with the fundamental character of the Psalter, as that of subjective responsiveness to the divine approach and embrace in religion. Devotion, worship, the giving answer to God, cannot but spiritualize. It is, as it were, the projection into the objective sphere of the intrinsically trans-

---

[48] Cfr. Cheyne, *Origin,* pp. 387, 388; Beer, p. 62, refers in connection with Ps. lxxiii. 28 to the Jewish Kirbath Elohim, the unio mystica, as eschatologically approached; Montefiore, *Mystical Passages in the Psalms, Jewish Qurterly Review* 1889, pp. 143-161.

[49] Ps. xcv. 11; xlvi. 4; xlviii. 1.

[50] Cheyne, *Origin,* pp. 314-327; Beer, p. 47.

[51] Cheyne, *Origin,* p. 428.

lucent essence of the religious soul itself. And it is called to enter into the direct presence of and lay hold upon Jehovah Himself, in doing which it grasps the root of all spirituality. Truly, the new invisible throne of God, in distinction from the ark, rests in a yet higher sense upon the praises of Israel.[52]

In conclusion we may briefly consider the Messianic element in the eschatology of the Psalter. Here also the subjectively responsive and appropriative attitude has left some traces. To be sure, before speaking of such matters, one is at present compelled to raise the question whether in the old, familiar sense there is a "Messiah" in the Psalter at all. Belief in "typically-Messianic" Psalms has practically disappeared from contemporary critical exegesis. But not only this, the Psalms which used once to be quoted as directly-prophetically Messianic are now frequently understood as relating to the people of Israel as the real "Anointed of Jehovah." The curious fact results that on such a view the title "Messiah" in its technical sense, as the designation of the individual eschatological King, disappears from the Old Testament, for it is in the Psalter and in the Psalter alone, that, on the old interpretation, this title is found.[53] In this situation little comfort can be taken from the quasi-rehabilitation which the idea of typical Messianism has undergone at the hands of Babylonianizing interpreters such as Gunkel. Calling attention to the fact that in Babylonian and Assyrian documents the reigning king, especially at his accession, was invested by courtiers and court-poets with superhuman or eschatological predicates, they have found this custom back in certain Psalms,

---

[52] Cheyne, *Origin,* p. 327.

[53] This leaves out of account Dan. ix. 25, 26, of doubtful interpretation. Cheyne, *Origin,* p. 340 and others, can, of course, continue to speak of "Messianic Psalms," since the term "Anointed" is in a more or less technical sense, with eschatological associations, bestowed upon the people. Still, in view of the long traditional usage, it would be better for those adopting such exegesis to avoid the term.

notably Pss. ii., xlv., lxxii, cx.[54] On this view the users of such language might be said to have seen their present ruler in the mirror of the conception of the great eschatological King, which would involve a certain resemblance to the old typological scheme. Now, if this adaptation of Oriental court-style to the case of an Israelitish king could be taken as sincere and naïve in its intent, something might be made out of it, in connection with the fact, that at first no one knew which of the Davidic descendants would fulfill the promises, each new accession being capable of giving rise to new hopes. We are not allowed, however, to impose such a meaning upon the custom. These phrases formed a regular court-style; they were no more than "loyal hyperboles" to which no one, least of all those who flatteringly spoke them, attached any real significance. The only useful purpose which the discovery of this ancient ceremonial may serve to the conservative exegete consists in this, that it may prove the early existence of eschatological belief and eschatological interest in these pagan circles and so furnish an argument against the theory of a late emergence of such belief and interest among Israel.[55] If, refusing to assume such a style in the Psalter, and finding here not the insincerities of court-life, but a solid typical groundwork in-

[54] Cfr. Gunkel, *Ausgewählte Psalmen,* under the head of Pss. ii., xlv., cx. He does not discuss Ps. lxxii.

[55] Acording to Gressmann, *Ursprung,* p. 252, note 4, Gunkel is mistaken in assuming a transfer of Messianic-eschatological language to the human king. The extravagant language, then, would have nothing to do with eschatology. It would be court-style pure and simple: "Der Messias hat hier nichts zu suchen." We do not see how this is to be reconciled with the later statements on pp. 286-293 where we read that "the contemporaneous prince or dynasty is celebrated as the introducer of the golden age, as once the first King. This explains the chief activity of the Messiah, etc." According to this "mythical-paradise elements" have been received into the court-style. Gressmann further believes that the ceremonial must have originated in the great empires of the East, the kingdom of Israel having been too small for aught else than snobbish imitation. He compares the reproduction of the customs of the court of Louis XIV. in the courts of the little principalities of that period. This would emphasize the utter emptiness of the custom in Israel.

wrought by the Spirit of God in the religious experience of David and others, it will be obvious how significant this is for the nearness and intimacy which the figure of the Messiah had acquired for the religious consciousness. No matter what peculiar philosophy or psychology of the typical relation be adopted, this much will be common to all, that the thought of the Messiah must have had a vital existence in the hearts of the Psalmists in order to make this prefiguration of him in themselves more than an empty, unreal show. The David, who could speak of himself in Messianic terms, must have held the Messianic concept in a warm religious embrace.

So much for the typical side of the matter. The other question had reference to the directly-Messianic element in the Psalter. Here the phenomena are so peculiar that modern criticism, though obviously shrinking and moving away from the old, solid Messianic ground, has not succeeded in finding a satisfactory substitute. The chief peculiarity of the passages in question is, that they speak of the King or the Anointed as a present, existing figure.[56] To account for this three possibilities offer themselves. If one, with Gunkel and Gressmann, applies the court-style hypothesis, the King spoken of or addressed is simply a contemporary ruler and has nothing to do with the Messiah.[57] Or, if one has recourse to the collectivistic theory,

---

[56] The Psalms constituting this group of so-called "King-Psalms" are the following: ii; xviii. 50; xx; xxi; xxviii. 8; xlv; lxi. 6, 7; lxiii. ii; lxxii; lxxxiv. 10; lxxxix. 38. 51; cx; cxxxii. Cfr. Buchanan Gray, *The references to the King in the Psalter in their Bearing on Questions of Date and Messianic Belief in Jewish Quarterly Review*, vii. pp. 658-686.

The only exception to the above statement about the present existence of the King or Messiah is Ps. ii., on the view that this Psalm from beginning to end, with all the speakers in it, the writer included, is projected into that point of the future, when the last great attack of the nations against Zion takes place. In that case, of course, the existence of the King at the actual time of writing would not be necessarily implied.

[57] Here what was once supposed to be directly-Messianic is turned into the quasi-typical, *i.e.* into the embellishment of the character

the King or Messiah fades away into the figure of Israel. Again, if one is prepared to attach the extraordinary language employed in such Psalms as ii. and cx. to one or the other of the Maccabaean rulers, he may yet save the directly-Messianic character at the expense of having it connected with an unworthy figure. But on all three views the present existence of the "King" is explained. It would require, however, a combination of at least two of them to cover all the facts. In the case of Pss. xlv.; lxxii. and cx. the collectivistic exegesis is, of course, excluded, and the attempt to carry it through in Ps. ii. is open to most serious objections.[58] Here then it will be necessary to fall back upon either the one or the other or both of the two other proposals. We believe orthodox exegetes will find it difficult to get rid of the feeling, that neither of these two is in keeping with the dignity of revelation. Subjectively the insincerities of a court-ceremonial, and objectively the char-

of an existing king with originally eschatological traits. Gunkel admits that, contrary to the intent of the writers, very early readers of such Psalms found in them a direct-Messianic import, *Ausgewähte Psalmen*, p. 18. "So ist also dieser Stoff, der ursprünglich eschatologisch war, schliesslich auch wieder eschatologisch verstanden worden."

[58] The subject of the equation Israel=the Messiah is a most interesting one, but too large to be handled in the present connection. There can be no *a priori* objection to the investment of Israel not only with the predicate of "anointed," but even with the title of "The Anointed One." The anointed king and the people are closely related, and the parallel case of the attribution of sonship to both, suggests a common possession by both of the anointing. In the New Testament the anointing is bestowed upon both Christ and believers. Besides, the anointing was not strictly confined to the kings. It is quite plausible, therefore, to understand the term of Israel in such passages as Hab. iii. 13; Ps. xxviii. 8, where the *parallelismus membrorum* favors it. The serious objection to the theory arises from the concrete way in which it is applied, viz. that the Messianizing of the nation shall have been an intentional substitute for the hope of a Davidic individual Messiah. Usually Isa. lv. 3 is cited as furnishing either an instance, or the original precedent of the replacement of the Messiah by Israel. But the passage does not require this interpretation, and in view of the fact that it calls the mercies of David "sure" *i.e.* unalterable, reliable, it is absurd to find in a statement emphasizing this very thing the idea of their abrogation or even transfer.

acter and life of the later Maccabaean leaders seem unfit to be the bearers of such a high and sacred conception.[59] As compared with these, there is at least a kernel of attractive truth in the collectivistic idea. Not as if the Messiahship of the Davidic prince could have been abrogated and the Messiahship of Israel substituted for it, but in this way that in certain Psalms a strong sense of the close appurtenance of the Messiah to Israel and of Israel to the Messiah reveals itself. It is not identity, but identification of life that creates the appearance as if Israel were the real Messiah to the exclusion of the personal figure. These Psalmists, when they call Israel the Anointed of Jehovah, do so because they realize the significance of the Messiah's office for the religious life of Israel. Even Wellhausen observes that in a representation, like that of Ps. ii. the Messiah and Israel can be scarcely distinguished.[60] Such a close identification is after all what may and must be expected, if the root-idea of the Messiahship is taken into account. The deepest motivation of the Messianic conception lies in the absolute, concrete, palpable assurance it affords of Jehovah's permanent presence among his people as the supreme bliss of the future.[61] He is sacramental in the profoundest sense of the word. Consequently it cannot be indifferent which

---

[59] The Maccabaean reference is, even in the case of Ps. cx. where it might seem to be most plausible, rejected by Gunkel, *Ausgewaählte Psalmen,* p. 223. Cfr. Sellin, *Der Alttestamentliche Prophetismus,* pp. 168, 169.

[60] *The Book of Psalms* in *Sacred Books of the Old and New Testaments,* 1898, p. 164: "The Messiah is the speaker, and the whole Psalm is composed in his name . . . the Messiah is the incarnation of Israel's universal rule. He and Israel are almost identical, and it matters little whether we say, that Israel *has* or *is* the Messiah." But we cannot agree with the clause "It matters little," for, as above stated, the Messiah has his whole significance in this, that he stands as the God-given pledge of Israel's religious privilege and salvation. Israel become itself the Messiah would be thrown back upon itself, and the whole concept would be useless. Baethgen, *Die Psalmen,*[3] p. 4 well observes that while the name "son" might fittingly apply to Israel this can not be said of the title "king (over Zion)."

[61] Cfr. Cheyne, *Origin,* pp. 338, 340.

of the two is considered the prius, the Messiahship of the people, or that of the eschatological King. There is in this respect a difference between the joint-application of the idea of sonship to Israel and the coming King, and the joint-application of the idea of Messiahship to the same two subjects. In regard to the sonship, the sonship of Israel comes first in order of revelation; in regard to the Messiahship the anointed character of the Davidic heir has the precedence. Israel has its anointing because of the Messiah.[62] The question involuntarily occurs whether such a close religious embrace as seems indicated by the facts is conceivable with regard to a mere concept, a person purely seen through the medium of futurity. To speak of the pre-existence of the Messiah in the Psalms may sound preposterous in many critical ears, but there is no escape from the force that draws in that direction, once the actual occurrence of the individual Messianic figure in the Psalter is recognized. The Messiah leads, as it were, a mysterious life, that is somehow woven into the life of his people. After all those who place the Psalter in so late a period, have least reason to ridicule such a view. Will it not be necessary to assign to a date older than most of the Psalms the mysterious statement of Micah according to which the "goings forth" of the great coming ruler in Israel, are "from of old, from everlasting"?[63] If we might assume that in this way the Messiah, apprehended as a present reality, played a vital part in the piety of the Psalmists, this would furnish another illustration of the penetrating sub-

[62] The analogy of the collective "Servant of Jehovah" in Isaiah is often quoted to support the collective Messiahship of Israel. But this would be an analogy only if the individual idea of the Servant were entirely absent from these prophecies, as Giesebrecht and others contend. Criticism, however, seems to be well on the way of receding from this extreme position. And, if "the Servant of Jehovah" be both individual and collective, and the two closely united, the individual Messiah will have to be recognized in the Psalter also, and that in close union with the people in order to make a true parallel with Isaiah. Cfr. Sellin, *Das Rätsel des deuterojesajanischen Buches,* 1908. Gressmann, *Ursprung,* pp. 301, 333.

[63] Mic. v. 2.

jectivity with which the truth of revelation is appropriated here and enable us to feel more strongly than at any other point, how profoundly at one the Christian's Messianic orientation of faith is with that of those who could say: "Behold O God our shield, and look upon the face of thine Anointed."[64]

In concluding our rapid survey of the eschatology of the Psalter, a few words may be added in regard to its practical bearing on present-day conditions in the religious and social world. Perhaps our study of the Psalms can be of some help to us in taking our bearings in the midst of the loud and universal demand for what is called "reconstruction." It cannot be denied that the eschatological teaching of the Psalms, and Old Testament eschatology in general, bear a certain striking resemblance to the desires and ideals of this eminently modern drift of life. In the Psalter we meet not only with the conception of a reconstruction of things on the grandest of scales, but this is actually projected on the stage of earthly existence. Here, then, an opportunity is afforded for testing, and, if necessary, correcting the ends and methods with which the modern movement for world-reconstruction occupies itself. This is all the more timely, since the Church herself is invited to lend a helping hand in the making over of things, and to let herself be registered as one of several coëqual and coöperative forces making ready for this gigantic enterprise. Now it is plain from the eschatological teaching of Scripture in general and from the Psalms in particular, that the Church has already in advance an outlook and a program towards an absolute and ideal future, which is governed by certain distinct and definite principles, to such a degree bound up with her very essence of belief, that to ignore these principles or to cease insisting upon them in any line of altruistic work, would mean self-abdication and disloyalty to her charter as the Church of God. The foremost of these pinciples is that the end of existence for all things lies in

---

64 Ps. lxxxiv. 9.

God, and that, therefore, to religion must be assigned the highest place in every ideal condition contemplated as a goal. It is the special function of the Church to speak unceasingly and unfalteringly for this one supreme aspect of the future world, to insist in season and out of season that in it God and the service of God are to the highest good and satisfaction of mankind, that without which all other desirable things will lose their value and abiding significance. To work for the amelioration of the world without putting at the top of its program the bestowal upon this world of the baptism of religion as the primal requisite, should be impossible for the Church so long as she retains a clear consciousness of her own specific calling. Nor is this merely one or the foremost of the tasks of the Church, it is in such a unique sense her "business," that every other activity in order to legitimatize itself as a church-function should be able to prove its vital connection, direct or indirect, with the service of God and of religion as her one unique mission in the world. For the Church to indulge in the advocacy of social and economic programs, without taking the time or the trouble of deriving these from her religious root-consciousness, and subordinating them to the glory of God, is a precarious undertaking, not only because in so doing the Church would speak without authority, but also because by every form of experimentizing in such a field she endangers the authority, which within the sphere of strictly-religious principles is properly hers. Undoubtedly the Church even so, will do her royal share in making the world better, and that more effectually than she could possibly do in any other way. The by-product of the genuinely-religious activity will be more abundant and more valuable, than any scheme to substitute it for the main product could possibly make it. For the Church, to keep this in mind is not to be indifferent to the lesser and secondary needs and distresses of mankind; it is in reality to obey the conviction that in no other way her deep solicitude for the sinful world, and the resources she carries within herself for its healing, can be successfully brought to bear upon it. There can be no doubt that the Church owes the success with which in the past she has contributed to the progress of the world in civilization to her fidelity to this fundamental principle and the self-limitation it imposes upon her; through it mainly she has become and remained the *antiqua mater* out of whose blessed womb the liberties and reforms among mankind have been born and reborn. When measured by this standard of a genuinely-religious and God centered consciousness, it will have to be confessed that, taken as a whole, the modern reconstruction-movement is sadly deficient. It appears to be more humanistic than religious, to derive its motives and ideals from man rather than from God. In the vision of the land to be reached there seems to be little of the worship and enjoyment of him who is the center of every hope worth cherishing for man. God is enthroned but seldom in these Eutopian palaces. And the fear is not altogether groundless, that the Church, in her pragmatic desire to accomplish concrete and speedy results, has opportunistically fallen in line with such humanitarian efforts, and for the moment waived the consciousness of her unique and privileged position, as voicing the specific claims of God upon the service of man. A compromise of this kind born from opportunism is serious enough; far more serious would the situation be, if internal doubt as to the reality or primacy and efficacy of the God-ward side of religion within the consciousness of professed Christians should underlie this tendency. That would mean not merely the death of religion as such, but would result in the utter sterility, so far as lasting, deeper results are concerned, of all uplifting work conducted in its name. Christianity can make the world better in the sign of religion; that standard abandoned she will not only fail of success, but face actual defeat.

The second principle with which the biblical prospect of a better order of affairs is inseparably bound up is that of supernaturalism. The Psalter expects the marvelous future from no other source or cause than a God who only doeth wonders. Whatever there may be in it of teaching and learning and meditating upon the law, these human endeavors or performances are not credited with bringing on the world-change. It is not through evolution from beneath, but through descent and theophany and interposition from above, that the face of the earth is to be renewed. The comparison with and the appeal to the supernatural past is sufficient proof of this. That the help of man is vanity is a conviction deeply inwoven into the consciousness of the Psalmists. Their true help is in the name of Jehovah who made heaven and earth. Here again a sad difference is to be observed between this frame of mind, and that in which much of the reconstructive effort of the present time is being applied. The latter often cherishes a most doctrinaire and tenacious belief in the inherent and endless perfectibility of human nature, a humanistic optimism which manages to thrive, no one knows how, in the face of the most discouraging circumstances. It is a faith and has some of the noble characteristics of faith, its imperviousness to discouragement, its sovereign indifference to obstacles, its resiliency under apparent defeat, but it is after all a faith in man rather than in God, and since faith in the last analysis can be glorified only through its object, it lacks the supreme glory of the faith of Christianity. It cannot overcome the world, because it has its resources in the world itself. Even much of its unshakable confidence in man is due to this that it feels itself shut up within the sphere of the purely-human, and so tied down to man and his natural potentialities, that to doubt of man would mean to despair of itself and its own mission. And unfortunately at this point also there is observable a certain tendency in the procedure of the Church to bend and lend itself to this mode of thinking. Some of its educative and reformatory work does not at least scorn the appeal to it as a motive force ,and gives the impression, if not by direct avowal, at least indirectly and through the assent of silence, that much can be made of man, if only his better nature is cultivated and his environment improved and his evil propensities repressed. True, this may seem a mere matter of temporary accommodation, an innocent shifting of the emphasis. Even as such, however, it is serious enough. The idea of God and his indispensable, all-determining part in the transformation of the world, and central place in the world as transformed, is not a thing that, like some secondary factor, can be for a while ignored or neglected with impunity. The Christian who allows himself to be drawn into this mode of thought, can not escape in the end having his whole religious consciousness deflected by it from its original and proper center. A dualism which reckons with God in the inner life of the soul and takes no account of Him in its outward activities for reclaiming others, is in the long run impossible. Moreover, the tendency in question minimizes and virtually denies the fact of sin as the primal element in the situation to be met. The slighting of the thought of God has for its inevitable correlate the weakening and ultimate loss of the specific consciousness of sin. But, serious as all this may be, there is sometimes reason to fear that the things enumerated are not simply consequences of a drift of thought superficially followed, but are the deeper-lying causes of an inclination to fall in with the drift. The humanitarian movement in its most pronounced and specific form, not seldom has for its background a weakened or tottering faith in the dependableness of God and the supernatural. Where this shows itself the Church should be on her guard, lest by countenancing it she deny herself and her Master and renounce the most precious heritage of power she has received from Him. To withdraw herself from participating in such action is not abandonment of the world to itself; it is the simple refusal to encourage a huge system of quackery, and, that, if for no higher reasons, in the interest of sinful, suffering humanity itself.

Finally the third lesson to be learned from the eschatology of the Psalter is the importance of the strand of otherworldliness in our Christian thought-fabric and love-service with reference to the future. It might seem, to be sure, as if the Psalter were ill-adapted to instruct us here, because its own outlook is confined to the earthly state, because while expecting another world-order, it postulates no other milieu for this than the terrestrial one already known. And so it might seem as if both the Psalter and Old Testament eschatology in general lent real support to the view that it is this lower earthly sphere, that must be transformed, and that, leaving the question of a higher sphere to itself, the Christian can be contented with directing his reclaiming effort to it alone. But this is only apparently so, and the Psalter is, of all biblical books, the best adapted to correct this impression, because it gives us a glimpse not merely of a higher future world objectively, but gives us a glimpse of the subjective psychological process by which the revelation of such a higher world was carried home to the minds of the Psalmists, and consequently of the depth to which it is rooted in the very heart of the religious consciousness itself. It was because they could not conceive of the communion between themselves and their God as other than endless, that the Psalmists projected it into a future life. It was the challenge of death flung into the face of religion that led to this supreme victory of faith. It was this that opened the gates of brass and broke the iron bars in sunder. Thus religion reached the consciousness of the inadequacy of the present life to meet its most instinctive and deepest desires, and threw its anchor into the greater, eternal beyond. And from that moment onward there could be no more doubt as to where the emphasis in biblical religion would finally lie. The New Testament has, of course, added to this the clearer and more principal knowledge, that not merely will God not withdraw himself from the believer in death, but that first on the other side of death the perfectly normal and satisfying, the true life can begin. It has brought life and immortality to light in their most positive self-evidencing aspect. This revelation is so rich and overwhelming; it shows such a tremendous disproportion between what religion can mean and bring to us here, and what it will mean and bring to us hereafter, that merely to believe it is bound to make other-worldliness the dominating attitude of the Christian mind. This is so much the case that the slightest shifting of emphasis here may justly be considered the symptom of some religious abnormality. The gauge of health in the Christian is the degree of his gravitation to the future, eternal world. The Christian train of thought in this respect is the reversal of that of the Old Testament: the eternal is not so much a prolongation of the temporal, but the temporal rather an anticipation of the eternal. And what is true of life is true of the ministering and self-propagating function. The Church of Christ in all its complex service to the world can never forget that its primary concern is to call men into and prepare them for the life eternal. Now, if one compares these obvious facts with the spirit in which the modern humanitarian movement estimates this life and the future life in their relative importance, it can not be denied, that the Christian point of view is not only not always consistently maintained, but that sometimes it is openly scorned and rejected. The taunt of the masses, who feel themselves discriminated against in the treasures and comforts of this world, is that religion seeks to reconcile them to their spoiling of the present with the promise of an illusory or at best doubtful future. The temptation is strong to overcome this prejudice through giving greater prominence to the secular advantage connected with the Christian life and promoted by Christian activity. There is some warrant for this, for we are taught that godliness is profitable unto all things, having promise of the life that now is and of that which is to come. At the same time the danger should not be underestimated that out of this strategic concession to the demand of the age, may spring an actual compromise with the spirit that would secularize and terrestrialize Christianity as to its essence. Leaving for a moment higher things out of account, it is obvious that from the Christian standpoint no greater injury can be done to the true progress and healing of humanity in this present evil world than to make it promises and offer it remedies which have no vital connection with the hope of eternal life. For this hope alone can in the long run feed and keep flowing every stream of altruistic activity that deserves the name of religion. The life of this earth as a mere passing episode in time is not worth the aeonian toil expended upon it. Precisely because the Christian other-worldliness is inspired by the thought of God and not of self, it involves no danger of monastic withdrawal from or indifference to the present world. The same thirst for the divine glory which is the root of all heavenly-mindedness, also compels the consecration of all earthly existence to the promotion of God's kingdom. Here also the by-product cannot continue, if the main object of pursuit is lost sight of or neglected. But, what is most serious of all, the vanishing of the belief in the transcendent importance of the world to come would most surely spell the death of the Christian religion itself. Whatever may have been possible under Old Testament conditions, in the beginnings of revelation, it is absolutely impossible now with the New Testament behind us to construe a religious relationship between God and man on the basis of and within the limits of the present life alone. A religion which touched only the little span of consciousness between birth and death would be a pseudo-religion and its God a pseudo-God. A God who treated the fugitive generations of the race as so many passing acquaintances, content to see them afloat in and float out of the luminous circle of his own immortal life, could not continue to evoke the worship of his creatures. Pagan cult He might receive, but Christian service not. Men would become, and in a far more tragic sense than the Psalmist meant it, strangers and sojourners with Him. The Psalter bears eloquent witness to the truth that a hope of indefinite perpetuation for the collective body is not enough. It requires the assurance of the eternity of religion in the individual soul to secure the permanence of religion as such. The Psalmists had their faces set towards this and through wrestlings of prayer with Jehovah won their way to the light. The modern, humanistic movement prefers to cultivate the secular and earthly in part because it has come to doubt the heavenly and eternal; its zeal for the improvement of the world often springs not from faith, but from scepticism. The Church by compromising and affiliating with this would sign her own death-warrant as a distinct institution. When religion submerges itself in the concerns of time and becomes a mere servant of these, it thereby renders itself subject to the inexorable flux of time. Kronos has eaten all his children and he will not spare even this noblest of his offspring, once it passes wholly into his realm and closes behind itself the doors of eternity. On the other hand, in a pure and firm eschatological conviction, which keeps eternal hopes and interests well to the front, lies the safeguard and pledge of the perpetual vigor of Christianity. It cannot lose its youth here, because it knows eternal youth is promised in the hereafter. Through faith in this promise alone it defies the attrition of time and history. Its eschatology is its greatest religious glory, for in this the Church expresses her faith in a future when all the accidents and externals of religion shall drop away, a great purging of the world-stage, which shall leave only the perfect and ripe fruitage of all God's intercourse with man from the beginning. The Gospel of the life to come is the Gospel of a Church sure of herself and her own endless destiny. No other creed can bring it, and the Christian Church can bring nothing less. In it lies the believer's own portion and it is the only portion he should think it worth while to offer to a spiritually empoverished and starving world. It is moreover the portion which has the promise that all other things shall be added to it.

Princeton. GEERHARDUS VOS.